AF411485

EXHIBITION/EXPOSICION

Curator / Comisario

George L. Aguirre

Coordination in New York / Coordinación en Nueva York

Suzanne L. Stratton

Transport of works Madrid - New York - Madrid

generously provided by Iberia Airlines of Spain

El transporte de las obras Madrid -Nueva York - Madrid

es por la generosidad de Iberia Líneas Aéreas de España

CATALOGUE / CATALOGO

Translations / Traducciones

María Angélica Fernández Diamante

Photcomposition / Fotocomposición

avalon Madrid

Photomechanicals / Fotomecánica

ADAN, S.L. Madrid

Printing / Imprenta

Gráficas IGAR, S.A. Madrid

Binding / Encuadernación

Huertas, S.A. Madrid

Photographs / Fotografía

The photographs of Joan Fontcuberta are courtesy of the Zabriskie
Gallery, New York City, and the rest are courtesy of the individual
photographers. Las fotografías de Joan Fontcuberta se hicieron
disponibles por la cortesía de la Galería Zabriskie de Nueva York, y las
demás por cortesía de cada autor individualmente.

ISBN : 84-604-2055-8

© 1992, The Spaninsh Institute, Inc.

Depósito Legal : M-7027-1992

Dust cover Photograph / fotografía de la sobrecubierta

by María José Gómez Redondo, Series "The Five Senses",
"The sense of vision". De su serie "Los cinco sentidos",
"El sentido de la vista".

Foreword

The Spanish Institute is a private, not-for-profit organization dedicated to broadening an understanding of Spain in the United States. Our mission is to support the study, understanding, teaching and exposition of Spanish arts, letters, and public affairs in the United States, with particular outreach made to our Hispanic communities.

The galleries of The Spanish Institute are the only exhibition spaces in the United States dedicated solely to Spanish art in all its richness and variety. The Spanish Institute has curated and organized exhibitions that included paintings by El Greco, Picasso and Miro and prints by Goya, Tápies and Chillida. We have shown works ranging from the tiny scale of miniature 16th and 17th century portraits to the site specific sculptures planned for the public spaces of Barcelona (shown here in maquettes and photographs). The wide variety of exhibitions has included Goya etchings, drawings done by Spanish children during the Civil War and Pictorialist photography from the turn of the century.

The mission of our gallery program, however, is not merely to reflect the riches of Spain's unique cultural heritage, but to celebrate the very real accomplishments of Spain today. This exhibition, *The Spanish Vision: Contemporary Art Photography, 1970-1990*, appropriately marks an "encounter" between Spain and the United States in the Columbus Quincentenary year of 1992.

We extend our warm thanks to the Fine Arts Advisory Committee of The Spanish Institute, chaired by Jonathan Brown, for unstintingly sharing their expertise in the planning of our exhibitions, and to Guest Curator George Aguirre for his unfailing enthusiasm and professionalism. This exhibition has been made possible by support from sevoral sources. We are grateful to the Ministery of Culture of Spain and José María Luzón, Director General de Bellas Artes y Archivo. The Robert Mapplethorpe Foundation provided a grant toward the publication of the catalogue we are grateful for both the support and recognition of a foundation dedicated to fostering the dissemination of developments in photography today. Transport has been generously provided by GRUPO IBERIA and IBERIA Airlines of Spain; we are thankful for the kind cooperation of Enrique Pérez Torres in Madrid and David González in New York.

Edward Schumacher
The *Director*

Suzanne L. Stratton
Director of Fine Arts and Cultural Programa

Carmen Soler Bultó de Hilton
Director of Special Projects

Presentación

El Spanish Institute es una organización privada con fines no lucrativos dedicada a ampliar el conocimiento de España en los Estados Unidos. Nuestra misión es apoyar el estudio, conocimiento, enseñanza y exposición de las artes, letras y asuntos públicos de España en los Estados Unidos, con particular interés en nuestras comunidades hispanas.

La galería del Spanish Institute es el único espacio en los Estados Unidos dedicado únicamente al arte español en toda su riqueza y variedad. El Spanish Institute ha comisionado y organizado exposiciones que han incluído a El Greco, Picasso, Miró y grabados de Goya, Tápies y Chillida. Hemos expuesto obras que van desde la diminuta escala de los retratos en miniatura de los siglos XVI y XVII, a las esculturas específicas concebidas para lugares públicos de Barcelona (mostradas aquí en maquetas y fotografías). La amplia variedad de exposiciones también ha incluído dibujos hechos por niños españoles durante la Guerra Civil y fotografía pictórica de fines del siglo pasado.

La misión del programa de nuestra galería, sin embargo, no es meramente reflejar las riquezas de la singular herencia cultural de España, sino celebrar los logros reales de la España de hoy. Esta exposición, *La visión española: fotografía contemporánea de autor, 1970-1990*, sella un "encuentro" entre España y los Estados Unidos en el 1992, año del Quinto Centenario del viaje de Colón.

Extendemos nuestro cálido agradecimiento al Comité Asesor de Bellas Artes del Spanish Institute, presidido por Jonathan Brown, por compartir incondicionalmente su pericia en la planificación de nuestras exposiciones y al comisario invitado George Aguirre por su profesionalidad y entusiasmo inagotable. Esta exposición ha sido posible por el patrocinio de varias instituciones. Estamos muy agradecidos al Ministerio de Cultura de España y en particular a Don José María Luzón, Director General de Bellas Artes y Archivo. La Fundación Robert Mapplethorpe ha patrocinado parcialmente la publicación del catálogo y estamos muy agradecidos no sólo de su patrocinio pero también por el reconocimiento de una fundación dedicada al estímulo de la difusión de los vertientes actuales de la fotografía. El transporte de las obras fue provisto por el GRUPO IBERIA e IBERIA Líneas Aéreas de España y en particular agradecemos la colaboración de Don Enrique Pérez Torres en Madrid y Don David González en Nueva York.

Edward Schumacher
Director

Suzanne L. Stratton
Directora de Bellas Artes y programas Culturales

Carmen Soler Bultó de Hilton
Directora de Proyectos Especiales

TABLE OF CONTENTS / INDICE

PAGE /PAGINA

Introduction

ALEJANDRO CASTELLOTE

A point of symbolic change took place in Spanish photography during the transition from dictatorship to democracy. An analysis of this period should thus look at not only the artistic viewpoint, but also the political, economic and socio-cultural conditions.

Contrary to other artistic expressions, photography had to wait for the democratic transition in order to mature. The fine arts and literature were obviously affected by the cultural drought after the Civil War, but either because of exile, or because of a broader uprooting in Spanish society, the truth is that writers survived censorship and repression, making the tragedy of the Civil War and its aftermath the background for their works. The writers whose political commitment confronted the dictatorship directly had their books published by Latin American publishers, mostly Mexican and Argentinean or European. The Spanish editions by "conflictive" writers penetrated Franco's Spain illegally, and reading them became a symbol of resistance.

The visual arts saw how their main practitioners who were deeply committed to the Republic continued their work in exile. In Spain the university level teaching of the fine arts and the powerful presence of the great Spanish classical painters who continued to be studied in the schools maintained alive an art which was not considered to be too subversive.

This relative permissiveness was one of the reasons why, together with the broader information they had about trends from abroad, restless groups of artists defined and developed an amazing avant-garde in the visual arts. Their proposals became known through a few galleries and Spanish art patrons who successfully wagered on a generation whose work was a breath of fresh air in the apathetic artistic panorama at the end of the '50s. Contemporary music also formed part of these renovating movements through their groups, such as ZAJ, which made room for the cutting-edge and multidisciplinary cultural avant-garde.

Photography had a prominence in the artistic panorama at the beginning of the century, especially during the period between the two Republics and even during the Civil War. Nonetheless, the dictatorship supposed its setback and the returno to pictorialism, an attitude that was stimulated by "salon" photography and the amateur photography associations whose main activity was to hold competitions. It is curious that from these emerged a faint divergence which sought a broadening of the narrow concerns which ruled Spanish photography of the '50s by using the language of documentary photography.

Through these groups which severed from the salons and contests, a series of photographers showed their work outside of Spain. They also took on the task of showing representative exhibitions here which were the model for the photographic language's evolution outside of our boundaries, as was the case of "The Family of Man". All of these contributed in stimulating interest in "another type of photography", one more enriching and innovative.

Sings of Identity

It is always risky, or inexact, to make generalizations, especially when referring to the personality of a nation, but the existence of certain characteristics common to different generations allow us to assert and define certain behaviours as specifically Spanish. The long period of isolation from the outside world gave rise to a feeling of inferiority and, consequently, to an overvaluation of "everything from Abroad". These were conflicting sentiments given that the Government aimed at exacerbating "national values" as an attempt for a collective defense vis-á-vis a community of nations which, from the U.N., promoted an embargo to fascist Spain. However, the fostering of a patriotism which presented Spain as "the spiritual reservoir of the West" contrasted with the provoked popular fervor that accompanied the rare visits of foreign dignitaries. Far from being an expression of solidarity, these embargoes always responded to economic or strategic interests. Franco's regime had adopted a neutral position in World War II with the objective of not worsening our deep isolation, but this did not result in a subsequent support from the Allies. The Marshall Plan, conceived as an aid for the economic reactivation of the countries affected by the war, left Spain out.

A glance at our recent past, the 20th Century, leaves clear that Spain had built its history trying to make its pulse coincide with our country's fate, either because of anticipation or delay. Thus, it is not difficult to understand that a certain fatalism impregnated Spanish society. An awareness of isolation always distorts a country's evaluation of its present and so an epic or catastrophic feeling passively emerges in daily life.

The Generational Change

The generation gap was especially evident among those who lived the postwar period. The youth brought up in a relative well being during the economic take-off the '60s stimulated social change after Franco's death. However, their eagerness to be different did not stop them from maintaining their devotion for foreign things. Culturally, travelling and having access to information of the latest artistic trends became a symbol of modernity and, in a certain manner, of power. It led to a deliberate and liberating rupture.

The protagonists of that "renaissance" had forcefully lavished an analysis of the change Spanish photography went through in those years with a heroic tinge. On those occasions when this period has been commented about (practically covering the '60s decade) it has served as an exaggerated platform for a reduced number of photographers who presented themselves as almost the "first inventors". An excessively narcissistic judgment, but to some extent comprehensible - the pioneers' epic.

Photography did not arouse any interest in official quarters as it might be expected. This was one of the reasons why it was not included in the public universities' curriculum. In programming exhibitions, there was no room for photography. After 1973, some private galleries, magazines and modest teaching centers were established. One of these magazines, *Nueva Lente*, has been considered by many as the flagship of "the fifth generation", a self-named group which was composed of photographers born in the '50s.

The breakthrough, and in a certain way the neo-surrealist proposals, of *Nueva Lente* implied an important change in the reduced quarters of amateur photography. Its energy gained it recognition abroad. It awakened a logical interest about an art which, except for rare occasions, was assumed to be anchored in photographic contests or salons previously discussed. From another magazine, *Arte Fotográfico*, official organ of Spanish "salonismo", emerged an innovative alternative: *Poptografía*. It published international portfolios, information about books and foreign activities, as well as criticism and texts disassociated from the usual language of contests, and created a different space where those recently arrived to the medium could end mutual support. Curiously enough, both *Nueva Lente* and *Poptografía* counted on members of the photographic societies.

A discreet simmering of photographic activities began. However, the economic pie was not big, or at least not big enough for everyone, and some of the newly created galleries went out of business or had to become schools.

The generation of pioneer photographers and instigators of alternatives had little to do with the photographers who had stood out in the past, except that like them, a considerable majority came from well-off families who could finance their offspring's expensive hobby. Photographic materials, especially cameras, were outside the reach of almost every social class as well as information, since books, which are scarce even now, could hardly be found The in Spain. They were for the privileged few. Because of this, or as well as another provocation, the idea of "poor photography" was launched from *Nueva Lente*. It saw this concept welcomed by photographers of differing social origins. Given their backgrounds, it was surprising to see Jorge Rueda, Cristina García Rodero or Joan Fontcuberta, to cite only a few, under the same flag.

Conceptual shifts are common in times when subtleties are not well considered, and when clear viewpoints with no middle ground are required. Granted that not everyone shared the same need to demonstrate his liberalism, but the adventure of challanging censorship generally excited the histrionic side of the creators. Now, perhaps, this might seem a naive or excessively adolescent attitude. That is why it is necessary to give the social and political environment during this movement's beginning.

As time went by, the need to find economic support arrived as their student life was ending. It was then when *Nueva Lente* vanished.

The then not-so-new generation was forced to mature. Knowing that photography's recent history had them as apostles, the most active ones began the road toward international recognition as the self-proclaimed Spanish photographic avant-garde. Success smiled at the first incursions into other countries which were the scions of democracy. Solidarity and the feeling of a common cause which united the young photographers in their first adventures was eclipsed as soon as they realized that the exciting hobby could become a means of support. The marketplace, public relations and the competition became the principal priorities for the most ambitious. The contacts they bragged about before were now silenced and became part of each individual's legacy, or, at most, part of a small group that shared the same interests.

But the schools that provided work for many of them as teachers inevitably produced students. This new generation had no need to cross the desert or fight "come what may" to get their basic training. Thus, photography gradually became what makes it most dignified: the most democratic art of the 20th Century.

The feudal kingdoms created after that Fifth Generation were rapidly challanged by the ceaseless stream of young photographers more interested in creating than in strengthening power positions. This evolution was welcomed with uneven joy, but, in truth, it must be said that the most honest promoters of photography in Spain have much to do with the talent developed in private schools, and, more timidly, in public universities.

The others, the few, continue to present their group of friends and acolytes as a summary and history of Spanish photography. But each time there are less and less naive persons to deceive. A process of normalization is taking place; culture, in both upper and lower case, has become part of Spanish society again. The mere fact of belonging to influential circles no longer implies an immediate passport to success. Both central and autonomous governments begin to be aware, in a larger or lesser degree, of photography's potential. It escapes no one's attention that the photography exhibitions are the most attended by the public, except for those of the great classical painters, and gradually they are becoming a habitual element in every type of cultural center. But if previously private initiative was ahead of the state's, in the '90s there are still problems for including photography in the art market. The successive failures of those galleries which were exclusively devoted to photography and which seemed to have had a promising future confirm the mistake involved in trying to walk it alone. Except for honorable, and sometimes isolated, exceptions, multi-disciplinary galleries are the ones who are betting timidly, but progressively, on photography. All in all, it is necessary to stabilize the structures and professionalize the sector through a complete formal training and the term "professionalize" should be undersood not in a corporate sense, but as one with honesty and respect towards its product. For obvious reasons those who are currently devoted to organizing photographic activities or teaching are mostly self-taught and certainly do not have *ad hoc* titles.

Slowly and ceaselessly Spanish photography is maturing, a process which takes from its origins without any remorse, and incorporating the trends which are being developed with the same direction in other countries in a natural way. Their work denotes wide knowledge of world photography'a great classics. The concept of a "global village" has also reached our country and in the artistic creation of our artists.

It is now, after overcoming an inferiority complex and other imposed burdens, when there is no desperate need to be known and recognized, and when it is really possible to talk about a corpus of Spanish photography.

Prefacio
ALEJANDRO CASTELLOTE PIÑUELA

El hecho fotográfico en España tiene en el paso de la dictadura a la democracia un punto simbólico de inflexión. El análisis de este período ha de contemplar por tanto, no sólo el punto de vista artístico, sino las circunstancias políticas, económicas y socioculturales.

Al contrario que otras expresiones artísticas, la fotografía ha de esperar a la transición democrática para madurar. La literatura o las artes plásticas se vieron lógicamente afectadas por la sequía cultural que sobrevino tras la guerra civil pero, bien por el exilio, bien por un mayor arraigo en la sociedad española, lo cierto es que los escritores sobreviven a la censura y la represión incorporando la tragedia de la guerra civil y la posguerra como escenario de sus obras. Los autores cuyo compromiso político se enfrenta directamente a la dictadura, publican sus libros en editoriales latinoamericanas -principalmente México y Argentina- o europeas; la ediciones en castellano de autores "conflictivos" penetran en la España franquista de forma clandestina y su lectura se convierte en símbolo de resistencia.

Las artes plásticas han visto como sus principales exponentes, profundamente comprometidos con la república, continúan su obra en el exilio. En el interior, la enseñanza de las Bellas Artes en la Universidad y la poderosa presencia de los grandes pintores clásicos españoles, que se siguen estudiando en los colegios, mantiene latente en nuestra sociedad un arte considerado no excesivamente subversivo.

Esta permisividad relativa es una de las razones que, junto a la mayor información que poseen los artistas plásticos sobre las tendencias del exterior, hace que grupos inquietos de autores conformen y desarrollen una sorprendente vanguardia plástica. Sus propuestas se dan a conocer en el ámbito de unas pocas galerías y mecenas españoles que, lúcidamente, apuestan por una generación cuya obra es una inyección de frescura en el abúlico panorama artístico de finales de los años 50. También la música contemporánea se adhiere a estos movimientos renovadores a través de colectivos como el grupo ZAJ, que dan cabida a la vanguardia cultural más fronteriza y multidisciplinar.

La fotografía tuvo un relieve relativamente importante en el panorama artístico de principios de siglo y, fundamentalmente, en los períodos de las 2 repúblicas e, incluso, durante la guerra civil, sin embargo, la dictadura supuso su declive y su retroceso al pictorialismo; una actitud que se vio fomentada desde el salonismo y las asociaciones de fotógrafos aficionados, cuya principal actividad se reducía al concurso. Curiosamente, es desde este ámbito donde se produce una suave escisión que intenta, utilizando el lenguaje del documentalismo, ampliar las estrechas miras que imperan en la fotografía española de los años 50.

A través de estos grupos escindidos de los salones y la concursística, una serie de autores muestran su obra fuera de España y, a la vez se ocupan de dar a conocer en nuetro país exposiciones paradigmáticas de la evolución del lenguaje fotográfico fuera de nuestras fronteras como fue el caso de "La Familia del Hombre"; todo ello contribuye a promover el interés por "otro tipo de fotografía" más enriquecedora y renovadora.

Señas de indentidad

Siempre es arriesgado y, cuando menos inexacto, hablar de generalizaciones, sobre todo al referirse a la personalidad de un pueblo, sin embargo, existen algunas características comunes a distitnas generaciones que permiten aventurarse a afirmar y definir determinados comportamientos como específicamente españoles.

El largo período de aislamiento del exterior hace emerger un sentimiento de inferioridad y, consecuentemente, una sobrevaloración de "lo extranjero". Un sentimiento conflictivo, ya que desde el Gobierno se intenta exacerbar "lo nacional" como medida de autodefensa colectiva frente a toda una comundiad de naciones que, desde la ONU, había promovido el bloqueo a la España fascista. Sin embargo, el fomento del patriotismo que presenta a España como "reserva espiritual de Occidente", contrasta con el provocado fervor popular que acompañaba a las escasas visitas de Jefes de Estado extranjeros.

Lejos de suponer un gesto de solidaridad estas "rupturas" del bloque obedecen siempre a intereses económicos o estratégicos. El régimen de Franco había adoptado una posición neutral en la II Guerra Mundial con objeto de no hacer más profundo nuestro aislamiento, pero ello no revertiría en un posterior apoyo del bloque aliado. El "Plan Marshall", concebido como una ayuda a la reactivación económica de los países afectados por la guerra, dejó de lado a España.

Una mirada a nuestro pasado reciente, el siglo XX, deja ver con claridad que España ha construído su historia tratando de hacer coincidir su pulso con el resto de los países homólogos; sin embargo, por anticipación o por retraso, la asincronía es el sino de nuestro país. No es difícil por ello, comprender que un cierto sentimiento fatalista impregne a la sociedad española. La conciencia del aislamiento siempre desproporciona la valoración de un pueblo sobre su presente y la épica o el catastrofismo afloran de forma inercial en la vida cotidiana.

El recambio generacional

La ruptura generacional, especialmente evidente entre quienes vivieron la posguerra y la nueva juventud criada en relativo bienestar y despegue económico de la década de los sesenta, promueve el relevo social tras la muerte de Franco. Sin embargo, su afán de ser diferentes, no impide que mantengan enquistada la devoción por lo foráneo. En el ámbito cultural, viajar y poseer información de las últimas tendencias artísticas se convierte en símbolo de modernidad y, en cierta manera, de poder. Se va hacia una ruptura deliberada y liberadora.

Las revisiones del proceso de transformación de la fotografía española en estos años son cada vez más frecuentes, y se ven fácilmente impregnadas de los tintes épicos que los protagonistas de este "renacimiento" se han esforzado en conferirle. Las sucesivas oportunidades en las que se ha glosado este período, que abarca prácticamente la década de los setenta, han servido de tribuna amplificadora a un reducido grupo de fotógrafos que se presentan poco menos que de "madres del invento"; un juicio excesivamente narcisista pero en cierto modo comprensible: la épica de los pioneros.

La fotografía, como era de esperar, no suscita en los ámbitos oficiales ningún interés; esta es una de las razones por las que no se incluye su enseñanza en las Universidades públicas. Asimismo, en la programación de exposiciones tampoco tienen cabida las muestras fotográficas. A partir de 1973, nacen en el sector privado algunas galerías, revistas y modestos centros de enseñanza. Una de estas revistas, Nueva Lente, es considerada por muchos como buque insignia de un colectivo que dio en llamarse "la quinta generación" y agrupaba fotógrafos nacidos en la década de los 50.

Las propuestas rupturistas y, en cierto modo, neo-surrealistas de Nueva Lente suponen un importante revulsivo en el reducido ámbito de la fotografía de aficionados. Su empuje la da a conocer fuera de nuestras fronteras, despertando un lógico interés sobre un arte que, salvo contadas excepciones ya mencionadas en las escisiones del salonismo, se suponía anclado en los concursos. Desde otra revista, Arte Fotográfico, órgano oficial de salonismo español, surge una innovadora alternativa: Poptografía. La publicación de porfolios internacionales, la información de libros y actividades foráneas, así como una crítica y unos textos desligados del lenguaje habitual de la concursística, va creando un espacio distinto, donde los recién llegados al medio fotográfico pueden encontrar materia y espíritu con el que solidarizarse. Curiosamente, tanto Nueva Lente como Poptografía contaron en su staff con miembros de las Sociedades Fotográficas.

Se comienza a gestar una discreta ebullición de actividades fotográficas. Sin embargo, el pastel, en términos económicos, no da para mucho o, más bien, no da para muchos y algunas de las recién creadas galerías de fotografía dan al traste con sus proyectos o se ven obligadas a reciclarse en escuelas.

La generación de fotógrafos pioneros e impulsores de alternativas tiene muy poco que ver con los fotógrafos que descollaban en el pasado, salvo que como ellos, una significativa mayoría proviene de familias de economía desahogada que puede financiar el caro ocio de sus vástagos. Los materiales fotográficos, fundamentalmente las cámaras, no están al alcance de todos los estamentos sociales; tampoco la información, pues los libros que aún ahora escasean, prácticametne no se encontraban en España y eran privilegio de unos pocos. Quizá conscientes de ello, o como un giro provocador más, se lanza desde Nueva Lente la idea de la "fotografía pobre". Una idea a la que se acogen autores de muy distinta extracción y que, a la vista de sus actuales trayectorias, no deja de sorprender el ver reunidos bajo la misma bandera a Jorge Rueda, Cristina García Rodero o Joan Fontcubierta por citar sólo algunos ejemplos.

Los bandazos conceptuales son moneda corriente en una época en la que están mal vistas las sutilezas y se exigen posicionamientos claros y adscripción ideológica sin paliativos. Bien es cierto que no todos comparten la necesidad de evidenciar su progresismo, pero en general, la aventura de desafiar a la censura excita el histrionismo de los creadores. Quizá ahora pueda parecer una actitud ingenua o excesivamente adolescente; es por ello que se hace necesario enmarcar social y políticamente el entorno en el que nace este movimiento.

Con el paso de los años llega para muchos la necesidad de buscar soporte económico ante el inmediato fin de una juventud de estudiante. En esos años se desvanece Nueva Lente.

La ya no tan nueva generación se ve forzada a madurar. A sabiendas de que la historia reciente de la fotografía tenía en ellos a sus apóstoles, los más activos inician el camino de darse a conocer fuera de España como autoproclamados representantes de la vanguardia fotográfica española. El éxito sonríe a las primeras incursiones en otros países de los retoños de la democracia. La solidaridad y el sentimiento de causa común, que unía a los jóvenes fotógrafos en sus primeras andanzas, se eclipsa tan pronto como se vislumbra que ese ocio excitante ha de convertirse en fuente de supervivencia. Son el mercado, las relaciones públicas y la competencia los argumentos prioritarios de los más ambiciosos. Los contactos que antes se cacareaban, ahora se silencian y pasan a pertenecer al patrimonio individual o, a lo sumo, a un reducido colectivo que comparte intereses comunes.

Pero las escuelas que dan trabajo a muchos de ellos como profesores, inevitablemetne producen alumnos. Otra nueva generación que esta vez no necesita hacer ninguna travesía del desierto ni luchar contra viento y marea para acceder a los conocimientos básicos. La fotografía se convierte poco a poco en lo que más la dignifica: ser el arte más democrático del siglo XX.

Los reinos de Taifas creados a partir de aquella Quinta generación se ven rápidamente contestados por el incesante fluir de autores jóvenes, más interesados en crear que en afianzar posiciones de poder. Este devenir es acogido con desigual alegría pero, en honor a la verdad, hay que decir que los más honestos de los impulsores de la fotografía en España tienen mucho que ver con el potencial gestado en las escuelas privadas y, más tímidamente, en las Universidades públicas.

Los otros, los menos siguen todavía presentando su grupo de amigos y acólitos como resumen y glosa de la fotografía española; pero cada vez quedan menos ingenuos a los que engañar. Se está entrando en la normalización, la cultura con mayúsculas y minúsculas se ha asentado en la sociedad española y el mero hecho de pertenecer a grupos de influencia ya no supone pasaporte inmediato al éxito. Los gobiernos, tanto el central como los autonómicos, comienzan a percatarse con mayor o menor lucidez del potencial de la fotografía. A nadie se le escapa que este tipo de exposiciones son las más visitadas por el público, si exceptuamos claro está a los grandes clásicos de la pintura, y poco a poco se han convertido en elemento habitual de todo tipo de centros culturales.

Pero si en épocas anteriores la iniciativa privada se ha adelantado al estado, en los noventa existen problemas para incluir la fotografía en el mercado del arte. Los sucesivos fracasos de galerías que han experimentado en exclusiva con la fotografía, suponiéndole un prometedor futuro, evidencian el error de prenteder caminar en solitario. Salvo honrosas y a veces numantinas excepciones, son las galerías multidisciplinares quienes están apostando tímida pero progresivamente por la fotografía.

Con todo, se hace necesario estabilizar las estructuras y profesionalizar el sector a través de una completa formación; bien entendido que se utiliza aquí el término profesionalizar, no en el sentido corporativista sino en lo que respecta a la honestidad y respecto hacia su trabajo. Por razones obvias, quienes ahora se dedican a la organización de actividades fotográficas o a la enseñanza, son en su gran mayoría autodidactas y por supuesto no disponen de titulación "ad hoc".

Lenta e imparáblemente está madurando una fotografía española que bebe sin complejos de sus orígenes, aprovechando e incorporando de forma natural las tendencias que paralelamente se desarrollan en otros países. Sus obras evidencian el amplio conocimiento de los grandes clásicos de la fotografía mundial. El concepto de "aldea global" también ha calado en nuestro país y en la expresión artística de nuestros creadores.

Es ahora, a posteriori, tras la superación de los sentimientos de inferioridad y de otros lastres impuestos, cuando ya no existe la necesidad desesperada de darse a conocer y ser reconocidos, cuando se puede realmente hablar de un corpus de fotografía española.

The Spanish Vision

GEORGE L. AGUIRRE
GUEST CURATOR

Spanish photography is just beginning to receive the attention traditionally given to Spanish painting, printmaking, drawing and sculpture. Yet, most of what is being seen outside of Spain, and particularly in the United States, is photography about Spain. Photographers have looked at "one day in the life", the disappearing, the profound, the mystical, the folkloric and the hidden faces of Spain. Unwittingly, these presentations prolong Spanish stereotypes long past their death. There is a folkloric or dark side to any Western society and its culture, and modern photographers have documented it. However, there is an aspect of Spanish photography which is much less known outside of Spain —art photography— photography as a medium for expressing one's inner world, whether or not using the external world as the subject. Spain, latecomer to the 20th Century as Americans understand it, is changing rapidly, and so are its artistic expressions including art photography.

Europeans long ago condemmed Spain as the last outpost of Africa, and cut Spain off from their world. When photography began, Spain entered into a turbulent period, and the turbulence continued. "I have lived through two monarchies, two dictatorships, two republics, and now a democracy", a friend commented not long ago.

The 20th Century began with the loss of Spain's last colonies —Puerto Rico and the Philippines to the United States, and Cuba to her independence. The world entered into its First World War, and new order began to reshape the face of the Old World. The Second World War caused another new order. This period of great change was reflected in the cultural scene through the various avant gardes formulated in Europe and the United States. European emigres stimulated great changes in American art, and just after the Second World War the G.I. Bill stimulated a growth in the Fine Arts schools, creating a "baby boom" in the arts and crafts of the United States.

Spain, however, did not participate in those two great wars and remained apart from the new world order. It was attempting to consolidate its nation-state and define its political systems. Just after the First World War, the Military Juntas found the revolt of their junior officers, general strikes were declared, labor stuggled in Catalonia, etc., ending with the dictatorship of Primo de Rivera. Then the Second Republic was formed, and with it, all the struggles culminating in the Civil War. The Spanish Civil War, in which other European interests entered as a test for the succesive European power struggle, was a testing ground for the power of photojournalism by the foreign press. Spain became the workplace for the European and American photographers. This was the period when photography was changing from an artistic or documentary process to the photomechanical process of informing. In the '20s and '30s a photographic revolution was taking place, with photographs and word merging, picturing world events. Spain closed in upon itself and was shunned by the rest. It was hardly the place where free expression could take place. Yet there were photographers in Spain, but materials were scarce and highly priced. The Catalans had some advantage since, when they could cross the border, they could acquire film, paper, chemicals.

But the Civil War devastated the economy, and all suffered. Even as the economy began to recover and some materials became available, there was still a suppression of cultural expression.

Although the period of the two dictatorships did not stimulate creativity, there were photographers who, despite the problems, formed their groups in almost every Spanish city. The Royal Photographic Society of Madrid, founded in 1899, continues to be active today, just as the Photographic Society of Zaragoza (1922), and the Photographic Group of Catalonia (1923). The were important for the exchage of ideas, techniques and mutual ecouragement. The societies formed competitions for the photographers, and displayed the photographs, or created Salons where photographers were invited to display their work. One of the benefits that these photographic societies provoved was the bulletins they published which included reproductions of the competition winners, or of some of the works exhibited in the Salons. One of the effects, however, was the continuation of pictoralism as a photographic expression in Spain long after it disappeared elsewhere. But these were not times for innovation, except among who had exiled themselves, such as Josep Renau, or others who were killed, like Nikolas Lekuona.

In 1952, a magazine independent of any Group and its bulletin started to be published, *Arte Fotográfico*. Still published today, *Arte Fotogáfico* provived an opening into the wider photographic world by translating and publishing articles from publications outside of Spain. It disseminated information about the photographic competitions being held by the photographic groups, published some of the prize-winning photographs, and even provived information on how to win them. In provived national standards that, in effect, supported the continuation of pictoralism as the mainstream of art photography in Spain. The Agrupación Fotográfica Almeriense (AFAL) began to publish its bulletin in 1956. This group and its publication began publishing works which were more "intuitive", less formally controlled, less studied. AFAL sought to advance the art of photography, since the salons had become too cautious for this group, by caring more about the photograph itself, rather than the person who made it. AFAL gained international recognition. Its members were invited to participate in exhibitions held in Paris, Milan, Venice, and were included by Edward Steichen in his Masterworks of Photography exhibition held at the Museum of Modern Art in New York City, in 1958. In that group was Alberto Schommer and Gabriel Cualladó, both included in *The Spanish Vision*.

During this period there was a small group of photographers working and living in Madrid who met occasionally at the Spanish Royal Photographic Society's offices, sharing their photographic concerns, and they became known as *La Palangana* (in 1959), so named because of a photograph of then made by one of the members with their six portraits placed in a washbasin. At the same time there were other young photographers who went to the Society's offices to learn and share photographic interests. Some of them formed another group knonn as *La Colmena* (The Hive). Rafael Sanz Lobato was one of the members of *La Colmena*.

The 1960s saw the end of the AFAL publication, and the beginning of another, *Imagen y Sonido*, en 1963. This was a period when some of the photographers began to attain real success, working for newspapers, magazines, television and cinema. *Imágen y Sonido* focused on well known photographers and groups. The foment begun in the '50s abated, competitions attracted amateurs, and the images slipped back to stereotypes. The end of the 1960s, with the Vietnam war, its protests, the Parisian May of '68, the flower children, saw tumult everywhere and repercussions in Spain as well. The photographic explosion that took place in those years was documented and nourished by the magazine, *Nueva Lente*. From its first number "0", published in July 1971, through the 1970s, *Nueva Lente* fomented new ways of thinking about photography. In the beginning Jorge Rueda served as Artistic Director, and the first cover was by Pablo Pérez Mínguez.

In *Nueva Lente* photographers could find a multi-disciplinary approach, through articles on design and esthetics. In 1975, Jorge Rueda became the Editor, and he began to get Joan Fontcuberta, Manuel Falces, Miguel Angel Yáñez Polo and others involved. *Nueva Lente* is now recognized as an important catalyst for establishing photography as one of the "fine" arts in Spain. One could find voice and support for a kind of photography af the inner self. The 1980s saw a proliferation of photography magazines, with *PhotoVision* beginning in 1981, *Foto Profesional* in 1982, *Diorama* in 1984 and *La Fotografía* in 1989. Except for *PhotoVision*, they tend to be like the American photography magazines, a mixture of technical and equipment advice, and publishing portfolios of all types of photography. *PhotoVision*, founded by Joan Fontcuberta and Rafael Levenfeld, among others, is more like a Spanish version of *Aperture*. Each issue is dedicated to a theme, or a photographer, and presented with some intellectual depth.

Photography was not taught in the universities until 1981. Before that, learning about photography groups, or the private academies which began to offer photography and Film courses. For the serious photographer, the professional structure long taken for granted in other countries did not begin to form until much later. The first commercial gallery opened in Barcelona, in 1973: the second in Madrid, in 1975. There is still no Spanish museum or arts institution devoted to photography only. Not until the end of 1991 did the new *Museo Nacional y Centro de Arte Reina Sofía* hold its first Spanish photography exhibition.

The art galleries are opening their doors to art photography little by little, often with one exhibition a year, usually with the work of a well recognized photographer. Galleries thar foster work by young artists sometimes include photography by photographers, as well as by artists who have adopted photography as only part of their technical spectrum. Among the most active are the *Galería Moriarty*, in Madrid and the photography galleries *Spectrum*, in Zaragoza; *Forum,* in Tarragona; and *Visor Centre Fotografic*, in Valencia. Some serious attention is being paid to photography in the art press and the newspapers, but, with rare exception (Joan Fontcuberta is a prime example), there are few critics in the best sense of the word. The Savings & Loan institutions of Spain have their cultural officers and exhibition halls where photographers have an opportunity to exhibit their work. The museums are beginning to pay attention to photography. The soon to be closed *Museo Español de Arte Contemporáneo* (it will fuse with the *Centro de Arte Reina Sofía*) began a photography department in 1984-85, and initiated an important series of exhibitions. Each Autonomous Community, provincial office, and city hall in Spain has its cultural office, and each is beginning to pay attention to photography, especially of that region. The Autonomous Community of Madrid, the City Government of Córdoba, the Catalonian and Barcelona governments have been particularly active in supporting photography. There are few photography collectors, and fewer professional "reps", but a professional scaffolding is slowly being formed, and the annual art fair in Madrid, ARCO, is exposing Spanish collectors to photography as a collectible art form.

The "new" Spain, organized into Autonomous Communities, has decentralized the country, weaning regional interests away from the influences of Madrid, and opening the way for more diverse exhibitions of a more diverse photographic production. Political change is also causing cultural tensions, reflected in the "regional" versus the "European" search for cultural expression. Spain's entry into the European community has also stimulated a "North" versus "South" dichotomy and a search for a characteristically Mediterranean means of expression, reflected in two recent books: Toni Catany's *La Meva Mediterrania* (Barcelona, Lunwerg Editores, 1990); and Manuel Falce's *Contrapunto Mediterráneo* (Sevilla, Productora Andaluza de Programas, S.A., 1990).

The Spanish Vision begins with photographs taken during the 1970s. Gabriel Cualladó demonstrated then and continues to demostrate this Mediterranean sensitivity in his portrait of his mother, with an empty rocking chair where his father once sat, or in his rural scenes so respectful of the people and their environment. Likewise, Rafael Lobato continues today to express his personal respect for the vanishing customs of a rapidly chaging rural society, where the State has separated from the Church, but where life otherwise continues as usual. Francesc Catalá-Roca continues his personalized urban vision through views taken while he attended his retrospective exhibition at The Spanish Institute in 1987. He is the son of another well-known photographer Pere Catalá Pic. Francesc Catalá-Roca is the first photographer to have received the Spanish National Award for Fine Arts, in 1983. The urban theme becomes prominent again in Spanish photography during the 1970s. Francesc Catala's photographs during the 1940s and '50s documented the black markets due to the rationing of that time. His son, one of two who continue photography into the third generation of the family, Andreu Catalá Pedersen, also continues with the urban scene. The sparkling scenes among Andreu's photographs reflect the emergence of "street theatre" in Catalonia, a very urban phenomenon.

Alberto Schommer is widely know in Spain for his books, his portraits of wellknown public figures and his current weekly series of portraits in one of the leading newspaper's Sunday magazine. Schommer is a very versatile photographer. In *The Spanish Vision* he is represented by a highly personal series, *Civilizations*, which show his versatility as a portraitist, in these examples, of objects, and which were previously exhibited at the Juana Mordó Gallery in Madrid.

Gerardo Vielba is represented here by works which are within a classical style, touched with his unique lyricism. He is currently devorting much time to his writing, and to the Royal Photographic Society as its Director. Not only does his photography indicate how he, and others, were able to stray from the "official" photography of an earlier period by including different attitudes from developments outside of Spain, but he is sharing many personal reflactions on what was the state of the photography art during his earlier experiences through his writing.

In the 1970s, Spanish photography changes, becoming more introspective, more free from the previous dicta, and color is added to the photographic language. Jorge Ruedas's photographs show us the shock of rapid changes that take place in his world through his personal, ironic, surreal and biting commentaries. Pablo Pérez Mínguez plays with traditional folkloric symbols, utilizing famous (and not-so-famous) persons as his models. Manuel Falces began his career in the 1970s. His work links the world between *Nueva Lente* and other European influences, purposefully using the lie of photography to show its truth, with wit and irony, and using a slightly blurred, out-of-focus image from time to time, as well as collage. Another of the prhotographers who returns to the possibilities of collage, as well as other experimental processes is Miguel Angel Yáñez Polo. His highly personal works reveal a surreal presentation of a world which combines many of his personal interests as well as a world changing quickly. His historical interest in Spanish Photography lead him, with others, to organize the *Society of the History of Spanish Photography* in the mid-' 80s.

Rafael Navarro, working in black and white, explores such themes as *Forms, Evasions, Presences*, culminating in his well-known series, *Diptychs*. His work is represented here with selections from his recent series, *Homage to a Century and a Half* referring to that anniversary of photography. Done while Navarro was exhibiting at the Chateau d'Eau in France, these works merge the photography of yesterday with that of today, bridging years, and points of view with reality and reflections of reality.

Joan Fontcuberta is the best known of the Spanish photographers in the United States. He is prolific, multifaceted and his writing and thinking about photography are equally influential as is his photographic work. The series of gardens presented here is especially quiet, lyrical, elegant and urbane.

The 1980s began with a consolidation of democratic procesess in Spain - and the "Movida" began, too. the "Movida" was to Madrid, and other Spanish cities, what the "Underground" was to New York, and other U.S. cities at an earlier time. Artists and photographers celebrated kitsch, and experiemental magazines, such as *Madrid Me Mata, La Luna De Madrid* and *Madriz* documented and comunicated the happenings, using graphics and photography. But with all the exuberance and extroversion thar this "Movida" contained, there was an interesting introspection as well.

Juan Ramón Yuste, one of these photographers who documented the persons of that time, did a series of self-portraits utilizing light in a special way. Part of this series is represented in *The Spanish Vision*. This group of photographs ends with a witty double self-portrait, where the photographer is both subject and picture-taker, using a flash on the camera in the one picture in which he, the photographer, uses light as part of the subject, but with the object which emits it.

Antonio Bueno is another photographer who also uses light as an object by "writing" with it, making it protagonist, as well as its being a source of illumination. In *The Spanish Vision*, there is a selection from his series *Graphis* which vividly demostrates this use of light in his examination of interiors.

Ouka Lele (Bárbara Allende) takes on an instrumental name and is instrumental in documenting the "Movida" through her "Pop" style, with strong colorations, and by various stagings of her models, in both interior and exterior settings. Madrid is her stage, and its people the actors. She expresses this renewed awareness of creative freedom in her unique photography, much of it hand-colored. In *The Spanish Vision* she is represented by a series of scenarios about woman, including a self-portrait.

Tony Catany is best known is Spain, France and the United States for his still-life photographs in color, although he also has done some series of travel scenes and nudes, and works in black and white as well. The series presented in this exhibition are of still-life photographs of fruits and flowers. These photographs are sensitive, introspective, lyrical and, sometimes, ironic. They are always beautiful.

Eduardo Momeñe is a photographer, working in black and white, who has explored the human body with an almost fetishistic and narcissistic approach by photographing various attitudes of a model posing with a foot poised over a draped object, or the model seated, but always without a face. These photographs resound with a classical and sculptural attitude.

Josep Batlle has created three series of still-life photographs in black and white. They are titled "Dead Nature", "Live Nature" (which is represented in this exhibition), and "Animated Nature". The series' titles play with the Catalan "natures mortes", meaning "dead nature", or still-life in art. He uses mixtures of objects and animals which form mysterious codes and clues to the nature of "living", "animated" or "dead" in very taut images created with harsh light and high contrast printing.

Rafael Levenfeld is a photographer who also works in black and white. His series of self-portraits uses Madrid as the scenario, with the street, or public and private inetriors for an introspective examination of himself, sometimes with a bit of disguise, but always intense, despite the humor, and with a elegant spatial composition.

Nestor Torrens is one of the two representatives in this exhibition from the Spanish "periphery", the Canary Islands. He produces particularly interesting work in color. This series, reflecting his environment, also uses light as one of the protagonists with its use in "writing" a circle of "stick figure" persons, or as a fountain falling over a rock. Here, Torrens acknowledges what most tourists knonw about the islands —its unique landscape.

Joaquín Columé, atlthough born in Andalucía, has lived most of his life in Las Palmas. Columé deals with another Spanish controversy —boxing— in the series of photographs included here. This sport is banned from Spanish public television. Since Columé is a boxing fan, he has displayed these images on a television screen, and photographed them from the screen. He reminds us that freedom is not totally free. The series is titled "K.O.".

Since the late 1980s, the possibilities for exploring old as well as new photographic processes are materially possible in Spain. The economy is recovering rapidly, and many imported goods are available at more reasonable prices. Travel is possible. Two photographers in this exhibition travelled to study in the United States. Paca Arceo received a scholarship to study photography in the United States. Her work shows an understanding of the American documentary approach. Her color photography is represented in this exhibition with a series of photographs which demostrate the "old-new" tensions in a highly personal way.

Isabel Muñoz works in black and white, and she is the only Spanish photographer who prints her work using the platinum process. Her *Tango* series, done in Argentina and Madrid, treats a nostalgic dance form in an appropriately seductive and sensous way, both with the imagery and with the process for printing them.

Nostalgia is not part of the Spanish emotional palatte, but the early gum bichromate processes which Rodrigo

Mosquera uses to print his black and white photographs creates a sense of nostalgia worthy of any fin-de-siècle remembrance. José Gómez Aparicio uses a selenium toned bromide printing process for completing his portraits imbuing them with a sense of mystery. Rafael Vargas's portraits are very accesible on one level, with a frontal approach, but our careful reading of them pays off in personal insight. José Malibran lets us peer through his window into a private woman's place. Printed in a small format, he makes our viewing as private as the place, and accomplishes it with elegance and respect. Chema Madoz, recent winner of the European Young Photographers Award (1991), is another black and white photographer. At first sight, one sees daily objects, and then quickly perceives that there is something unusual about them. Here is a key, but the lock appears in its handle, or a knife which usually reduces something by cutting, but this one measures, or a ladder that leads to a mirror. His view of daily life's objects is ironic, surreal, clean and witty.

Jorge Lens Leiva is one of the Spanish photographers to use the "new color" approach. In picturing his northern part of the country, he provides us a quiet space for contemplation, and in the photograph "Hand" demostrates and ability to show another way of picturing patience.

María José Gómez Redondo uses appropriations, double exposures and montages to create a dream-like work in which no monsters are allowed. In the series of her photographs in *The Spanish Vision*, she depicts the five senses,. leaving the "sixth" sense to be deduced from these depictions —and the one which forms a part of her technique along with the other, more apparent ones.

These photographers suggest what Spanish art photography will be like in the '90s, and beyond. They study fine arts, they explore and experiment with new techniques, and they travel. Some of these photographers attended the first major course on photographic creation in color as well as its history and esthetic held in Madrid at the Círculo de Bellas Artes during the first four months of 1990. Two Americans were among the instructors. One of them admitted privately her amazement at the high quality of work the attendees presented, revealing that her expection of Spanish photography was that of amateurs, or beginners.

Multicultural and multilingual Spain will continue to provide her photographers with inspiration for great visual expression. That expression has been characterized by Juan Ignacio Hernáiz as having "exaggeration, pomposity, tremendousness, radicalness, passion, exhuberance, imbalance, exhaltation and mmoderation". Spain is clearly no longer the place that Nobel prize-winner Camilo José Cela once described as a country "… so poor that one cannot have more than two ideas from the same person". With this exhibition, the New World has an opportunity to appreciate first hand the new Spanish Vision of photography today.

La visión española

GEORGE L. AGUIRRE MIRANDA
Comisario invitado

La fotografía española comienza a recibir la atención que tradicionalmente se le ha dado a la pintura, al grabado, a la escultura y al dibujo españoles. Aún así, la mayor parte de la obra que se expone fuera de España y sobre todo en los Estados Unidos, es fotografía sobre España. Los fotógrafos han mirado "un día en la vida de…", la España que desaparece, la cara profunda, mística, folklórica y oculta de España. De modo inconsciente, estas presentaciones prolongan estereotipos españoles mucho más allá de su extinción. Cualquier sociedad occidental y su cultura poseen un lado folklórico u oculto y los fotógrafos lo han retratado. Sin embargo, hay un aspecto de la fotografía española que es mucho menos conocido fuera de España, la fotografía de autor, medio de expresión de nuestro mundo íntimo, aún cuando utilice el mundo exterior como sujeto. España —uno de los últimos países en arrivar al siglo XX, tal y como lo entienden los norteamericanos— está cambiando rápidamente, y también evolucionan sus expresiones artísticas, incluida la fotografía como arte.

Antaño los europeos decidieron que Europa terminaba en Los Pirineos y aislaron a España de su mundo. En los comienzos de la fotografía, España entraba en su largo período turbulento. "He vivido dos monarquías, dos dictaduras, dos repúblicas y ahora una democracia", me comentaba no hace mucho un amigo.

El siglo XX comenzó con la pérdida de las últimas colonias españolas; Puerto Rico y Filipinas fueron adquiridas por los Estados Unidos, y Cuba se hizo "independiente". El viejo mundo entró en su primera Gran Guerra y el nuevo orden comenzó a redefinir su faz. La Segunda Guerra Mundial trajo otro nuevo orden. Este período de grandes cambios se reflejó en la escena cultural con el surgimiento de las vanguardias en Europa y los Estados Unidos.

Los intelectuales exiliados provocaron grandes transformaciones en el arte americano. Poco después de la segunda guerra mundial, la ley de reinserción de los veteranos de guerra, estimuló un crecimiento en las escuelas de bellas artes, creando un "boom" en el arte y las artesanías de los Estados Unidos.

España, sin embargo, no participó en las dos grandes guerras y se mantuvo apartada del nuevo orden mundial. Trataba de consolidar su nación-estado y de definir su sistema político. Poco después de la Primera guerra mundial, las juntas militares se enfrentaron a revueltas de jóvenes oficiales, a huelgas generales, a conflictos laborales en Cataluña, etc., hasta llegar a la dictadura de Primo de Rivera. Más tarde se proclamó la Segunda república y todos estos conflictos culminaron en la Guerra civil española. A partir de este momento, España se aisló y fue rechazada por los demás.

En la guerra civil, entraron otros intereses europeos para poner a prueba la lucha por el poder que luego le dio en el continente. También fue terreno experimental para la fuerza de fotoperiodismo por parte de la prensa extranjera. Así, España se convirtió en taller para los fotógrafos europeos y norteamericanos. Este fue el período en que la fotografía evolucionaba de un proceso artístico o documental, a un proceso fotomecánico de información. En los años 20 y 30 aconteció una revolución fotográfica, al fundirse fotos y palabras para retratar los sucesos mundiales. A pesar de las dificultades, había fotógrafos en España, pero los materiales eran escasos y caros. Los catalanes contaban con la ventaja de poder cruzar la frontera para comprar película, papel y químicos. Pero la guerra civil devastó al país y el sufrimiento se hizo general. Aunque la economía se recuperaba y algunos materiales comenzaban a estar disponibles, la expresión cultural era sofocada. A duras penas era el lugar adecuado para que floreciese la libre expresión.

Aunque en el período de las dos dictaduras no se estimulaba mucho la creatividad, hubo fotógrafos que, venciendo los obstáculos, formaron agrupaciones en casi todas las ciudades españolas. La Real Sociedad Fotográfica de Madrid, fundada en 1899, continúa activa, lo mismo que la Sociedad Fotográfica de Zaragoza (1922), y el Grupo Fotográfico de Cataluña (1923). Estas sociedades fueron importantes para el intercambio de ideas, técnicas y estímulo. Hacían concursos de fotografía, exponían las fotos ganadoras e instituían salones donde los fotógrafos eran invitados a mostrar sus obras. También publicaban boletines donde se reproducían las obras gandoras o las fotos que se exponían en los salones. No obstante, contribuyeron a que el pictoralismo fotográfico se prolongase en España hasta mucho después de haber desaparecido en otros países. No eran tiempos para la innovación, excepto entre aquéllos que se exiliaron, como Josep Renau y otros que fueron asesinados, como Nikolas Lekuona.

En 1952 comenzó a publicarse la revista independiente de todos los grupos y sus boletines, *Arte Fotográfico* (aún en circulación). Esta revista ofreció una apertura a un mundo de la fotografía más vasto, al publicar artículos de revistas de otros países. Difundía información sobre concursos fotográficos, publicaba algunas de las ganadoras e incluso proporcionaba normas que ayudasen a ganar. Definió pautas nacionales que, de hecho, afirmaron el pictoralismo como corriente principal del arte fotográfico en España.

En 1956 la Agrupación Fotográfica Almeriense (AFAL) lanzó su boletín. Este grupo y su publicación se comprometió con obra más "intuitiva", menos estudiada, menos controlada formalmente. Ya que los salones se habían tornado muy cautos, AFAL se orientó hacia el arte fotográfico de avanzada, al mostrar más interés en la fotografía que en la persona que la realizó. AFAL llegó a obtener reconocimiento internacional. Sus miembros fueron invitados a participar en exposiciones en París, Milán y Venecia y les incluyeron en la exposición *Masterworks of Photography* de Edward Steichen en el Museo de Arte Moderno de Nueva York en 1958. En este grupo estaban Alberto Schommer y Gabriel Cualladó, presentes ambos en *La visión española*.

En esta misma época se formó un pequeño grupo de fotógrafos que vivían y trabajaban en Madrid, y que se reunían de vez en cuando en las oficinas de la Real Sociedad Fotográfica, para compartir sus ideas sobre la fotografía, y quienes en 1959 llegaron a ser conocidos como *La Palangana*. Este nombre lo inspiró una fotografía que presentaba los retratos de seis del grupo dentro de una palangana. Al mismo tiempo otros fotógrafos jóvenes iban a las oficinas de la Sociedad para aprender e intercambiar ideas. Algunos de ellos formaron otro grupo conocido como *La Colmena*. Rafael Sanz Lobato, fue uno de sus miembros.

La década de los 60 vio el fin de la publicación de AFAL y el comienzo de otra, *Imagen y Sonido* (1963). Esta revista se centró en fotógrafos conocidos y en las asociaciones fotográficas. En cierto modo el fomento de la fotografía que comenzó en los años 50 se debilitó, la competencia atrajo a principiantes y las imágenes volvieron a caer en los estereotipos. Fue en esta época que algunos de aquellos fotógrafos comenzaron a tener éxito trabajando para periódicos, revistas, televisión y cine.

A finales de los 60, con la guerra del Vietnam y sus protestas, el mayo del 68 y los "hippies", se vivió una época tumultuosa que repercutió en España. La explosión fotográfica que tuvo lugar en esos años fue documentada y publicada por la revista *Nueva Lente*. Desde el número "0", de julio de 1971, y a través de los 70s, *Nueva Lente* fomentó nuevos modos de pensar sobre la fotografía. En un principio Jorge Rueda fue el director artístico y la primera portada fue de Pablo Pérez Mínguez.

En *Nueva Lente* los fotógrafos hallaron un enfoque multidisciplinar, a través de artículos sobre diseño y estética. Mientras desempeñó el cargo de editor en 1975, Jorge Rueda involucró a Joan Fontcuberta, Manuel Falces, Miguel Angel Yáñez Polo y otros. En la actualidad *Nueva Lente* se considera un catalizador importante en el reconocimiento de la fotografía como una de las bellas artes en España. En ella se podía encontrar voz y aliento para un tipo de fotografía personal, del yo interior. Los 80 vieron la proliferación de revistas de fotografía: *PhotoVision* 1981, *Foto Profesional* 1982, *Diorama* 1984 y *La Fotografía* 1989. Aparte de *PhotoVision* estas revistas siguieron la tendencia de las revistas de fotografía americanas, una mezcla de consejos sobre técnicas y equipos y la publicación de porfolios de todo tipo de fotografía. *PhotoVision*, fundada por Joan Fontcuberta y Rafel Levenfeld, entre otros, es más bien una versión española de *Aperture*. Cada número está dedicado a un tema, o a un fotógrafo y se presenta con cierta profundidad intelectual.

La fotografía comenzó a enseñarse en las universidades en 1981. Antes, el aprendizaje dependía de revistas, de los pocos libros disponibles, de lo grupos de fotografía, o de las academias privadas que ofrecían cursos de cine y fotografía.

La estructura profesional para el fotógrafo serio, que ya existía en otros países, se desarrolló aquí mucho más tarde. La primera galería comercial se abrió en Barcelona en 1973, la segunda en Madrid, en 1975, pero aún no hay un museo español o institución artística dedicada a la fotografía exclusivamente. La primera exposición de fotografía española del nuevo *Museo Nacional y Centro de Arte Reina Sofía*, se ha llevado a cabo a finales de 1991.

Las galerías de arte abren sus puertas a la fotografía artística poco a poco, en general con una exposición al año pero con frecuencia muestran la obra de fotógrafos bien conocidos. Las galerías que promueven el trabajo de jóvenes artistas a veces incluyen fotografía hecha por fotógrafos, y también de artistas que utilizan la fotografía sólo como un elemento de su abanico técnico. Entre las más activas está la *Galería Moriarty* de Madrid, las galerías *Spectrum* de Zaragoza, **Forum** de Tarragona y *Visor Centre Fotografic* de Valencia. Se le da consideración seria a la fotografía en la prensa del arte y los periódicos, pero con raras excepciones (Joan Fontcuberta en un buen ejemplo), hay pocos críticos en el mejor sentido de la palabra. Las Cajas de Ahorro de España tienen departamentos culturales y salas de exposición, donde los fotógrafos muestran su obra. Los museos se interesan en la fotografía. *El Museo Español de Arte Contemporáneo*, a punto de cerrar sus puertas, (se va a unir con el *Centro de Arte Reina Sofía*), estableció un departamento de fotografía en 1984-85, e inició una serie importante de exposiciones. Las Comunidades fotografían, sobre todo de sus regiones. La Comunidad Autónoma de Madrid, el Ayuntamiento de Córdoba, el Gobierno Catalán y el Ayuntamiento de Barcelona han dado respaldo a la fotografía. Hay pocos coleccionistas de fotografía y menos representantes de fotógrafos profesionales, pero un andamiaje profesional se construye paulatinamente y la feria de arte anual de Madrid, ARCO, expone la fotografía como arte a los coleccionistas españoles.

La "nueva" España, organizada en Comunidades Autónomas, se ha descentralizado, destetando los intereses regionales de las influencias de Madrid, y abre el camino para exposiciones fotográficas más diversas. El cambio político también crea tensiones culturales, que se reflejan en la búsqueda de una expresión cultural donde lo "regional" y lo "europeo" se enfrentan. A partir de la entrada de España en la Comunidad Europea también surge una dicotomía "norte"-"sur" y una búsqueda de medios de expresión característicos del mediterráneo, reflejados en dos libros publicados recientemente: *La meva mediterrania* de Toni Catany (Barcelona, Lunwerg Editores, 1990); y *Contrapunto Mediterráneo* de Manuel Falces (Sevilla, Productora Andaluza de Programas, S.A., 1990).

La visión española comienza con fotografías tomadas durante los 70. Gabriel Cualladó expresa esta sensibilidad mediterránea en un retrato de su madre, con la mecedora vacía donde solía sentarse su padre, o en escenas rurales tan respetuosas de las personas y su ambiente. Del mismo modo, Rafael Lobato comunica respeto hacia las costumbres que desaparecen en una sociedad rural que cambia a ritmo vertiginoso, donde el estado se ha separado de la iglesia, pero donde la vida continúa como siempre. Francesc Catalá-Roca persiste en una visión urbana personalizada con imágenes realizadas mientras visitaba su exposición retrospectiva en el Spanish Institute en 1989. Hijo de otro fotógrafo muy conocido, Pere Catalá Pic, Francesc Catalá-Roca es el primero de su profesión que recibe el Premio Nacional de las Artes, en 1983. En los años 70 el tema urbano vuelve a ocupar un lugar importante en la fotografía española. Las fotos de Catalá-Roca de los años 40 y 50 son un documento de los mercados negros que brotaron a causa del racionamiento de esa época. Uno de sus hijos, Andreu Catalá Pedersen, también trabaja con la escena urbana. Las escenas chispeantes en las fotos de Andreu representan el "teatro de la calle" en Cataluña, un fenómeno muy urbano.

Aberto Schommer es muy conocido en España por sus libros, sus retratos de figuras públicas y una serie semanal de retratos en la revista dominical de uno de los principales periódicos. Schommer es un fotógrafo muy versátil. De su obra, *La visión española* contiene una serie muy personal, *Civilizaciones*, (antes expuesta en la galería Juana Mordó de Madrid), la cual demuestra su habilidad como retratista de objetos.

Gerardo Vielba está representado aquí con obras que pertenecen a un estilo clásico, con un toque único de lirismo. En la actualidad dedica gran parte de su tiempo a escribir y a la Real Sociedad Fotográfica, como director. Su obra fotográfica pone de manifiesto cómo él y otros fueron capaces de salir de la fotografía "oficial" de un período anterior, al asimilar diferentes actitudes resultantes de corrientes fuera de España mientras que su obra escrita manifiesta también una forma de compartir sus ideas personales sobre la situación del arte fotográfico de antaño.

En la década de los 70, la fotografía española cambia, se hace más introspectiva, más libre de los dictados previos, y se añade color al lenguaje fotográfico. Las fotos de Jorge Rueda nos muestran el choque de los cambios rápidos que se dieron en su mundo a través de comentarios personales, irónicos, surreales y mordaces. Pablo Pérez Mínguez juega con los símbolos folklóricos tradicionales. Para ello utiliza personas famosas (y no tan famosas) como modelos. Manuel Falces comenzó su carrera en los años 70. Su obra enlaza el mundo entre *Nueva Lente* y otras influencias europeas, con el uso intencional de la mentira de la fotografía para mostrar su verdad, con humor e ironía y de vez en cuando con imágenes un poco borrosas, a veces fuera de foco, así como el collage. Otro de los fotógrafos que regresa a las posibilidades del collage, y otros procesos experimentales es Miguel Angel Yáñez Polo. Su obra, muy personal, revela una visión surreal de un mundo que combina muchos de sus intereses personales así como un mundo que cambia velozmente. Su interés en la historia de la fotografía española le llevó, junto a otros, a organizar la *Sociedad de Historia de la Fotografía Española* a mitad de los años 80.

Rafael Navarro explora en blanco y negro temas como *Forma, Evasiones, Presencias,* culminando en su muy conocida serie de *Dípticos*. Su obra está representada por una selección de su reciente serie *Homenaje a siglo y medio*, que alude al aniversario de la fotografía. Realizada mientras exponía en el Museo Chateau d'Eau en Francia, esta obra funde la fotografía de ayer con la de hoy, acercando años y puntos de vista con la realidad y la reflexión sobre la realidad.

Joan Fontcuberta es el más conocido de los fotógrafos españoles en los Estados Unidos. Es prolífico, multifacético y sus escritos y sus ideas sobre la fotografía son tan influyentes como su obra fotográfica. La serie de jardines presentada aquí es especialmente callada, lírica, elegante y sofisticada.

La década de los 80 comenzó en España con una consolidación de los procesos democráticos, y a su vez, el movimiento conocido como la Movida. La Movida fue para Madrid y otras ciudades españolas, lo que fue el "underground" para Nueva York en un tiempo anterior. Los artistas y fotógrafos celebraron el "kitsch" y las revistas experiementales, tales como *La Luna de Madrid, Madriz* y *Madrid me mata*, documentaron y comunicaron los "happenings", por medio de las artes gráficas y la fotografía. Pero con toda la exhuberancia y extroversión que esta movida contenía, también hubo un interesante proceso de introspección.

Juan Ramón Yuste, uno de los fotógrafos que retrataron personalidades de aquel tiempo, realizó una serie de autorretratos con un uso de la luz muy especial. Una selección de esta serie forma parte de *La visión española*. Este grupo de fotografías termina con un gracioso doble autorretrato. Para esta imagen se usa un "flash" en la máquina fotográfica, de este modo tanto la luz como el objeto que le emite, se convierten en tema.

Antonio Bueno es otro fotógrafo que también utiliza la luz como objeto. Al "escribir" con ésta, la hace protagonista y fuente de iluminación. En *La visión española*, hay una selección de su serie *Graphis*, la cual demuestra de modo vivaz, el uso de esta luz para examinar espacios interiores.

Ouka Lele (Bárbara Allende) adopta un nombre instrumental, y su documentación de la "Movida" también lo es, a través de un estilo "pop", con colores fuertes, y de la puesta en escena de diferentes modelos tanto en exteriores como en interiores. Madrid es su escenario y sus habitantes son los actores. Esta artista expresa una conciencia renovada de la libertad creativa en fotografías que son únicas, casi siempre coloreadas a mano. Esta exposición contiene una muestra de su serie de escenarios sobre la mujer, y un autorretrato.

Tony Catany es más conocido en España, Francia y los Estados Unidos por sus fotografías a color de naturalezas muertas, aunque también ha realizado una serie de escenas de viaje y desnudos y ha incursionado en el blanco y negro. La serie presentada en esta exposición es de bodegones de frutas y flores. Son fotos sensibles, introspectivas, líricas y a veces, irónicas. Siempre hermosas.

Eduardo Momeñe trabaja en blanco y negro y explora el cuerpo humano con un enfoque casi fetichista y narcisista, al fotografiar varias actitudes de una modelo posando con un pie puesto sobre un objeto drapeado, o sentada, siempre sin rostro. Son imágenes con resonancias de actitud clásica y escultural.

Josep Batlle ha creado tres series de bodegones en blanco y nego. Se titulan "Natures Mortes", "Natures Vives" (representada en esta exposición) y "Natures animades". Los títulos de la serie juegan con la frase catalana *natura morta* que en arte, se refiere a, "naturaleza muerta" o bodegón. Utiliza mezclas de objetos y animales que forman códigos misteriosos y dan pistas para la naturaleza de lo "vivo", lo "animado" o lo "muerto", en imágenes muy bien amarradas, con una luz dura y un positivado muy contrastado.

Rafael Levenfeld también trabaja en blanco y negro. Su serie de autorretratos utiliza a Madrid como escenario —la calle o espacios exteriores o interiores— para un examen introspectivo de sí mismo, a veces un tanto disfrazado, pero siempre intenso, no obstante el humor, y con una composición elegante.

Nestor Torrens, es uno de los dos representantes de la "periferia" española, Las Islas Canarias. Ha producido una obra a color muy particular. Esta serie refleja su ambiente, y usa la luz como protagonista al "escribir" un círculo o figura de líneas, o como un chorro de agua cayendo sobre una piedra. Aquí Torrens reconoce lo que la mayoría de los turistas saben de las islas —su paisaje único. Joaquín Columé, nació en Andalucía pero ha vivido la mayor parte de su vida en Las Palmas. La obra de Columé en esta exposición trata un tema que ha causado mucha controversia en España; el boxeo. Fanático de este deporte —prohibido en la televisión pública española— Columé ha desplegado estas imágenes en un televisor y las ha fotografiado de la pantalla. Esta serie, titulada "K.O.", nos recuerda que la libertad no es completamente libre.

Desde finales de los 80, ha sido materialmente posible explorar procesos nuevos y antiguos. La economía se recupera rápido y muchos productos importados están disponibles a precios más razonables. Es posible viajar. Dos fotógrafos de esta exposición estudiaron en los Estados Unidos. Paca Arceo recibió una beca para estudiar en este país. Su estilo manifiesta una comprensión del enfoque norteamericano. La obra que le representa en esta exposición es una serie que demuestra la "nuevas" y "viejas" tensiones de un modo muy personal.

Isabel Muñoz estudió fotografía en los Estados Unidos desde 1984 a 1987. Muñoz trabaja en blanco y negro, y es de todos los fotógrafos españoles la única que utiliza el proceso de platino. Su serie *Tango*, realizada en Argentina y Madrid, aborda este baile nostálgico de una manera apropiada, seductiva y sensual, con este antigüo método.

La nostalgia no forma parte de la paleta emocional española, pero los procesos antiguos de bicromato que Rodrigo Mosquera utiliza para realizar sus fotografías en blanco y negro crean un sentido de nostalgia digno de cualquier remembranza de fin de siglo. José Gómez Aparicio retoca sus retratos con un baño de selenio, rodeándolos de una sensación de misterio.

En primera instancia los retratos de Rafael Vargas son muy accesibles, dado su enfoque frontal, pero una lectura cuidadosa nos recompensa con una revelación muy personal. José Malibrán nos permite atisbar a través de su ventana, hacia el ámbito privado de una mujer. Copiados en tamaño pequeño, hace nuestra visión del lugar tan privada como el lugar mismo, y lo logra con elegancia y respeto. Chema Madoz, ganador del premio de Fotógrafos Jóvenes Europeos (1991), también trabaja en blanco y negro. A primera vista, se ven objetos cotidianos, pero luego se percibe algo poco usual en ellos. Vemos una llave, pero la cerradura aparece en su empuñadura, o el cuchillo, que usualmente reduce algo al cortarlo, en este caso mide, y la escalera conduce a un espejo. Su visión de los objetos cotidianos es irónica, surreal, nítida.

Jorge Lens Leiva es uno de los pocos fotógrafos españoles que utiliza el enfoque del "nuevo color". Al representar la parte norte de su país, nos provée un espacio silencioso para la contemplación, y en la imagen titulada "Mano", demuestra una habilidad para mostrar otro modo de representar la paciencia.

María José Gómez Redondo utiliza "apropiaciones", exposiciones y montajes para crear un trabajo de ensoñación en el cual no se permite ningún monstruo. Su serie de fotos en *La visión española* representa los cinco sentidos, el "sexto" —que es elemento fundamental de su técnica— lo deja a la deducción del espectador.

Estos fotógrafos dan una idea de cómo será la fotografía de autor en los 90 y después. Estudian bellas artes, viajan, exploran y experimentan con técnicas nuevas. Algunos participaron en el primer gran taller sobre la historia y estética de la creación fotográfica a color, llevado a cabo en el Círculo de Bellas Artes de Madrid durante el invierno-primavera de 1990. Dos de los conferenciantes eran norteamericanos. Uno de ellos admitió en privado su sorpresa ante la alta calidad de la obra de los participantes; había pensado que la fotografía española estaría más cercana al trabajo de aficionados.

La España multicultural y multilingüe no dejará de ofrecer inspiración a sus fotógrafos para una gran expresión visual. Expresión que ha sido caracterizada por Juan Ignacio Hernáiz como cargada de "exageración, ampulosidad, tremendismo, radicalismo, apasionamiento, exhuberancia, desequilibrio, exaltación y desmesura". Está claro que España no es el lugar que el premio Nobel Camilo José Cela una vez describió como "... un país tan pobre que no se puede tener dos ideas de la misma persona".

A través de esta exposición, el Nuevo Mundo tiene la oportunidad de observar directamente la Visión Española en la Fotografía de la nueva España.

SELECTED BIBLIOGRAPHY / BIBLIOGRAFIA SELECTA

CARR, Raymond. *Modern Spain, 1875 - 1980*. New York, Oxford University Press, 1980.

FONTANELLA, Lee. *La historia de la fotografía en España desde sus orígenes hasta 1900*. Madrid, Ediciones El Viso, 1981.

FONTCUBERTA, Joan. *Crítica y nuevas tendencias*, en LA CRITICA FOTOGRAFICA. Bilbao, Caja de Ahorros Vizcaína, 1988.

HAHN, Betty, ed. *Contemporary Spanish Photography*. Albuquerque, University of New Mexico Press, 1987.

HERNAIZ, Juan Ignacio. *Análisis estético de la fotografía española*, en FOTO PROFESIONAL, julio 1991, p. 45.

Idas & Chaos, Trends in Spanish Photography, 1920-1945. Madrid, Ministerio de Cultura, 1945.

LOPEZ MONDEJAR, Publio. *Las fuentes de la memoria: Fotografía y sociedad en la España del siglo XIX*. Barcelona, Lunwerg Editores, 1989.

MUSEO ESPAÑOL DE ARTE CONTEMPORANEO. *Fotografías de la escuela de Madrid, obra 1950 - 1975*. Madrid, Ministerio de Cultura, 1988.

MUSEO NACIONAL CENTRO DE ARTE REINA SOFIA. *Cuatro direcciones: Fotografía contemporánea española, 1970 - 1990*. Barcelona, Lunwerg Editores, 1991.

PEREZ SIQUIER, Carlos. *Grupo AFAL, 1956 - 1991*. Almería, Almediterránea con la Junta de Andalucía, 1991.

SANZ LOBATO, Rafael y DE JUAN y PEÑALOSA, Koncha. *La fotografía y la Guerra Civil Española*, en LA GUERRA CIVIL ESPAÑOLA, EXPOSICION ITINERANTE. Madrid, Ministerio de Cultura, 1983.

VIELBA, Gerardo. *Una revista de las revistas fotográficas*, en FOTO PROFESIONAL, mayo 1991, pp. 28 - 34.

CATALOG OF THE EXHIBITION / CATALOGO DE LA EXPOSICION

THE PHOTOGRAPHERS INCLUDED / LOS FOTOGRAFOS INCLUIDOS

PACA ARCEO
JOSEP BATLLE
ANTONIO BUENO
ANDREU CATALA PEDERSEN
FRANCESC CATALA-ROCA
TONI CATANY
JOAQUIN COLUME
GABRIEL CUALLADO
MANUEL FALCES
JOAN FONTCUBERTA
JOSE GOMEZ APARICIO
MARIA JOSE GOMEZ REDONDO
JORGE LENS LEIVA
RAFAEL LEVENFELD
RAFAEL S. LOBATO
CHEMA MADOZ
LUIS MALIBRAN
EDUARDO MOMEÑE
RODRIGO MOSQUERA
ISABEL MUÑOZ
RAFAEL NAVARRO
OUKA LELE
PABLO PEREZ MINGUEZ
JORGE RUEDA
ALBERTO SCHOMMER
NESTOR TORRENS
RAFAEL VARGAS
GERARDO VIELBA
MIGUEL ANGEL YAÑEZ POLO
JUAN RAMON YUSTE

PACA ARCEO

Born Madrid, 1945 / Nació en Madrid, 1945

Individual Exhibitions
Exposiciones individuales

1981   "Puertas y ventanas". París, Munich,
        Viena, Londres.
1982   El Ateneo de Madrid. Madrid, España.
1983   Posada del Potro. Córdoba, España.
1984   Exposición sobre Arquitectura Medieval
        en España. Biblioteca Española. París,
        Francia.
1987   Centro de Estudios de la Imagen.
        Madrid, España.
1989   Museo Español de Arte Contemporáneo.
        Madrid, España.

Group Exhibitions
Exposiciones colectivas

1979   Club de Amigos de la UNESCO.
        Madrid, España.
1982   Arteder 82. Bilbao, España.
        Artistas por la libertad. Centro Cultural de
        la Villa. Madrid, España.
1983   ARCO 83. Galería Redor. Madrid,
        España.
        Cultural Center La Peña. Berkeley.
        California, EE.UU.
1984   ARCO 84. Galería Imágenes. Madrid,
        España.
        Centro de la Juventud Marqués de Riscal.
        Madrid, España.
1985   Isabel Percy West Gallery. Oakland,
        California, EE.UU.
        Artist's Gallery. Oakland, California,
        EE.UU.
        Camerawork. San Francisco, California,
        EE.UU.
1986   FOCO 86. Círculo de Bellas Artes.
        Madrid, España.
        PROCESOS. Museo Nacional Centro de
        Arte Reina Sofía. Madrid, España.
        Centro Cultural del Conde Duque.
        Madrid, España.
        Palacio Aguirre. Cartagena, España.
1987   Palau Sollerio. Palma de Mallorca,
        España.
        Palacio San Esteban. Murcia, España.
        Palacio de Cristal. Madrid, España.
1988   Art et Nouvelles Technologies. Montreal,
        Quebec, Canadá.
        El Ayuntamiento de Siena. Italia.
1989   Palacio de la Cultura. Praga,
        Checoslovaquia.

Photographs included in the exhibition
Fotografías contenidas en la exposición

1. El jueves. 1990. Cibachrome. 27,5 x 40 cm.
2. El jueves siguiente. 1990. Cibachrome. 27,5 x 40 cm.
3. La oferta y la demanda. 1990. Cibachrome.
    27,5 x 40 cm.
4. Vivir en Madrid. 1990. Cibachrome.
    27,5 x 40 cm.
5. A su aire. 1990. Cibachrome. 27,5 x 40 cm.

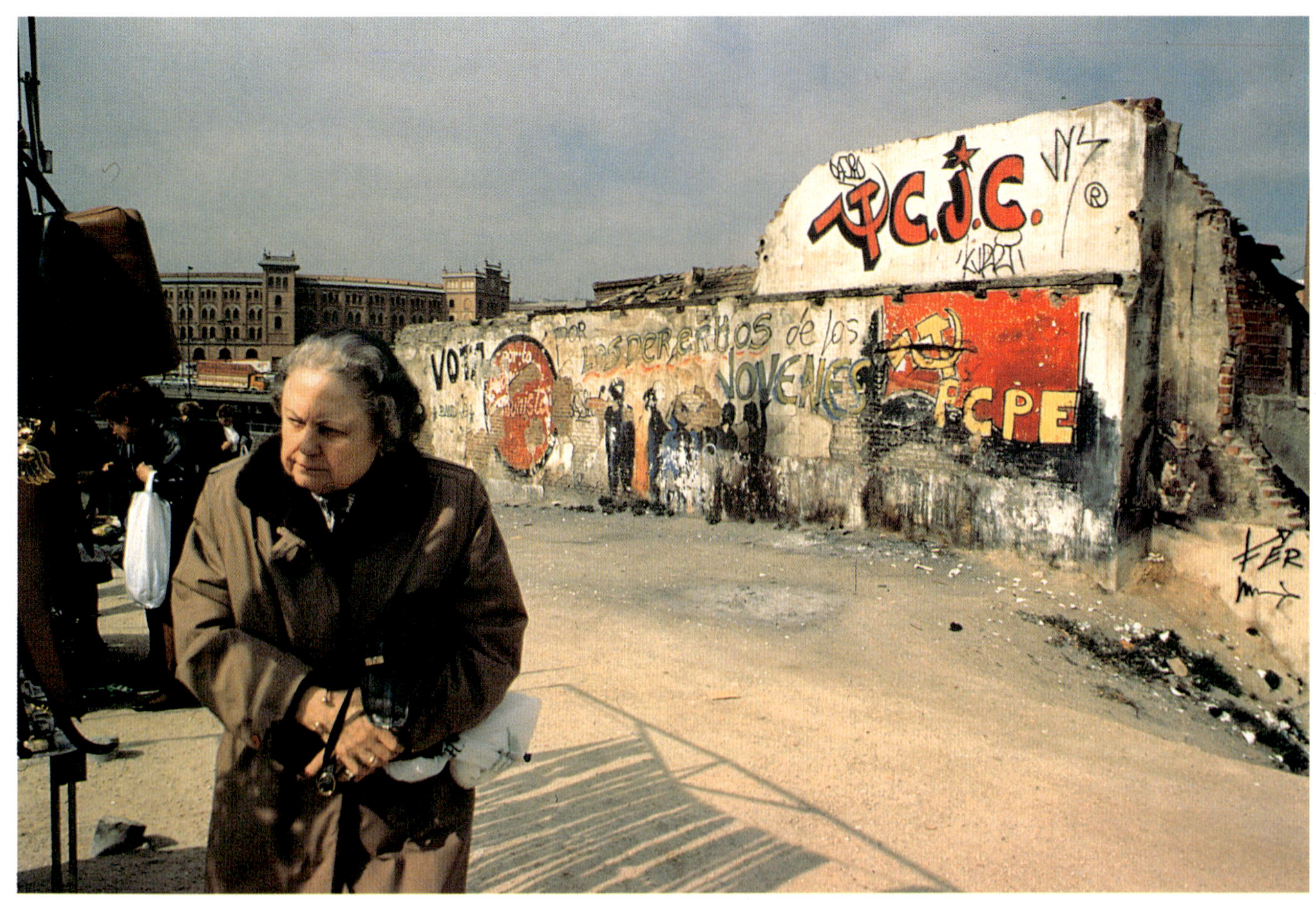

El jueves

1990

Cibachrome

27,5 x 40 cm.

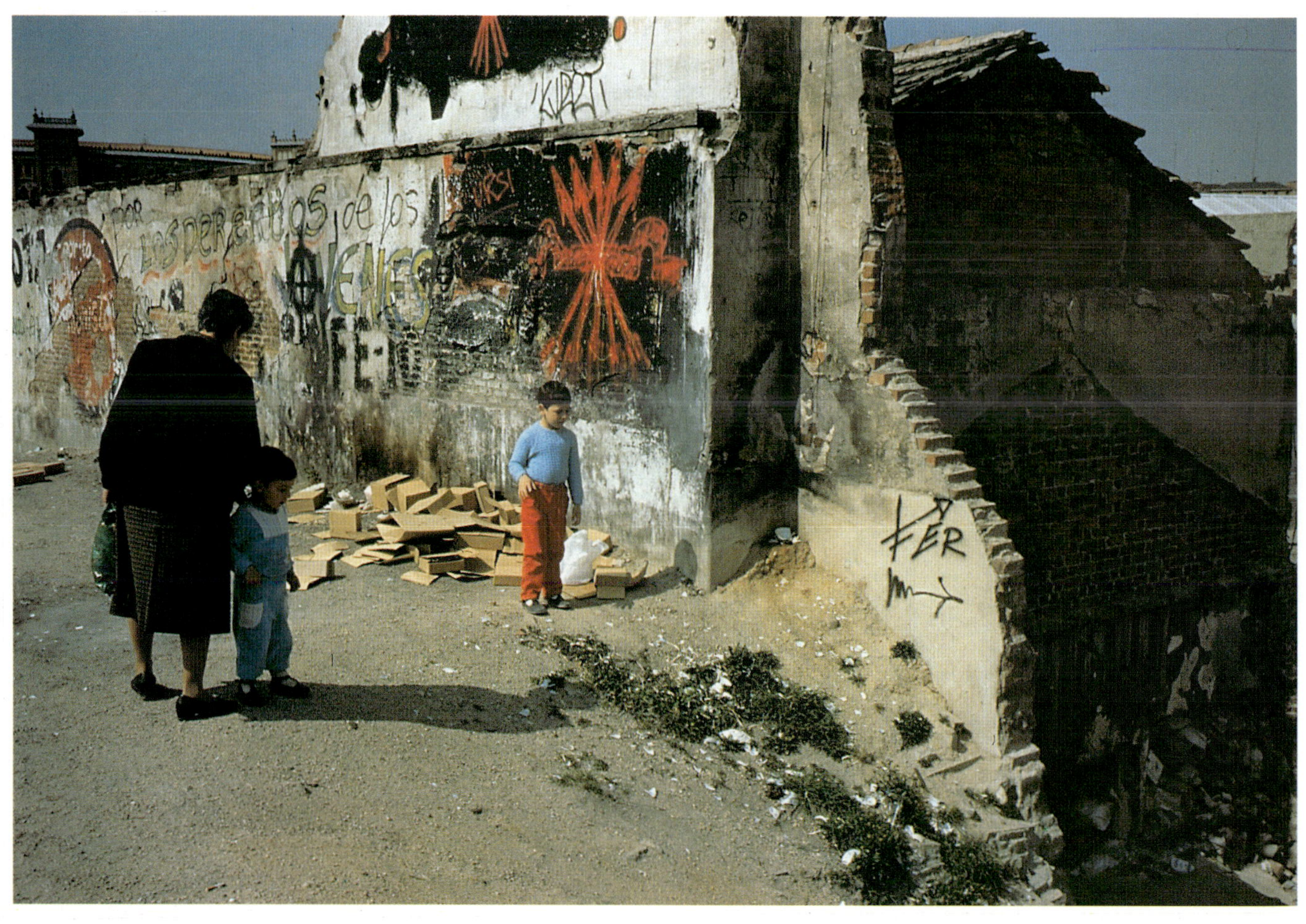

El jueves siguiente

1990

Cibachrome

27,5 x 40 cm.

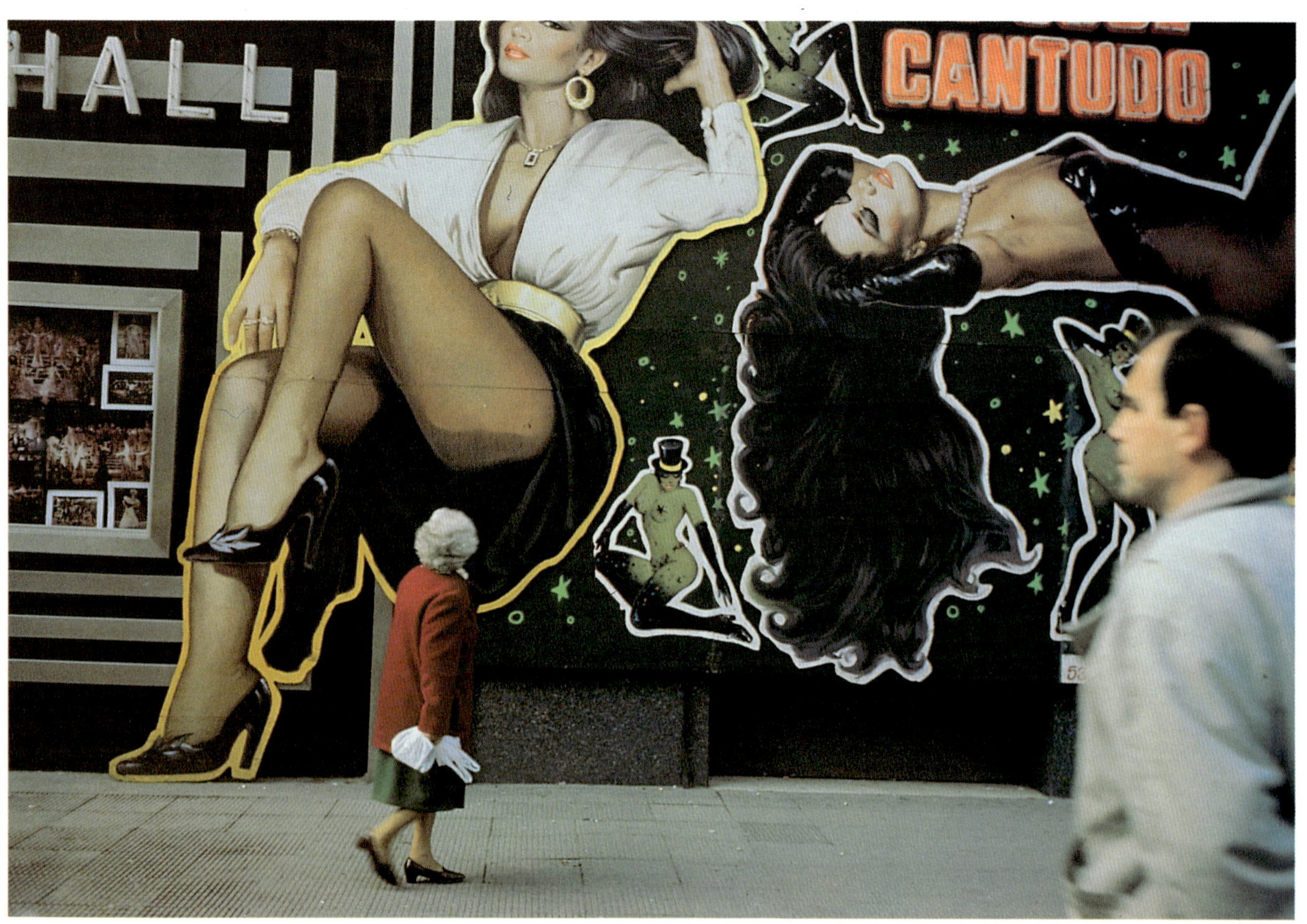

La oferta y la demanda

1990

Cibachrome

27,5 x 40 cm.

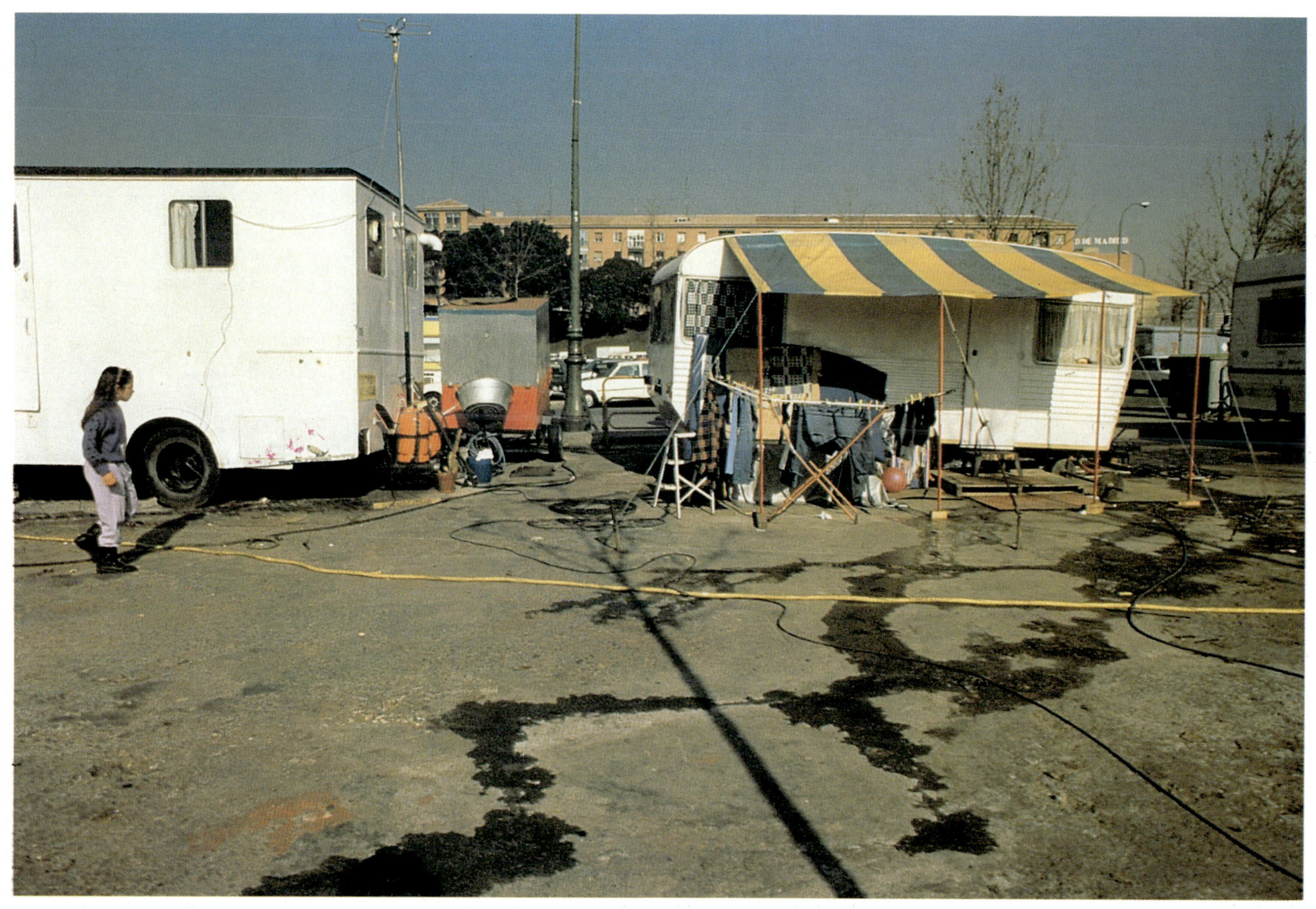

Vivir en Madrid
1990
Cibachrome
27,5 x 40 cm.

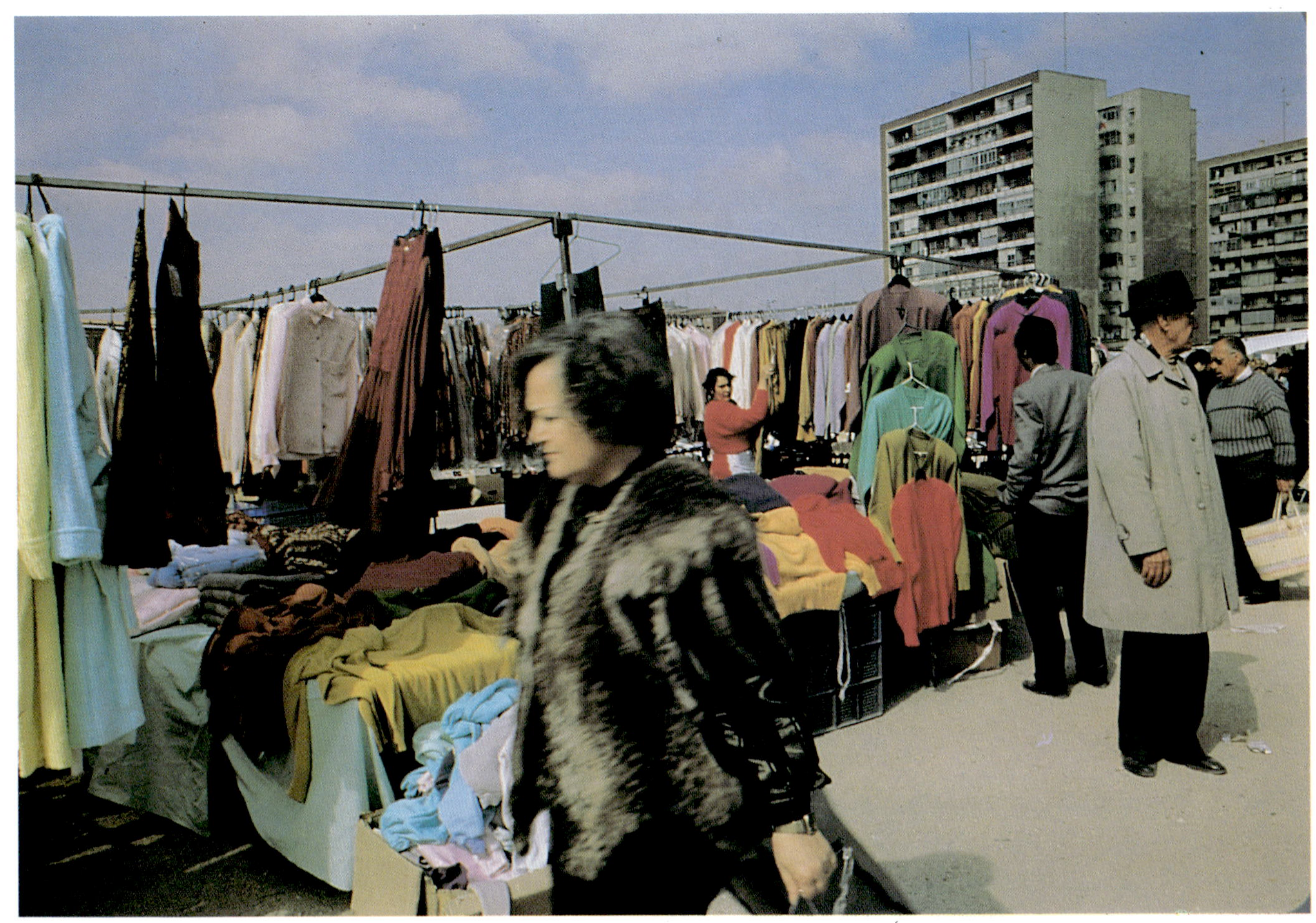

A su aire
1990
Cibachrome
27,5 x 40 cm.

JOSEP BATLLE

Born Barcelona, 1958 / Nació en Barcelona 1958

Individual Exhibitions
Exposiciones individuales

1988   "Natures Mortes" La Cantonada.
        Granollers. Barcelona, España.
1989   Sala Minerva. Círculo de Bellas Artes.
        Madrid, España.
1990   Colour Art Photo. Valencia, España.
        La Florida. Hospitalet, España.

Group Exhibitions
Exposiciones colectivas

1985   Bienal Producions Juvenils de l'Europa
        Mediterrània. Barcelona, España.
1986   Tres Historias. C. Masellera. S. Boi.
        Barcelona, España.

1987   Bienal P. S. M. Casa Caritat. Barcelona,
        España.
1989   Deu Fotografs a Barcelona. Barcelona,
        España.
        Bienal P. S. M. Casa Caritat. Barcelona,
        España.
1990   Semana Internacional de fotografía.
        Ateneo Peninsular de Mérida, México.

Photographs included in the exhibition
Fotografías contenidas en la exposición

1. Helix Aspersa I. 1988. 30 x 30 cm. B/N.
2. Helix Aspersa II. 1988. 30 x 30 cm. B/N.
3. Bombix Mori, IV. 1988. 30 x 30 cm. B/N.
4. Bombix Mori, VIII. 1988. 30 x 30 cm. B/N.
5. Spinculus Nuous. 1988. 30 x 30 cm. B/N.

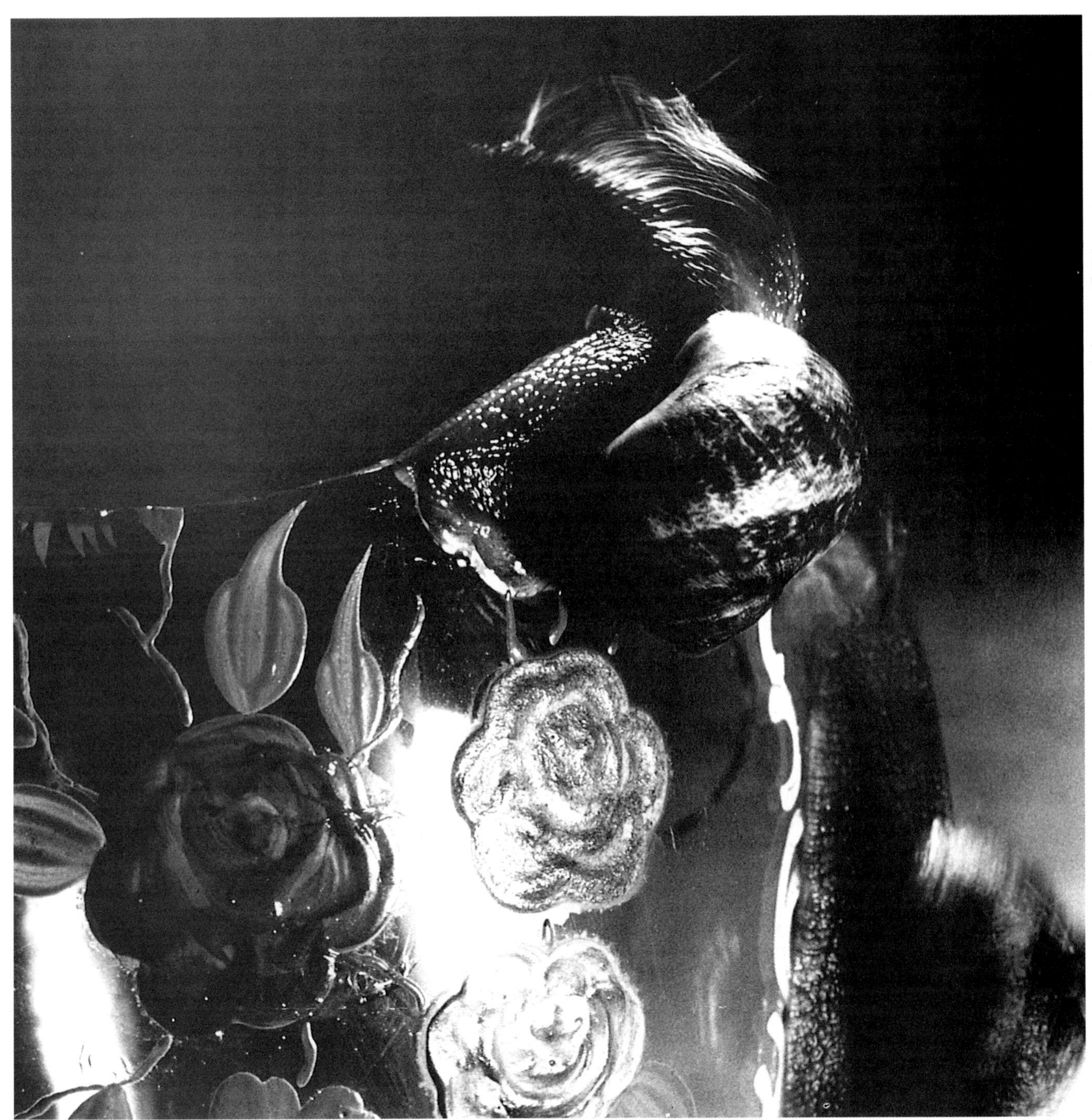

Helix Aspersa I

1988

30 x 30 cm.

B/N

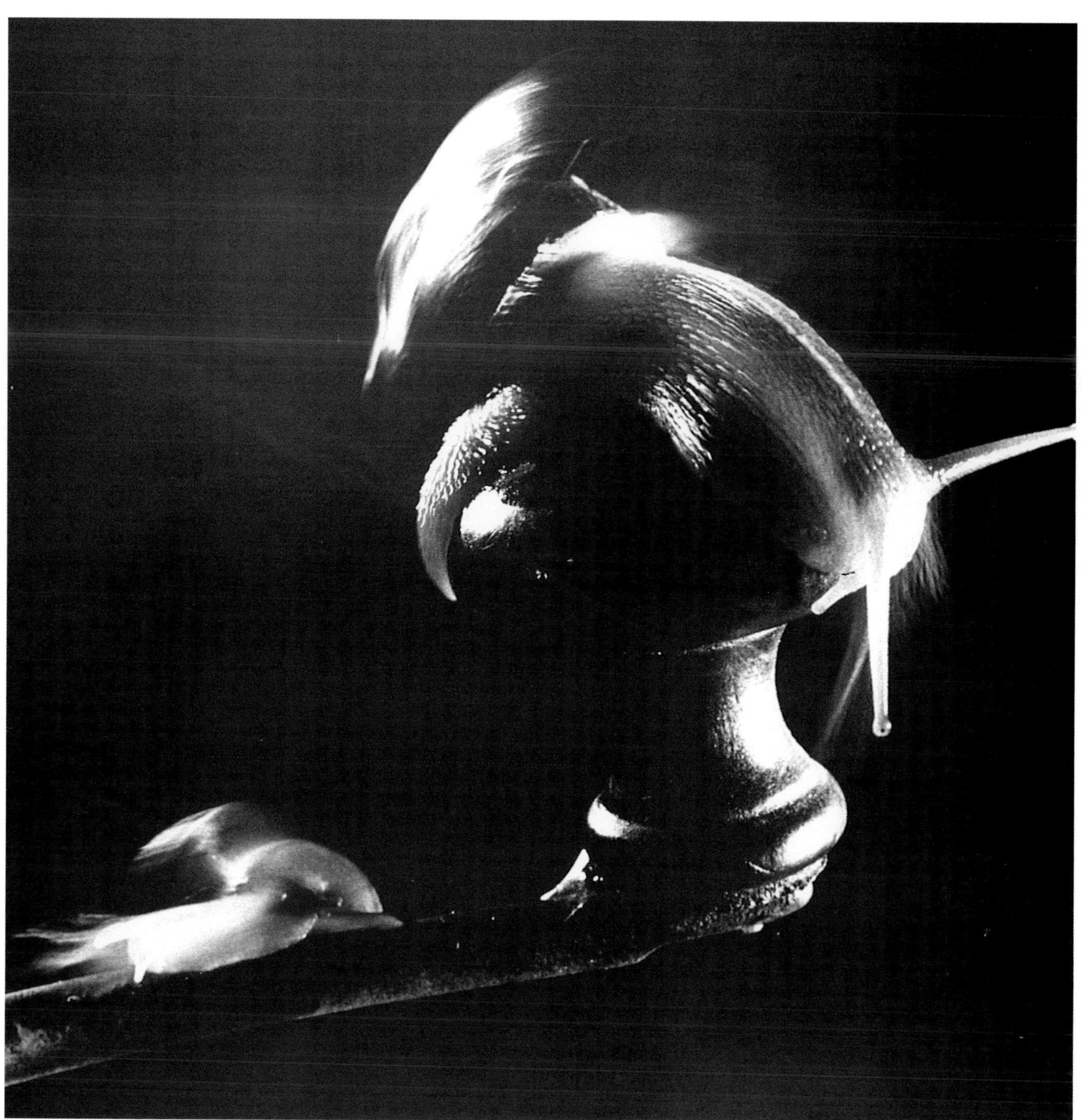

Helix Aspersa II
1988
30 x 30 cm.
B/N

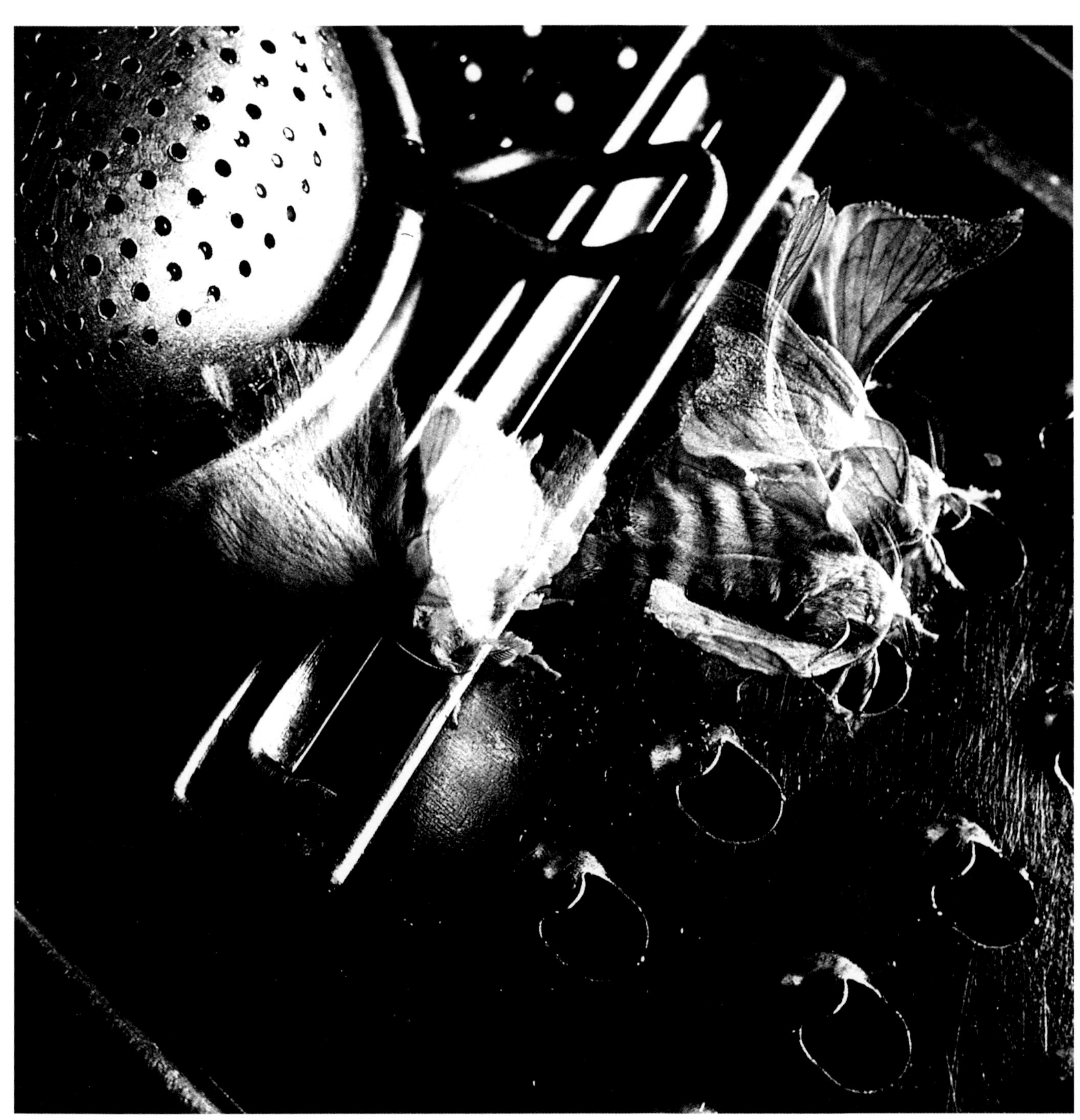

Bombix Mori, IV
1988
30 x 30 cm.
B/N

ANTONIO BUENO

Born Madrid, 1956 / Nació en Madrid, 1956

Individual Exhibitions
Exposiciones individuales

1980	Galería Redor. Madrid, España.
1981	Galería Procés. Barcelona, España.
	Galería Spectrum. Zaragoza, España.
1983	Instalación "'El bosque de las sombras". Museo Porvincial de Bellas Artes. Zaragoza, España.
	Galería Mixto-4. Zaragoza, España.
1984	Galería Cámara Oscura. Logroño, España.
1985	Galería Gualdalquivir. Sevilla, España.
	Galería Kem Dammy. Brescia, Italia.
1986	Sala Dos Peiraos. Vigo, España.
1988	"Foco 88". Círculo de Bellas Artes. Madrid, España.
	Sala Pallarés. León, España.
	Galería Spectrum. Zaragoza, España.
1989	Palacio Condes de Gavia. Granada, España.
1990	Colegio Oficial de Arquitectos de Canarias. Tenerife, España.
	Galería Jorge Kreisler. Madrid, España.
1991	Caja de Ahorros de Asturias. Itinerante por Gijón, Avilés y Mieres, España.

Main Group Exhibitions
Principales Exposiciones colectivas

1980	Instalación "Ambientación en negro, 15 artistas de Bellas Artes". Palacio de Velázquez. Madrid, España.
1981	Museo Español de Arte Contemporáneo. Madrid, España.
1982	Galería Redor, "Arco 82". Madrid, España.
	"Cinco". Galería Kreisler Dos. Madrid, España.
1983	Palacio de la Madraza. Granada, España.
	Galería Kreisler Dos. Madrid, España.
	"259 Imágenes". Círculo de Bellas Artes. Madrid, España.
	Exposición itinerante. España.
	"Madrid, Madrid, Madrid". Centro Cultural de la Villa. Madrid, España.
1985	"Nuevos Imagineros". Europalia. Charleroi, Bélgica.
	"Fotografien aus Spanien". Museum Folkwang. Essen, R. F. Alemania.
1986	"Cometel cometa". Galería Ovidio. Madrid, España.
	"La Fotografía en el Museo". Museo Español de Arte Contemporáneo. Madrid, España.
	"A Cor". Universidad Internacional Menéndez Pelayo. La Coruña, España.
1987	"La Guerra Civil". Sala Canal Isabel II, itinerante por ciudades españolas.
1988	"Arco 88". Galería Spectrum. Zaragoza, España.
	"Foco 88". Círculo de Bellas Artes. Madrid, España.
1989	"Spanish Eyes". Clarence. Kenedy Gallery. Boston, Massachusetts, EE.UU.
1990	"Colección 50 x 60 Polaroid". Escola Massana, Primavera fotográfica 90. Barcelona, España.
	"Fotografía española contemporánea". Bienal de Fotografía de Mérida. México.

Photographs included in the exhibition
Fotografías contenidas en la exposición

1. T.V. y puerta. 1984-85. Cibachrome. 60 x 60 cm.
2. Abriendo puerta. 1984-85. Cibachrome. 60 x 60 cm.
3. Cama y teléfono. 1984-85. Cibachrome. 60 x 60 cm.
4. Silla y sombra. 1984-85. Cibachrome. 60 x 60 cm.
5. Maleta. 1984-85. Cibachrome. 85 x 85 cm.

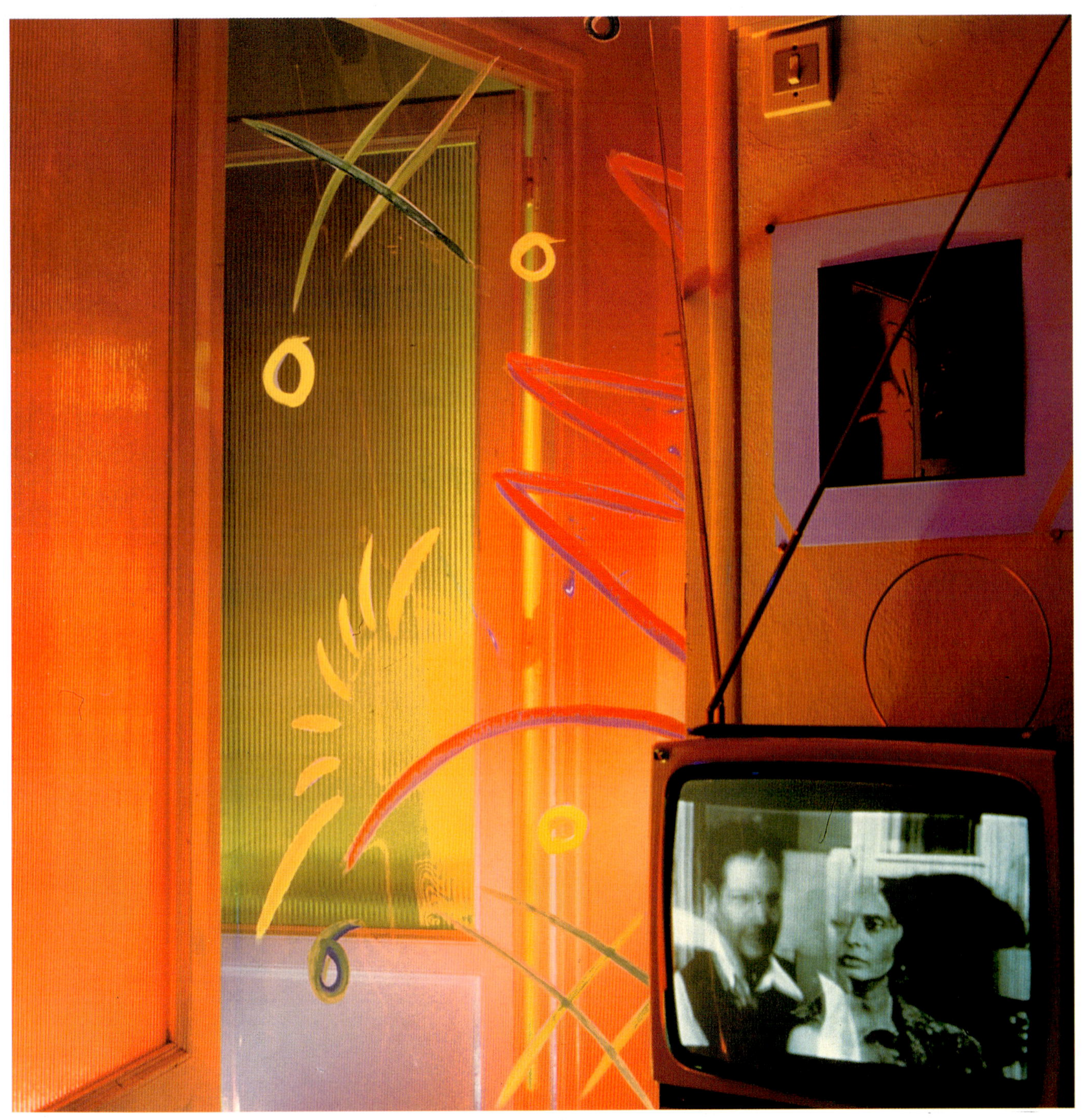

T. V. y puerta

1984-1985

Cibachrome

60 x 60 cm.

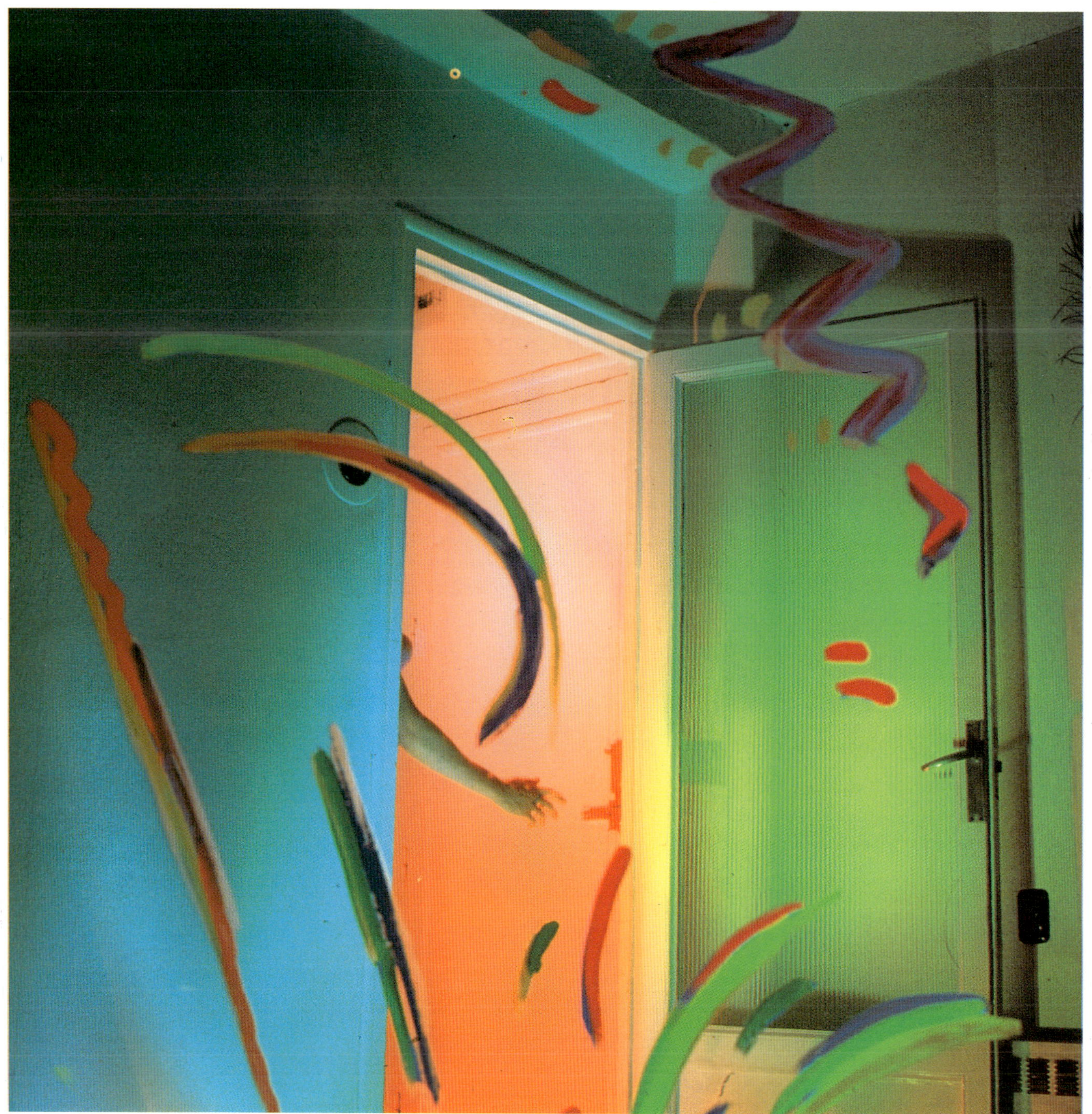

Abriendo puerta

1984-1985

Cibachrome

60 x 60 cm.

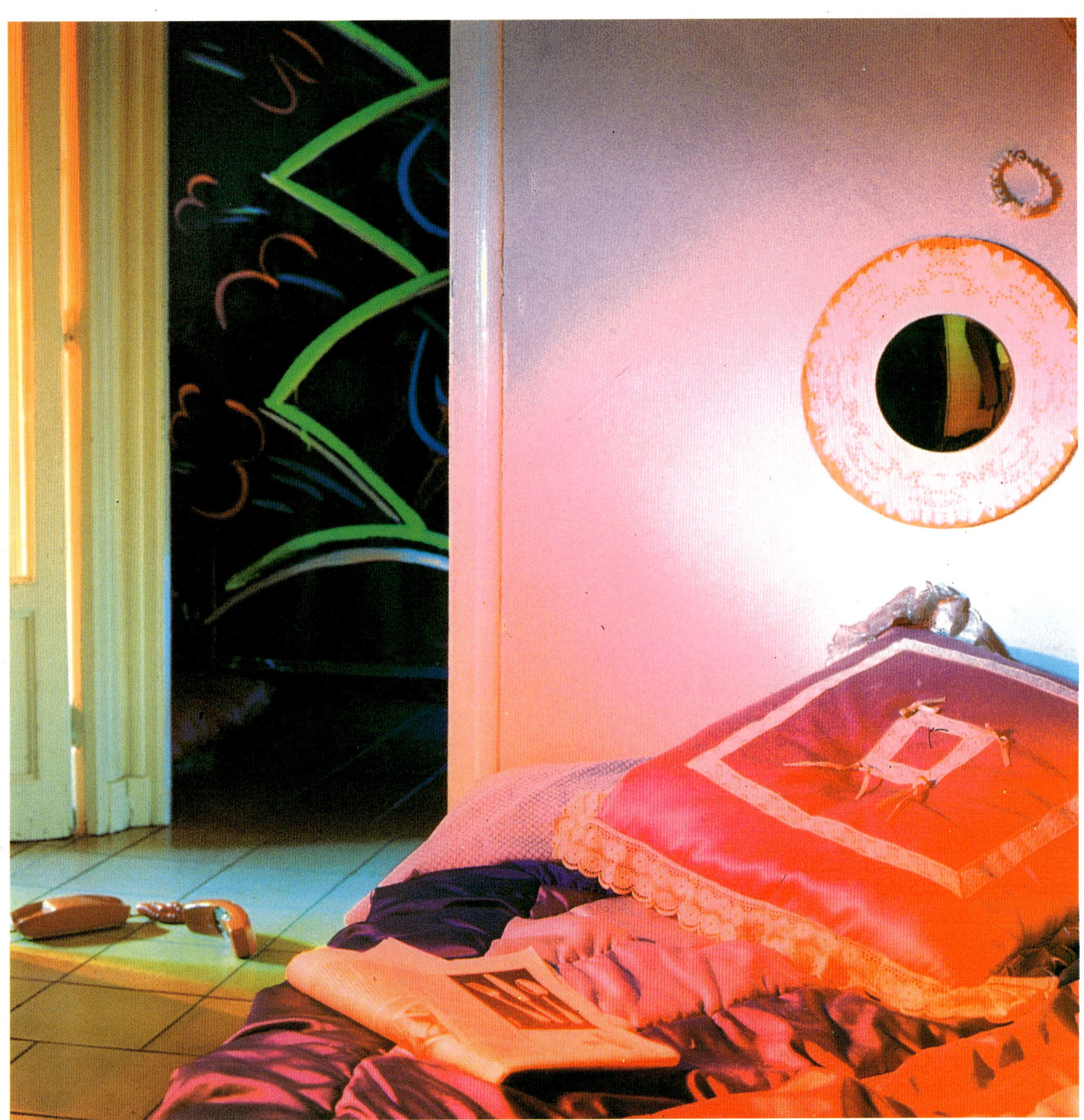

Cama y teléfono

1984-1985

Cibachrome

60 x 60 cm.

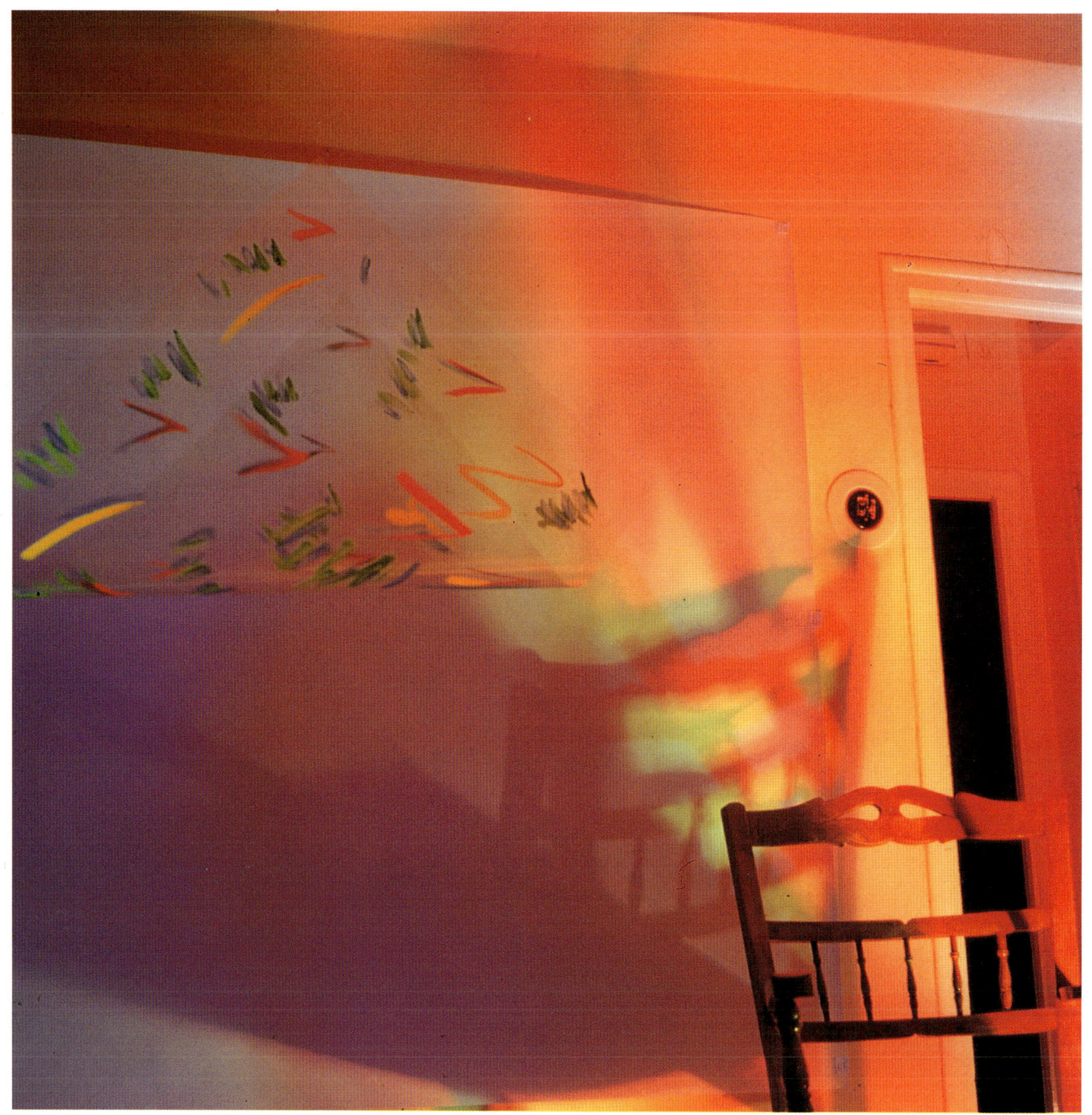

Silla y sombra

1984-1985

Cibachrome

60 x 60 cm.

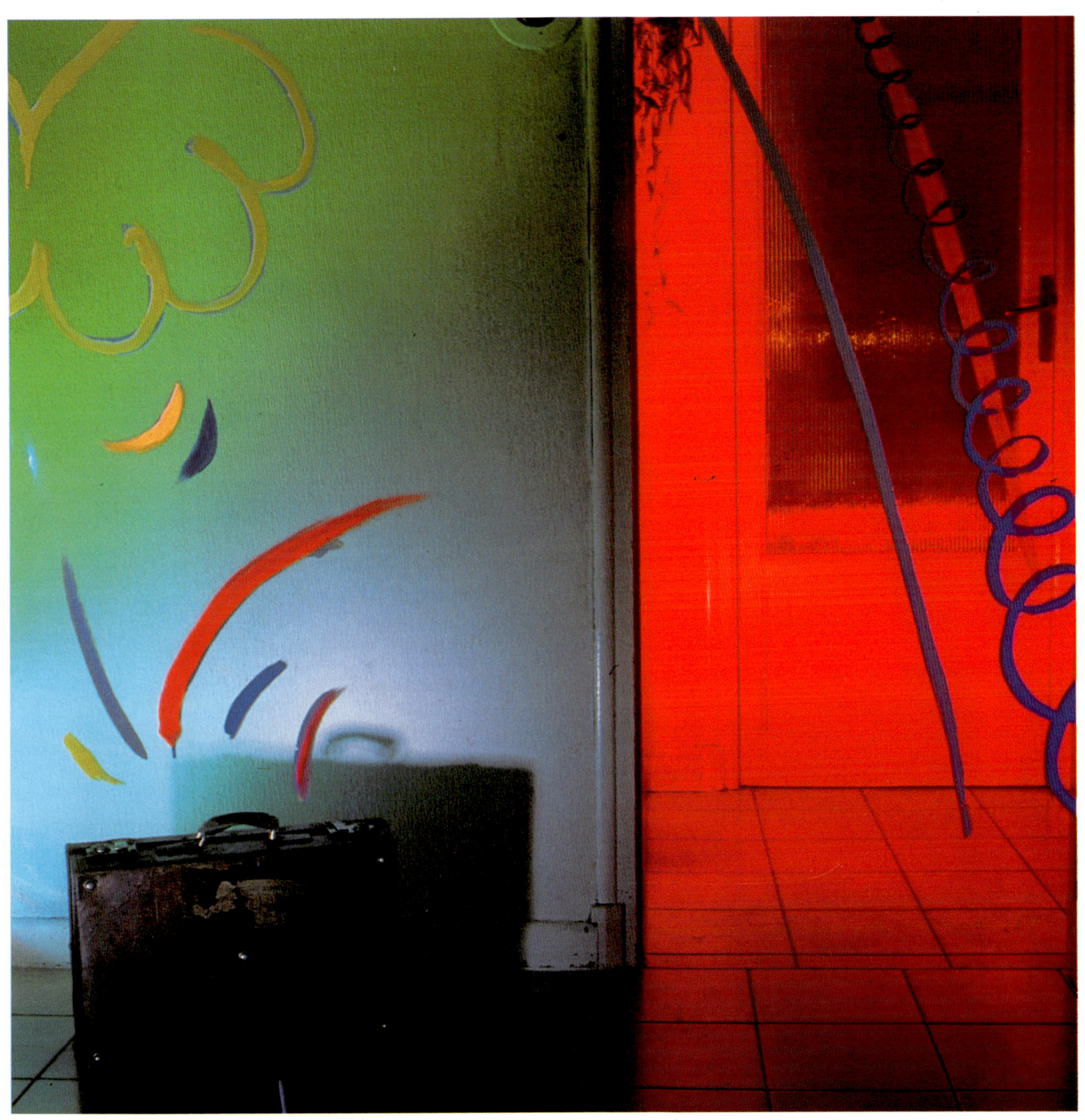

Maleta

1984-1985

Cibachrome

85 x 85 cm.

ANDREU CATALA PEDERSEN

Born Barcelona, 1963 / Nació en Barcelona, 1963

Individual Exhibitions
Exposiciones individuales

1989   La Mutua de Mataró. Cataluña, España.
1990   Can Miramar de Sitges. XXII Edición del
        Sitges Teatre Internacional. Cataluña,
        España.
        La Mutua de Mataró. Cataluña,
        Barcelona.
        Institut del Teatre de Barcelona.
        Barcelona, España.
1991   La Mutua de Mataró. Cataluña, España.

Group Exhibitions
Exposiciones colectivas

1984   "París-Barcelona". Instituto de Barcelona.
        Exposición itinerante por Cataluña,
        Francia y Dinamarca.
1988   "Extact". Centro Cívico La Sedeta de
        Barcelona. España.
1989   "El Gran Teatre del Liceu". Casal de

        Joves de Sant Feliu. Barcelona, España.
        "El Mon de L'Espectacle". L'Aixernador
        de Argentona, España.
        "Detail" Casa Elizalde de Barcelona,
        España.
        "Espectaclick". Casa Elizalde de
        Barcelona, España.
1985   "Els Catala, Tres generacions de
        fotografs". Patronat Municipal de Cultura
        de Mataró, España.
1991   "Onze de Barcelona". Ayuntamiento de
        Bludenz, Austria.

Photographs included in the exhibition
Fotografías contenidas en la exposición

1. Vicky con Máscara. 1984. Cibachrome. 40 x 50 cm.
2. Pas à deux contemporràneo. 1985. Cibachrome.
   40 x 50 cm.
3. Pink. 1988. Cibachrome. 40 x 50 cm.
4. Foll. 1990. Cibachrome. 40 x 50 cm.
5. Fuente. 1990. Cibachrome. 40 x 50 cm.

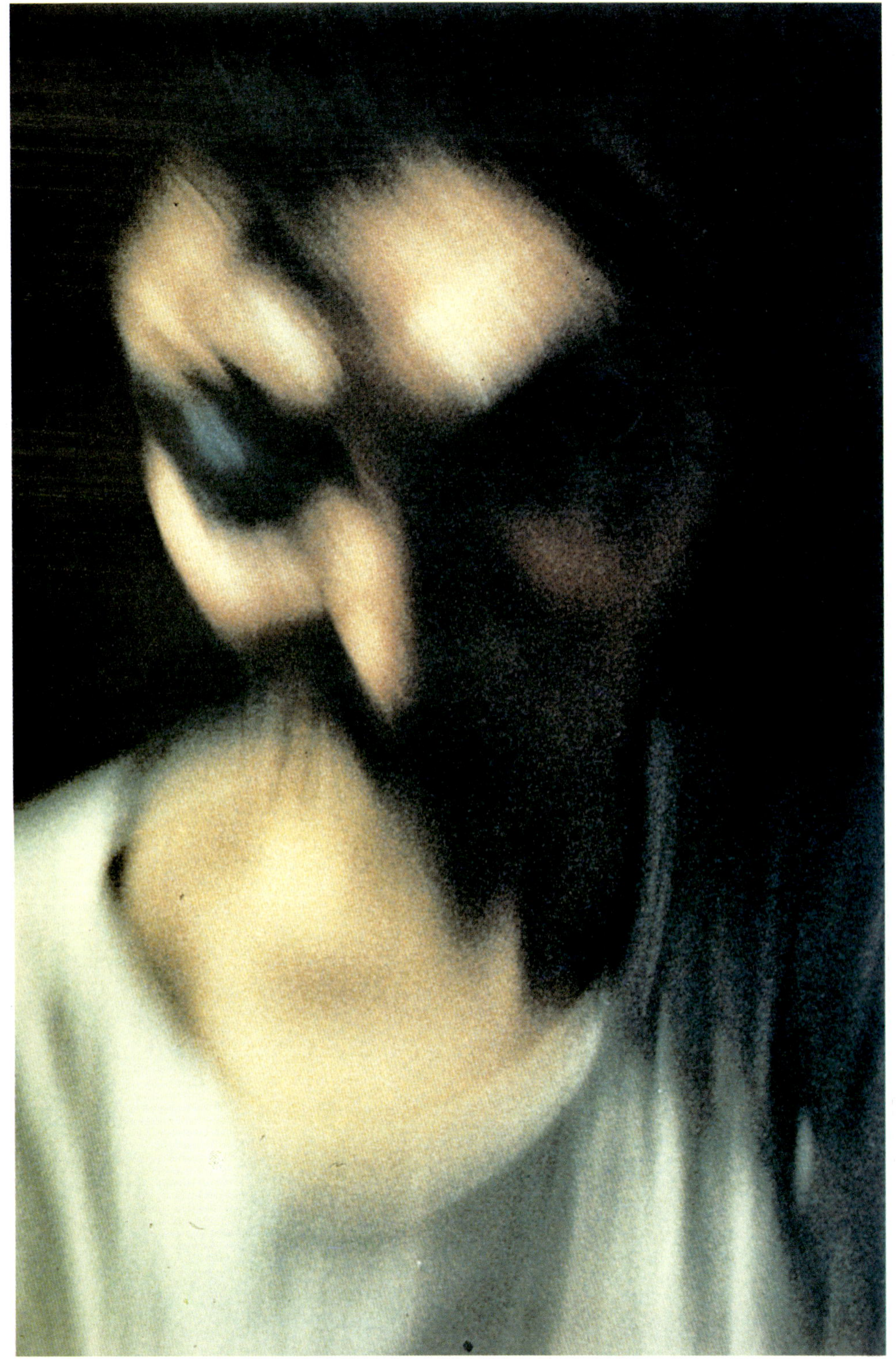

Vicky con Máscara

1984

Cibachrome

40 x 50 cm.

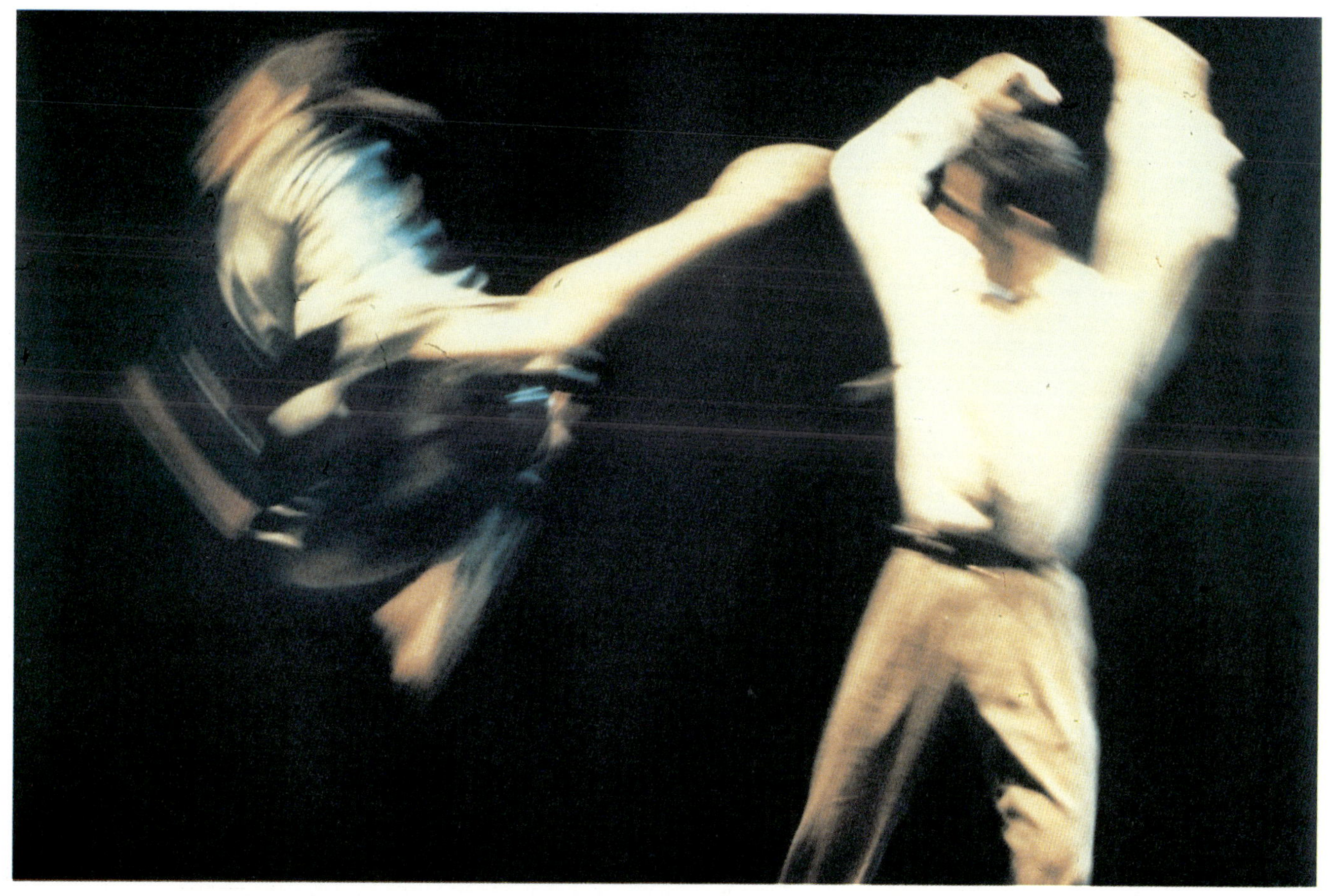

Pas à deux contemporàneo

1985

Cibachrome

40 x 50 cm.

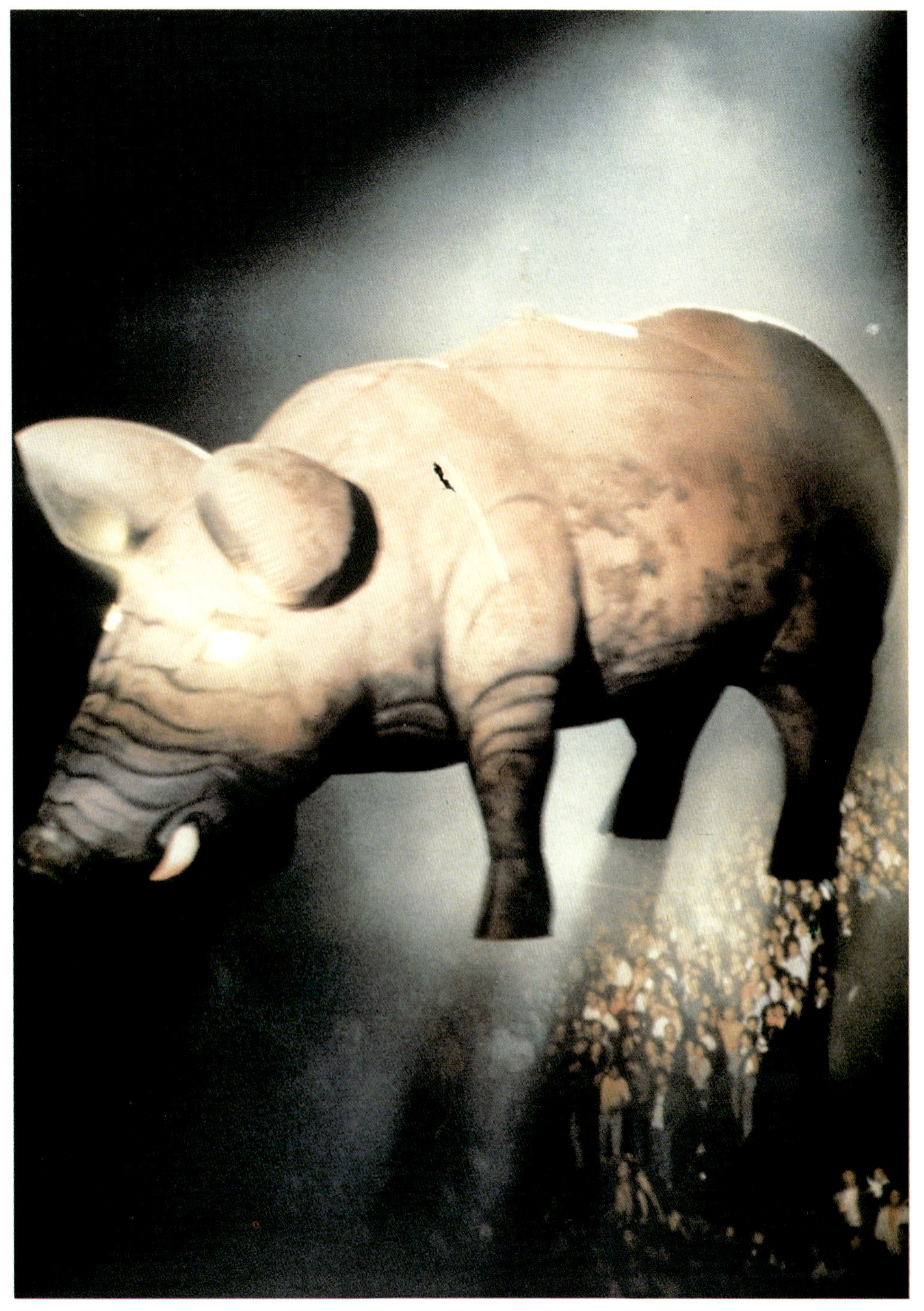

Pink

1988

Cibachrome

40 x 50 cm.

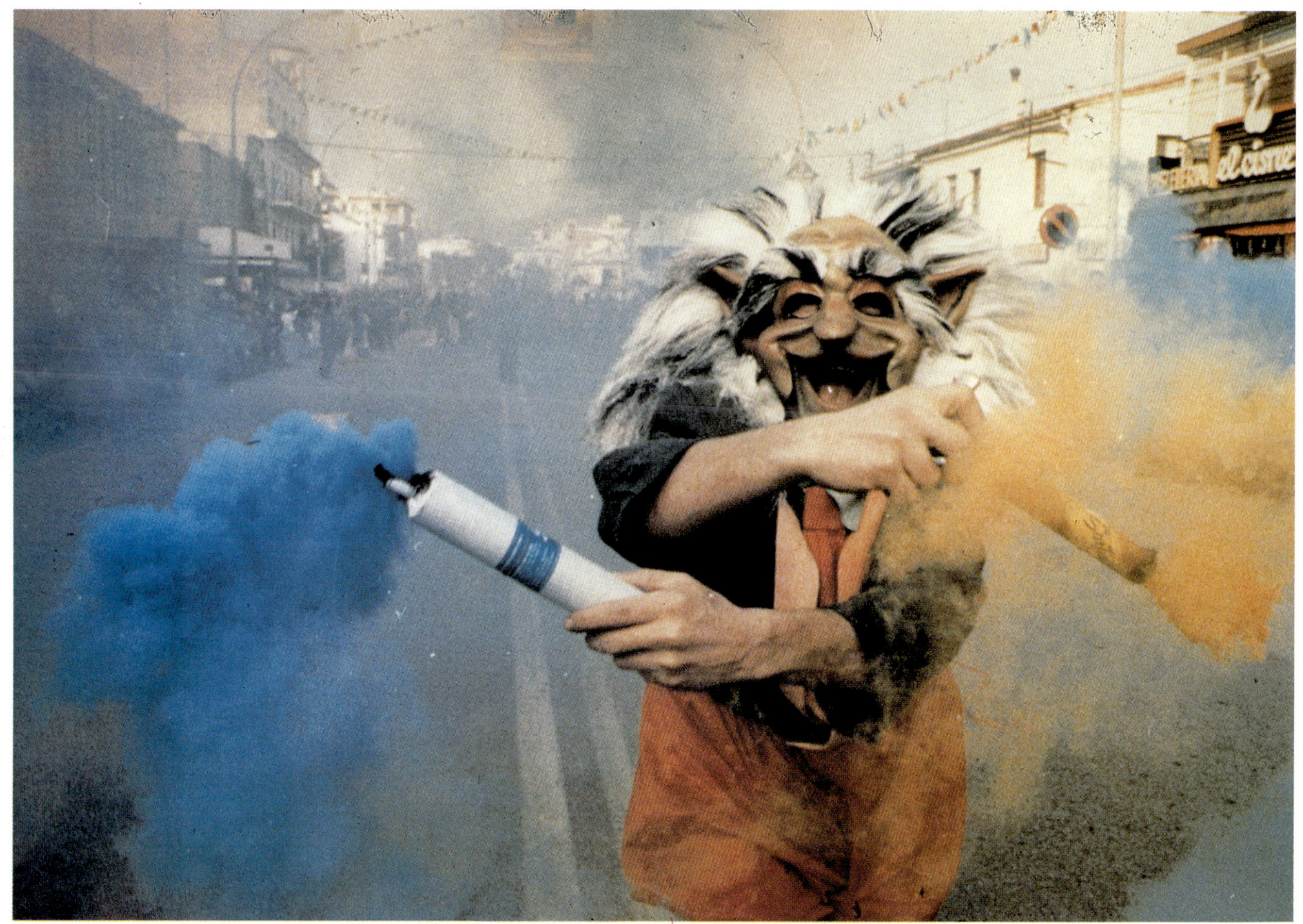

Foll
1990
Cibachrome
40 x 50 cm.

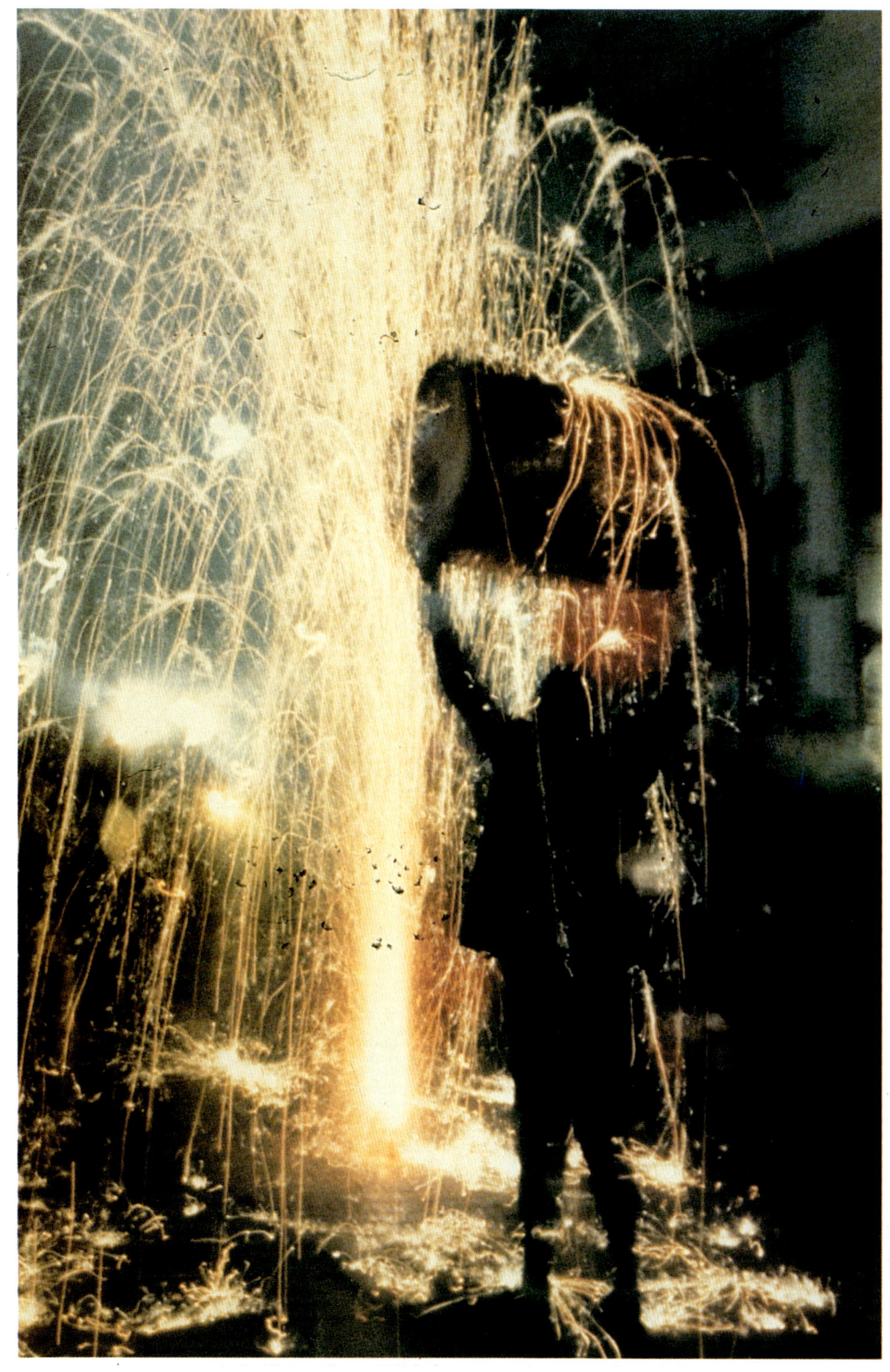

Fuente
1990
Cibachrome
40 x 50 cm.

FRANCESC CATALA-ROCA

Born Tarragona, 1922 / Nació en Tarragona, 1922

Main Individual Exhibitions
Principales Exposiciones individuales

1953   Sala Queralt. Barcelona, España.
1959   Sala Neblé. Madrid, España.
1966   Collegi d'Arquitectes de Barcelona.
        Barcelona, España.
1982   Galería Maeght. Barcelona, España.
1983   Galería Maeght. Barcelona, España.
        Agrupació Fotográfica de Catalunya.
        Barcelona, España.
1984   Biblioteca Nacional de Madrid.
        Itinerante de 1984-87, España.
1985   Museu Picasso, Barcelona, España.
        Centre Cultural de Terrassa. Cataluña.

España.
1987   The Spanish Institute. Nueva York, EE.UU.

Group Exhibitions
Exposiciones colectivas

1982   Galería René Metras. Barcelona,
        España.

Photographs included in the exhibition
Fotografías contenidas en la exposición

5 Fotografías. Manhattan. 1987. 40 x 50 cm. Copia "C"

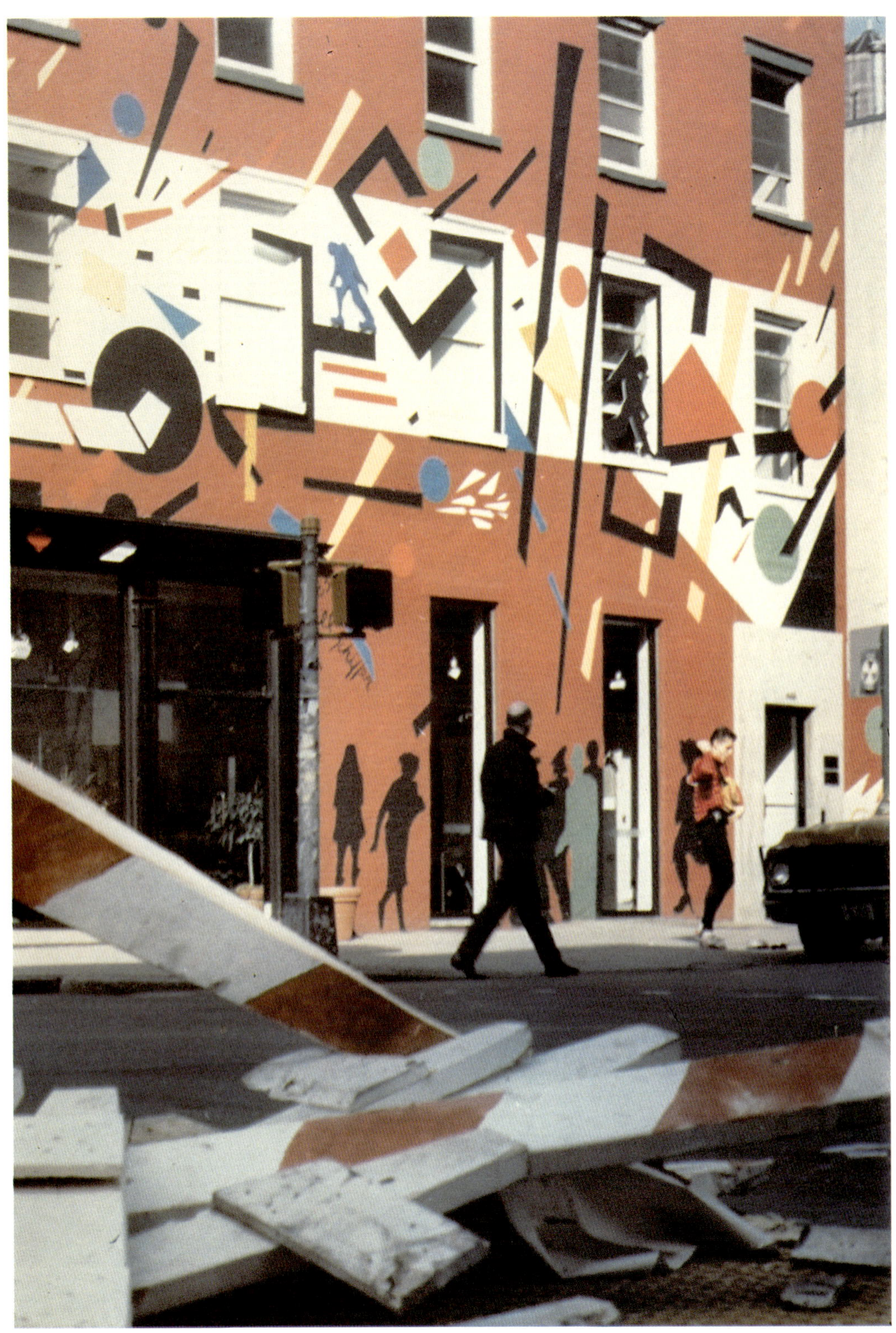

Manhattan

1987

40 x 50 cm.

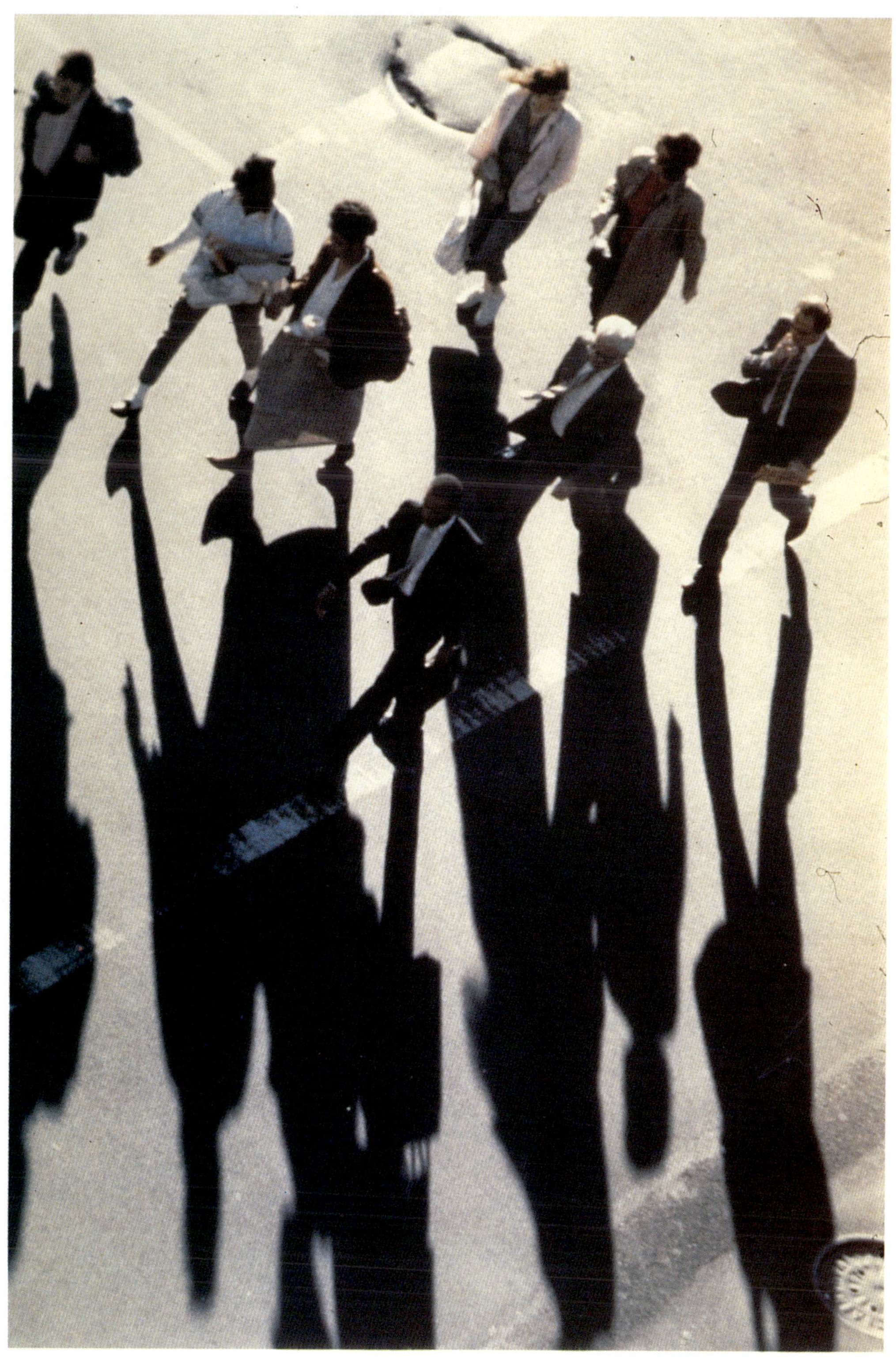

Manhattan

1987

40 x 50 cm.

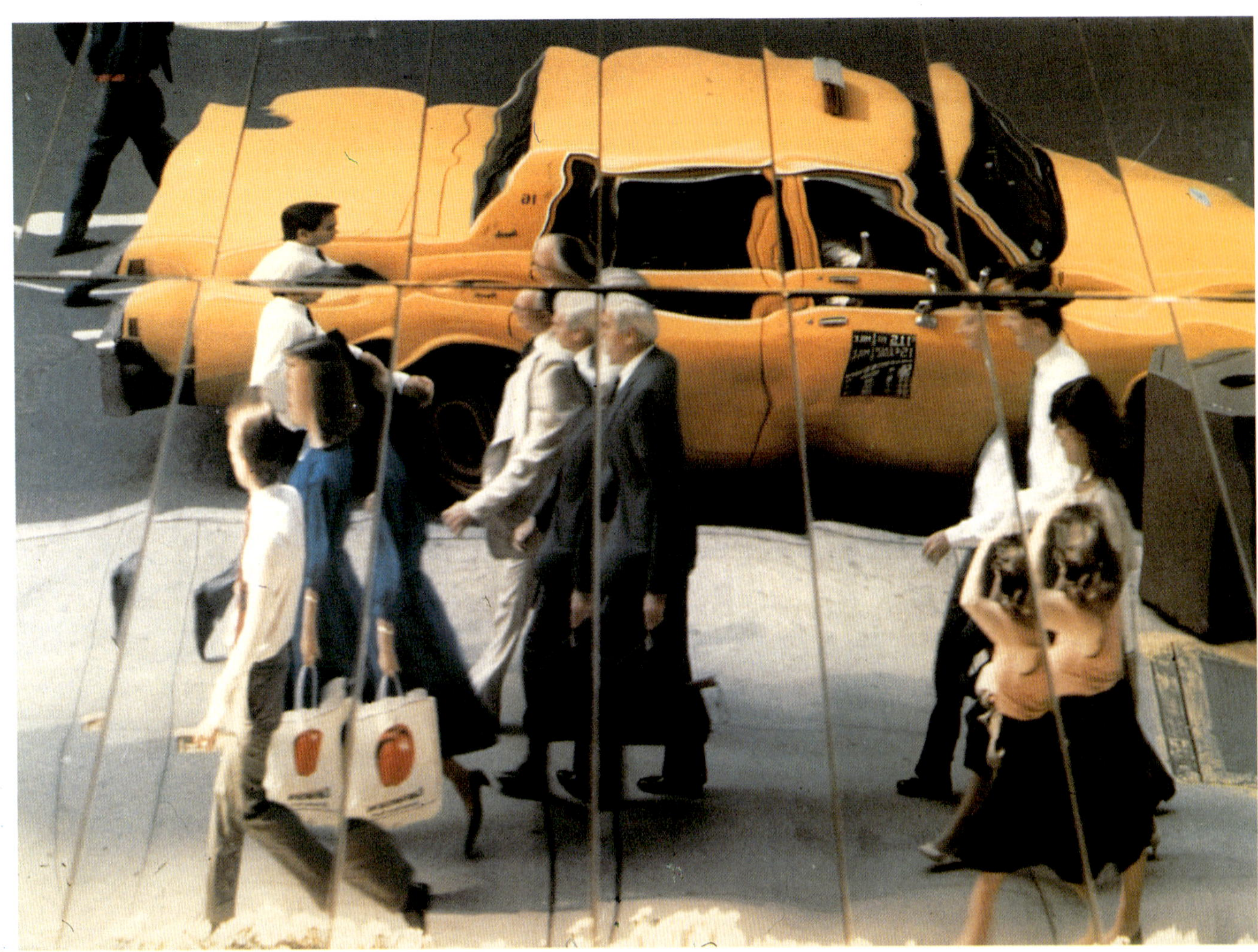

Manhattan

1987

40 x 50 cm.

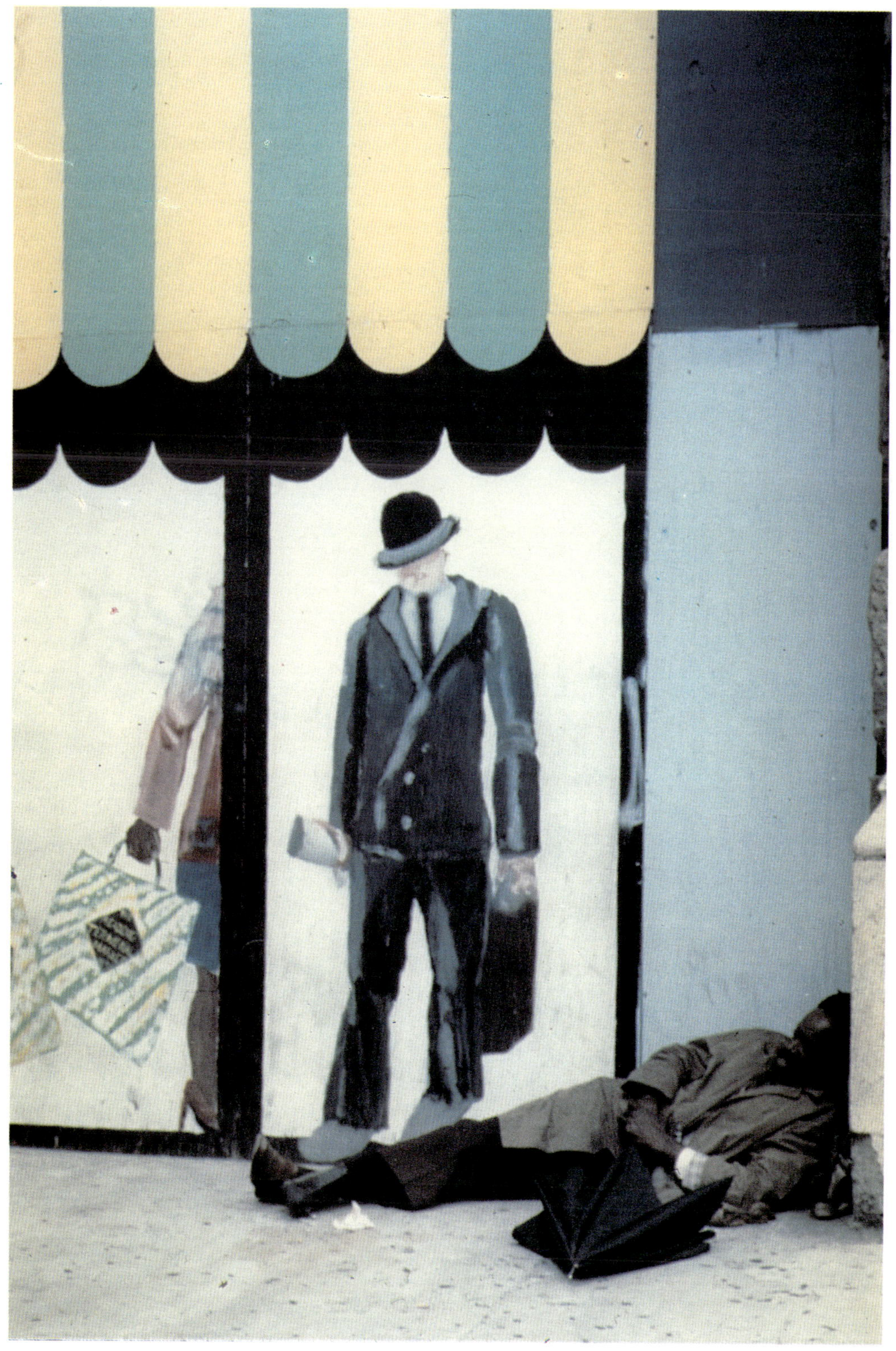

Manhattan

1987

40 x 50 cm.

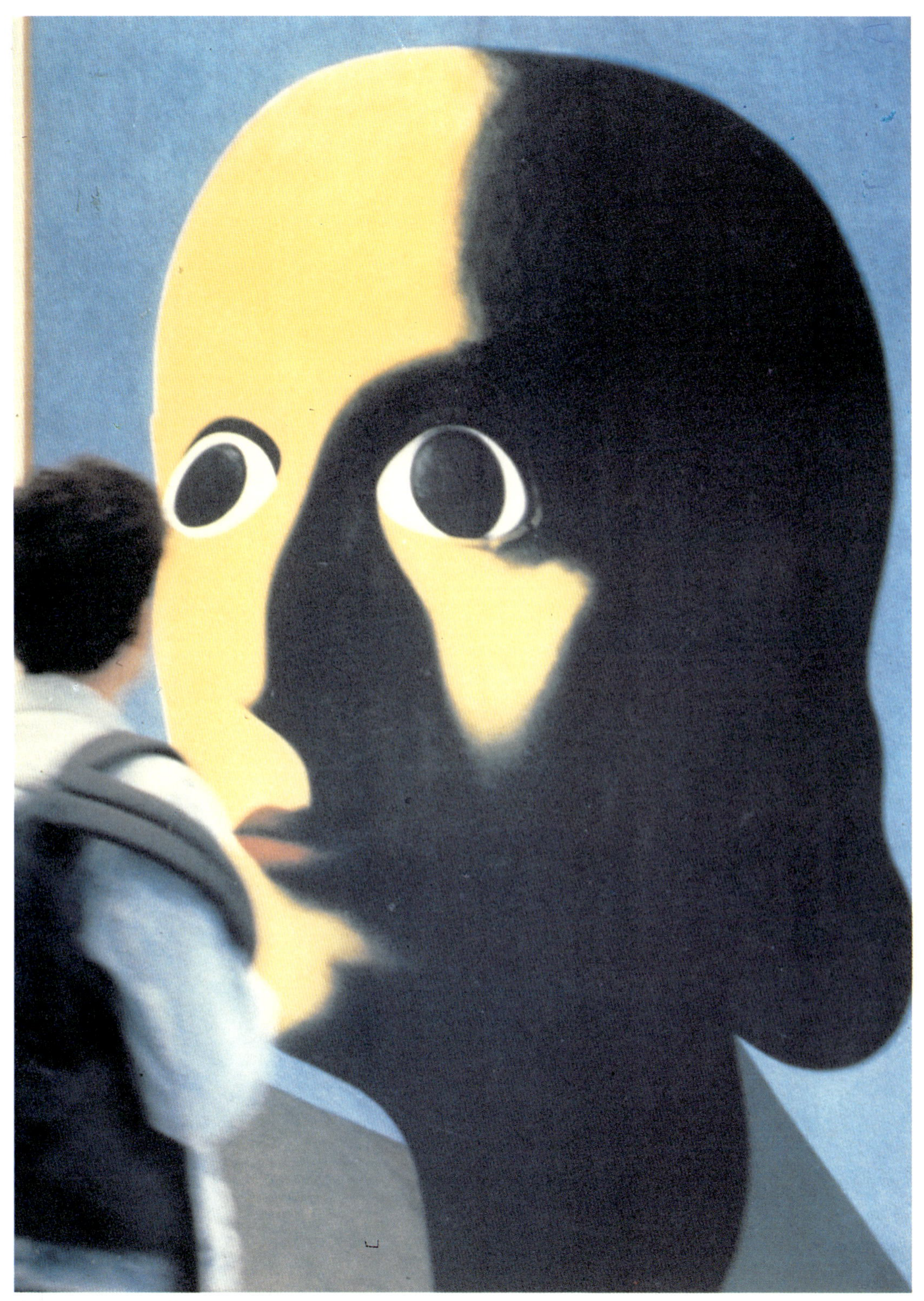

Manhattan

1987

40 x 50 cm.

TONY CATANY

Born Mallorca, 1942 / Nació en Mallorca 1942

Main Individual Exhibitions
Principales Exposiciones individuales

1987   Galerie Municipale du Cháteau-d'Eau.
        Toulouse, Francia.
        Musée Nicéphore Niepce.
        Chalon-sur-Saone, Francia.
        Fundació Caixa de Barcelona.
        Barcelona-Tarragona-Lleida-Girona,
        España.
        "Foco". Círculo de Bellas Artes. Madrid,
        España.
        Alsace-Mecenat. Strasbourg, Francia.
        Galerie Agathe Gaillard. París, Francia.
        R.I.P. Arles, Francia.
        Fundació Batomeu March. Palma de
        Mallorca, España.
        Hall de l'Image. Lyon, Francia.
        Galerie de The Seibu. Tokio. Japón.
        Galerie Le Salon d'Art. Bruxelles, Bélgica.
        Musée Municipale. Orange, Francia.

1988   "10e Festival Photographique du Tregor".
        Centre des Congrés. Tregastel, Francia.
        Fundació Bartomeu March. Palma de
        Mallorca, España.
        Hall de l'Image. Lyon, Francia.

1989   "Mes de la Foto Iberoamericana".
        Huelva, España.
        "Setembre de la Photo 89". Galerie
        Mossa. Nice, Francia.
        "Tarazona Foto". Palacio Episcopal.
        Tarazona, España.
        "Artothèque". Nantes, Francia.
        Galería Lienzo y Papel. Sevilla, España.
        Galería Agathe Gaillard. París, Francia.
        Galería Forum. Tarragona, España.

1990   Museo Municipal. Sta. Cruz de Tenerife.
        España.
        Galerie Suzel Berna. Antibes, Francia.
        Palau Sollerich. Palma de Mallorca,
        España.
        Galerie Past Rays. Yokohama, Japón.
        The Special Photographers Company.
        Londres, Gran Bretaña.

Main Group Exhibitions
Principales Exposiciones colectivas

1987   Marcuse Pfeifer Gallery. New York,

EE.UU.
"Del bell al sinestre" Sala Arcs.
Barcelona, España.
"Haute Sensibilite". Gal. d'Art du Centre
Sainte-Vicent. Herblay, Francia.
"Mois de la Photo". Liege, Bélgica.
"Corps et ame". Arles, Francia.
"Les miroirs qui se souviennent".
Cormeilles-en-Paris, Francia.
"Les Imagiques". Aix-en-Provence,
Francia.

1988   "Flores". Círculo de Bellas Artes.
        Valencia, España.
        Club Mediterranée. Gregolimano,
        Grecia.
        "50 Photographes a Gregolimano".
        Galería FNAC. París, Francia.
        "Fotoporto/Mes de la Fotografía". Porto,
        Portugal.
        "Imatges d'Eivissa". Galera Carl van der
        Voort, Suiza.
        "Splendeurs et Miséres du Corps".
        Fribourg. París, Francia.

1989   "10 Fotógrafos Españoles". Palacio de
        Sástago. Zaragoza, España.
        "Objectiu Ciutat Vella". Sala Picasso.
        Collegi Arquitectes. Barcelona, España.
        Clichés "Le choix des sens". Musée
        Botanique.
        Bruxelles, Bélgica.
        "Spanish Eyes". Clarence Kennedy
        Gallery. Cambridge, Massachussetts,
        EE.UU.

1990   "Spanish Fine Art Photo". The Special
        Photographers Company. Londres, Gran
        Bretaña.
        "Zoom on Europe". The R.H.A. Gallagher
        Gallery. Dublín. Irlanda.
        "Regards sur la Photo-Catalane". Teâtre
        de l'Agora. Evry, Francia.

Photographs included in the exhibition
Fotografías contenidas en la exposición

1. Natura Morte # 159. 1989. Cibachrome. 30 x 40 cm.
2. Natura Morte # 160. 1989. Cibachrome. 30 x 40 cm.
3. Natura Morte # 142. 1988. Cibachrome. 30 x 40 cm.
4. Natura Morte # 115. 1986. Cibachrome. 30 x 40 cm.
5. Natura Morte # 102. 1986. Cibachrome. 30 x 40 cm.

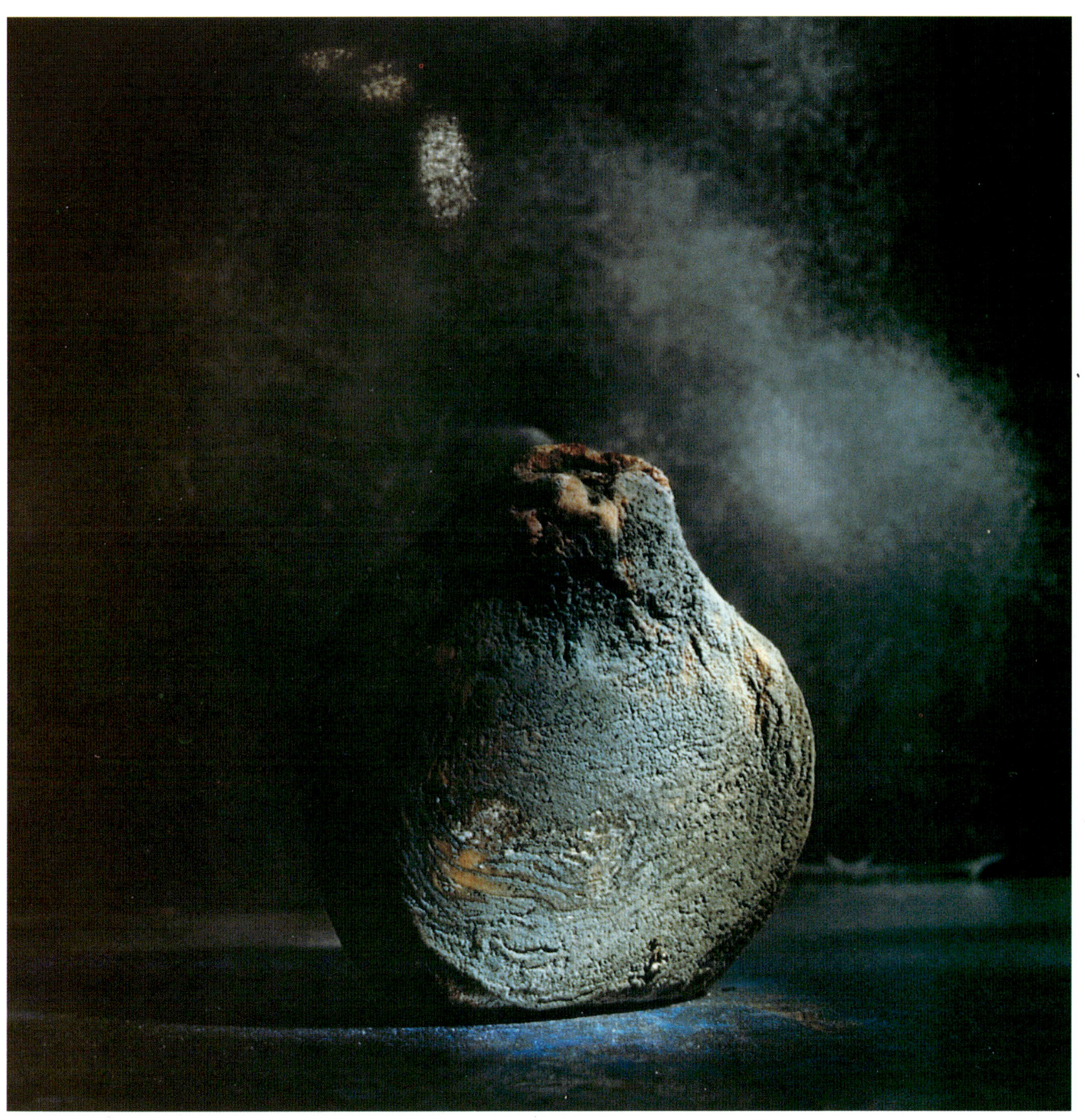

Natura Morte # 159

1989

Cibachrome

30 x 40 cm.

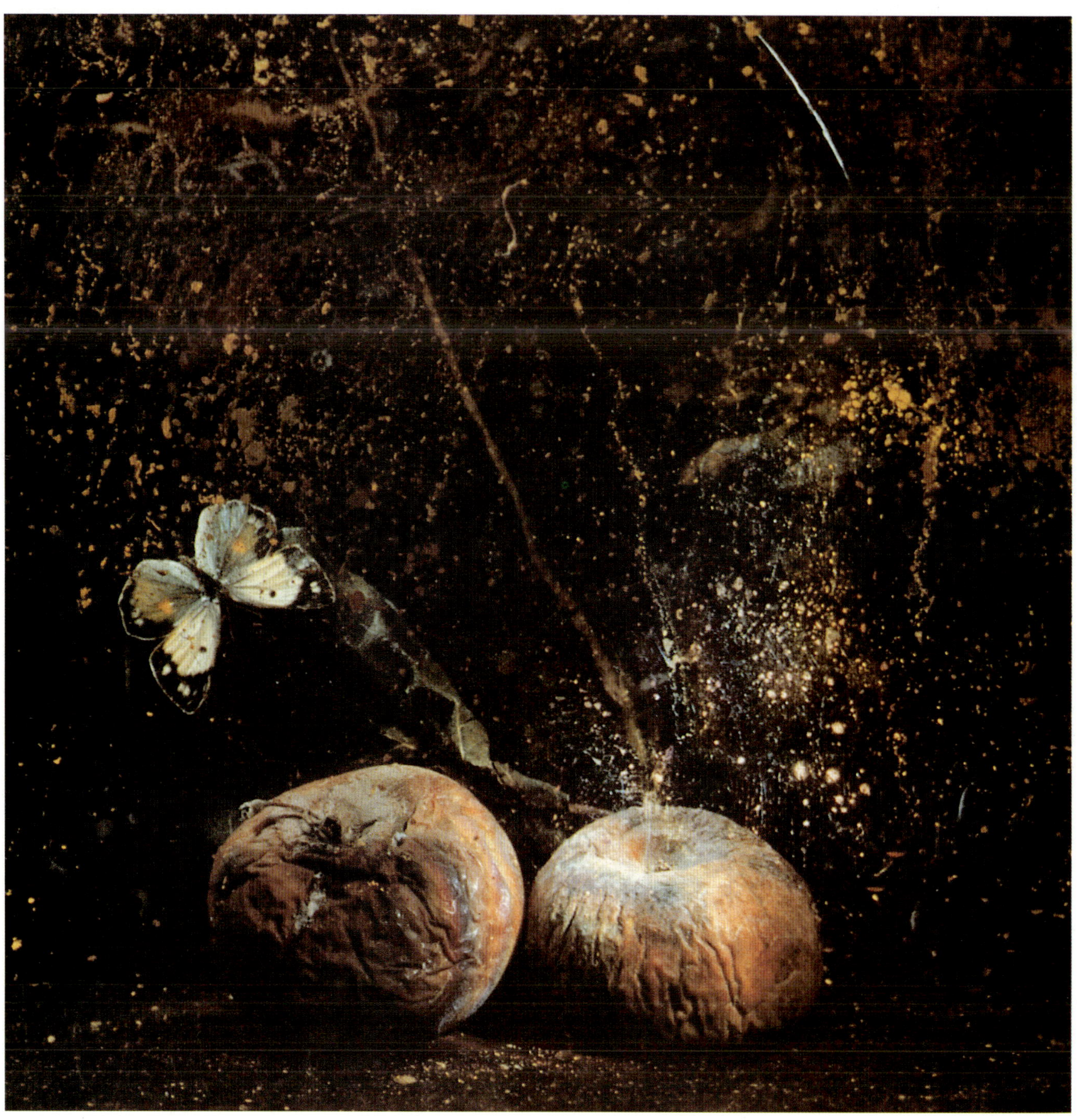

Natura Morte # 160

1989

Cibachrome

30 x 40 cm.

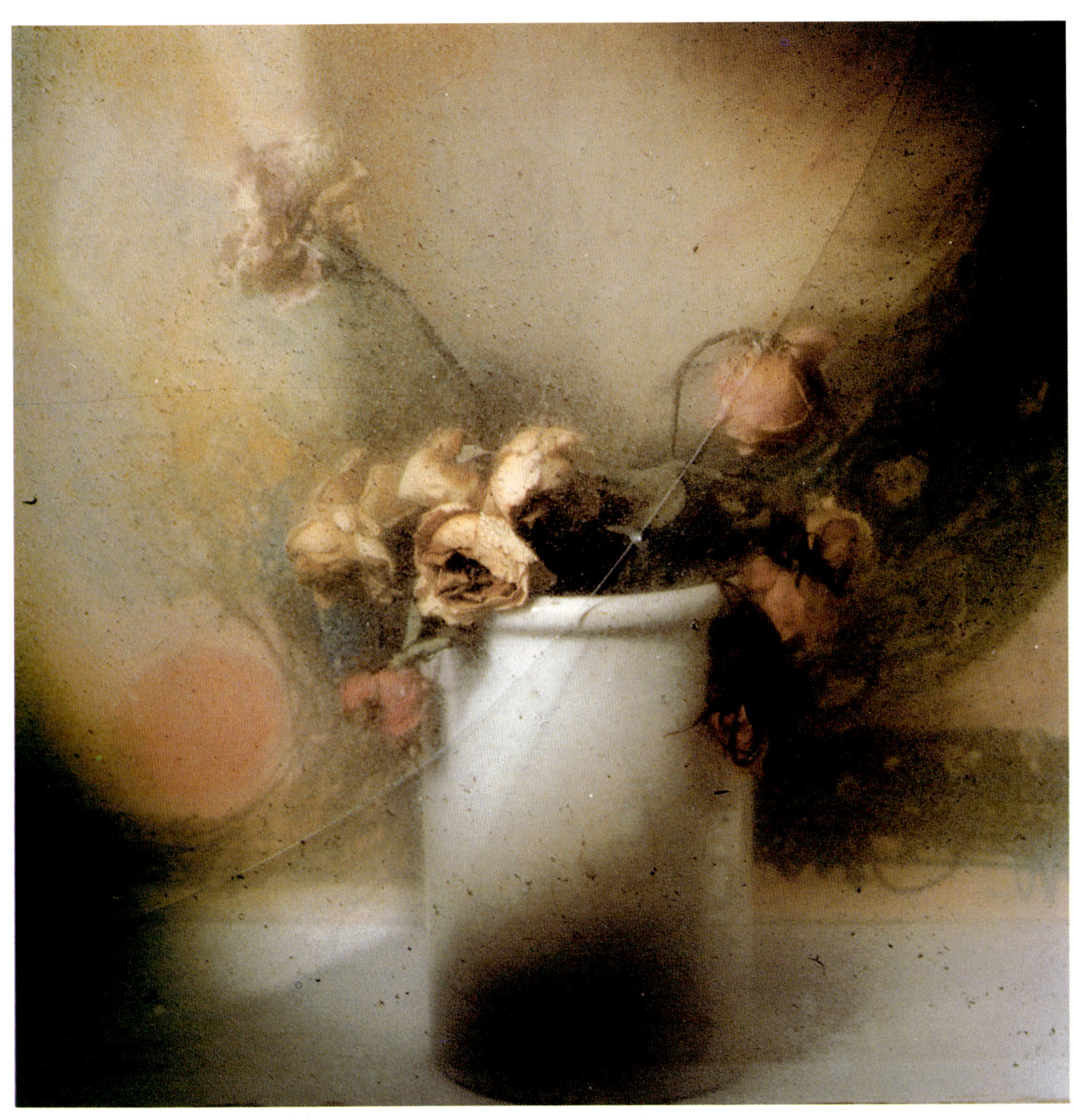

Natura Morte # 142

1988

Cibachrome

30 x 40 cm.

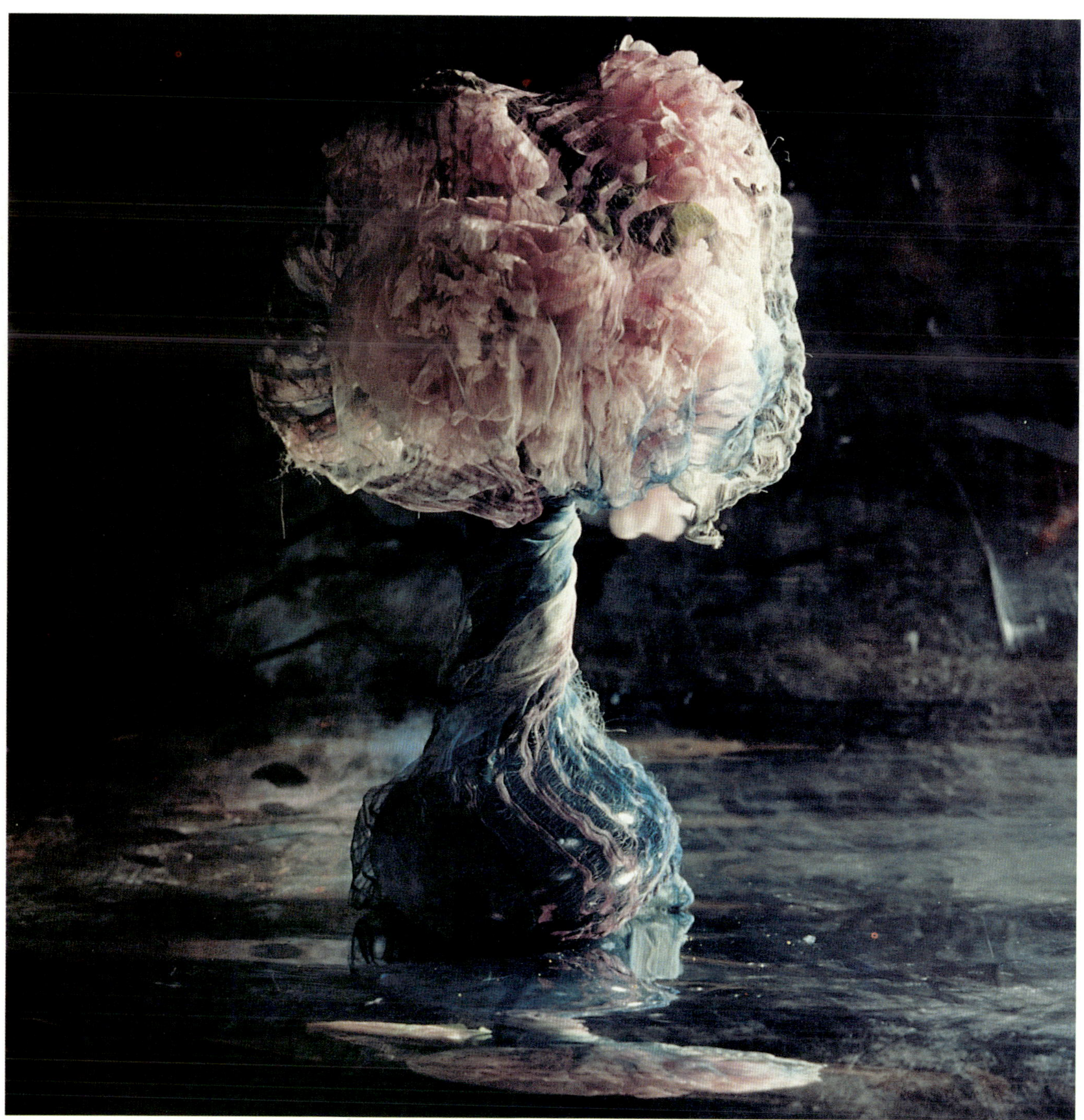

Natura Morte # 115

1986

Cibachrome

30 x 40 cm.

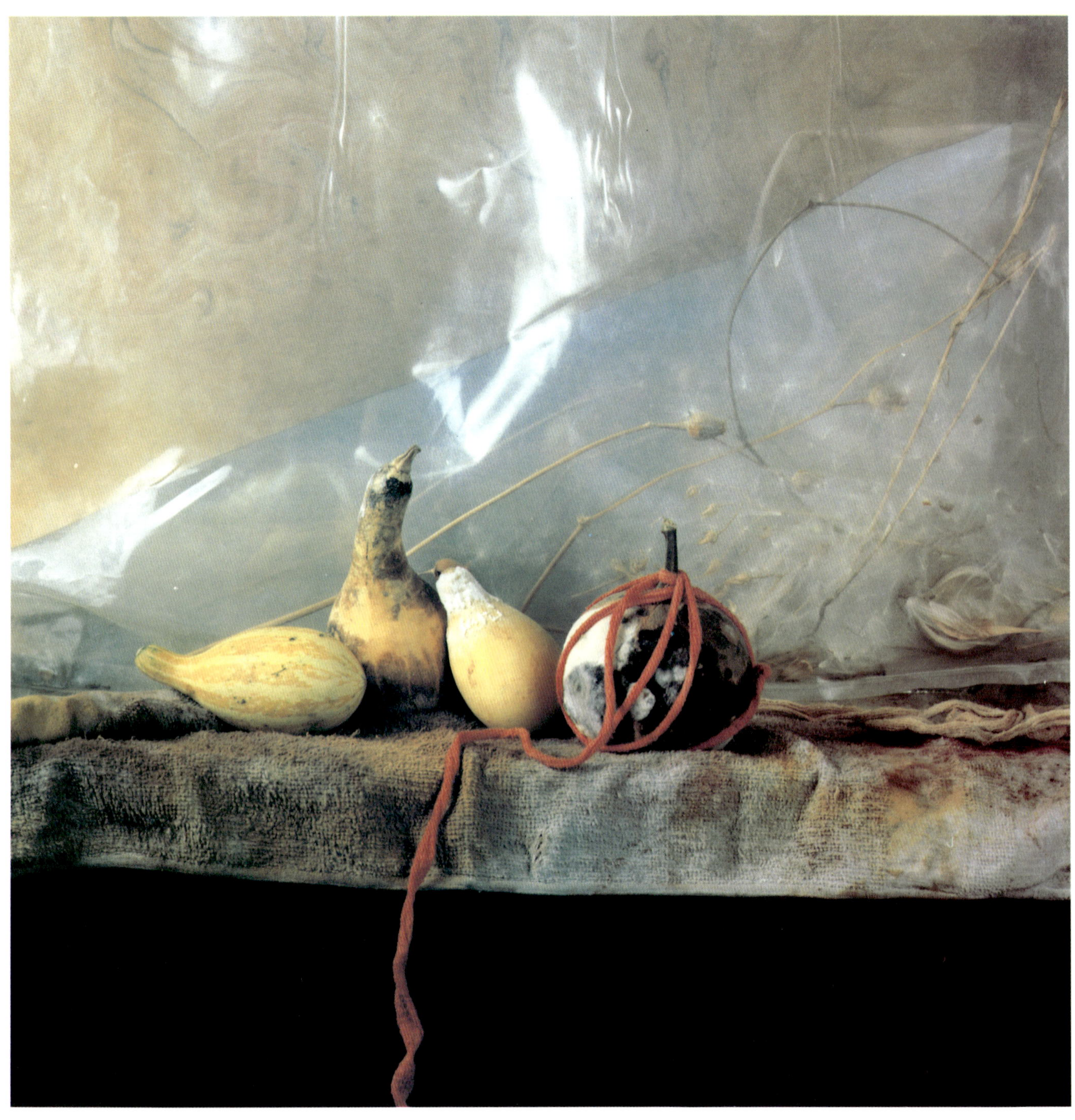

Natura Morte # 102

1986

Cibachrome

30 x 40 cm.

JOAQUIN COLUME

Born Isla Cristina, 1962 / Nació en Isla Cristina, 1962

Individual Exhibitions
Exposiciones individuales

1987	II Festival de Música de Canarias. Teatro Pérez Galdós. Islas Canarias, España.
1988	"El teatro del Comediants". Centro Insular de Cultura. Islas Canarias, España.
1988	Sala Maple Syrup. Barcelona, España.
1989	Escuela de Artes Aplicadas y Oficios Artísticos. Palama de Mallorca, España. Asociación Fotográfica Artística Linense. La Línea, Cádiz, España. Sala Gil Marraco. Sociedad fotográfica de Zaragoza. Zaragoza, España. Sociedad Fotográfica de Salamanca. Salamanca, España. Plasencia, Guipúzcoa, España.
1990	Agrupación Fotográfica de Gran Canaria.

Group Exhibitions
Exposiciones colectivas

1987	"Foto-Muestra'87 II". Centro Insular de Cultura.
1988	"Primer Aniversario". Centro Insular de Cultura.
1989	"K.O." Colectivo Formato Libre. Centro Insular de Cultura.

Photographs included in the exhibition
Fotografías contenidas en la exposición

1. K. O. 1989. Cibachrome. 24 x 30 cm.
2. El pensador, peso pluma. 1989. Cibachrome. 24 x 30 cm.
3. Kid Kiriki, peso gallo. 1989. Cibachrome. 24 x 30 cm.
4. Peso pluma. 1989. Cibachrome. 24 x 30 cm.
5. Pensador. 1989. Cibachrome. 24 x 30 cm.

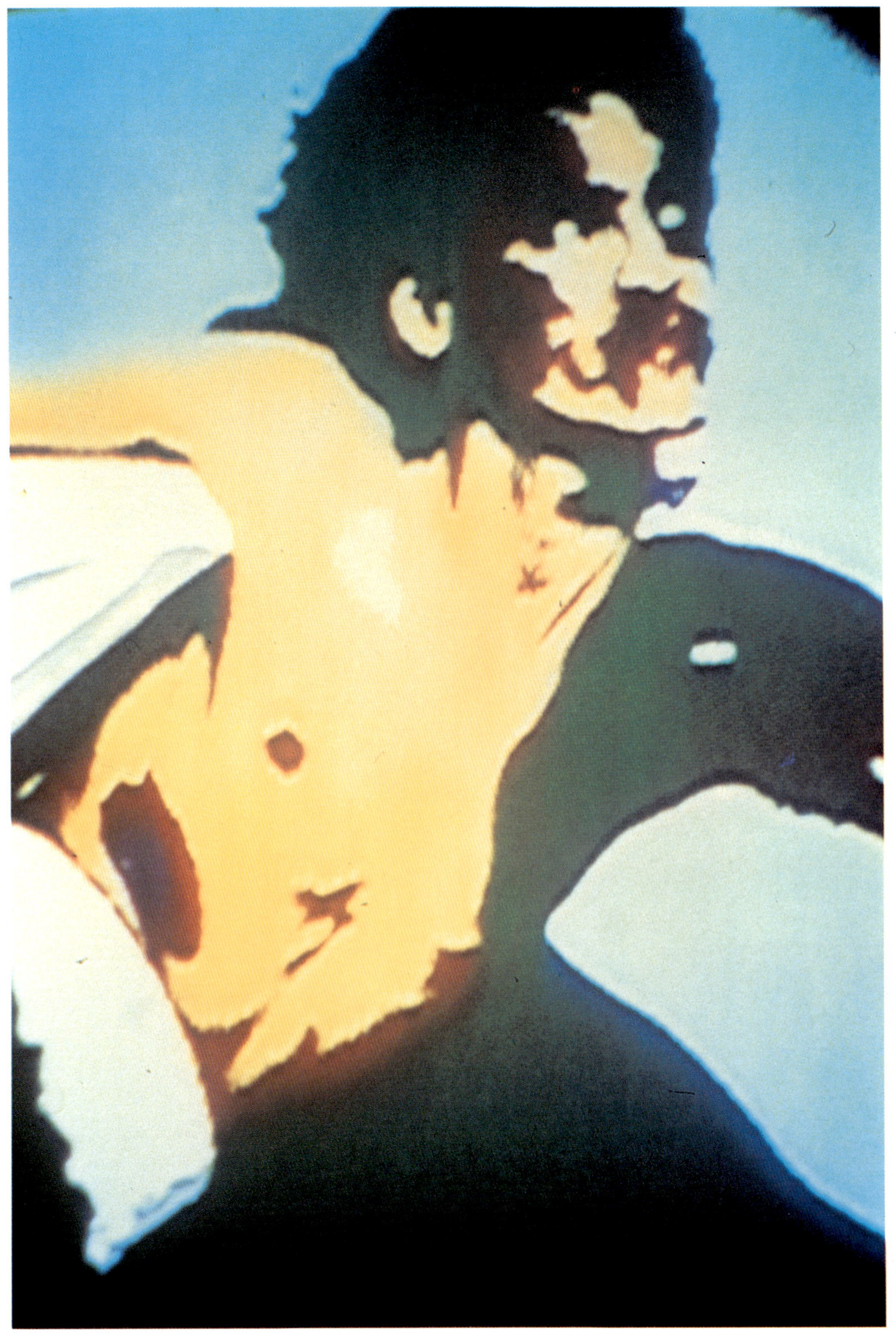

K. O.
1989
Cibachrome
24 x 30 cm.

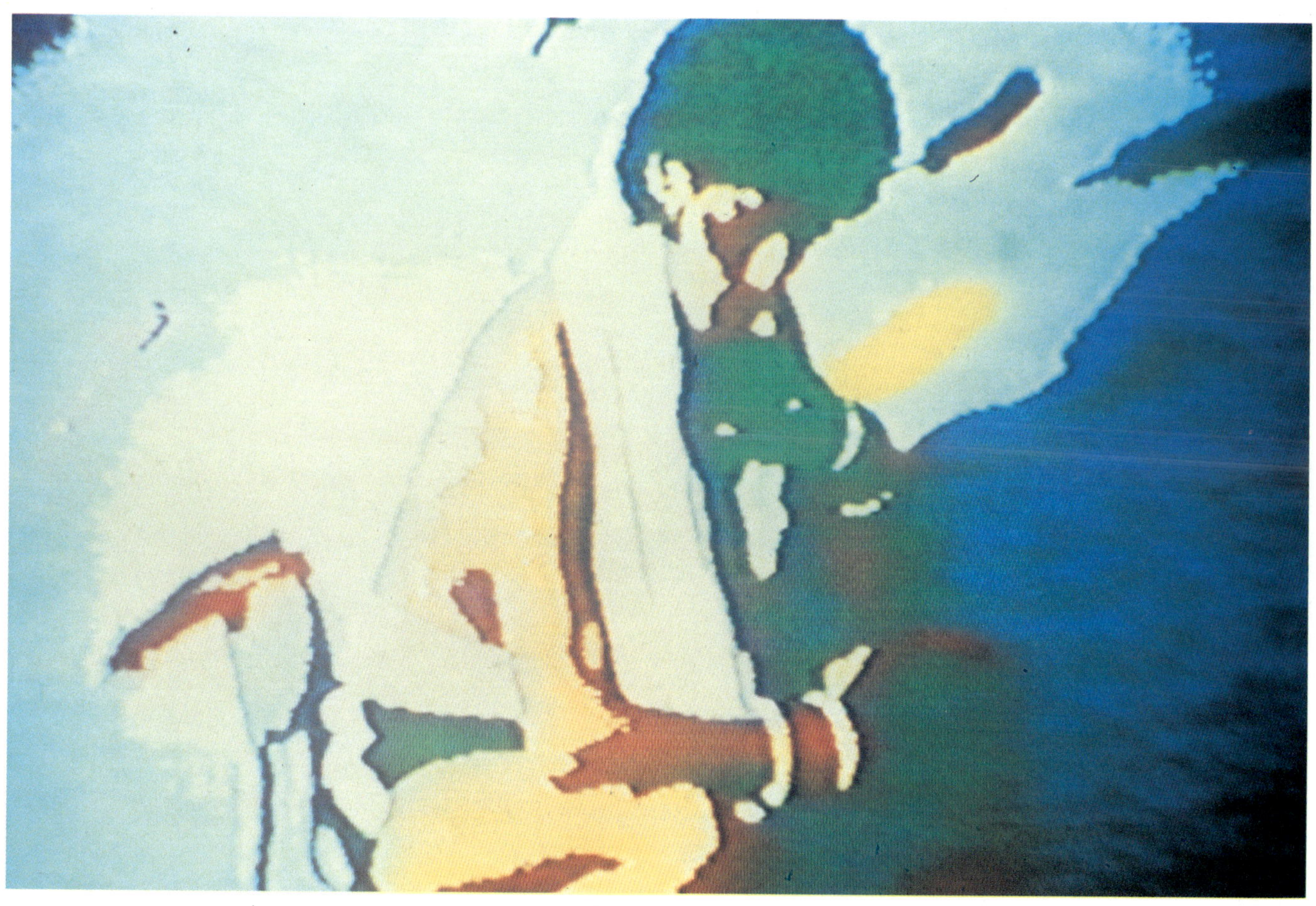

El pensador, peso pluma

1989

Cibachrome

24 x 30 cm.

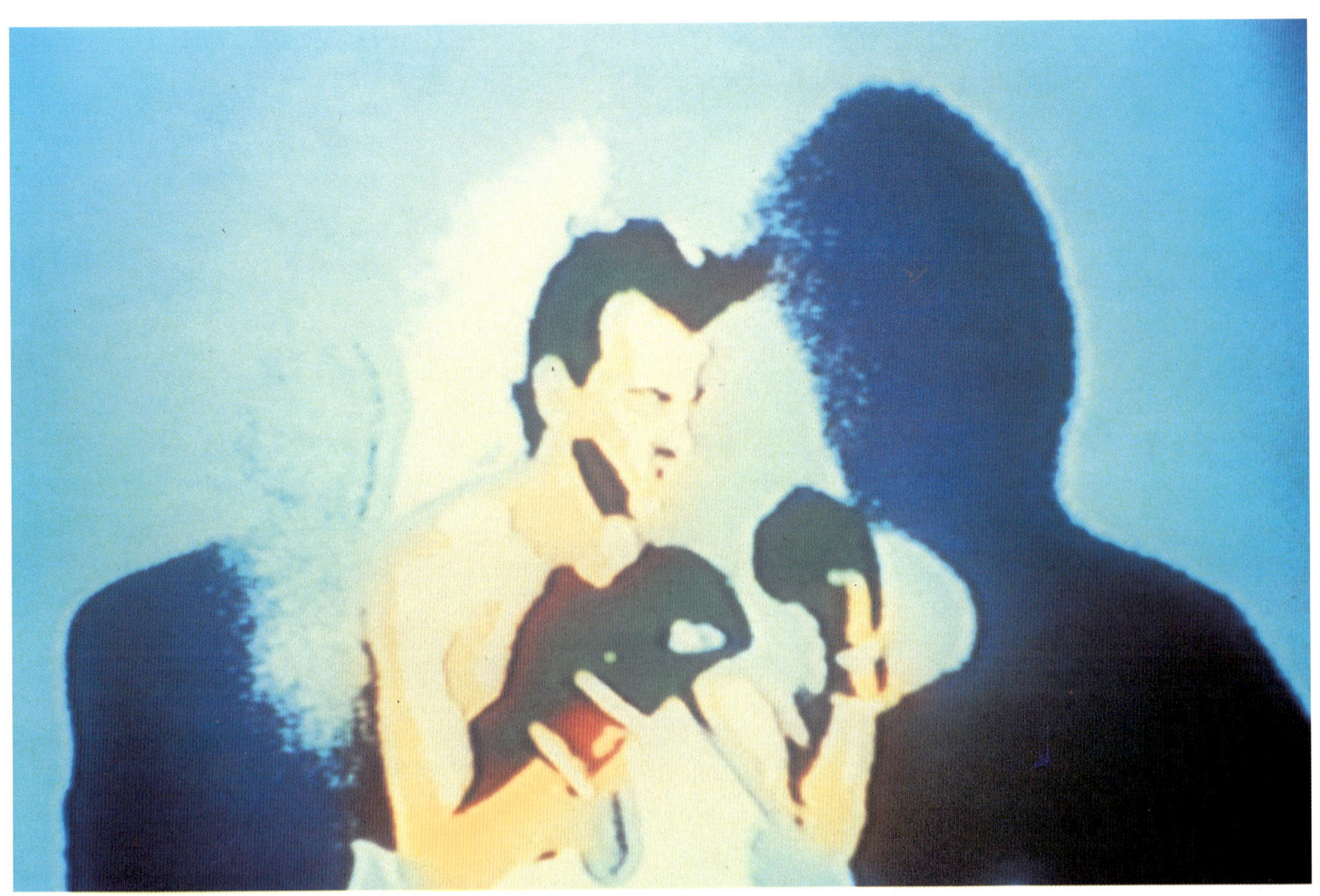

Kid Kiriki, peso gallo

1989

Cibachrome

24 x 30 cm.

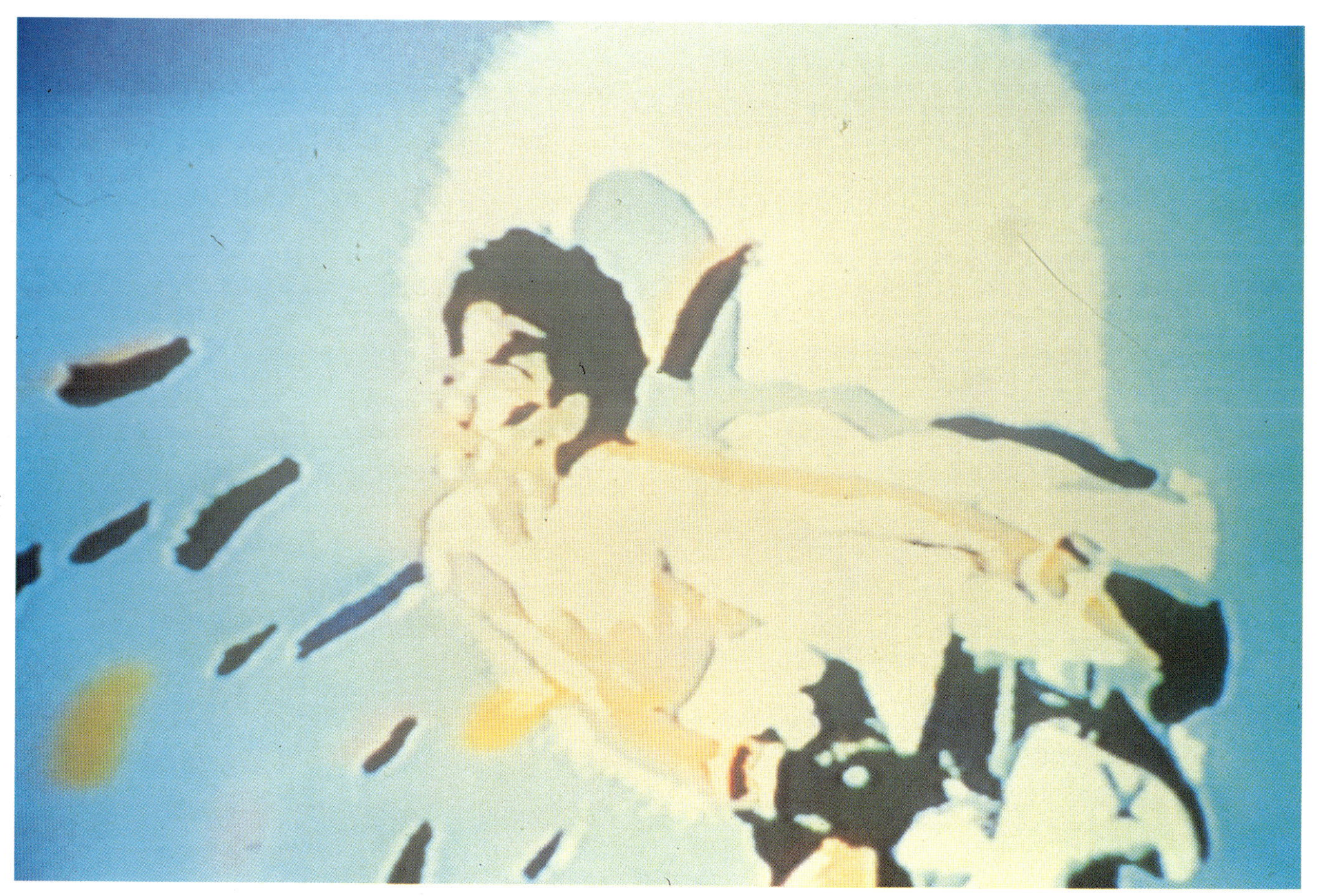

Peso Pluma

1989

Cibachrome

24 x 30 cm.

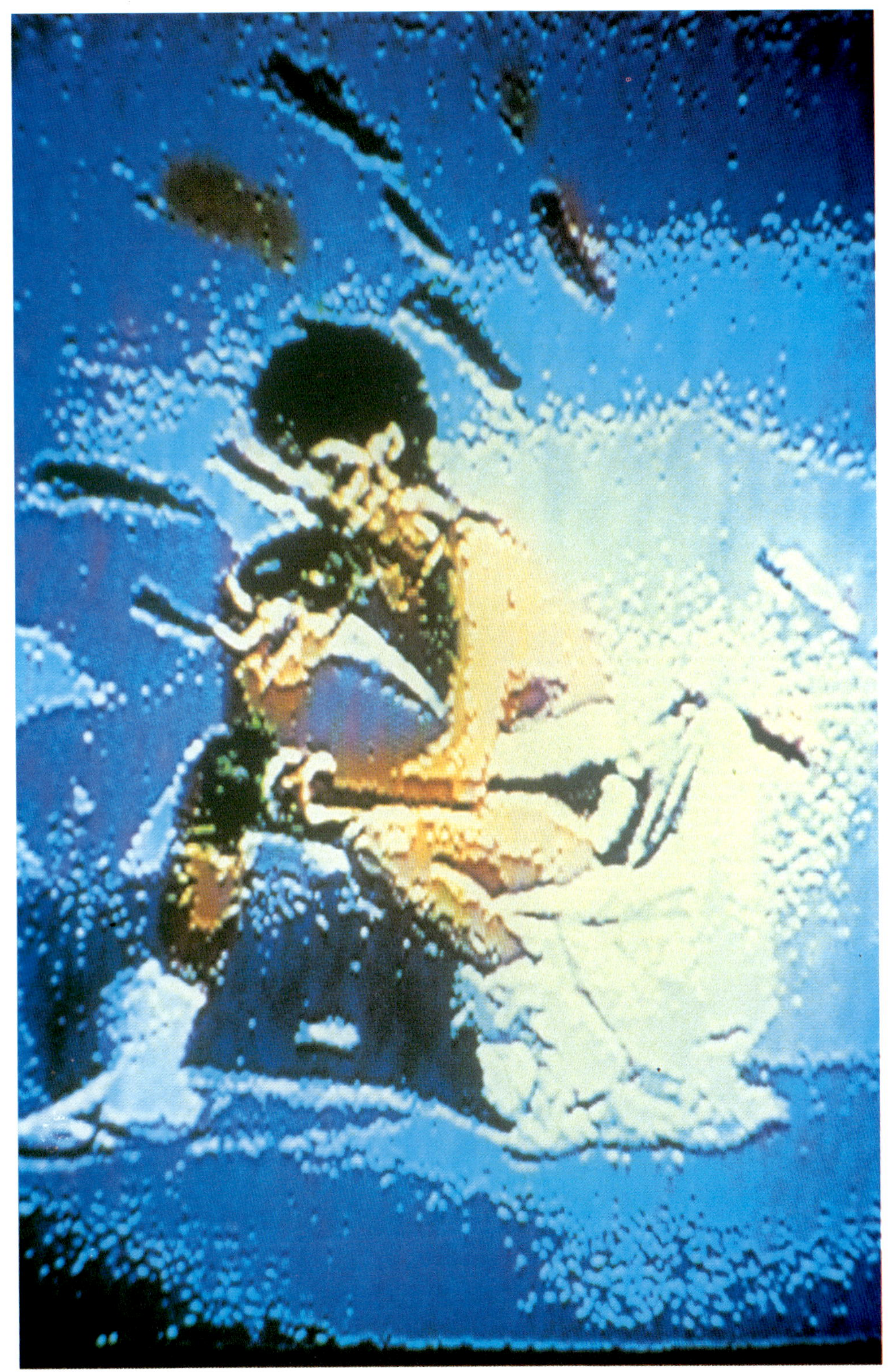

Pensador

1989

Cibachrome

24 x 30 cm.

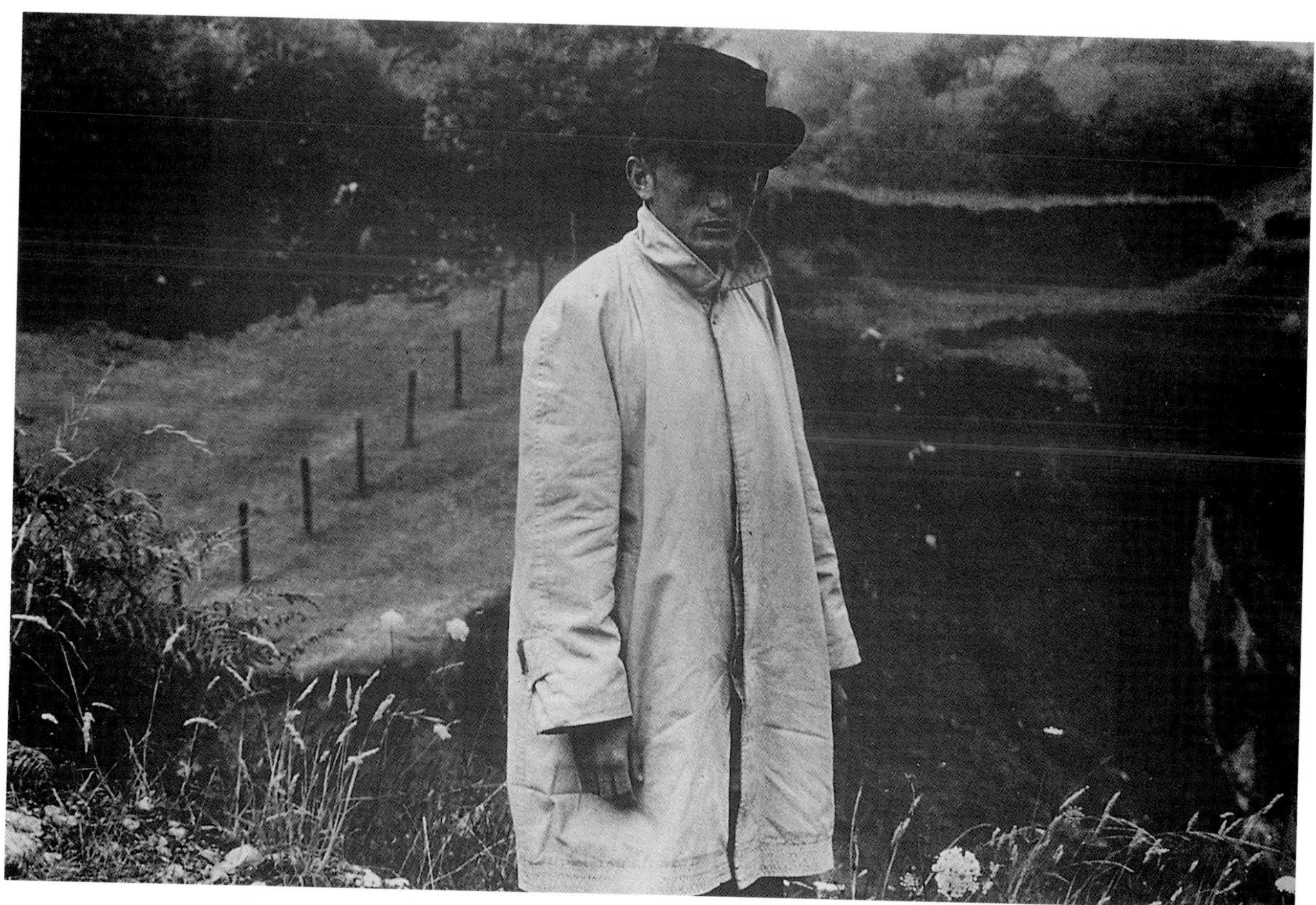

José Luis, El Pito

1975

41 x 50 cm.

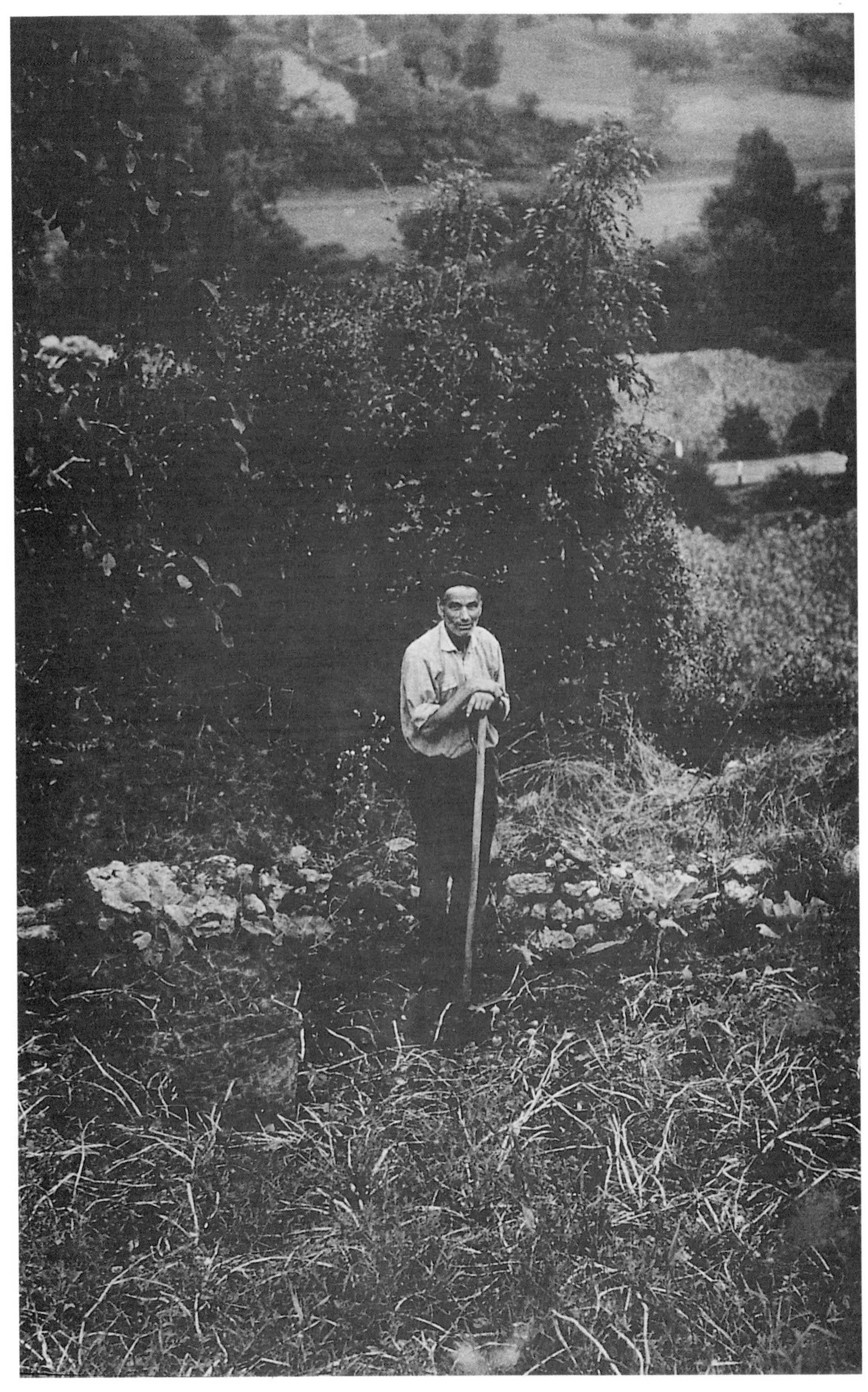

Isidro Sobra Piedra
1967
23,5 x 35,5 cm.

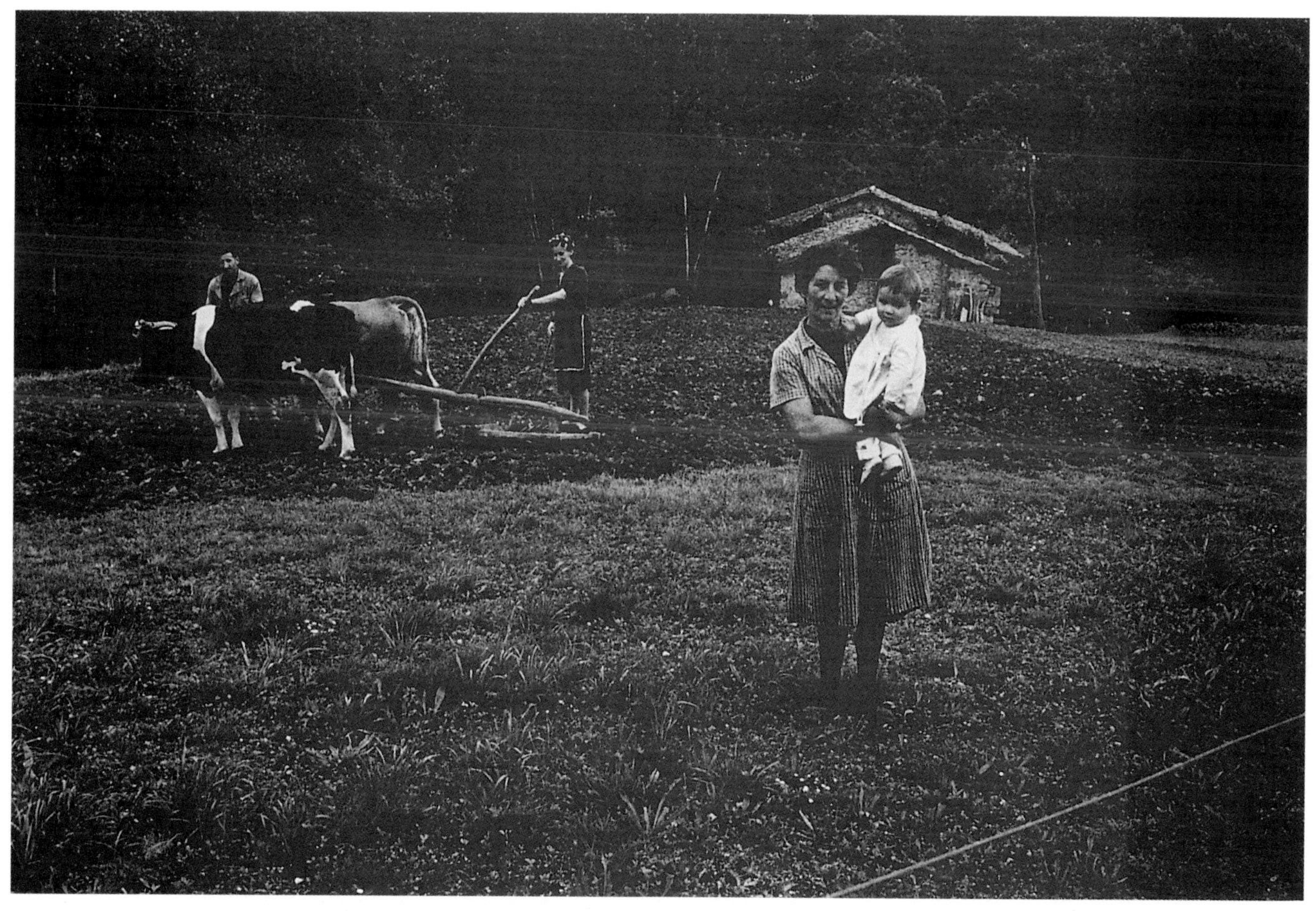

Familia Campesina Asturiana
1970
25 x 35,5 cm.

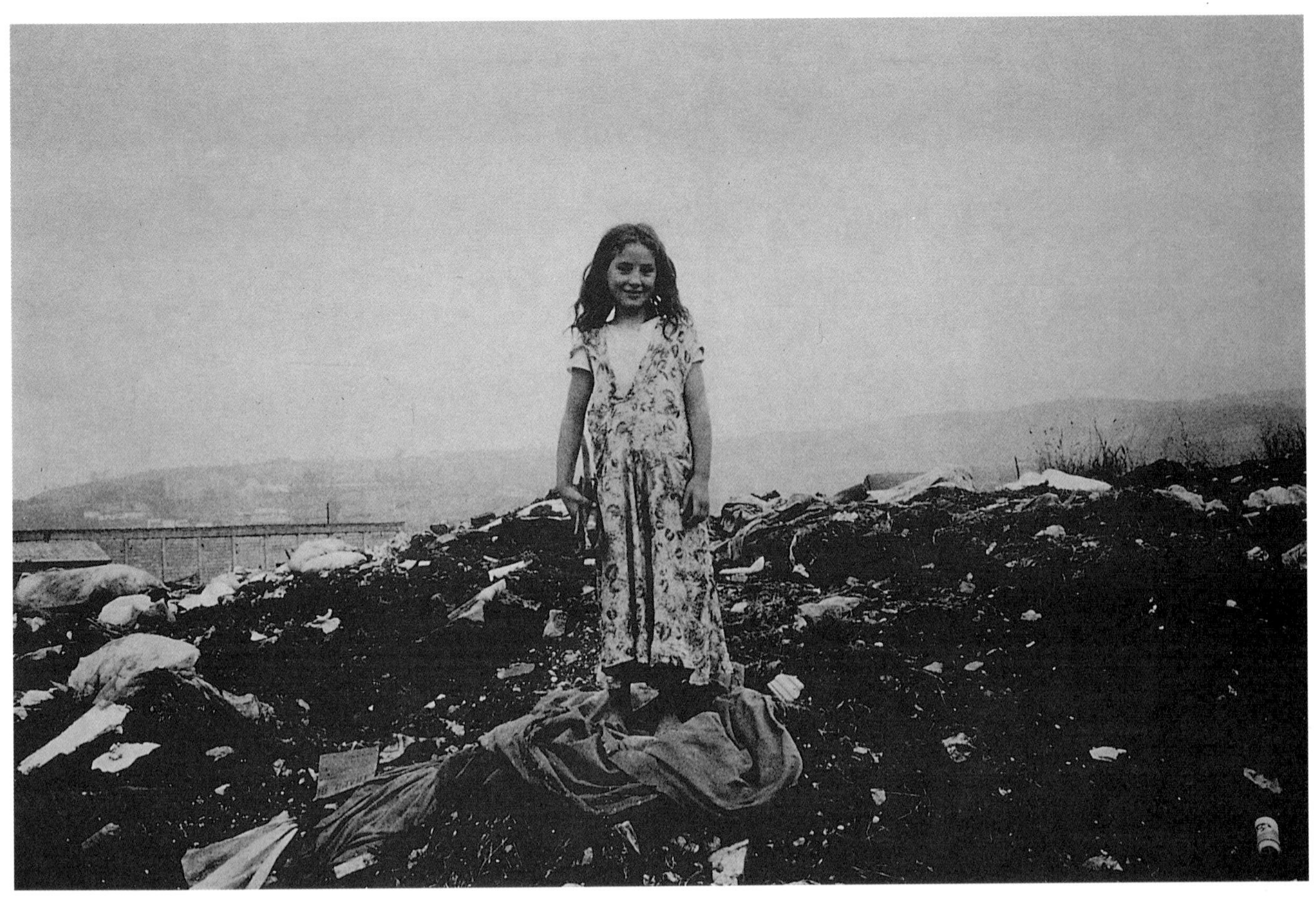

Gitanilla
1978
25 x 35,5 cm.

MANUEL FALCES

Born Almería, 1952 / Nació en Almería, 1952

Individual Exhibitions
Exposiciones individuales

1977   Photogalería. Madrid, España.
1988   IX Encuentros Internacionales de la
        Fotografía y lo Audiovisual. Monpellier,
        Francia.
1990   El Tránsito. Museo de Arte
        Contemporáneo. Sevilla, España.

Group Exhibitions
Exposiciones colectivas

1976   Kunsthalle. Colonia, Alemania.
1977   Fotografía Española Contemporánea.
        París, Francia.

1978   Fotografía Española de Vanguardia.
        Centro Cultural Juana Mordó. Madrid,
        España.
        IX Recontres Internationales de la
        Photographie d'Arles. Francia.
1988   Instituto Valenciano de Arte Moderno.
        Valencia, España.

Photographs included in the exhibition
Fotografías contenidas en la exposición

1. El año en que vivimos peligrosamente. 1973. Ciba. 50 x 60 cm.
2. Terraza de verano. 1973. Cibachrome. 50 x 60 cm.
3. Caballero de la rosa. 1984. Cibachrome. 50 x 60 cm.
4. V Centenario, Sevilla. 1985. Cibachrome. 50 x 60 cm.
5. Marco Polo. 1988. Cibachrome. 50 x 60 cm.

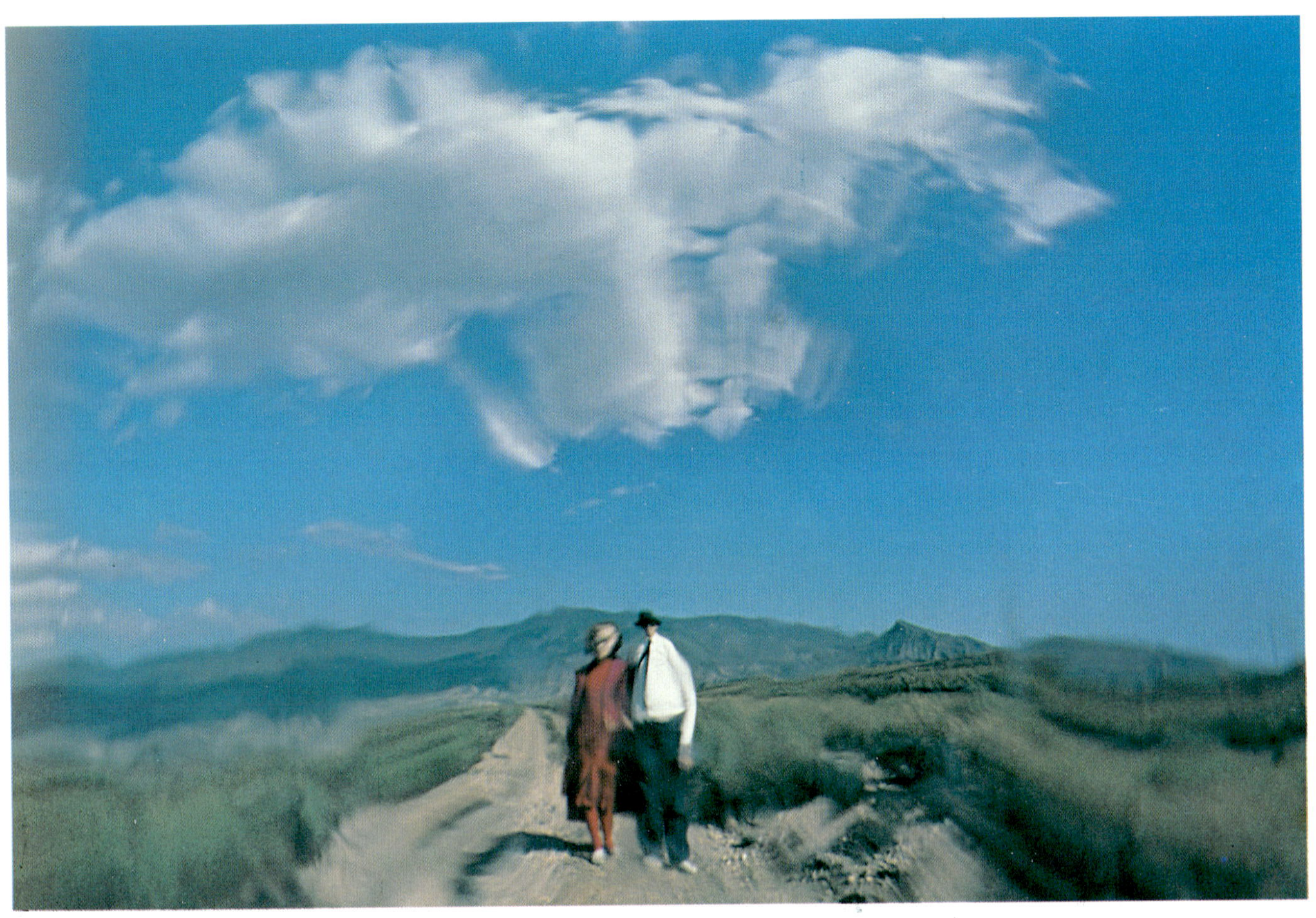

El año en que vivimos peligrosamente

1973

Cibachrome

50 x 60 cm.

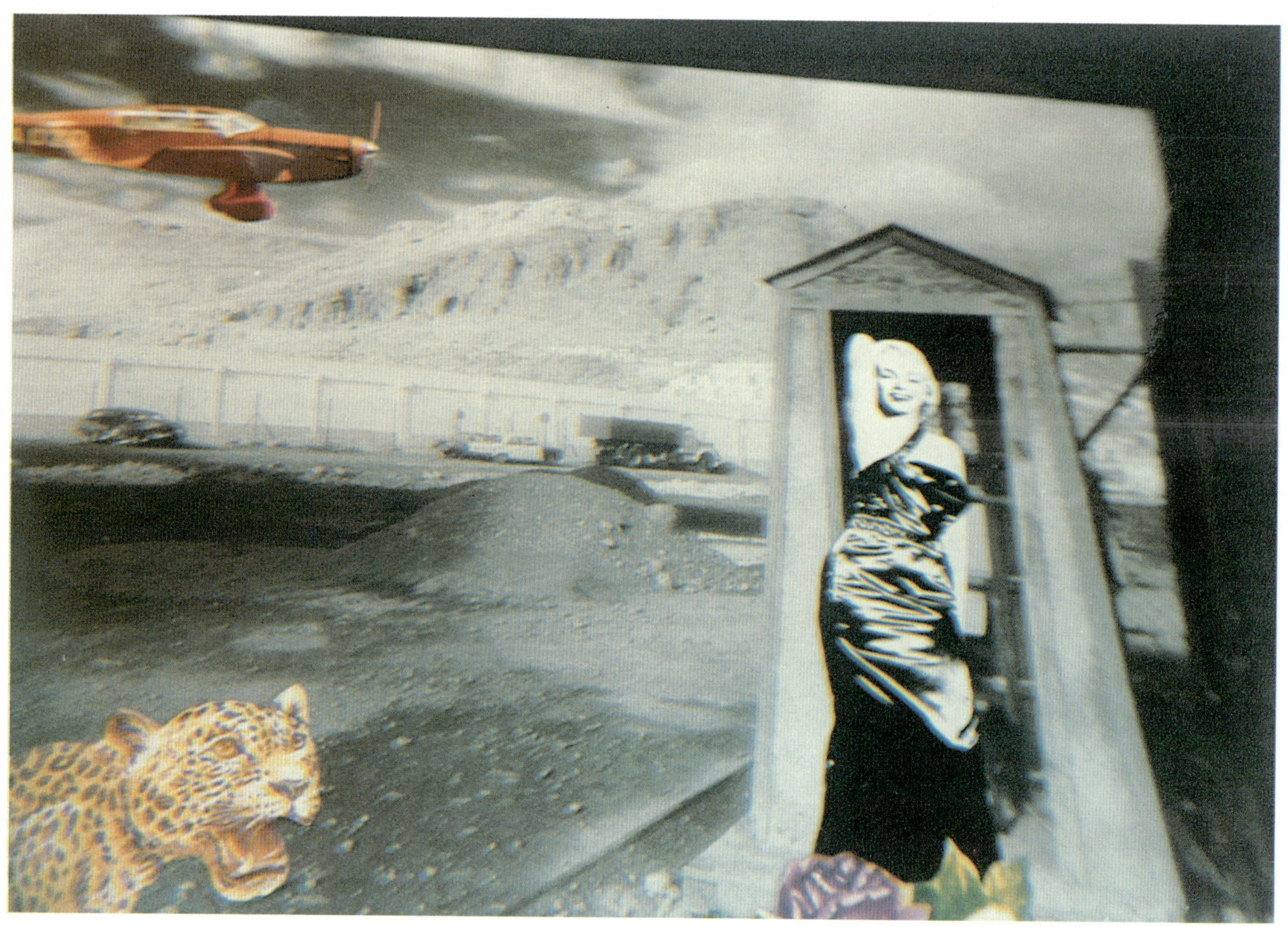

Terraza de verano

1973

Cibachrome

50 x 60 cm.

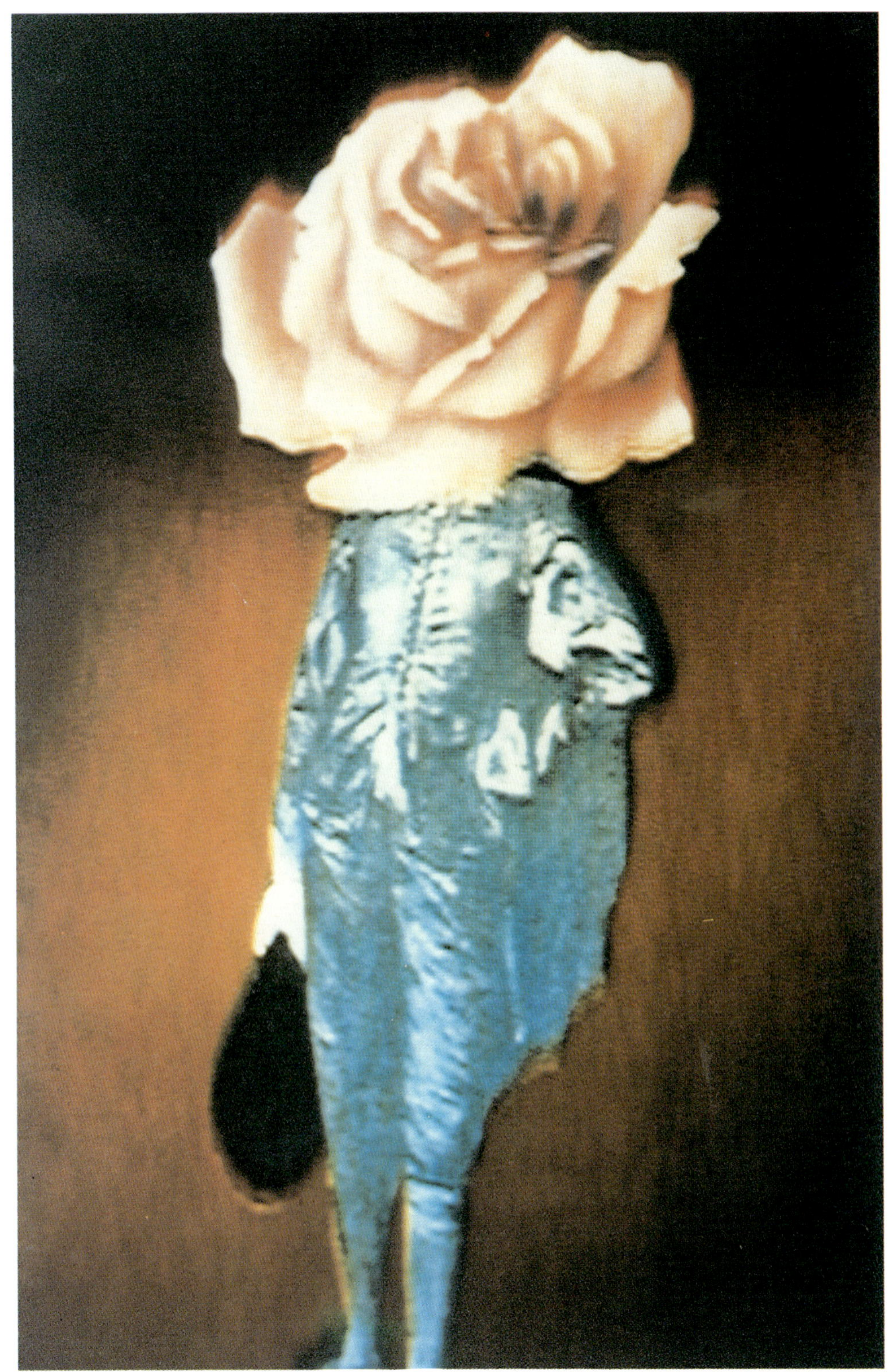

Caballero de la rosa

1984

Cibachrome

50 x 60 cm.

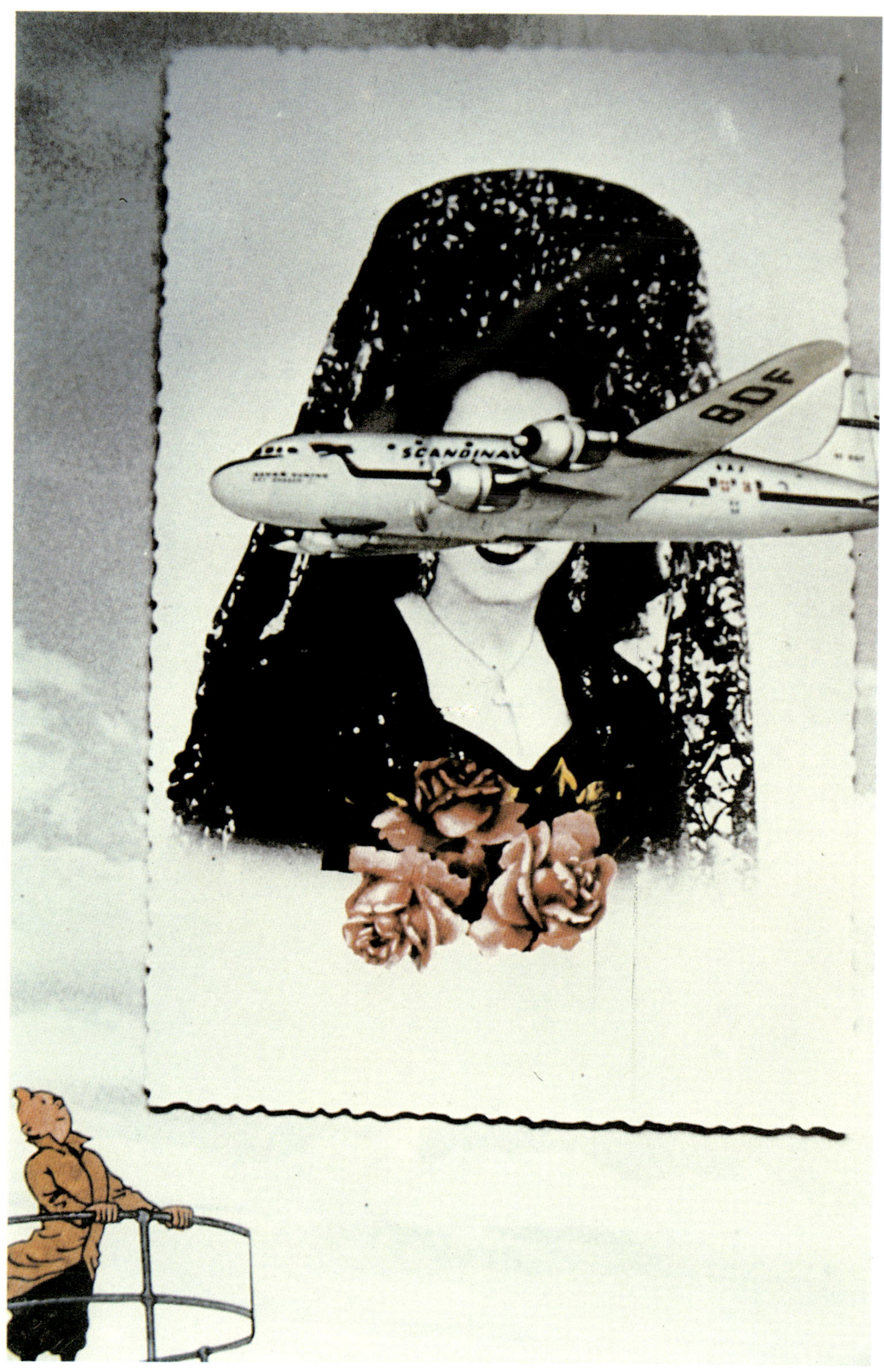

V Centenario, Sevilla

1985

Cibachrome

50 x 60 cm.

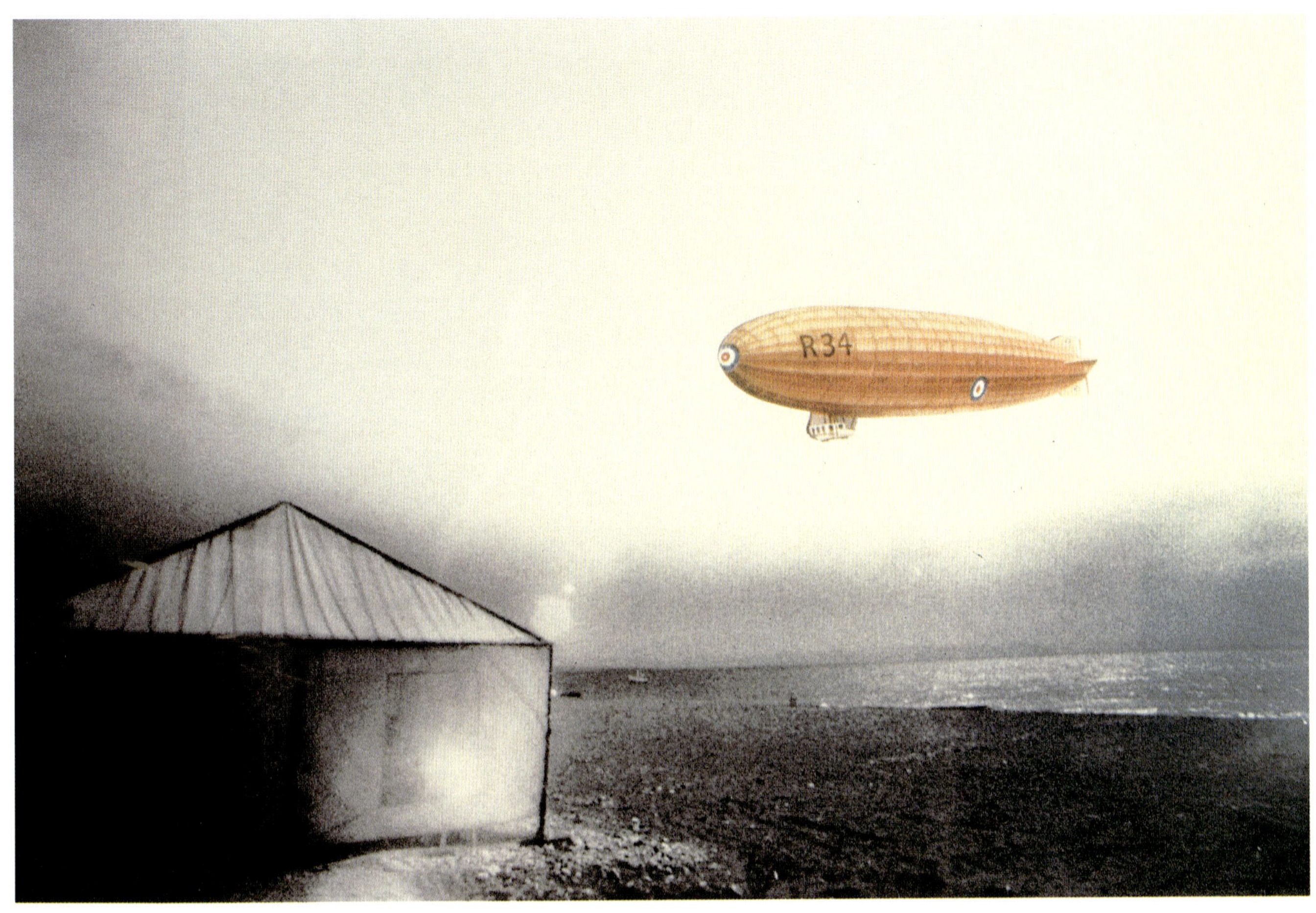

Marco Polo

1988

Cibachrome

50 x 60 cm.

JOAN FONTCUBERTA

Born Barcelona, 1955 / Nació en Barcelona, 1955

Main Individual Exhibitions
Principales Exposiciones individuales

1974   Sala Aixelá. Barcelona, España.
        Galería Spectrum. Barcelona, España.
1975   La Photogalería. Madrid. España.
1976   Galería Spectrum. Barcelona, España.
1977   Galería Upsilon. Nantes, Francia.
        Canon Gallery. Amsterdam, Holanda.
1978   Galería Fotomanía. Barcelona, España.
        Galería Voir. Toulouse, Francia.
1979   Galería Agathe Gaillard. París, Francia.
        Il Laboratorio d'If. Palermo, Italia.
        Galería Trackempresse. Berlín, Alemania.
        Galería Tretze. Valencia, España.
        Work Gallery. Zurich, Suiza.
1980   Paule Pia Galerij. Amberes, Bélgica.
        P. C. A. Atenas, Grecia.
1981   The Photographic Gallery. Cardiff,
        Inglaterra.
        Centro Cívico Irnerio. Bolonia, Italia.
1982   Galería Il Diaframma. Milán, Italia.
1983   Galería Profoto. Nuremberg, Alemania.
        Galería Municipale de Chateau d'Eau.
        Toulouse, Francia.
1984   Fotoforum. Bremen, Alemania.
1985   Galerie Zabriskie. París, Francia.
1986   Zabriskie Gallery. Nueva York, EE.UU.
1987   Folkwang Museum. Essen.
        Galería Zabriskie. París, Francia.
        Museo de Historia Natural. Coimbra,
        Portugal.
1988   Galería Jütta Rössner. Stuttgart.
        Zabriskie Gallery. Nueva York, EE.UU.
        The Photographers' Gallery. Londres,
        Inglaterra.
        Museo de Arte Moderno de Nueva York.
        Nueva York, EE.UU.
        The Museum of Art. Tucson, Arizona,

EE.UU.
Visual Arts Center. Cambridge,
Massachusetts, EE.UU.
Galería Nueva Imagen. Pamplona,
España.
Museo de Arte Contemporáneo. Sevilla,
España.
Galería Juana Mordó. Madrid, España.
1989   Rosenthal Art Center, Queans College.
        New York, EE.UU.
        Artotheque Antonin Artaud. Marsella,
        Nueva Francia.
        Museo de Zoología. Barcelona, España.
        Museo de Bellas Artes. Málaga, España.
1990   The Art Institute of Chicago. Chicago,
        Illinois, EE.UU.
        Museo Nacional de Ciencias Naturales.
        Madrid, España.
        Centre d'Art Santa Monica. Barcelona,
        España.
        Lehigh University Art Gallery, Bethlehem.
        Pennsylvania, EE.UU.
        Museum of Natural Historu, Aarhus.
        Dinamarca.
1991   Zabriskie Gallery. Nueva York, EE.UU
        Galerie Zabriskie. París, Francia.
        L.A. Galerie. Frankfurt, Alemania.
        Museo de Bellas Artes. Bilbao, España.

Fotografías contenidas en la exposición
Photographs included in the exhibition

1. Mont of Venus Botanical Garden. '78. Plata.
   35 x 35 cm.
2. Elogi de la Follia. '80. Plata. 35 x 35 cm.
3. Parc de la Ciutadella. '79. Plata. 35 x 35 cm.
4. Alba d'Aligues. '79. Plata. 35 x 35 cm.
5. Villa Aldobrandi Frascati. '80. Plata. 35 x 35 cm.

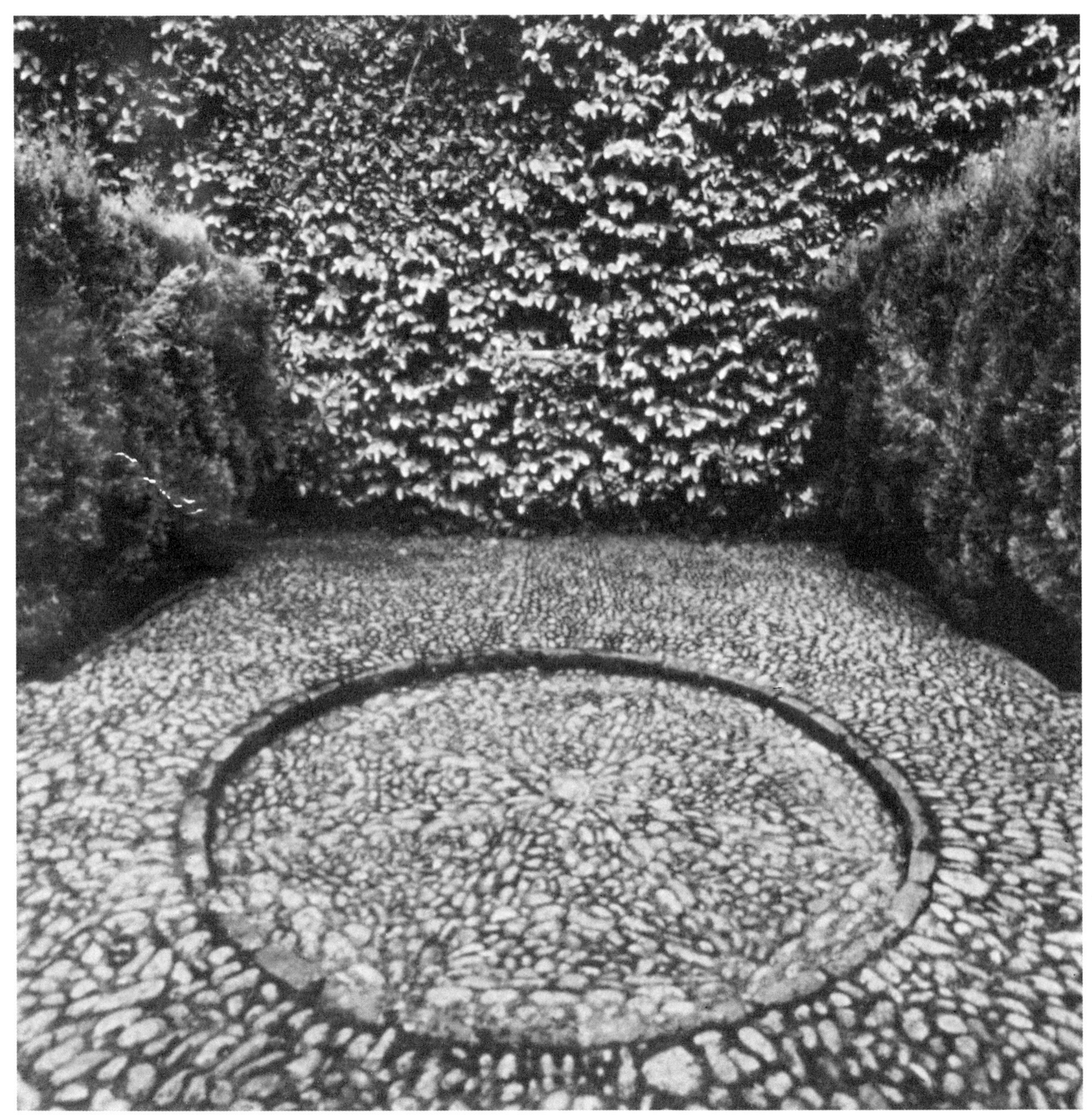

Mont of Venus Botanical Garden
Plata
35 x 35 cm.

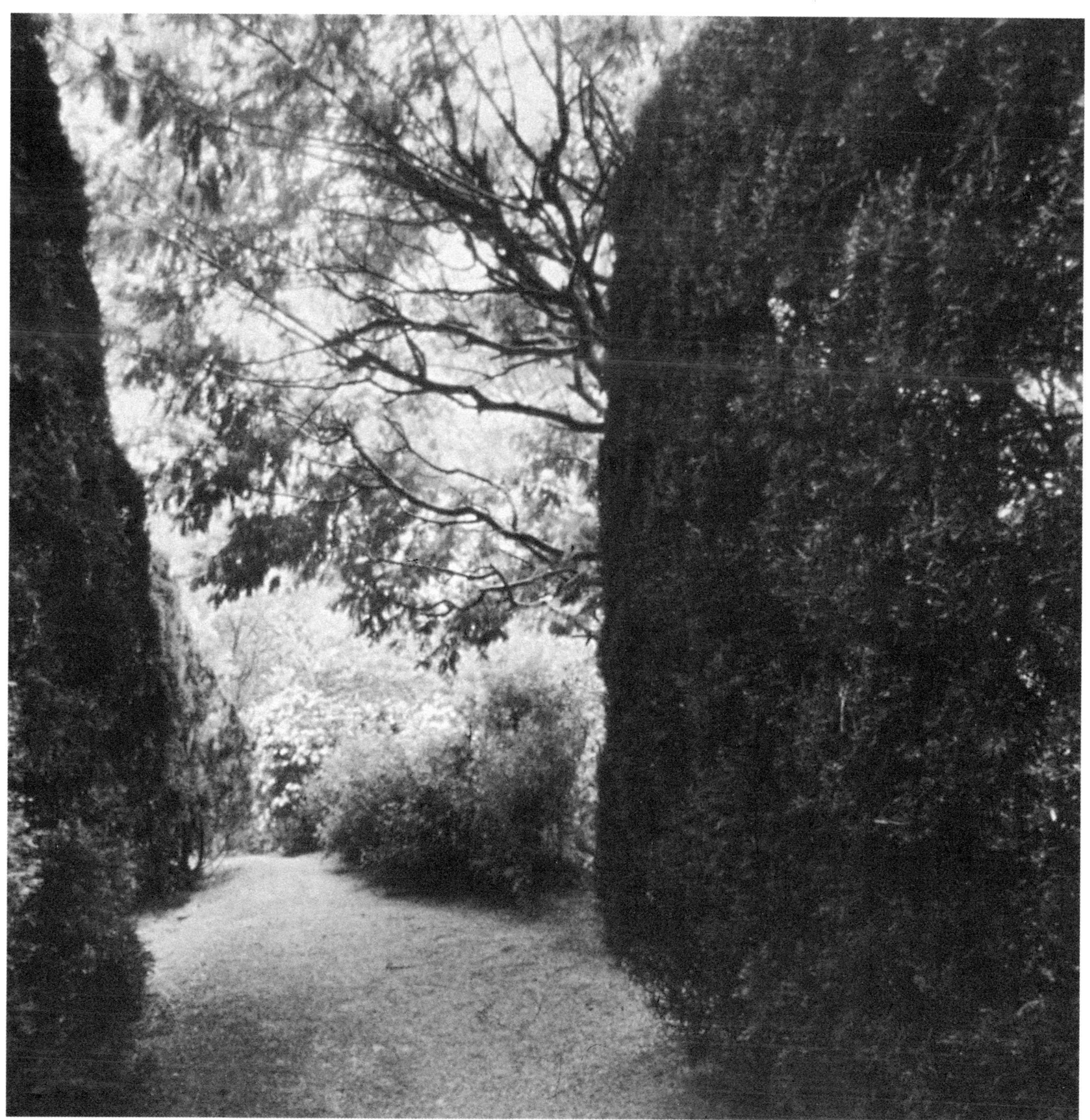

Elogi de la Follia
Plata
35 x 35 cm.

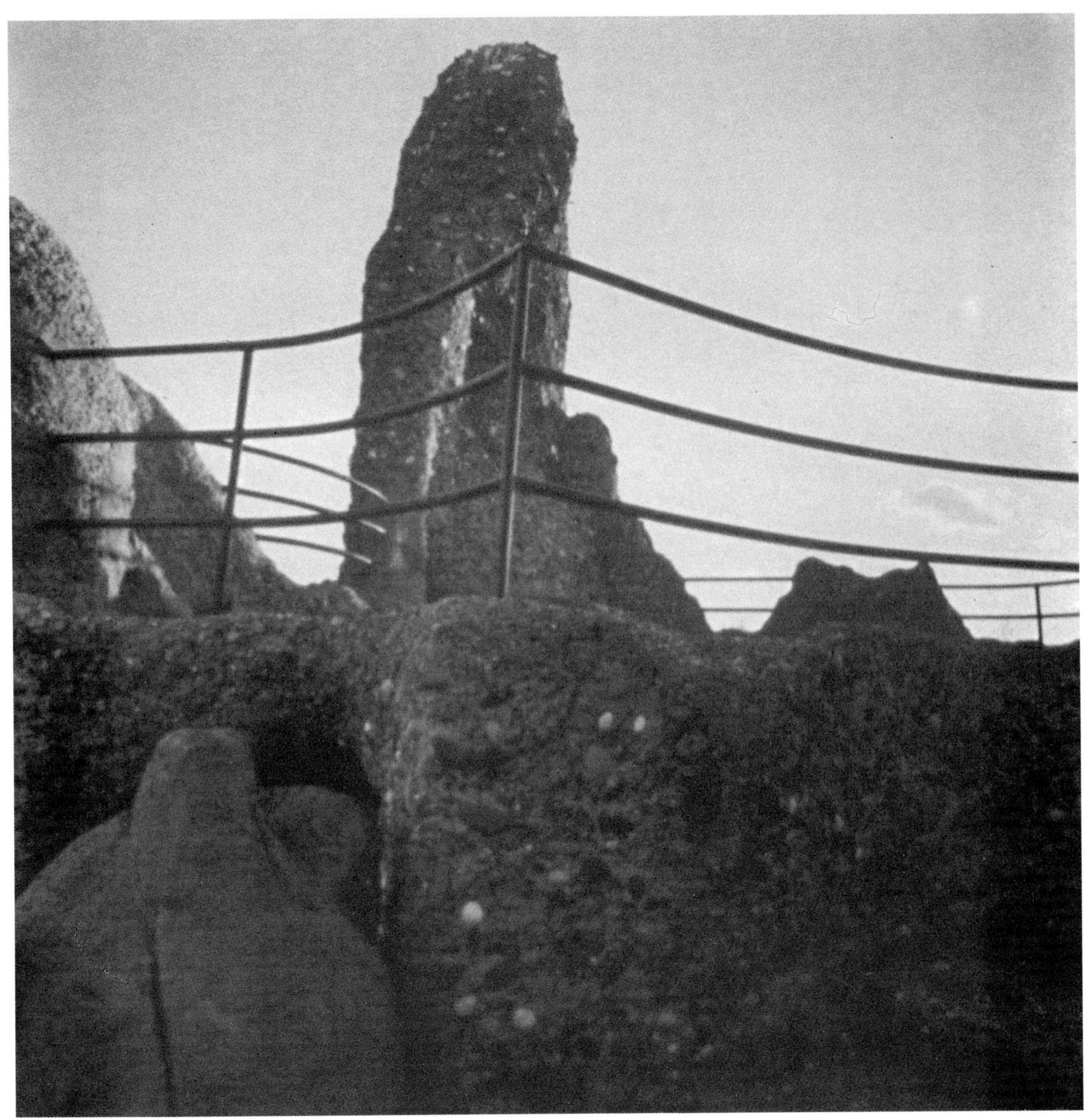

Parc de la Ciutadella
Plata
35 x 35 cm.

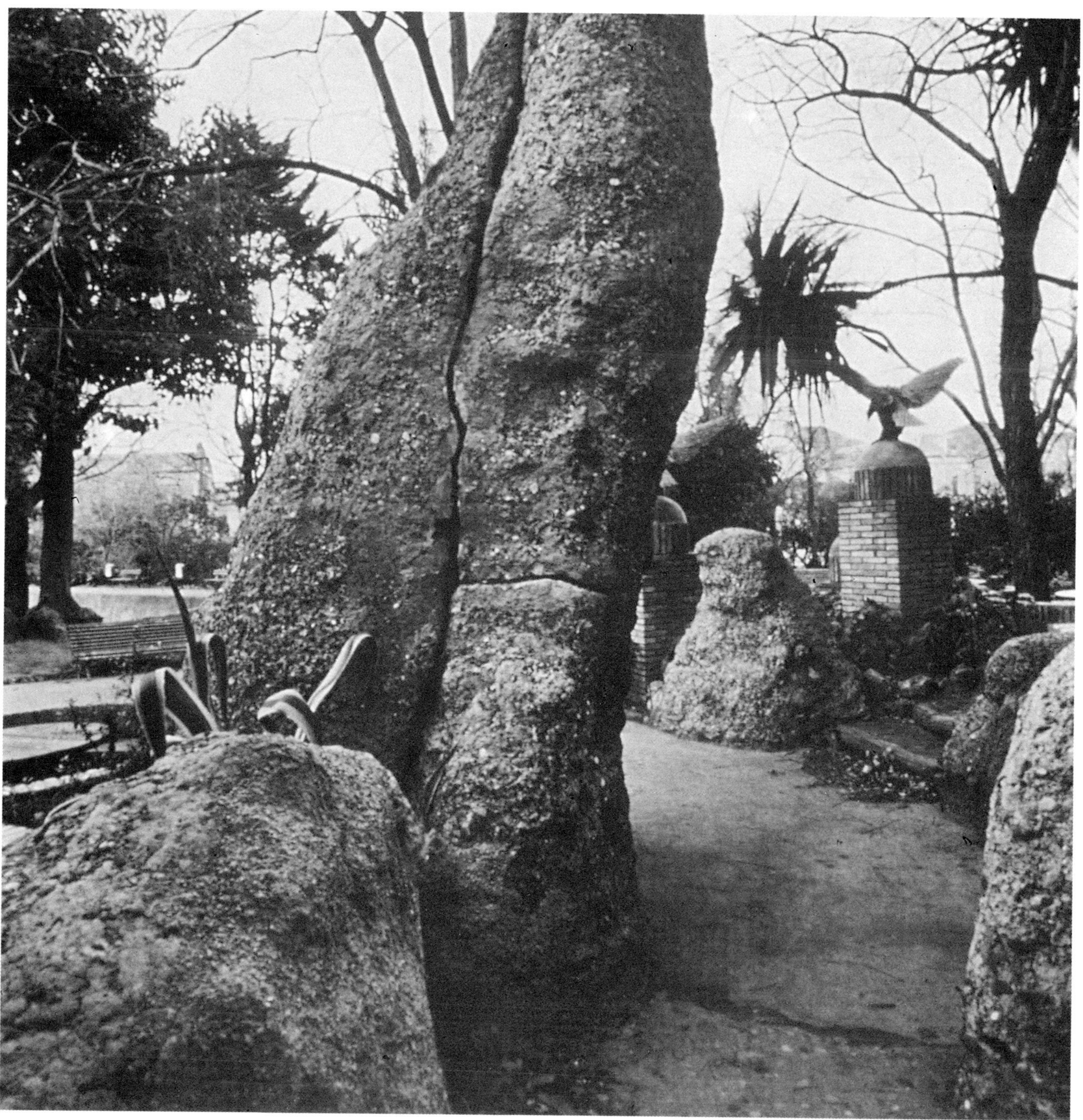

Alba d'Aligues
Plata
35 x 35 cm.

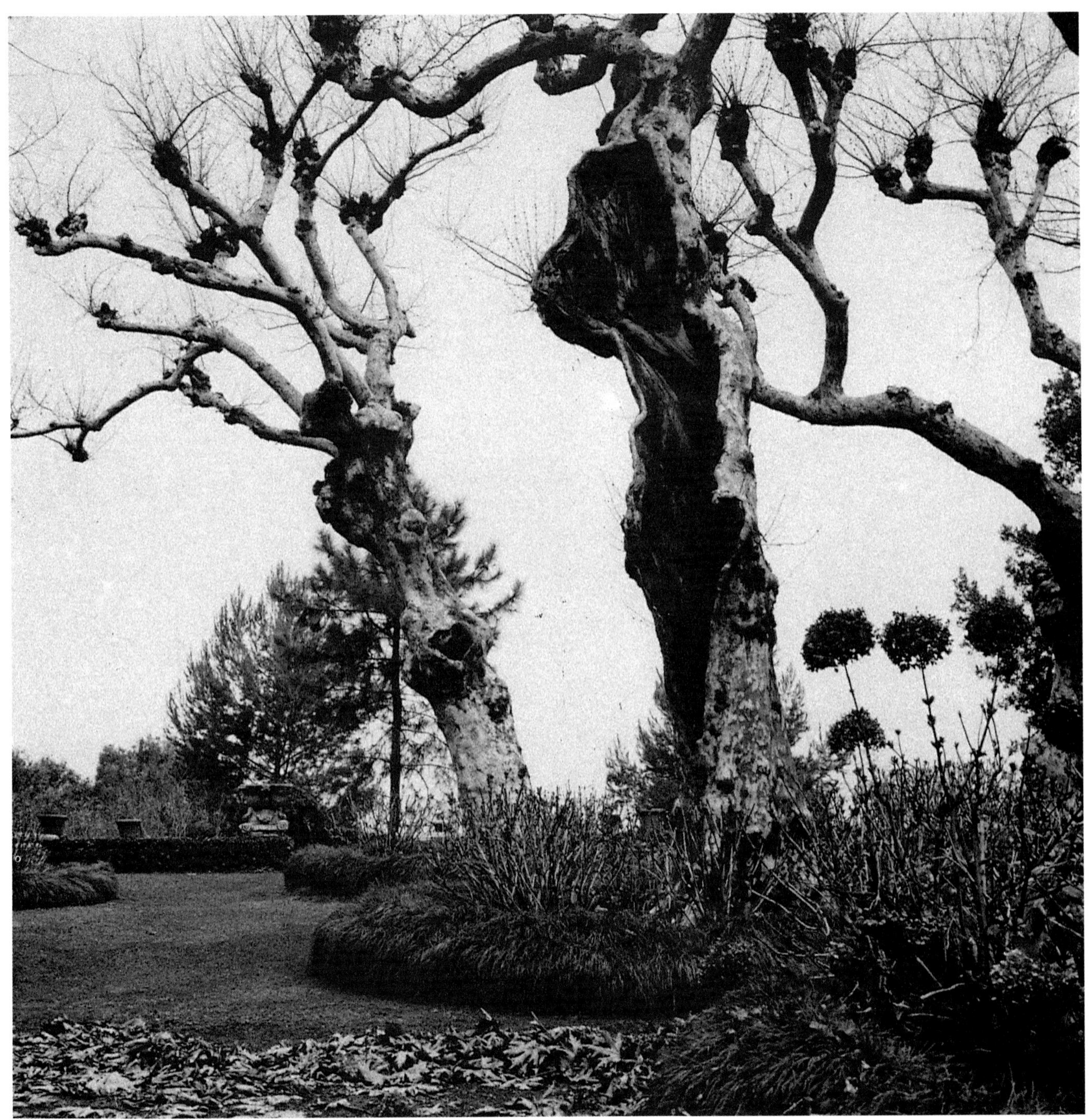

Villa Aldobrandi Frascati
Plata
35 x 35 cm.

JOSE GOMEZ APARICIO

Born Segovia, 1964 / Nació en Segovia, 1964

Individual Exhibitions
Exposiciones individuales

1985   "Fografías". Sala de exposiciones de la
Agrupación Fotográfica de Guadalajara.
Guadalajara, España.

Group Exhibitions
Exposiciones colectivas

1986   "Los jóvenes vistos por los jóvenes".
Círculo de Bellas Artes. Madrid, España.

1987   "Jóvenes Fotógrafos". Sala Amadís.

       Instituto de la Juventud. Madrid, España.

1988   "Ambitos de la fotografía". Ayudas a
jóvenes fotógrafos 1987. Sala Amadís.
Instituto de la Juventud. Madrid, España.

Photographs included in the exhibition
Fotografías contenidas en la exposición

1. Famosos VII. 1988. 38 x 20,5 cm. Bromuro / Baño selenio.
2. Famosos IV. 1988. 30 x 22 cm. Bromuro / Baño selenio.
3. Famosos II. 1988. 30 x 19,5 cm. Bromuro / Baño selenio.
4. Famosos III. 1988. 30 x 23 cm. Bromuro / Baño selenio.
5. Famosos IX. 1988. 34,5 x 28,5 cm. Bromuro / Baño selenio.

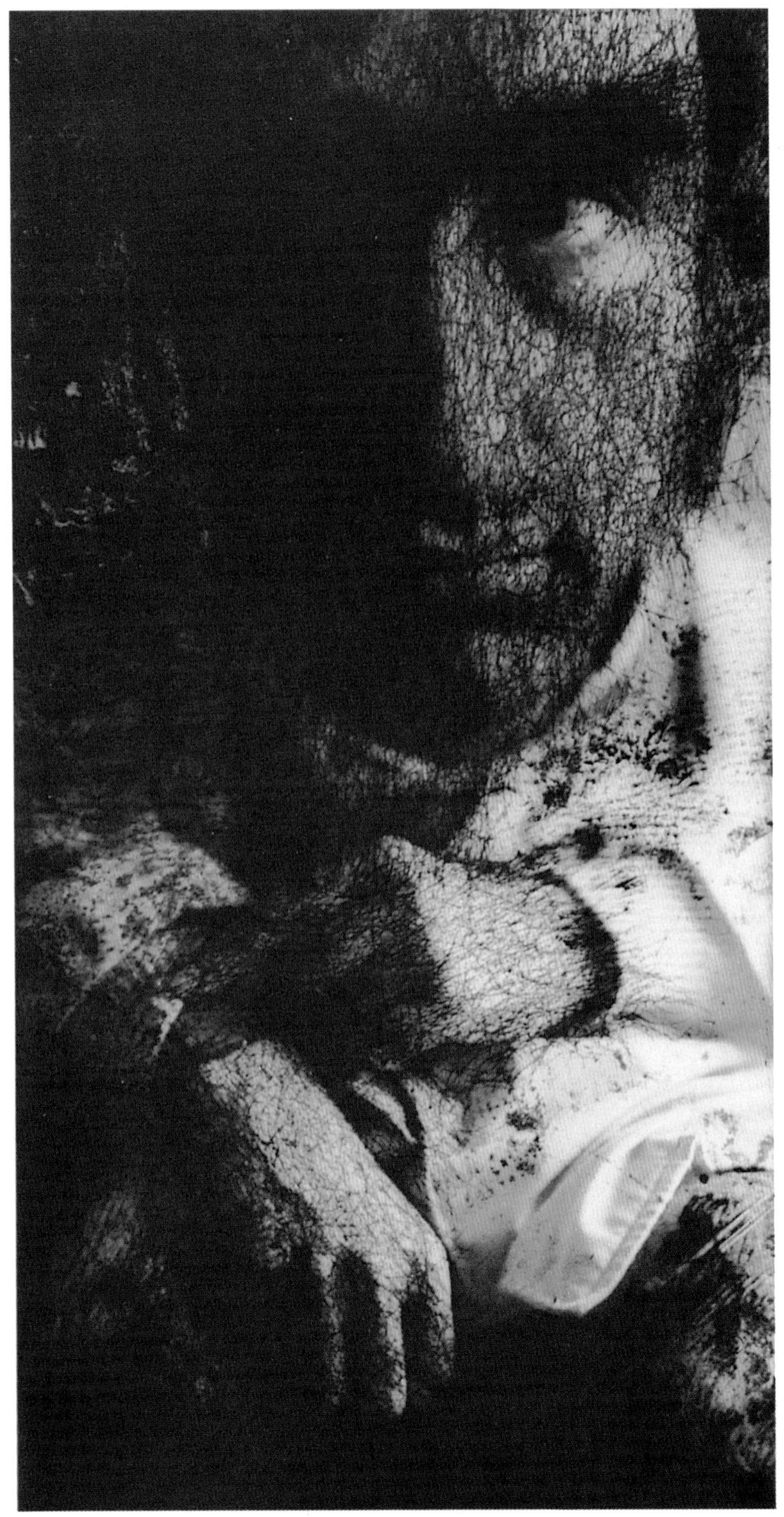

Famosos VII

1988

Bromuro / Baño selenio

38 x 20,5 cm.

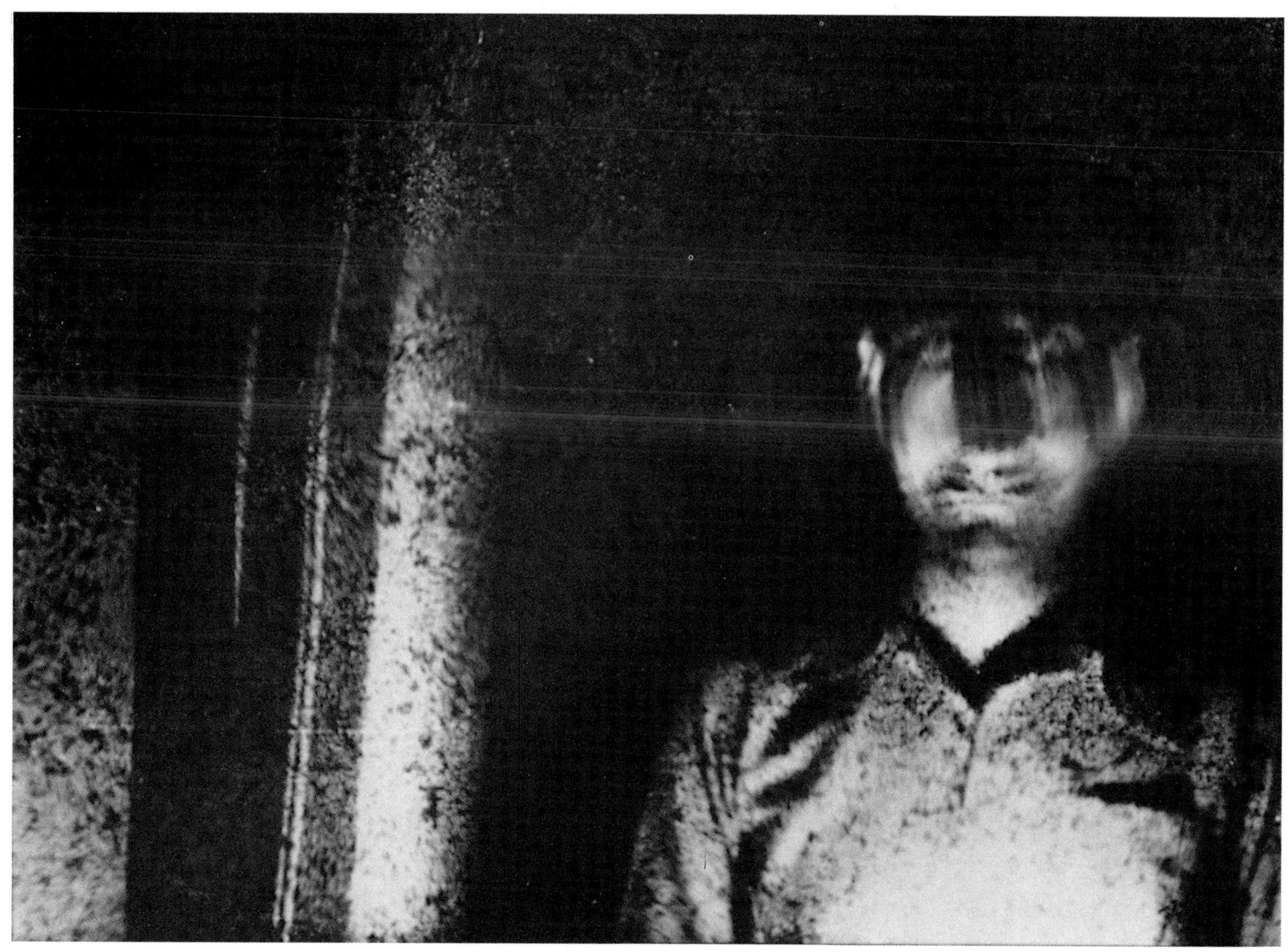

Famosos IV

1988

Bromuro / Baño selenio

30 x 22 cm.

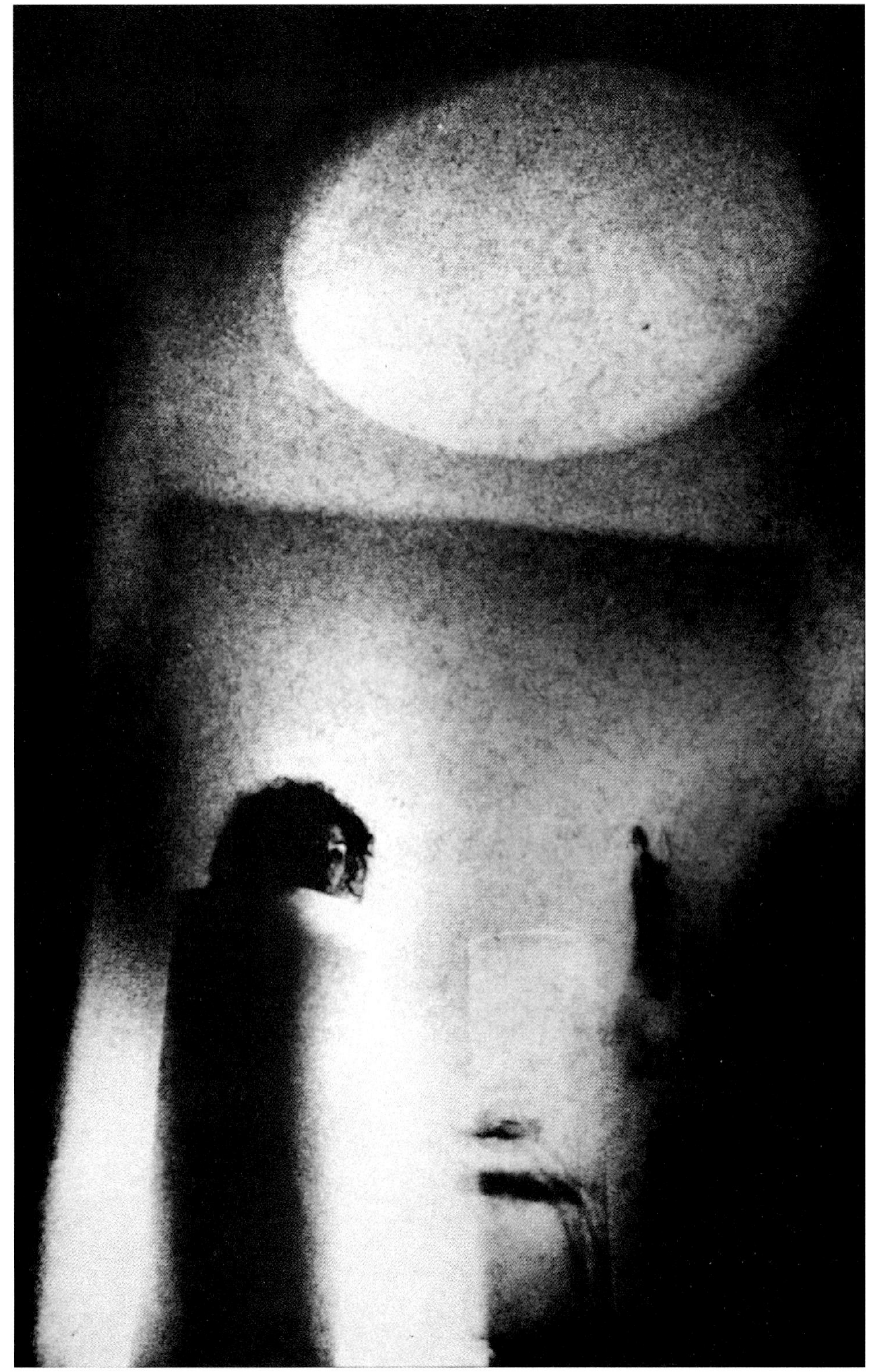

Famosos II

1988

Bromuro / Baño selenio

30 x 19,5 cm.

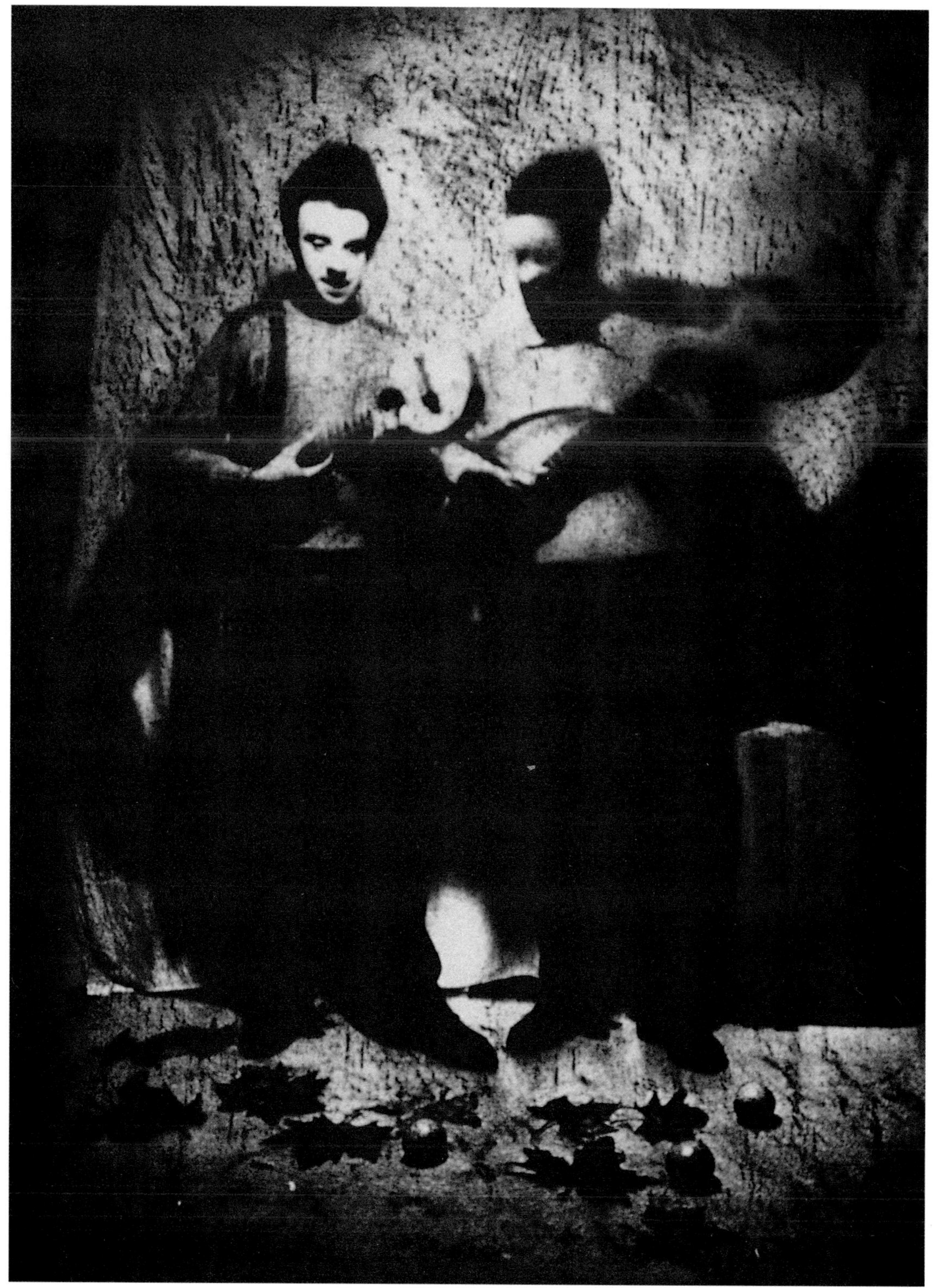

Famosos III

1988

Bromuro / Baño selenio

30 x 23 cm.

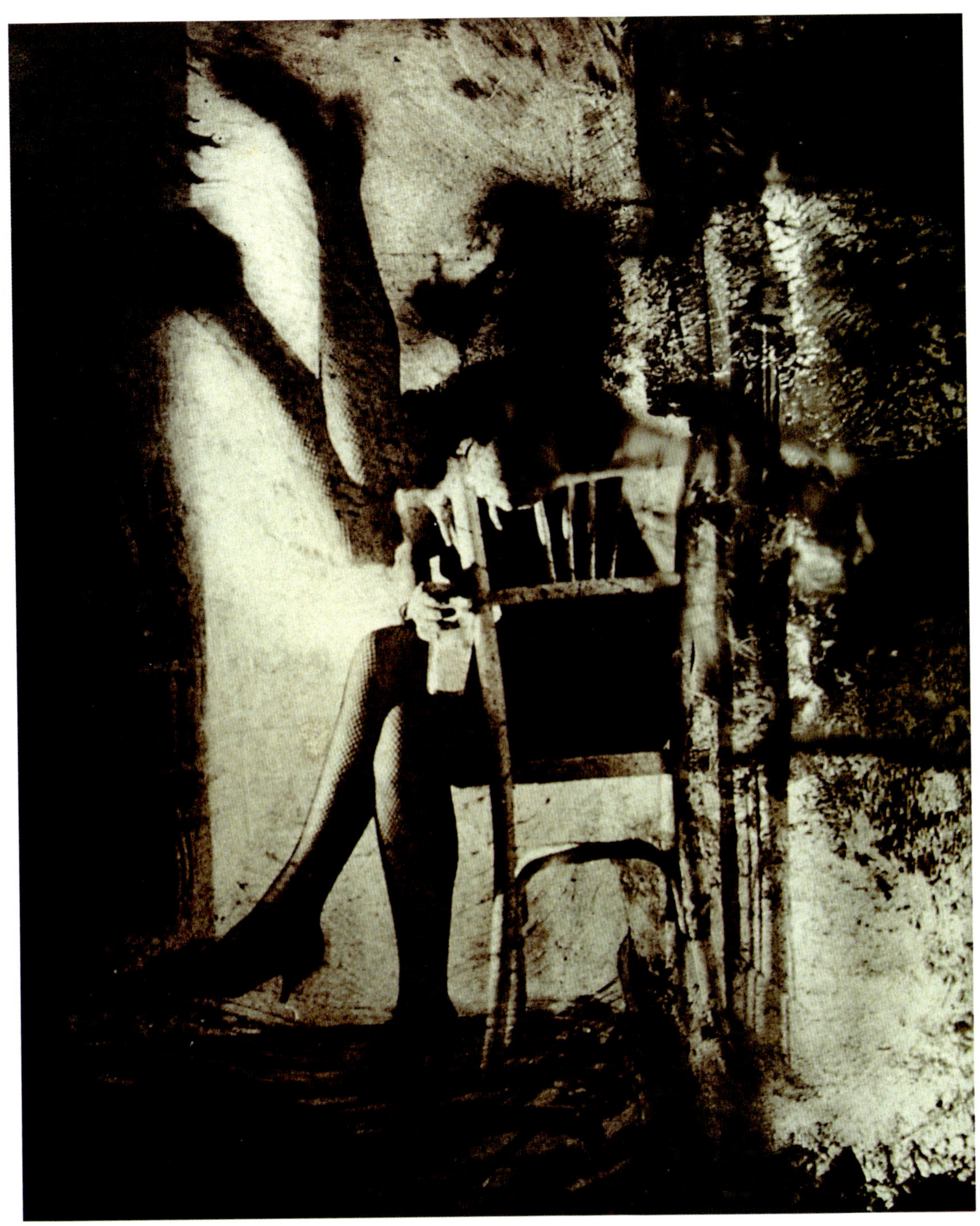

Famosos IX

1988

Bromuro / Baño selenio

34,5 x 28,5 cm.

MARIA JOSE GOMEZ REDONDO

Born Valladolid, 1963 / Nació en Valladolid, 1963

Individual Exhibitions
Exposiciones individuales

1990	Círculo de Bellas Artes. Madrid, España.
1991	Casa del Siglo XV. Segovia, España.
	Galería Emilio Navarro. Madrid, España.
	Galería Rafael Ortíz. Sevilla, España.

Group Exhibitions
Exposiciones colectivas

1982	Artistas Noveles. Torreón de Lozoya. Segovia, España.
1984	Espacia. Torreón de Lozoya. Segovia, España.
1985	Los novísimos son Diez. Casa del Siglo XV. Segovia, España.
1987	Madrid en Vanguardia. Centro Cultural Fernando de los Ríos. Madrid, España.
1988	Exposición de Alumnos Becarios. Facultad de Bellas Artes. Madrid, España.
1989	Jóvenes Fotógrafos. Sala Amadís. Instituto de la Juventud. Madrid, España.

	Talleres de Arte Actual. Círculo Bellas Artes de Madrid. Madrid, España.
	Imaginada. Torreón de Lozoya. Segovia, España.
	Muestra Internacional. Fundación Vía. Valkenswaard. Holanda.
1991	Fotografía Contemporánea Española: nuevas tendencias. Pohjoinen Valokuvakeskus. Oulu, Finlandia.
	Tentoonstelling. Fundación Vía. Valkenswaards, Holanda

Photographs included in the exhibition
Fotografías contenidas en la exposición

1. En la noche parecemos grises o el sentido del tacto. 1990. 50 x 34 cm. Copia "C".
2. Descubrir es ver por dentro o el sentido de la vista. 1990. 50 x 34 cm. Copia "C".
3. Tiene una voz transparente o el sentido del oído. 1990. 50 x 34 cm. Copia "C".
4. Jaime corta una rama verde o el sentido del olfato. 1990. 50 x 34 cm. Copia "C".
5. Sara comerá las frutas o el sentido del gusto. 1990. 50 x 34 cm. Copia "C".

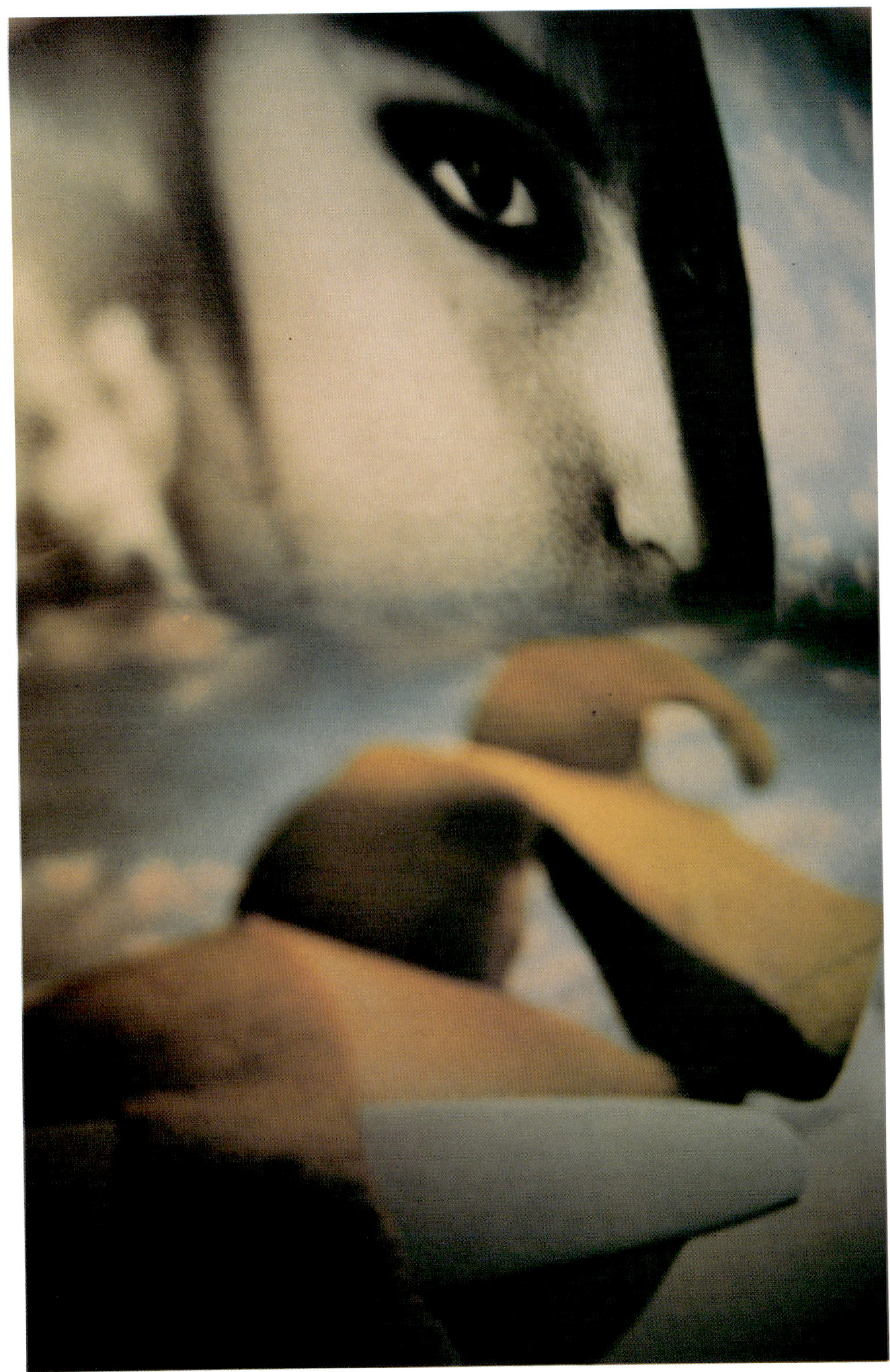

En la noche parecemos grises o el sentido del tacto
1990
50 x 34 cm.

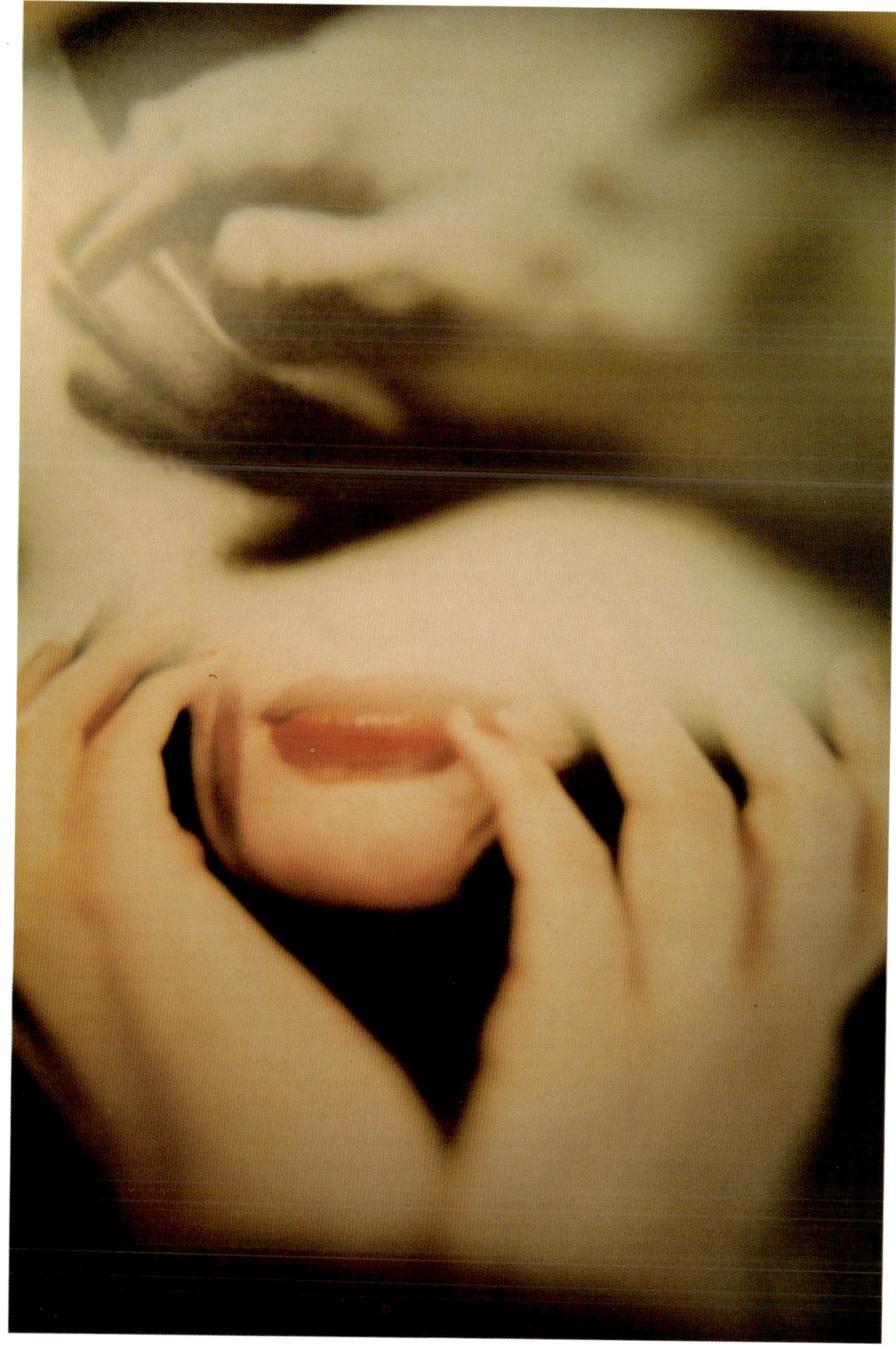

Descubrir es ver por dentro o el sentido de la vista
1990
50 x 34 cm.

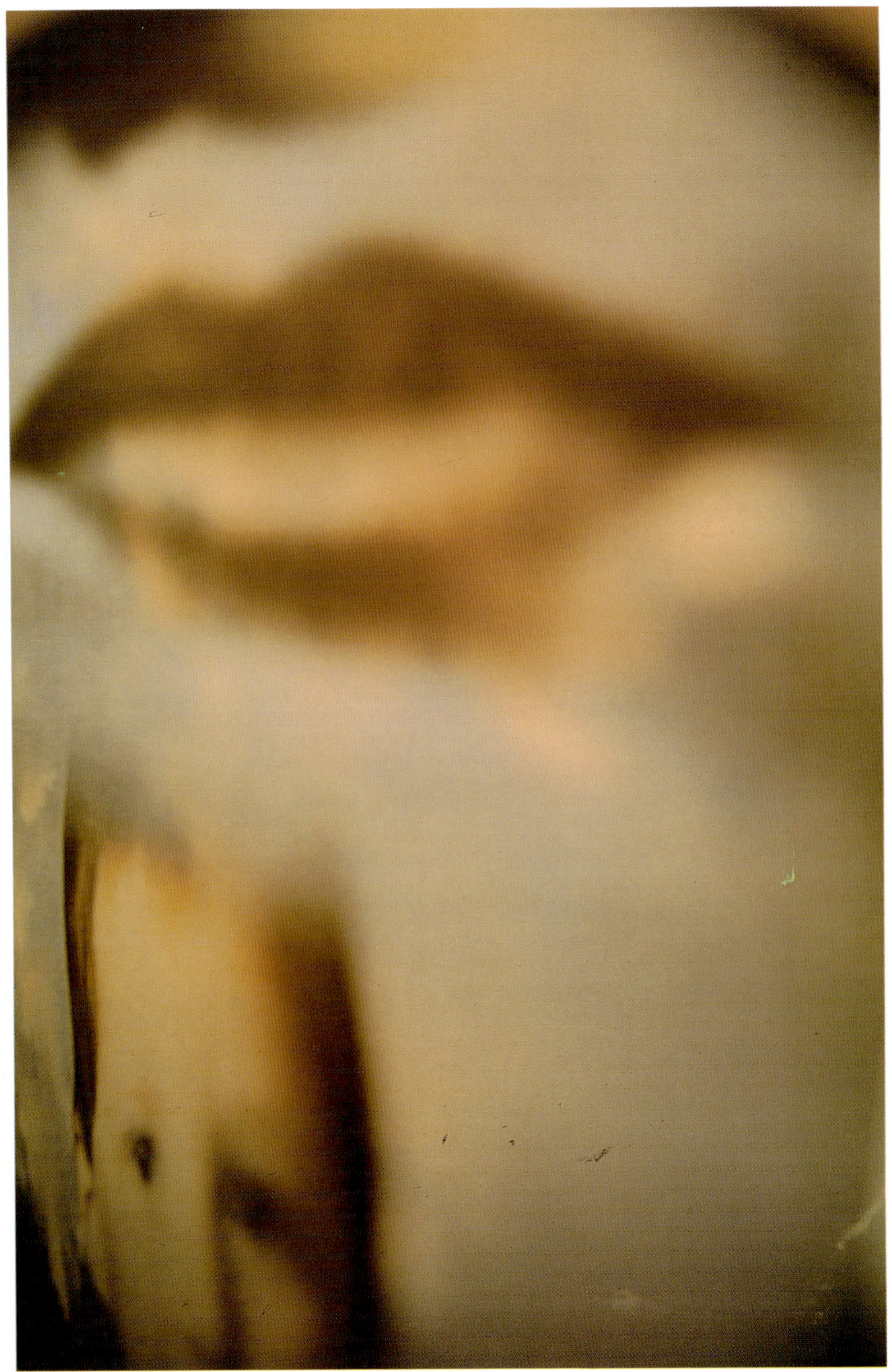

Tiene una voz transparente o el sentido del oído

1990

50 x 34 cm.

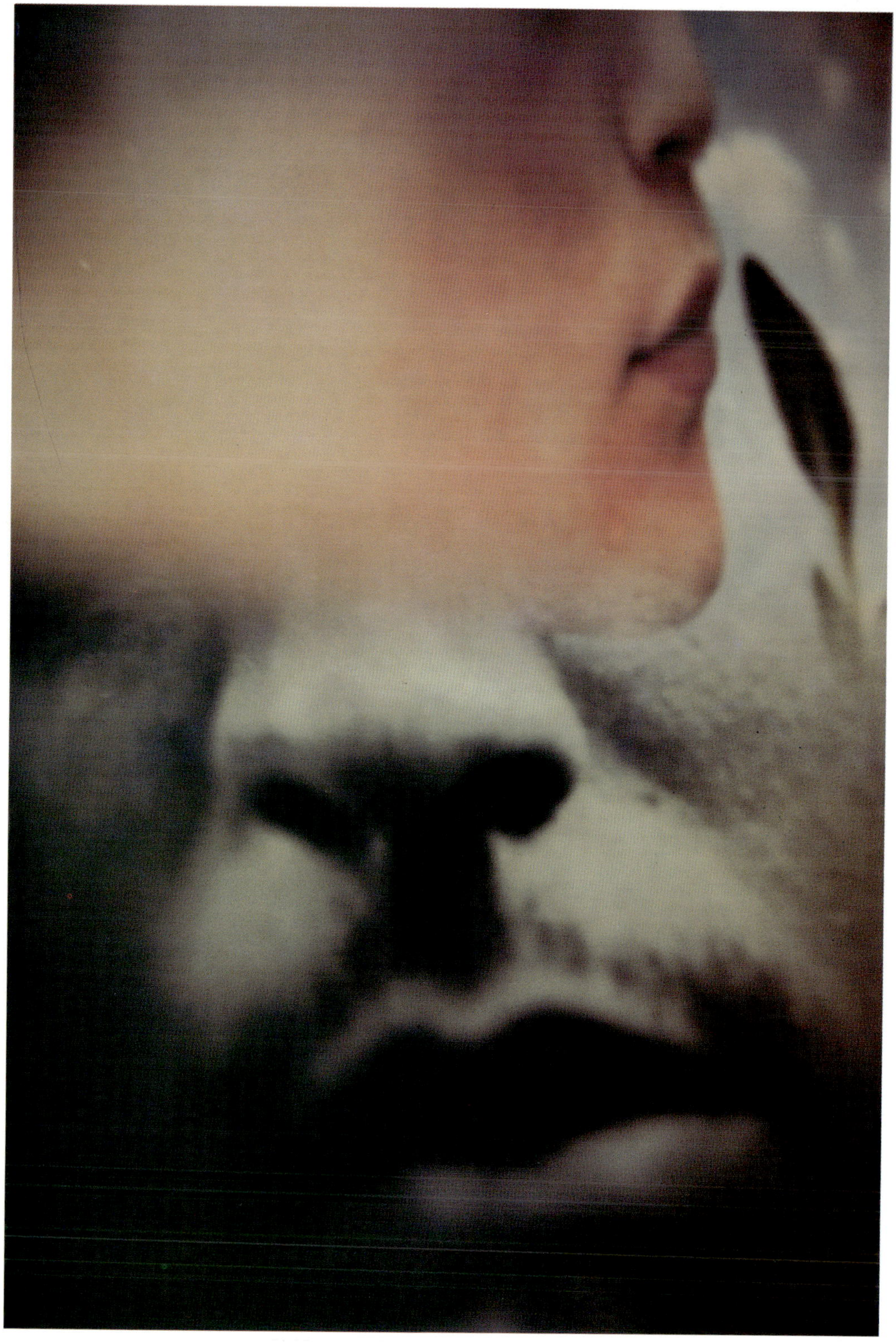

Jaime corta una rama verde o el sentido del olfato

1990

50 x 34 cm.

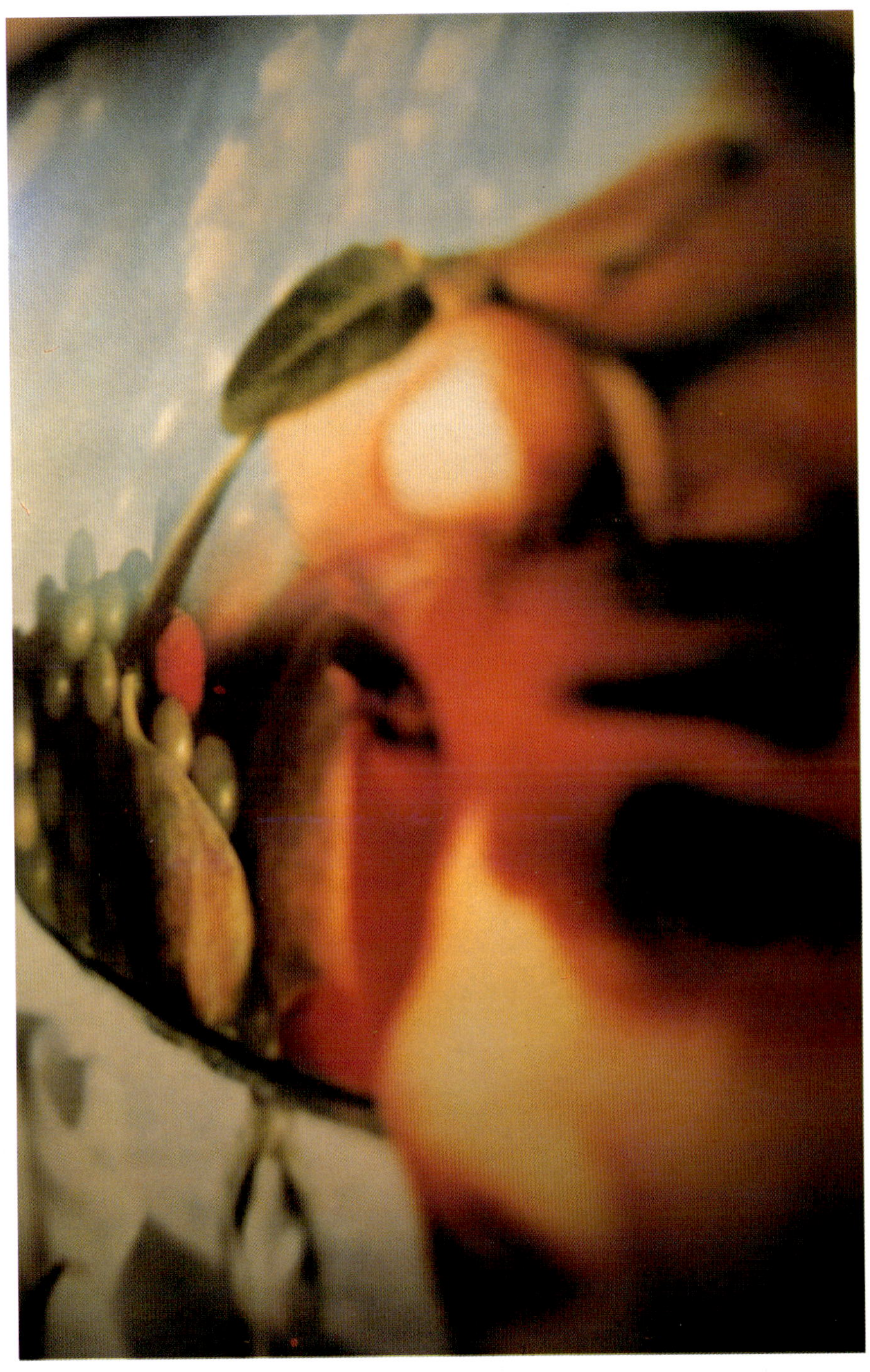

Sara comerá las frutas o el sentido del gusto
1990
50 x 34 cm.

JORGE LENS LEIVA

Born Vigo, 1967 / Nació en Vigo, 1967

Individual Exhibitions
Exposiciones individuales

1989   "Home mesmo". Sala dos Peiraos. Vigo,
España.

Photographs included in the exhibition
Fotografías contenidas en la exposición

1. Caseta. 1990. Cibachrome. 27 x 40 cm.
2. Canasta. 1989. Cibachrome. 27 x 40 cm.
3. Banco. 1989. Cibachrome. 27 x 40 cm.
4. Caja. 1989. Cibachrome. 27 x 40 cm.
5. Mano. 1989. Cibachrome. 27 x 40 cm.

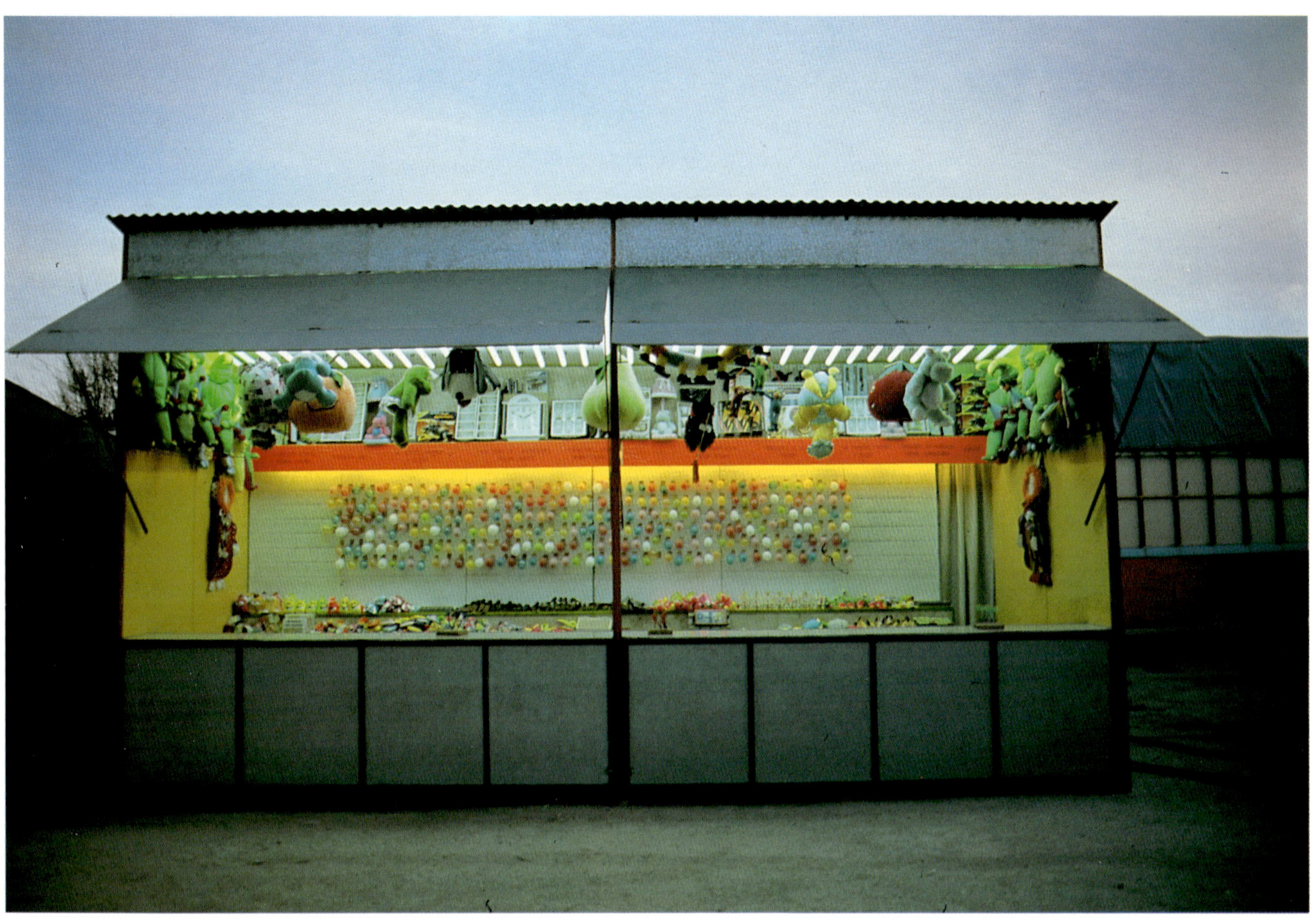

Caseta

1990

Cibachrome

27 x 40 cm.

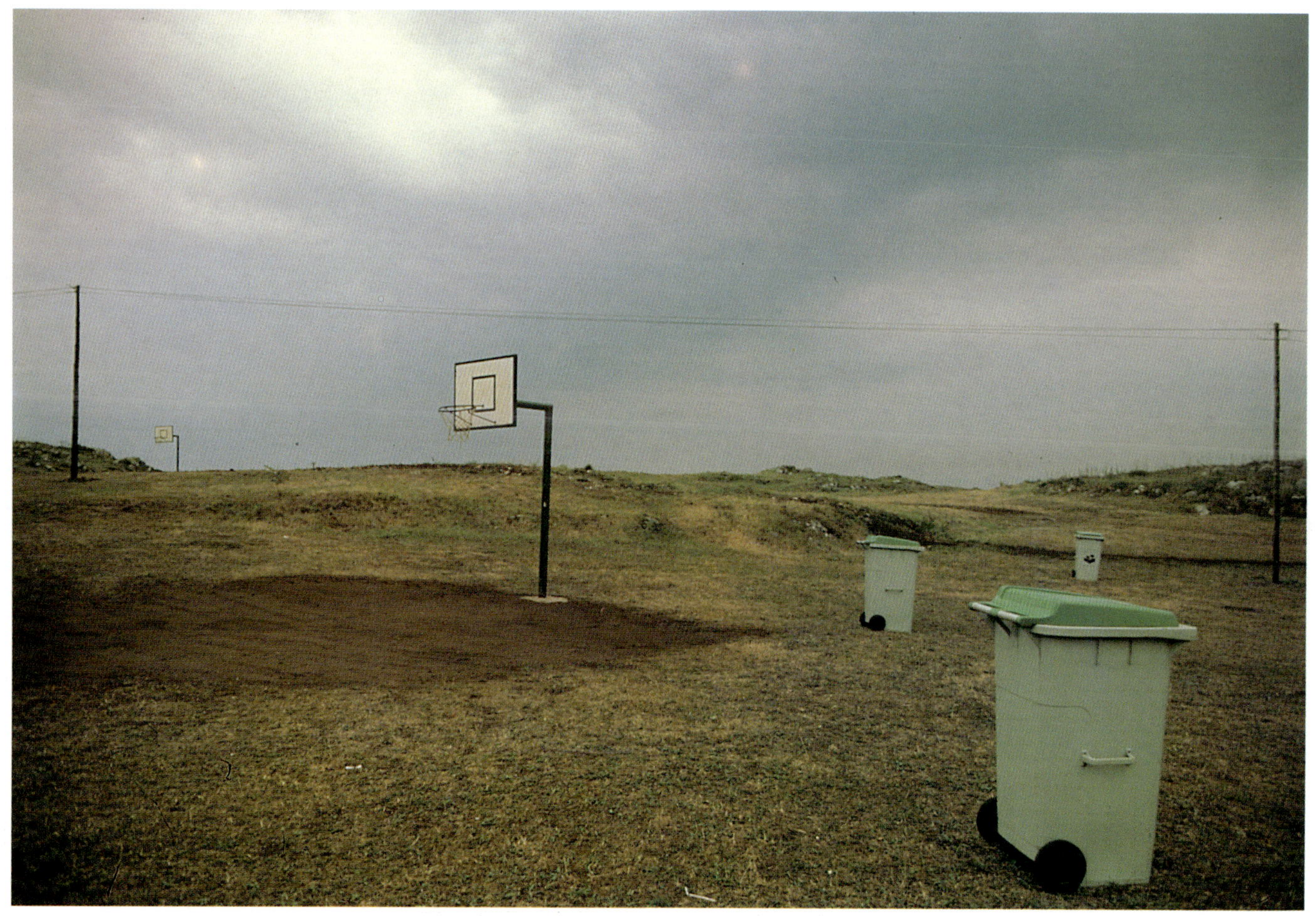

Canasta

1989

Cibachrome

27 x 40 cm.

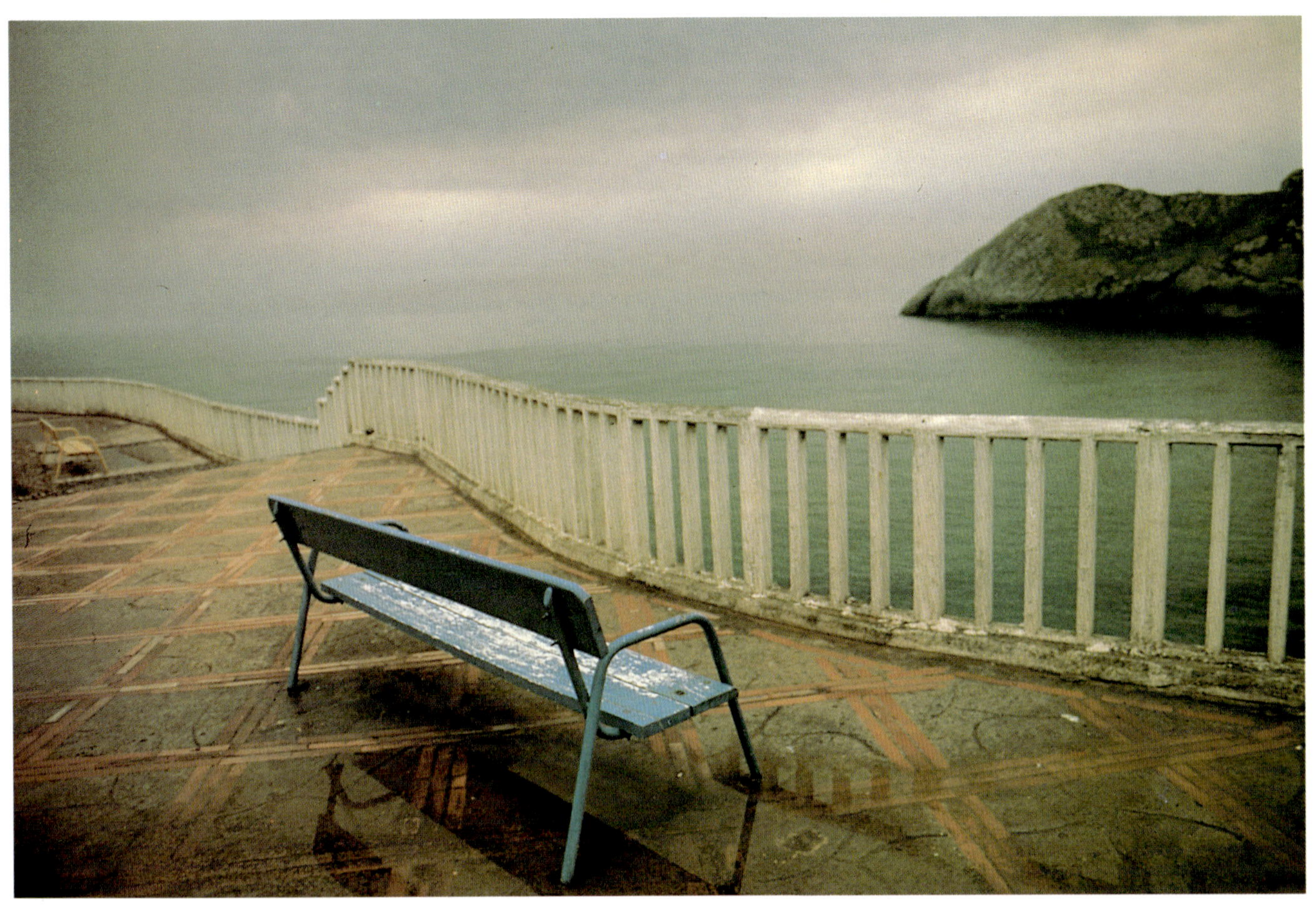

Banco

1989

Cibachrome

27 x 40 cm.

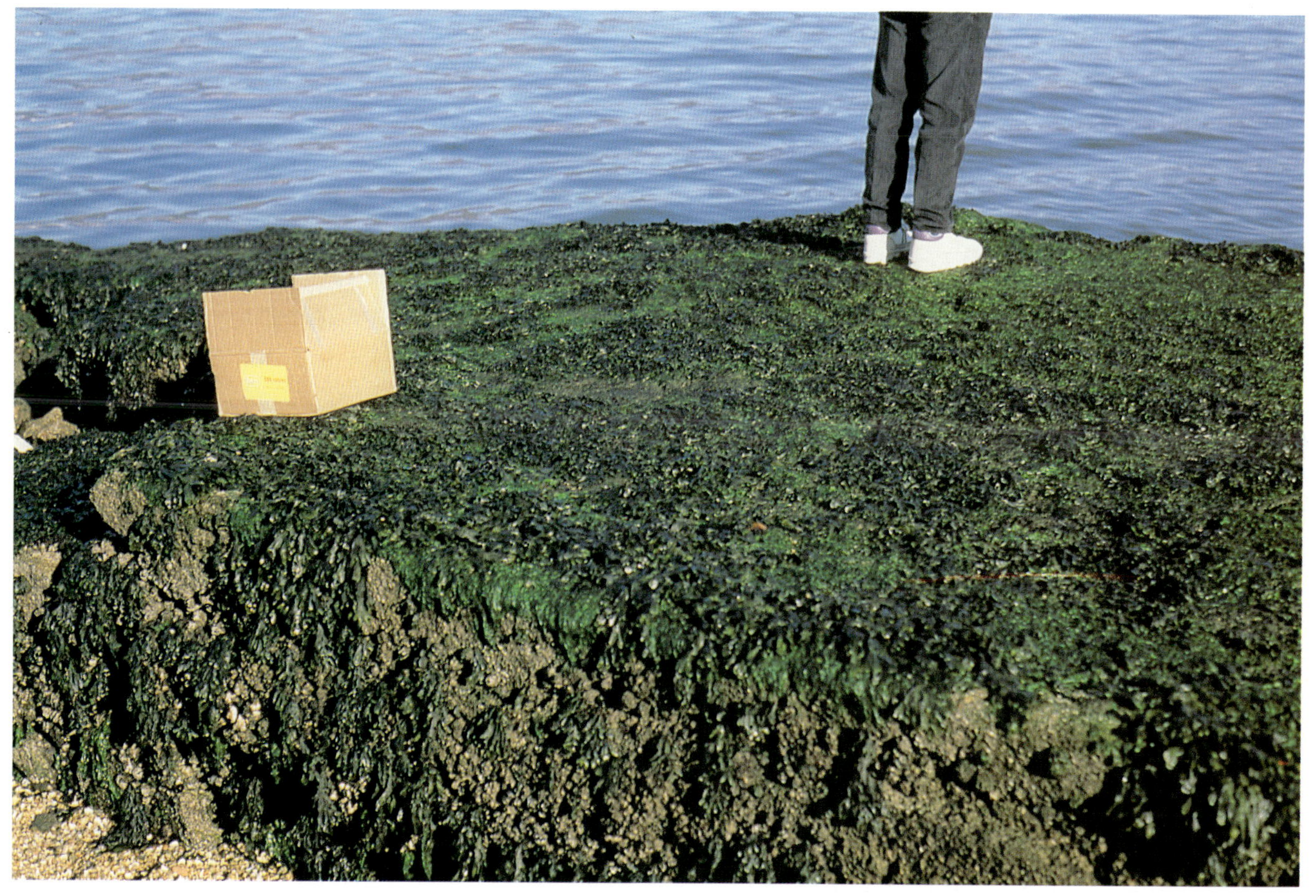

Caja

1989

Cibachrome

27 x 40 cm.

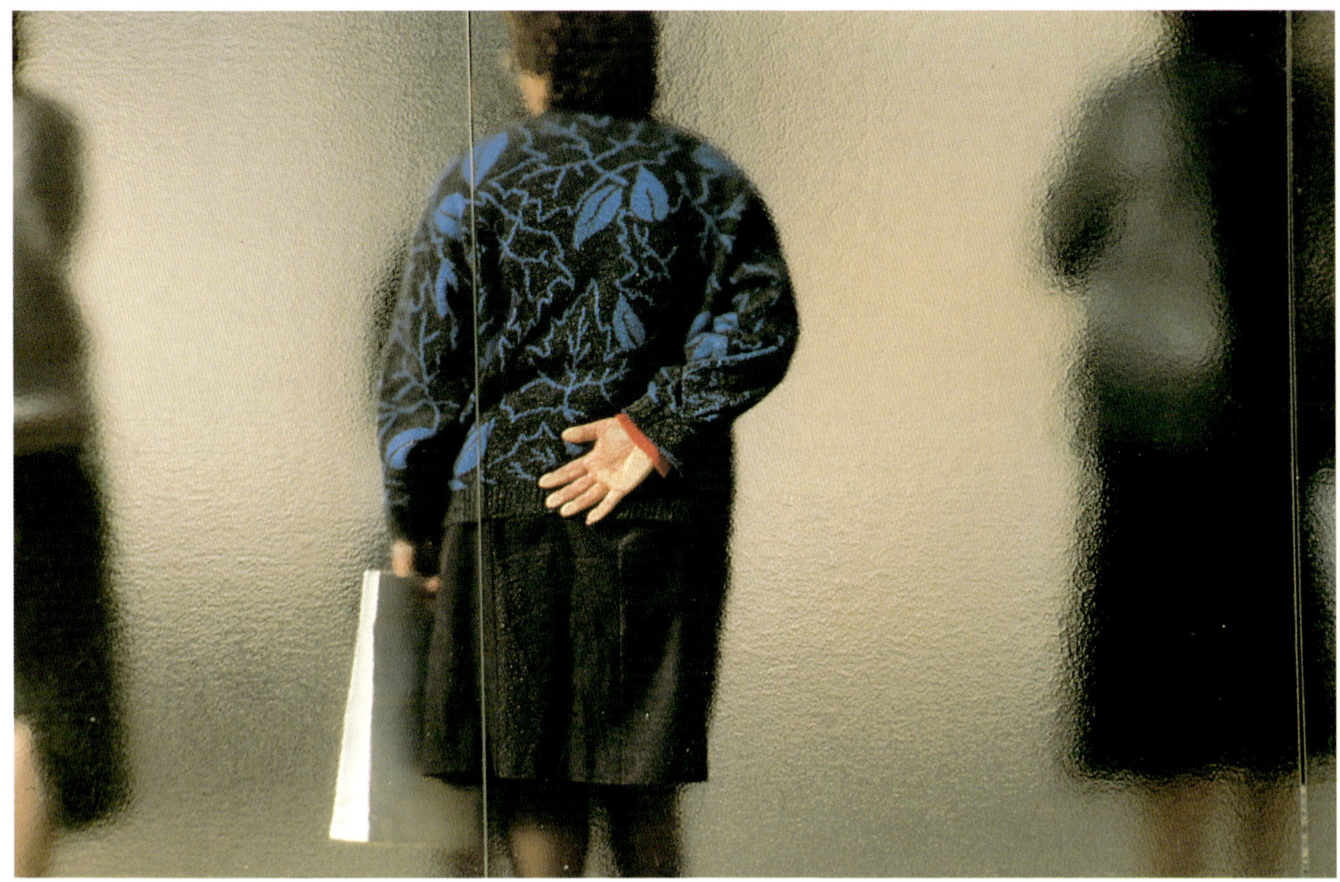

Mano

1989

Cibachrome

27 x 40 cm.

RAFAEL LEVENFELD

Born Madrid, 1955 / Nació en Madrid, 1955

Individual Exhibitions
Exposiciones individuales

1978   Real Sociedad Fotográfica. Madrid,
        España.
1979   Galería Bruixes. Tarragona, España.
1980   Sala La Caixa. Lérida. España.
1981   Galería Spectrum. Zaragoza, España.
1982   C. M. El Parque. Madrid, España.
1983   C. M. Ensenada. Madrid, España.
1984   Real Sociedad Fotográfica. Madrid,
        España.
1985   Sala E. D. Guadalajara, España.
1986   Sala E. D. Guadalajara, España.

Group Exhibitions
Exposiciones colectivas

1979   Nikon Photo International. Tokio, Japón.
        Fotomostra Lérida, España.
        Fotografía Española. Sonimag.
        Barcelona, España.
1980   Spanish Photography. Exposición
        itinerante en Gran Bretaña.

Fotografía española. Palacio del
Infantado. Guadalajara, España.
1983   ARCO 83. Madrid, España.
1984   Jornadas fotográficas. Valencia,
        España.
        ARCO 84. Madrid, España.
1985   ARCO 85. Madrid, España.
1987   "Echos d'Espagne". Burdeos, Francia.
1988   "Crèation photographique en Espagne".
        Musée Cantini. Marsella, Francia.
        "Autoretrato; ¿narcismo o provocación?.
        Círculo de Bellas Artes. Madrid, España.
1989   "Creación fotográfica en España. 1968 -
        1988". Centro de Arte Santa Mónica.
        Barcelona, España.

Photographs included in the exhibition
Fotografías contenidas en la exposición

1. Autoretrato. 1985. Bromuro. 90 x 90 cm.
2. Autoretrato. 1985. Bromuro. 90 x 90 cm.
3. Autoretrato. 1986. Bromuro. 90 x 90 cm.
4. Autoretrato. 1987. Bromuro. 90 x 90 cm.
5. Autoretrato. 1987. Bromuro. 90 x 90 cm.

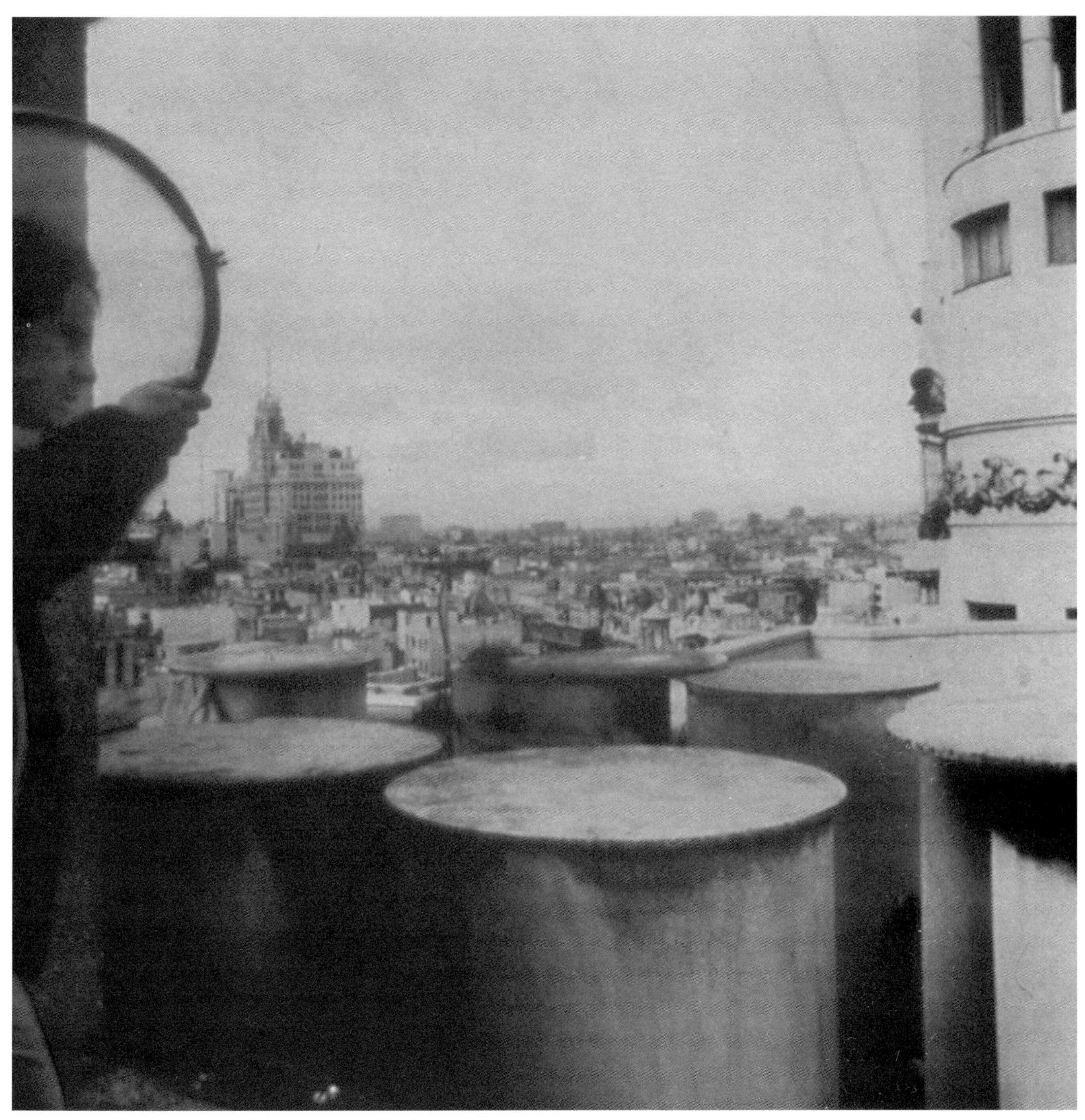

Autoretrato

1985

Bromuro

90 x 90 cm.

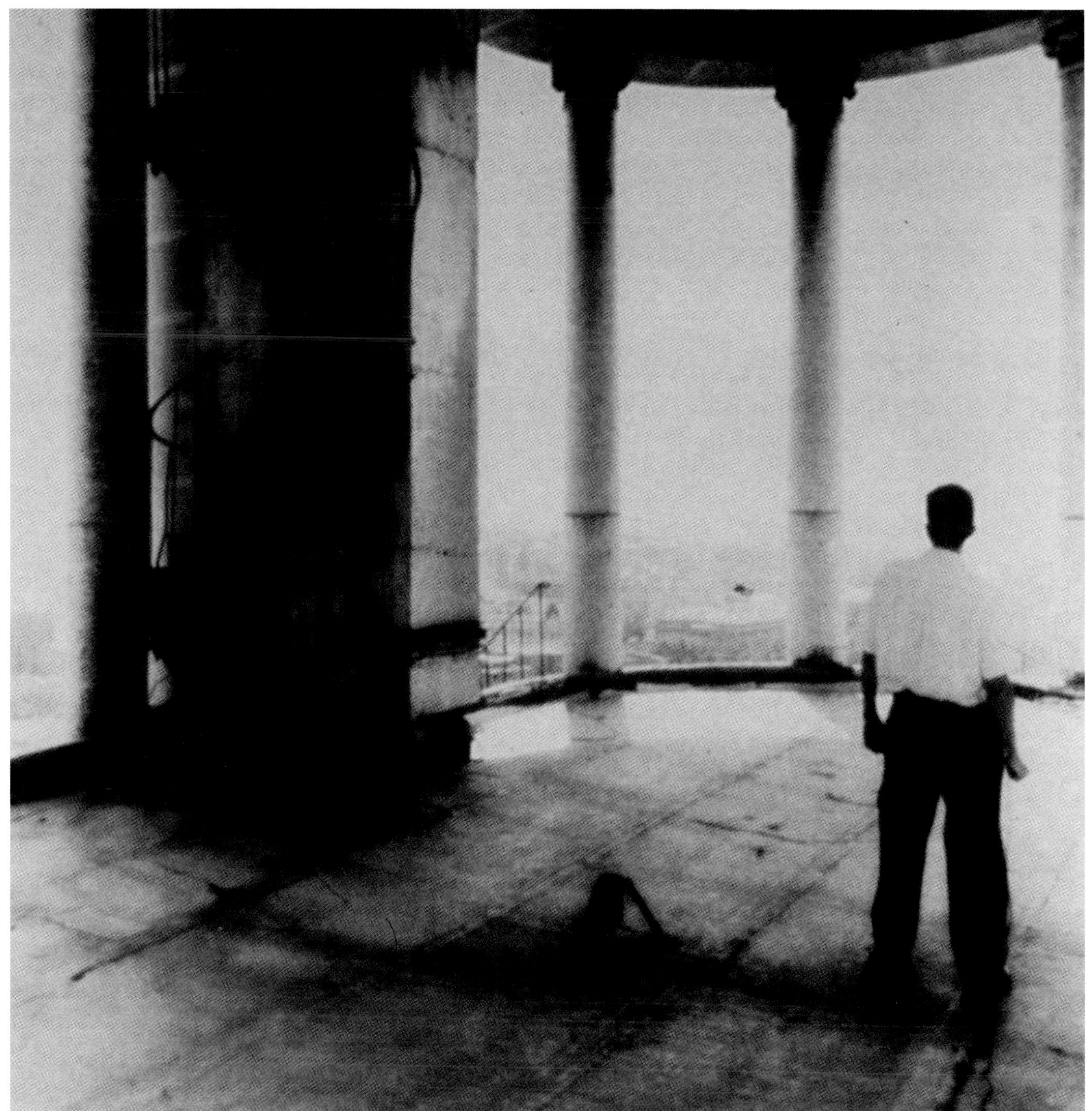

Autoretrato
1985
Bromuro
90 x 90 cm.

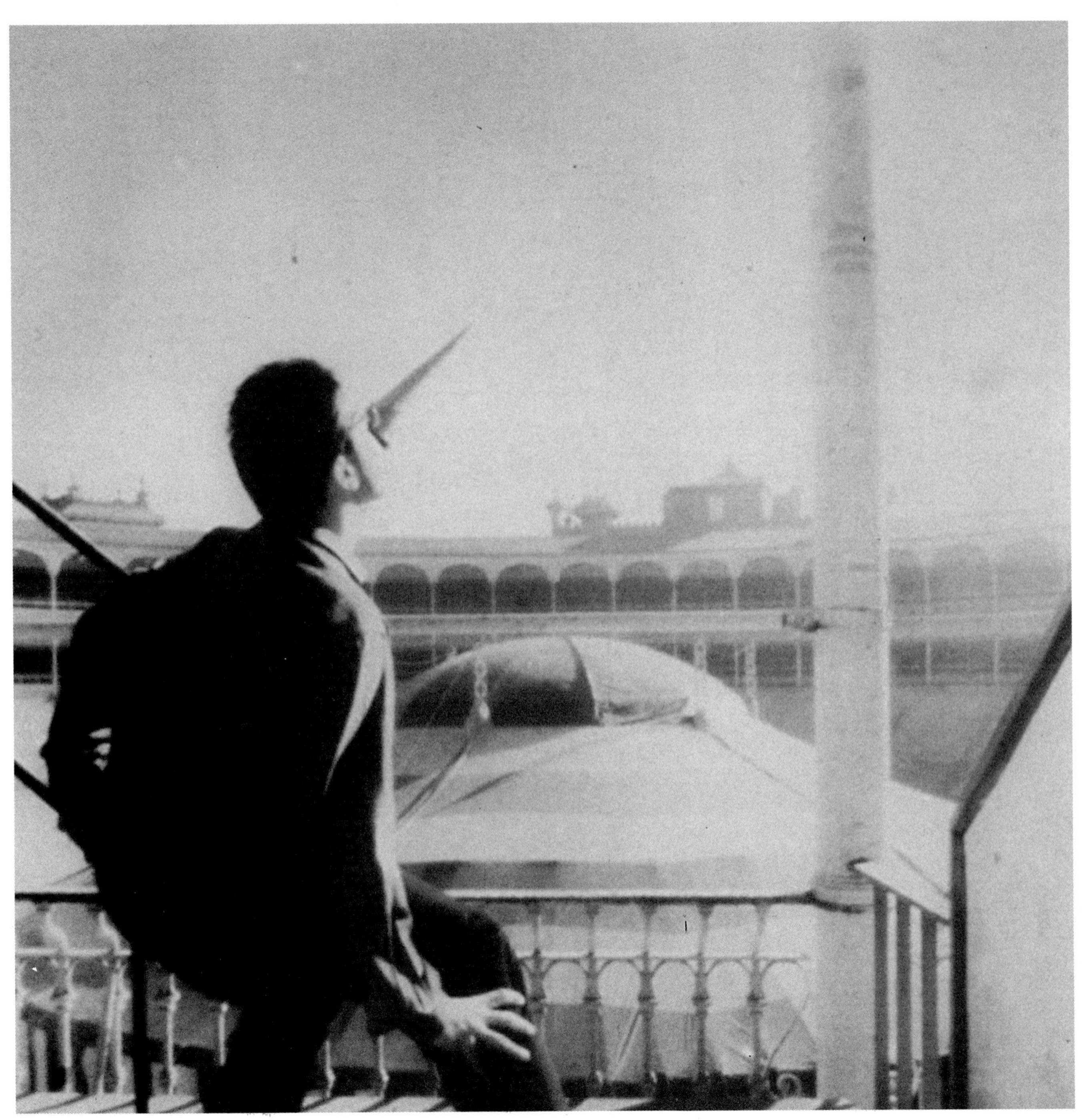

Autoretrato
1986
Bromuro
90 x 90 cm.

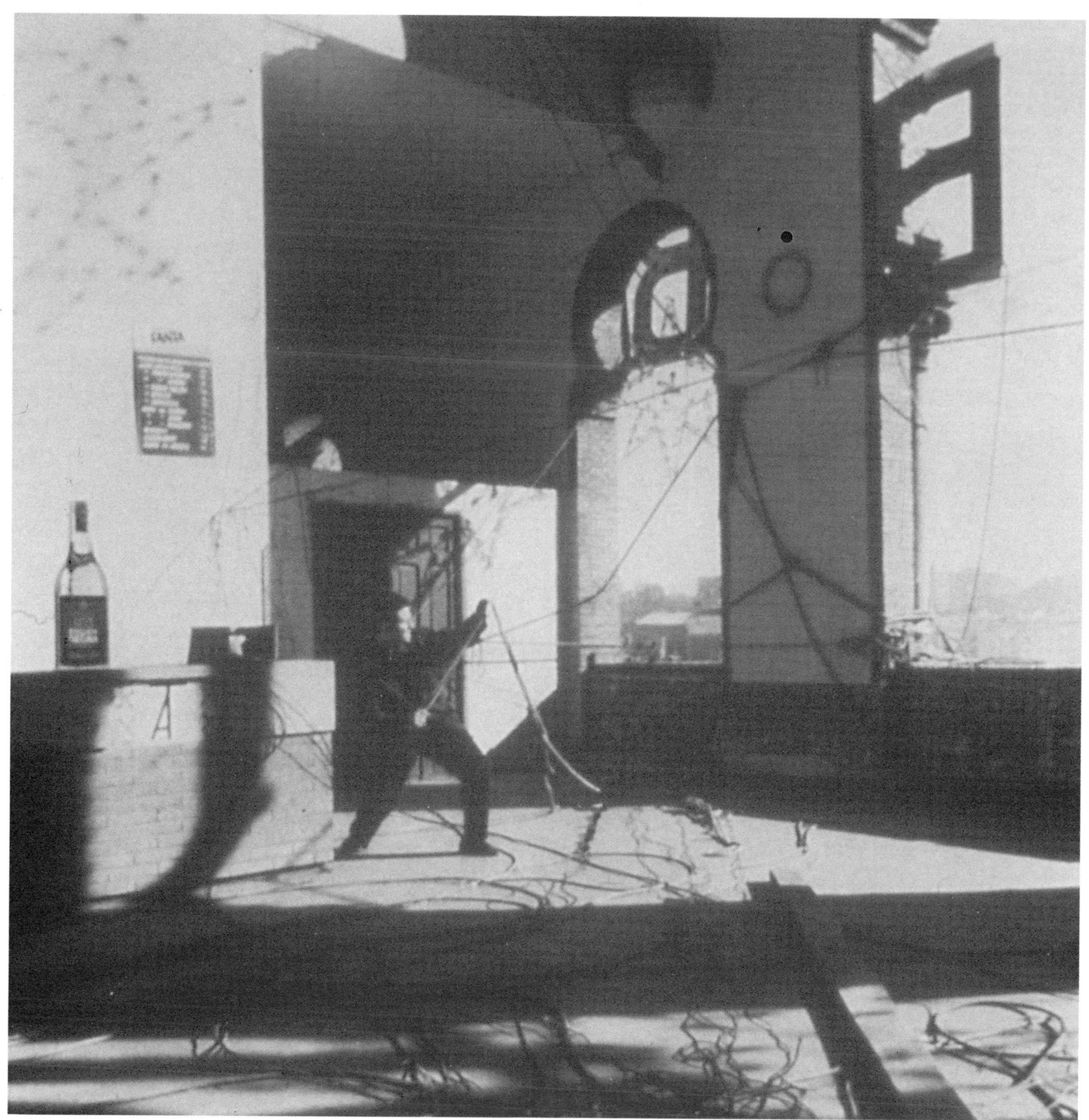

Autoretrato
1987
Bromuro
90 x 90 cm.

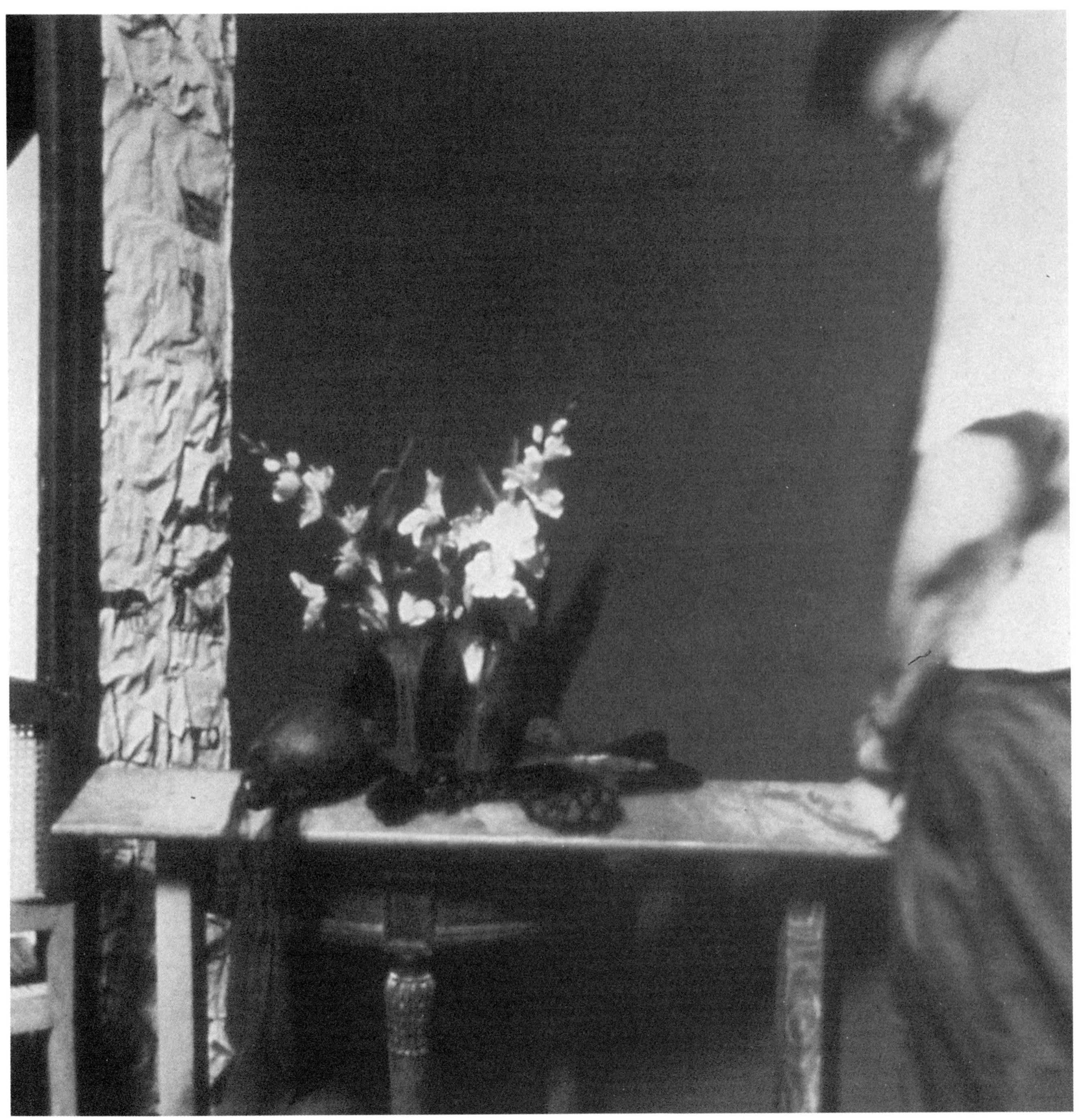

Autoretrato

1987

Bromuro

90 x 90 cm.

RAFAEL S. LOBATO

Born Sevilla, 1932 / Nació en Sevilla, 1932

Individual Exhibitions
Exposiciones individuales

1970   Agrupación Fotográfica de Cataluña.
        Barcelona, España.
        Real Sociedad Fotográfica de Madrid.
        Madrid, España.
        Aula Fotográfica de Madrid. Madrid,
        España.
1971   Sala de Exposiciones de la Caja de
        Ahorros de Zaragoza, Aragón y La Rioja.
        Guadalajara, España.
        Sala de Exposiciones de la Caja de
        Ahorros de Soria. España.
1990   Casa de la Entrevista. Fundación Colegio
        del Rey. Alcalá de Henares, Madrid,
        España.

Group Exhibitions
Exposiciones colectivas

1973   Componentes del Grupo 5. Sala Aixelá.
        Barcelona, España.
1978   "9.º Recontres Internationales de la
        Photographie". Arles, Francia.
1985   "La Generación 85". Capilla del Oidor.
        Fundación Colegio del Rey. Alcalá de
        Henares, Madrid, España.
1986   "50 Fotógrafos de la Historia de la
        Fotografía Española 1950-1986".
        Sevilla, España.
1987   Salón Nacional de la Comunciación, la
        Publicidad y el Marketing. IMPACT.
        Madrid, España.
1988   "Fotógrafos de la Escuela de Madrid".
        Museo Español de Arte Contemporáneo.
        Madrid, España.

Photographs included in the exhibition
Fotografías contenidas en la exposición

1. San Lázaro de Sabucedo. '70. Bromuro / selenio. 27 x 34 cm.
2. Bercianos de Aliste '71. Bromuro / selenio.   23 x 34 cm.
3. Bercianos de Aliste '71. Bromuro / selenio. 23 x 34 cm.
4. Bercianos de Aliste '71. Bromuro / selenio. 23 x 34 cm.
5. Bercianos de Aliste '70. Bromuro / selenio. 23 x 34 cm.

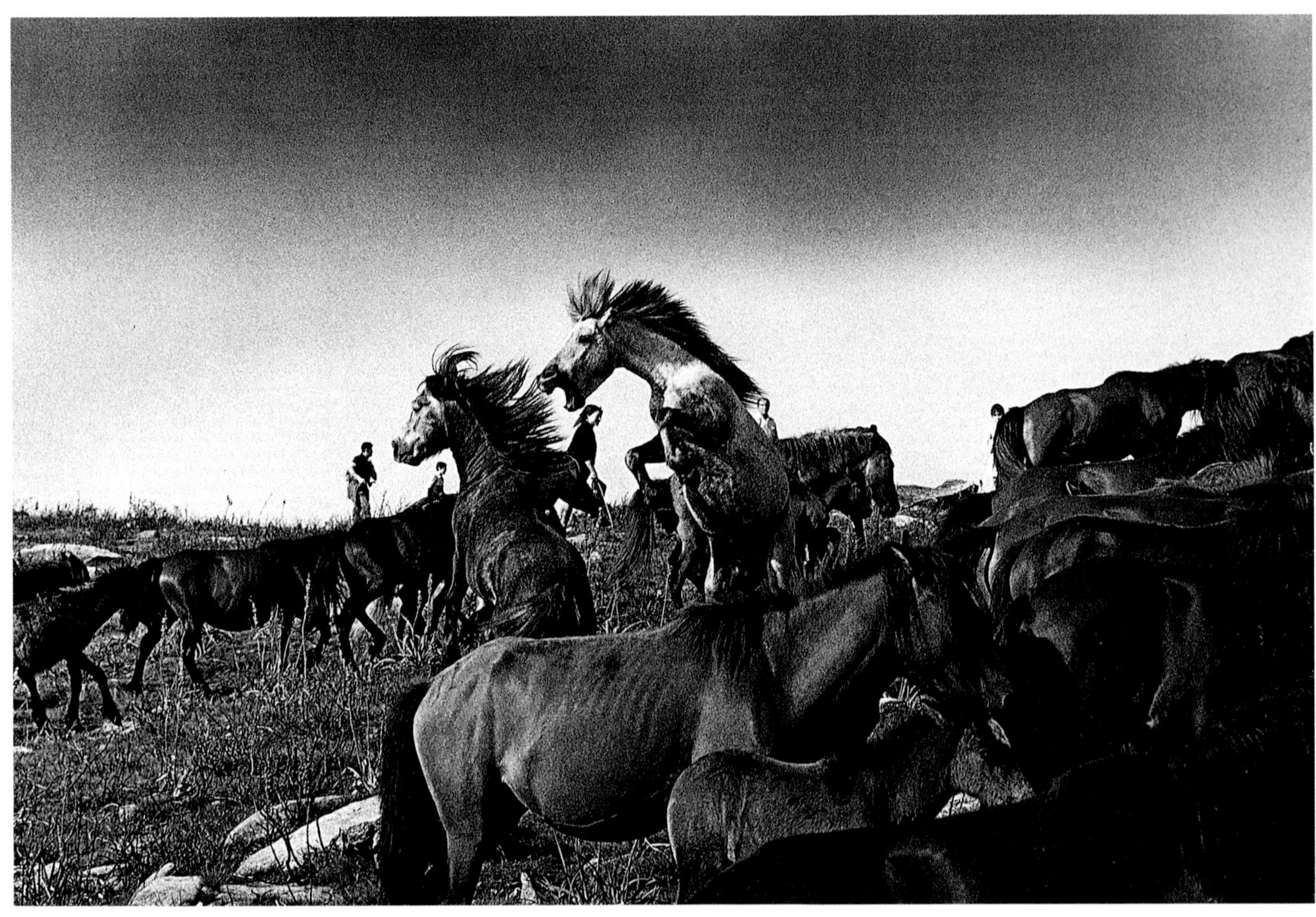

San Lázaro de Sabucedo
1970
Bromuro / selenio
27 x 34 cm.

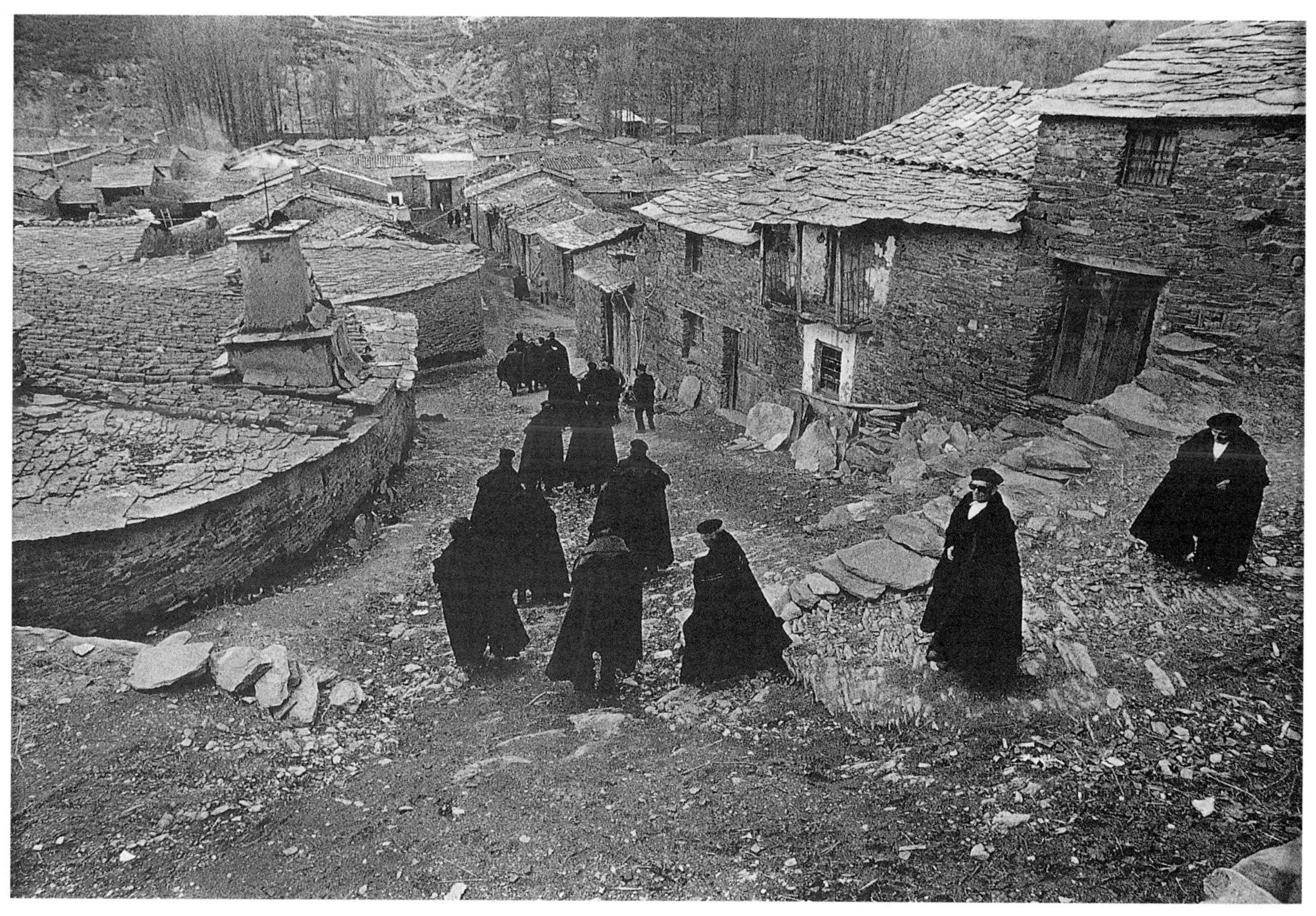

Bercianos de Aliste
1971
Bromuro / selenio
23 x 34 cm.

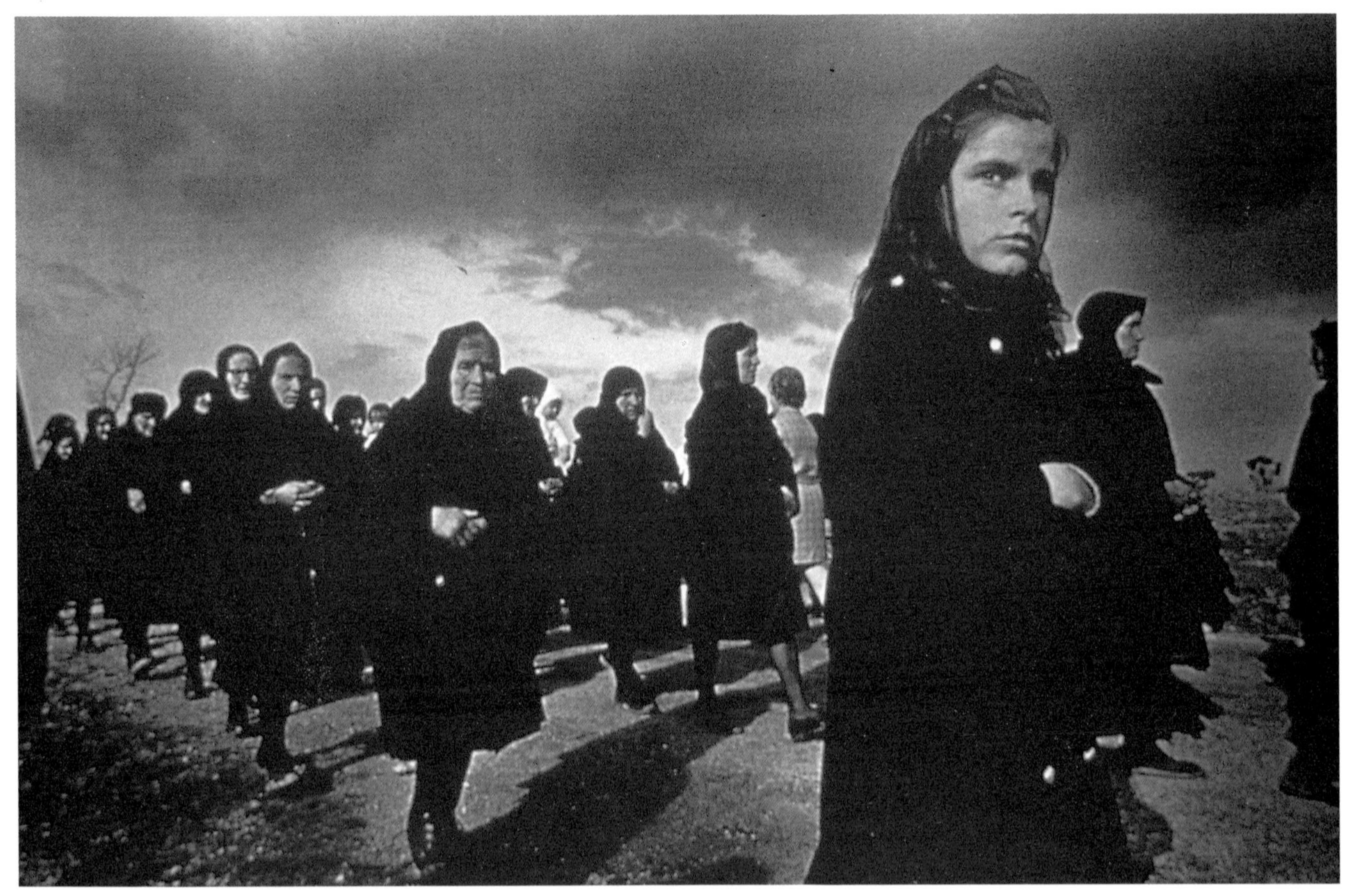

Bercianos de Aliste

1971

Bromuro / selenio

23 x 34 cm.

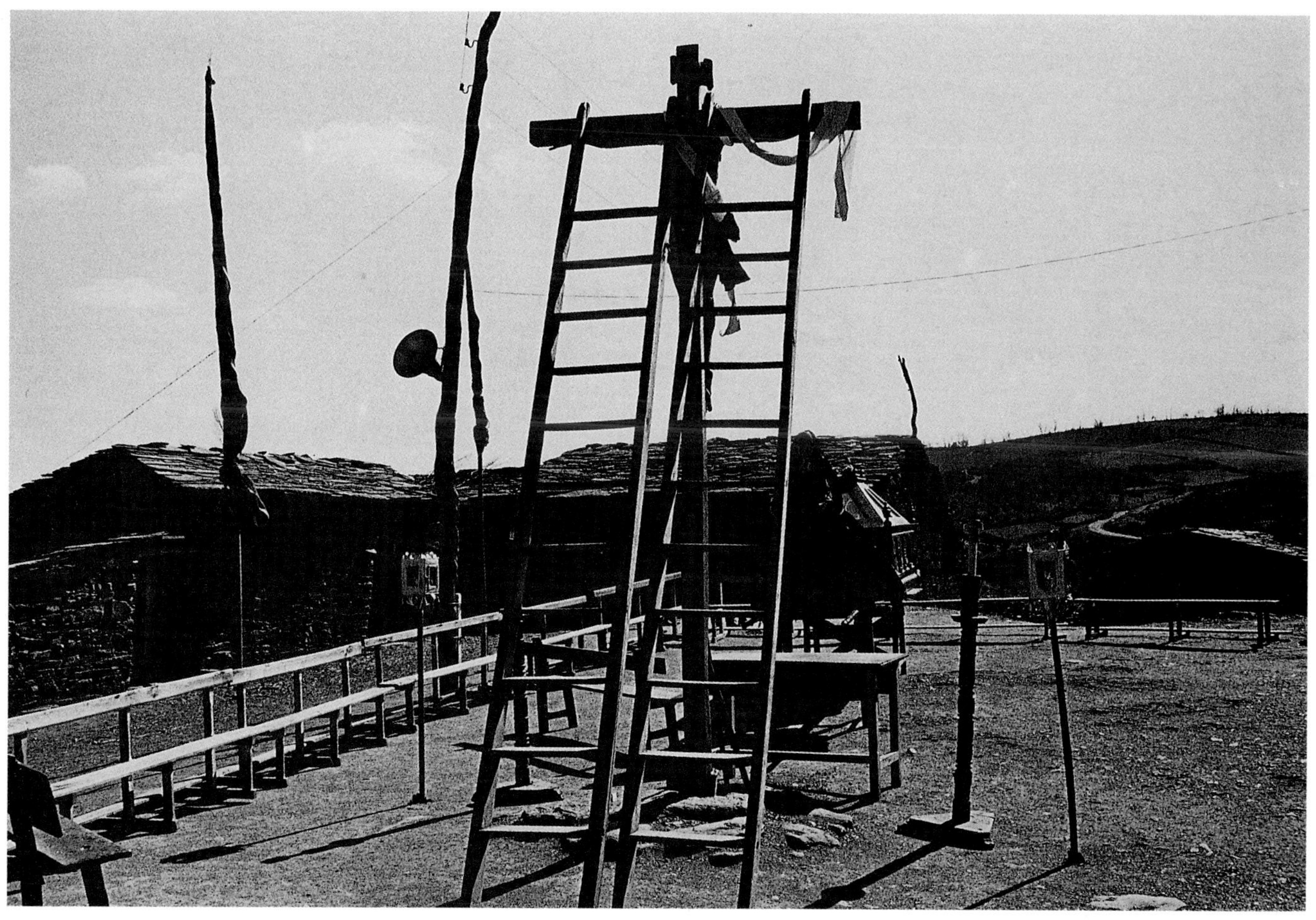

Bercianos de Aliste

1971

Bromuro / selenio

23 x 34 cm.

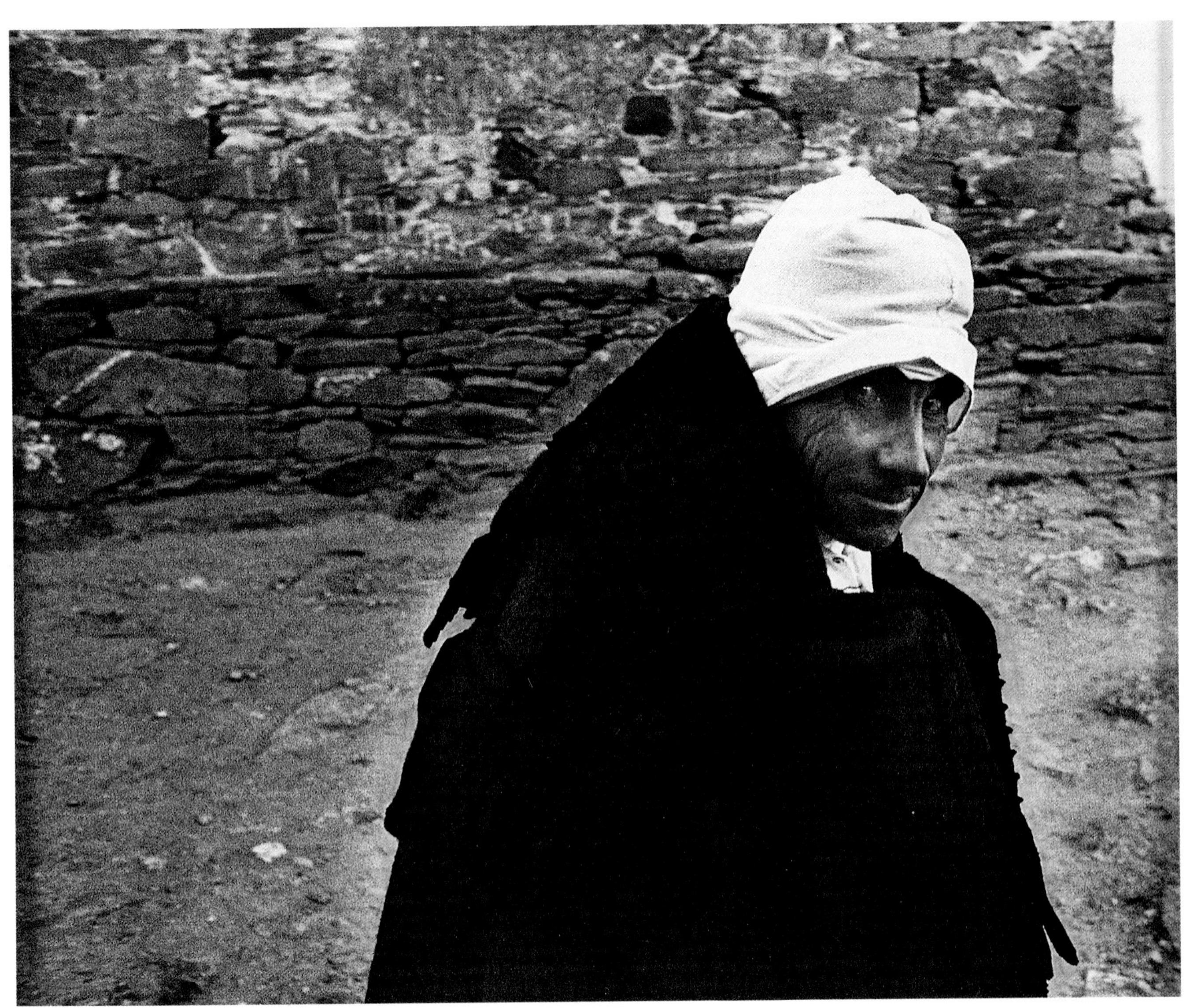

Bercianos de Aliste

1970

Bromuro / selenio

23 x 34 cm.

CHEMA MADOZ

Born Madrid, 1958 / Nació en Madrid, 1958

Individual Exhibitions
Exposiciones individuales

1985   Real Sociedad Fotográfica. Madrid,
        España.
        Cámara Oscura. Logroño, España.
        Railowsky. Valencia, España.
1987   Galérie Frederic Bazille. Montpellier,
        Francia.
        Galérie Perraine. París, Francia.
1988   Círculo de Bellas Artes, Sala Minerva.
        Madrid, España.
1989   Galería Contraluz. Barcelona, España.

Group Exhibitions
Exposiciones colectivas

1985   Galería Moriarty. Madrid, España.

1986   Galería Perspektief, "Imagen Nueva".
        Rotterdam, Holanda.
1988   Nikon-Galérie. Zurich, Suiza.
1990   Galería Moriarty, "La Imagen Indeleble".
        Madrid, España.
        Galería Fúcares. Almagro, España.

Photographs included in the exhibition
Fotografías contenidas en la exposición

1. Angulo de reflexión. 1990. Bromuro / Virado. 41 x 50,5 cm.

2. Terapia. 1990. Bromuro / Virado. 41 x 50,5 cm.

3. Cautela. 1990. Bromuro / Virado. 41 x 50,5 cm.

4. Apertura. 1990. Bromuro / Virado. 41 x 50,5 cm.

5. Util. 1990. Bromuro / Virado. 41 x 50,5 cm.

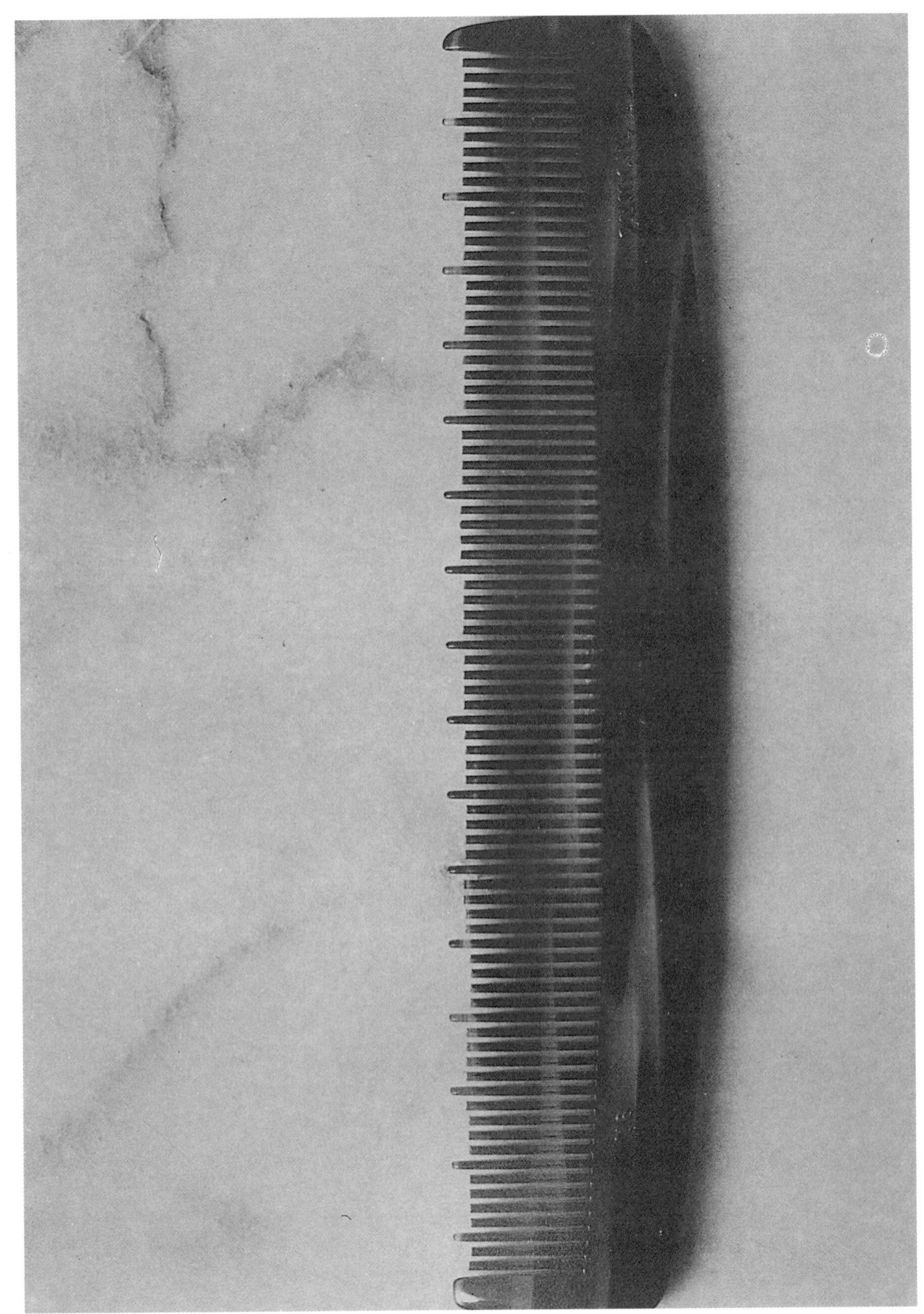

Angulo de reflexión
1990
Bromuro / Virado
41 x 50,5 cm.

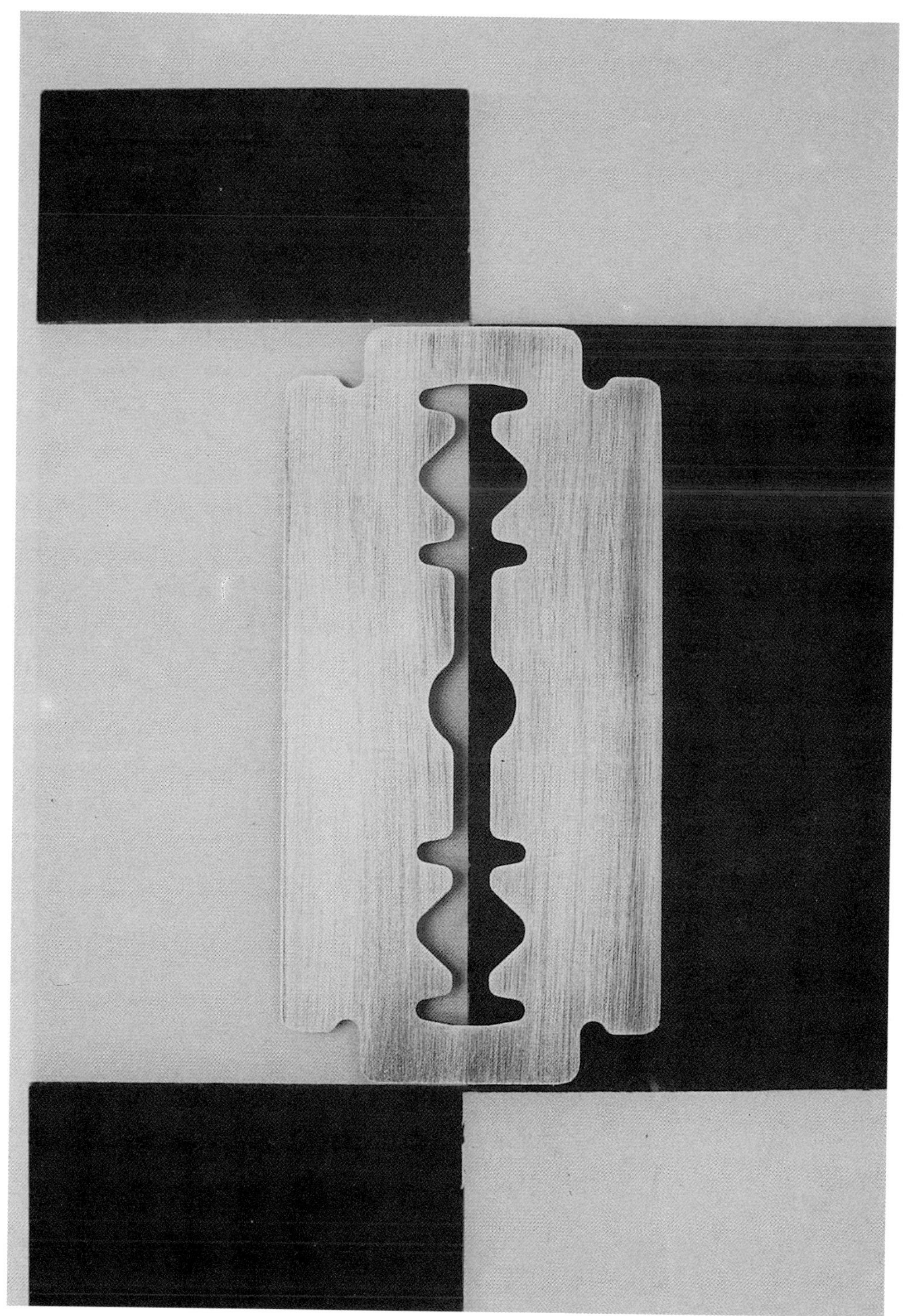

Terapia

1990

Bromuro / Virado

41 x 50,5 cm.

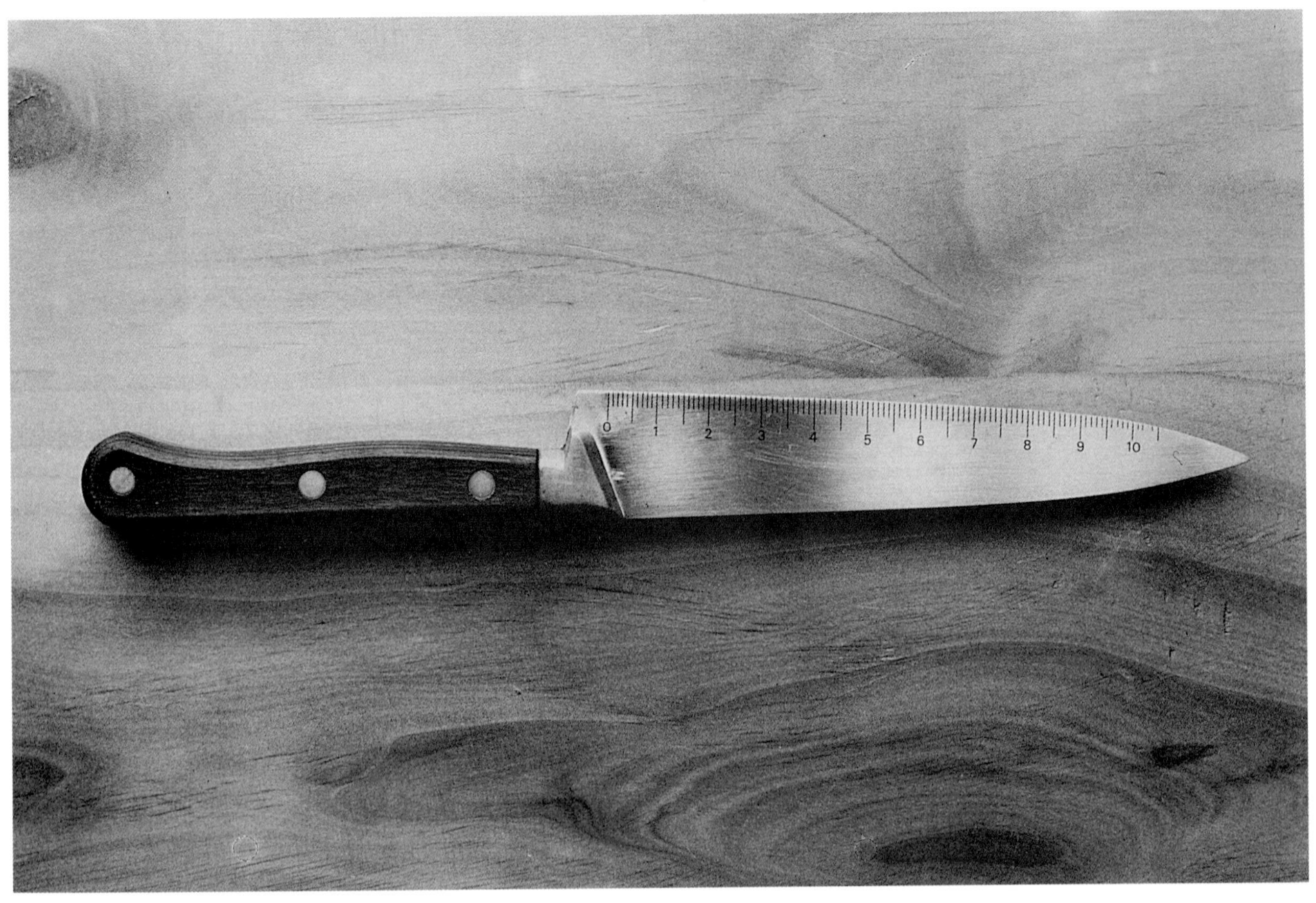

Cautela

1990

Bromuro / Virado

41 x 50,5 cm.

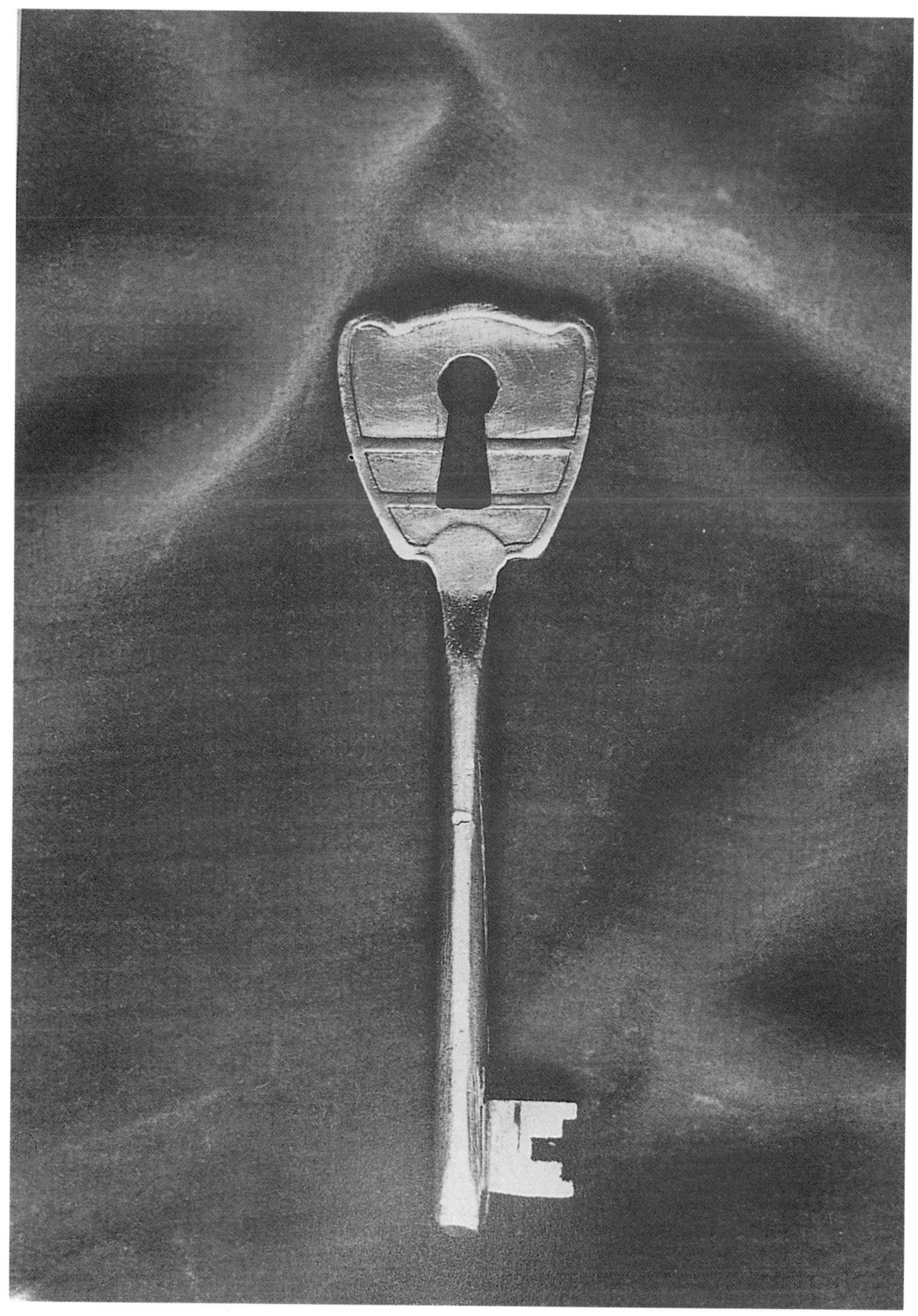

Apertura

1990

Bromuro / Virado

41 x 50,5 cm.

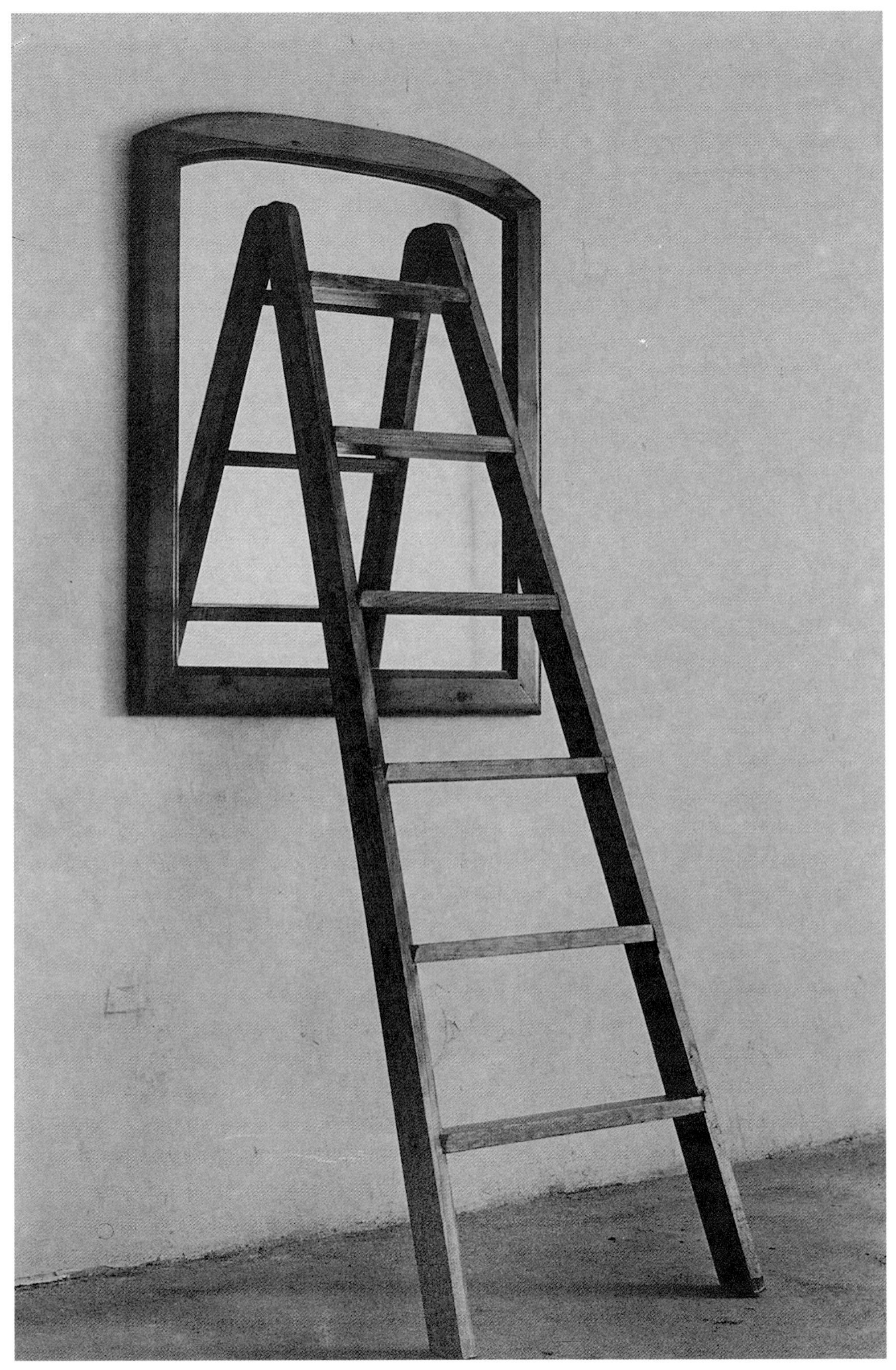

Util
1990
Bromuro / Virado
41 x 50,5 cm.

LUIS MALIBRAN

Born Madrid, 1960 / Nació en Madrid, 1960

Individual Exhibitions
Exposiciones individuales

1978   Primeros catálogos industriales y porfolios
        de actores.
        First industrial catalogues and actors'
        portfolios.

1981   Trabajo independiente como fotógrafo
        de moda.
        Free-lance work in fashion photography.

1984-
1985   Participa en exposiciones colectivas del
        Centro Cultural de la Villa de Madrid y
        del Instituto de la juventud.
        Participates in group exhibitions of the
        Madrid Cultural Center and the Youth
        Institute.

1987-
1991   Abre su propio estudio y realiza trabajo
        independiente de moda, retrato,
        publicidad. Enseña cursos de fotografía.
        Opens his own studio and free-lances in
        fashion, portrait and advertising
        photography.

Photographs included in the exhibition
Fotografías contenidas en la exposición

1. Gemma. 1988. Bromuro / sepia. 24 x 30 cm.
2. Alicia. 1987. Bromuro / sepia. 24 x 30 cm.
3. Rosa I. 1989. Bromuro / sepia. 24 x 30 cm.
4. Rosa II. 1989. Bromuro / sepia. 24 x 30 cm.
5. Rosa III. 1989. Bromuro / sepia. 24 x 30 cm.

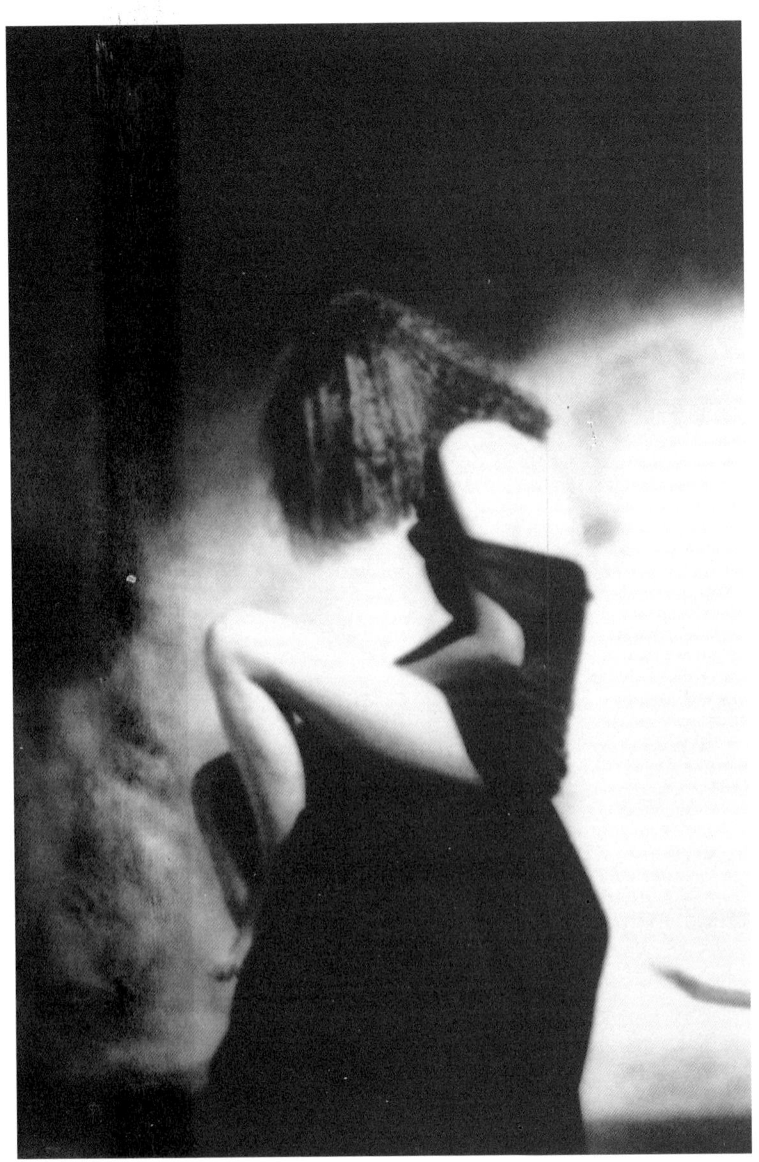

Gemma

1988

Bromuro / sepia

24 x 30 cm.

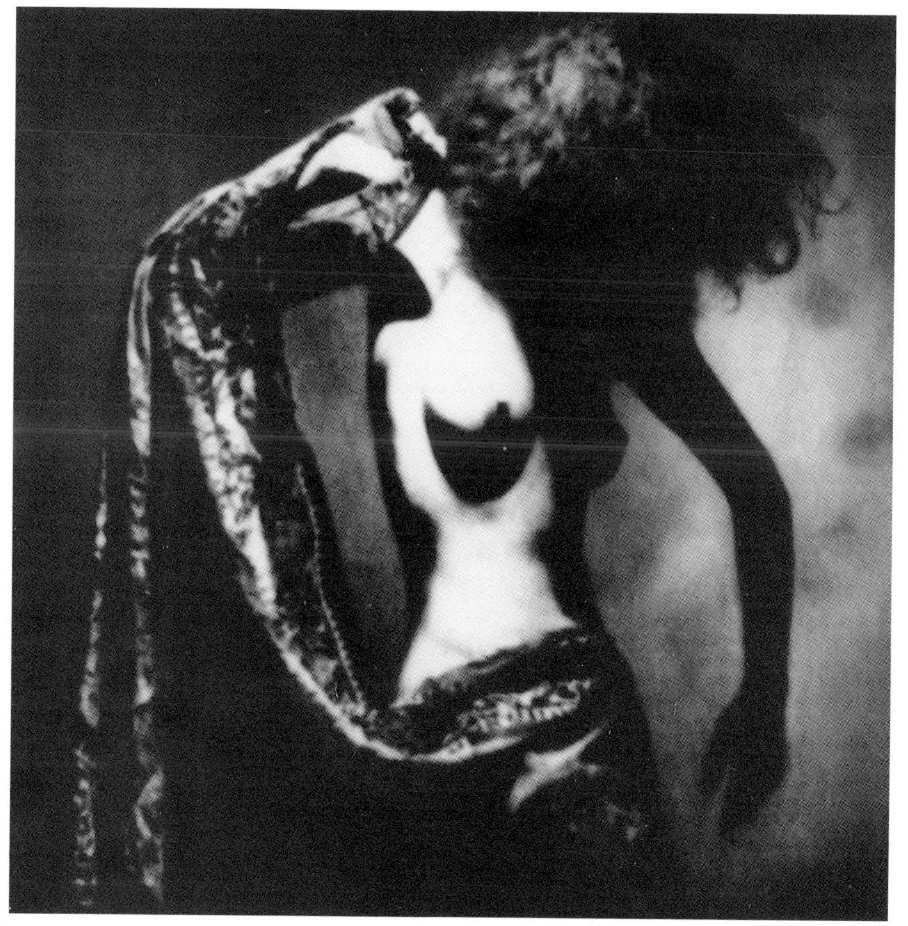

Alicia

1987

Bromuro / sepia

24 x 30 cm.

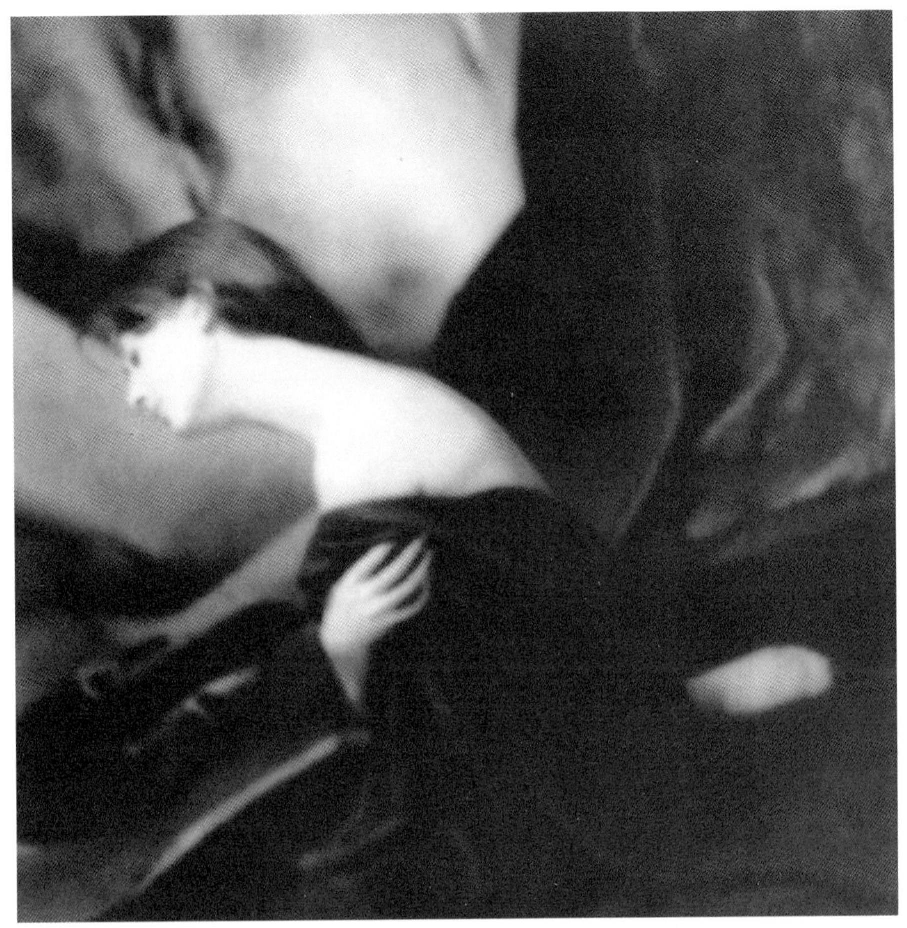

Rosa I
1989
Bromuro / sepia
24 x 30 cm.

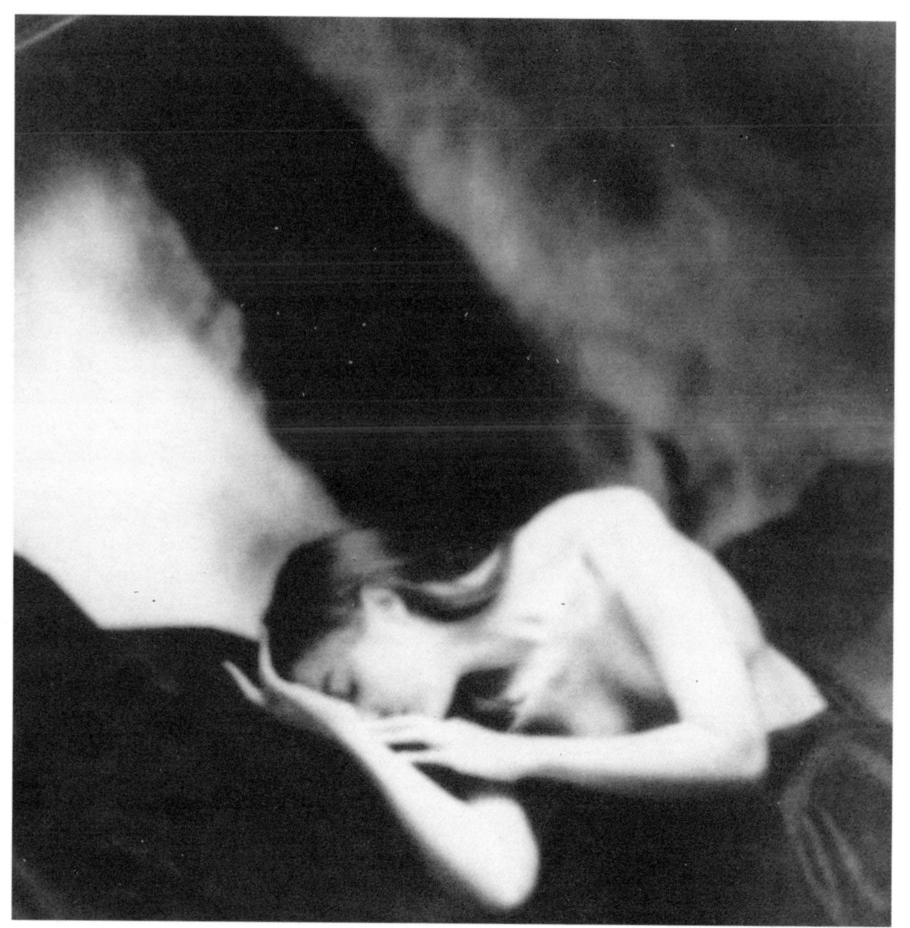

Rosa II
1989
Bromuro / sepia
24 x 30 cm.

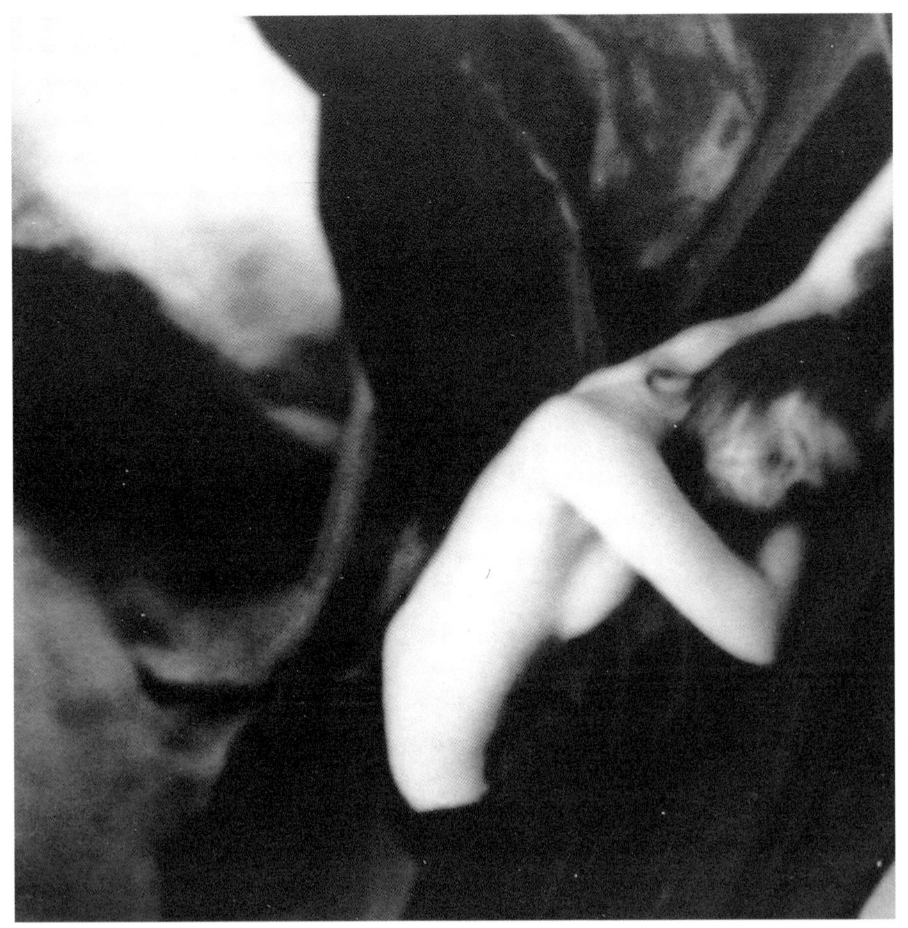

Rosa III

1989

Bromuro / sepia

24 x 30 cm.

EDUARDO MOMEÑE

Born Bilbao, 1952 / Nació en Bilbao, 1952

Individual Exhibitions
Exposiciones individuales

1974   Galería Nikon. Barcelona, España.
1981   Caja de Ahorros Municipal de Bilbao,
        España.
1982   Galería Pentaprisma. Barcelona,
        España.
        Galería Sen. Madrid, España.
1984   Galería Spectrum. Zaragoza, España.
        Universidad de Granada. Granada,
        España.
        Galería Tórculo. Madrid, España.
        Galería Nueva Imagen. Pamplona,
        España.
1987   "Puesta en Página". Biler '87. Durango,
        España.
1989   Museo de Bellas Artes de Córdoba.
        Córdoba, España.
1990   Sala del Colegio de Arquitectos. Santa
        Cruz de Tenerife, España.

Group Exhibitions
Exposiciones colectivas

1983   Galería Moriarty. Madrid, España.

Museo Español de Arte Contemporáneo.
Madrid, España.

1986   Museo de la Universidad de Nuevo
        México. Albuquerque, Nuevo México.
        EE.UU.
        "De lo Bello a lo Siniestro". Fundació
        Caixa de Barcelona. Exposición
        itinerante. España.
        "Galicia visto por…". UIMP. La Coruña,
        Galicia, España.
        "Escenarios de la Guerra". Exposición
        itinerante. España.
1988   "Creation Photographique en Espagne
        1968-1988". Musée Cantini. Marsella,
        Francia.
1989   "10 Fotógrafos Españoles". Palacio de
        Sástago. Zaragoza, España.

Photographs included in the exhibition
Fotografías contenidas en la exposición

1. Sin título. 1983. Papel baritado. 36 x 36 cm.
2. Sin título. 1983. Papel baritado. 36 x 36 cm.
3. Sin título. 1983. Papel baritado. 36 x 36 cm.
4. Sin título. 1983. Papel baritado. 36 x 36 cm.
5. Sin título. 1985. Papel baritado. 36 x 36 cm.

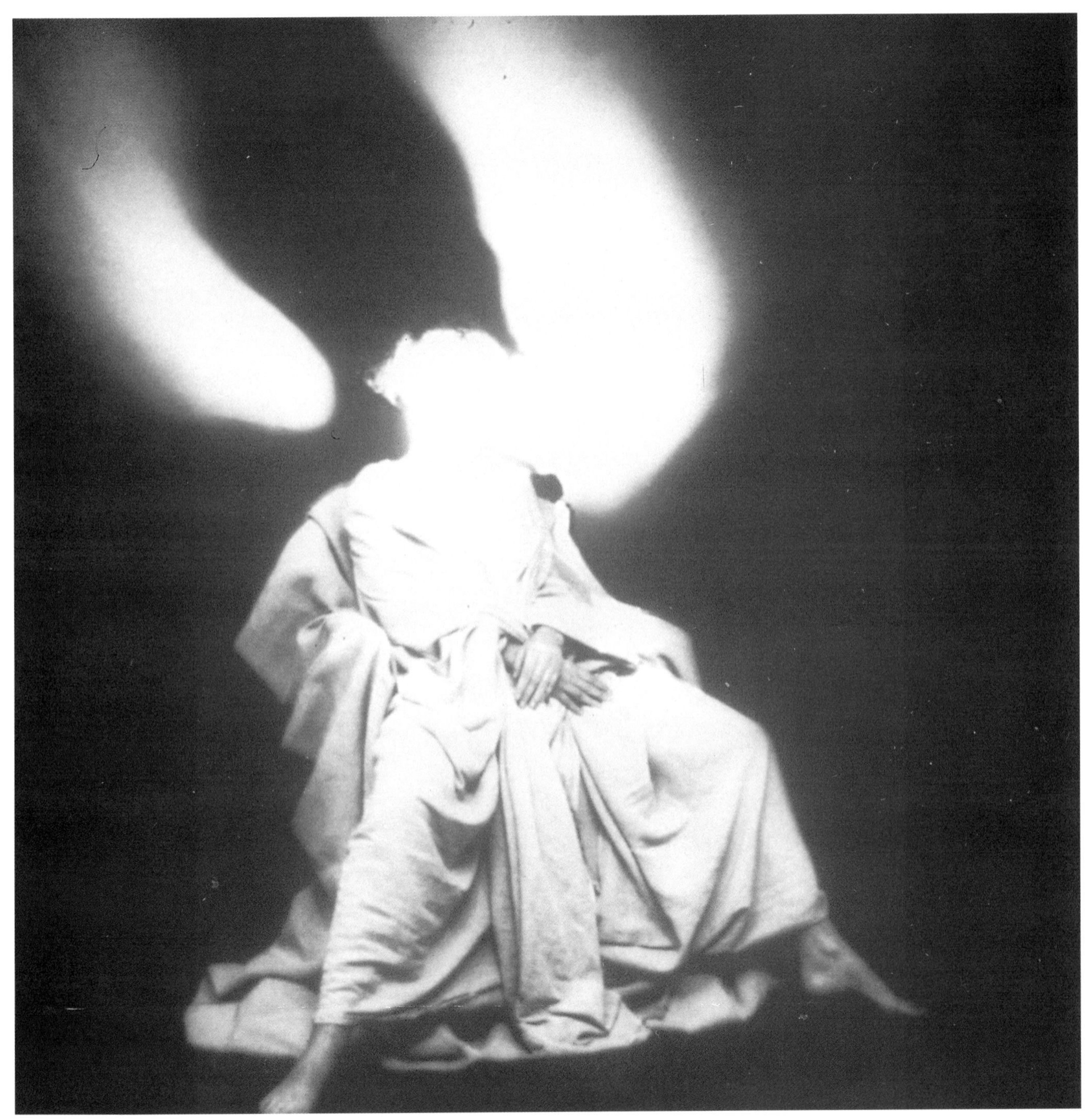

Sin título

1983

Papel baritado

36 x 36 cm.

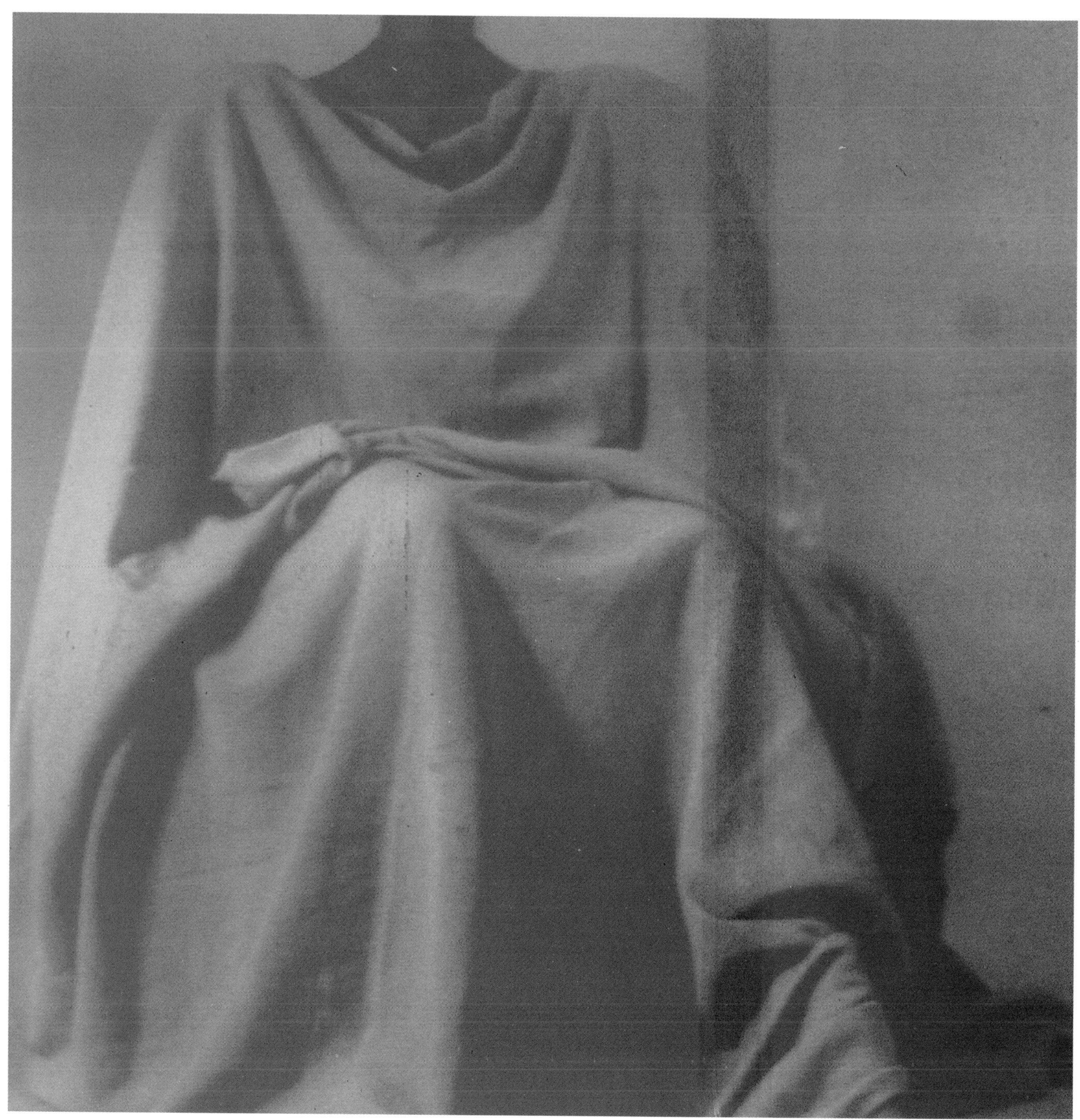

Sin título
1983
Papel baritado
36 x 36 cm.

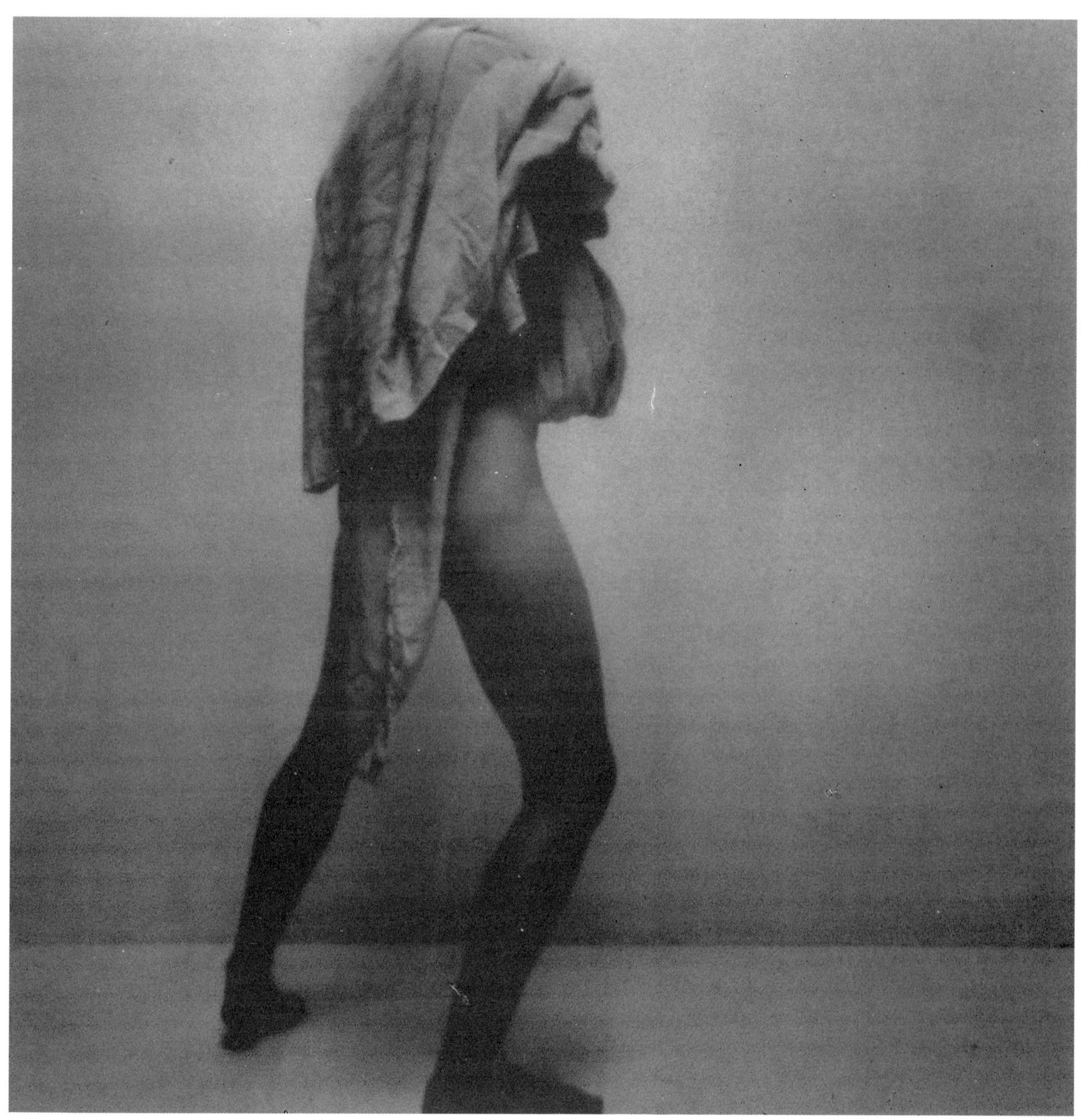

Sin título

1983

Papel baritado

36 x 36 cm.

RODRIGO MOSQUERA MARTINEZ

Born Madrid, 1962 / Nació en Madrid, 1962

Individual Exhibitions
Exposiciones individuales

1985   Sala Bradomín. Madrid, España.

Group Exhibitions
Exposiciones colectivas

1988   Centro Cutlrual "Alberto Sánchez".
            Madrid. España.
            "Circuitos de Fotografía". Rompeolas.
            Exposición itinerante. España.

1990   "Caminos de hierro". Exposición
            itinerante. España.

Photographs included in the exhibition
Fotografías contenidas en la exposición

1. Dos amigos. 1989. Van Dyke. 26,5 x 33 cm.
2. Las Navas del Marqués. 1988. Van Dyke. 30 x 40 cm.
3. Pomo Veneciano. 1988. 30 x 40 cm. Bicromatado.
4. Venecia, 1981. 1989. 30 x 40 cm. Van Dyke.
5. Tato I. 1989. 30 x 40 cm. Van Dyke.

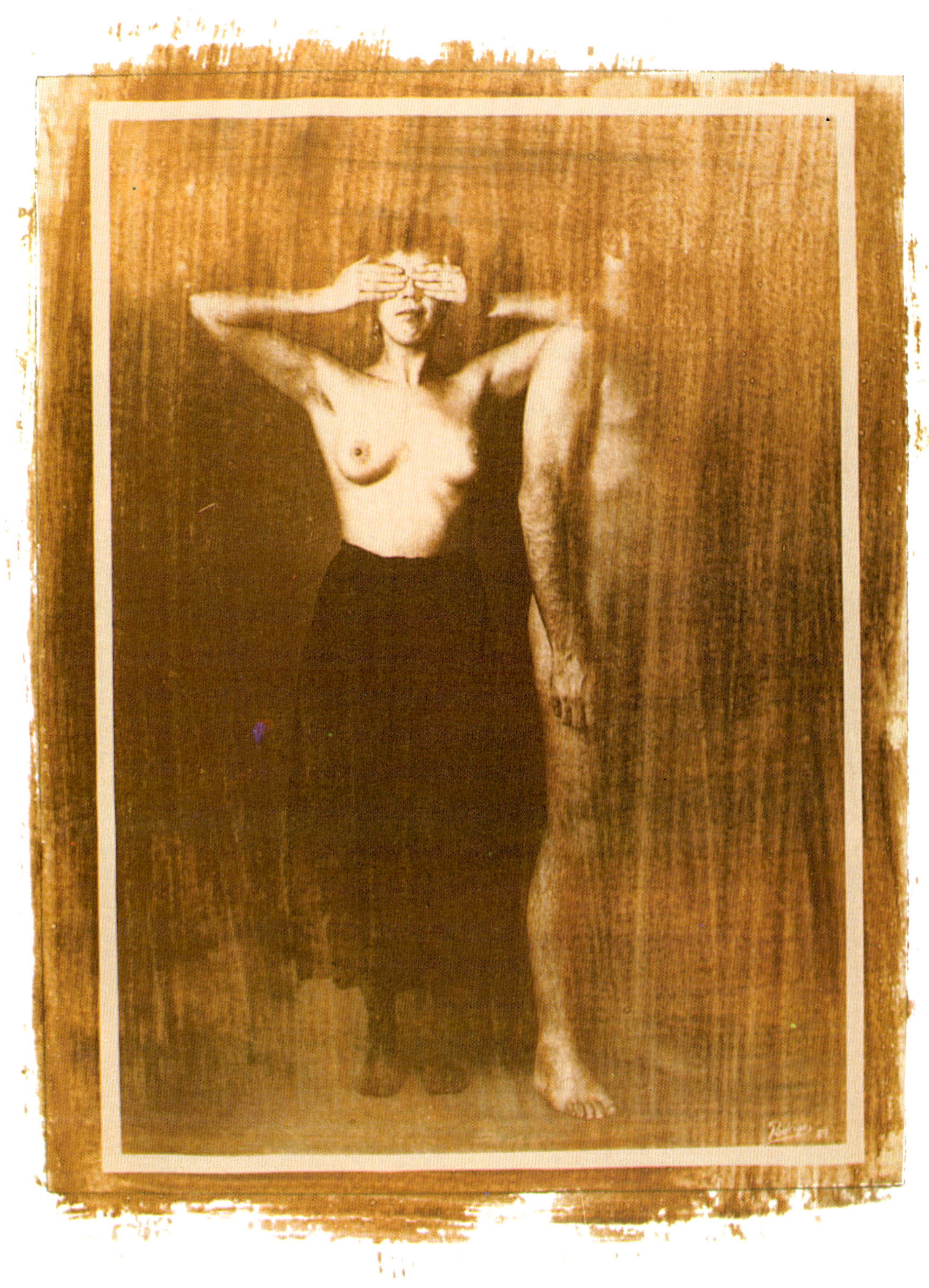

Dos amigos

1989

Van Dyke

26,5 x 33 cm.

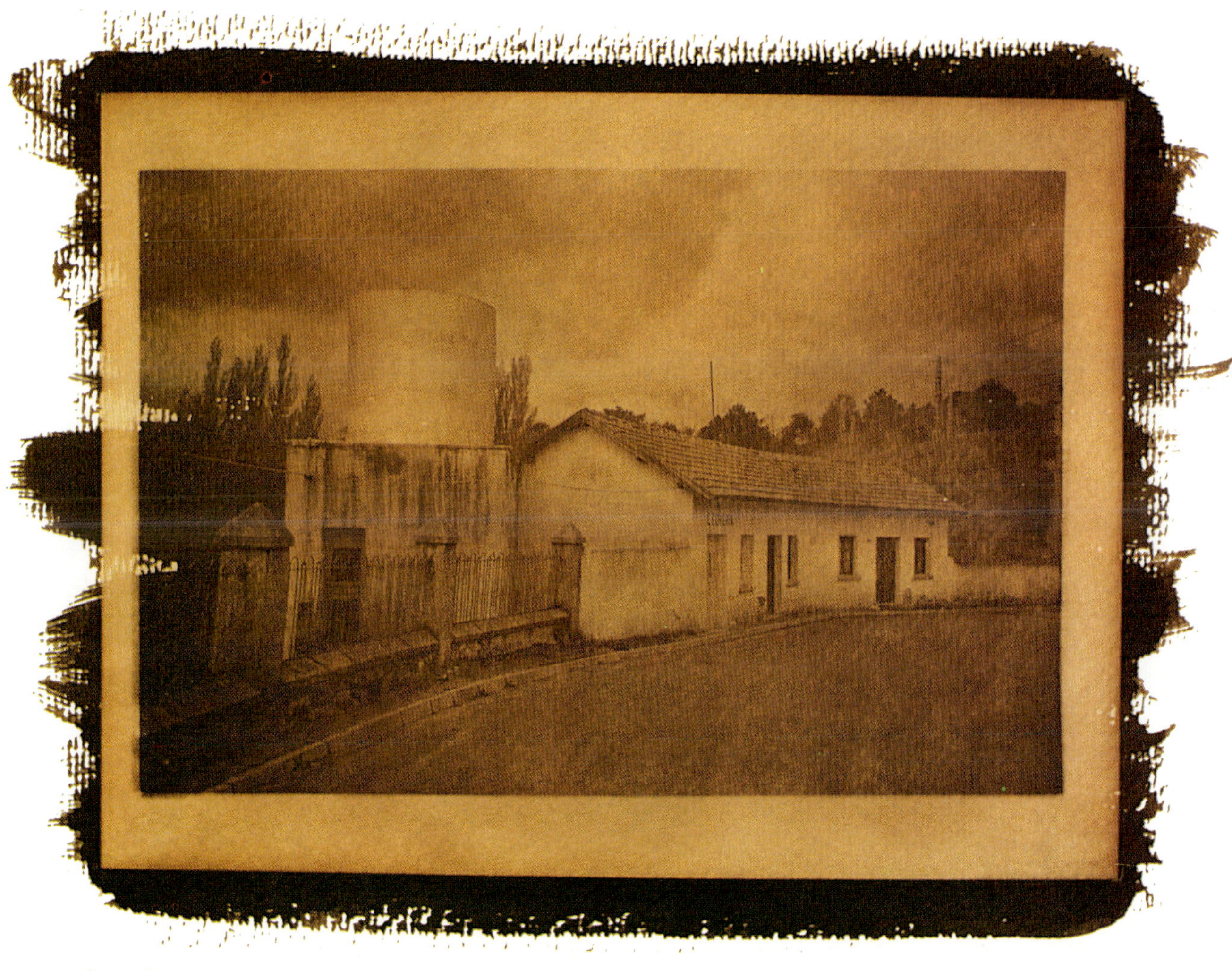

Las Navas del Marqués

1988

Van Dyke

30 x 40 cm.

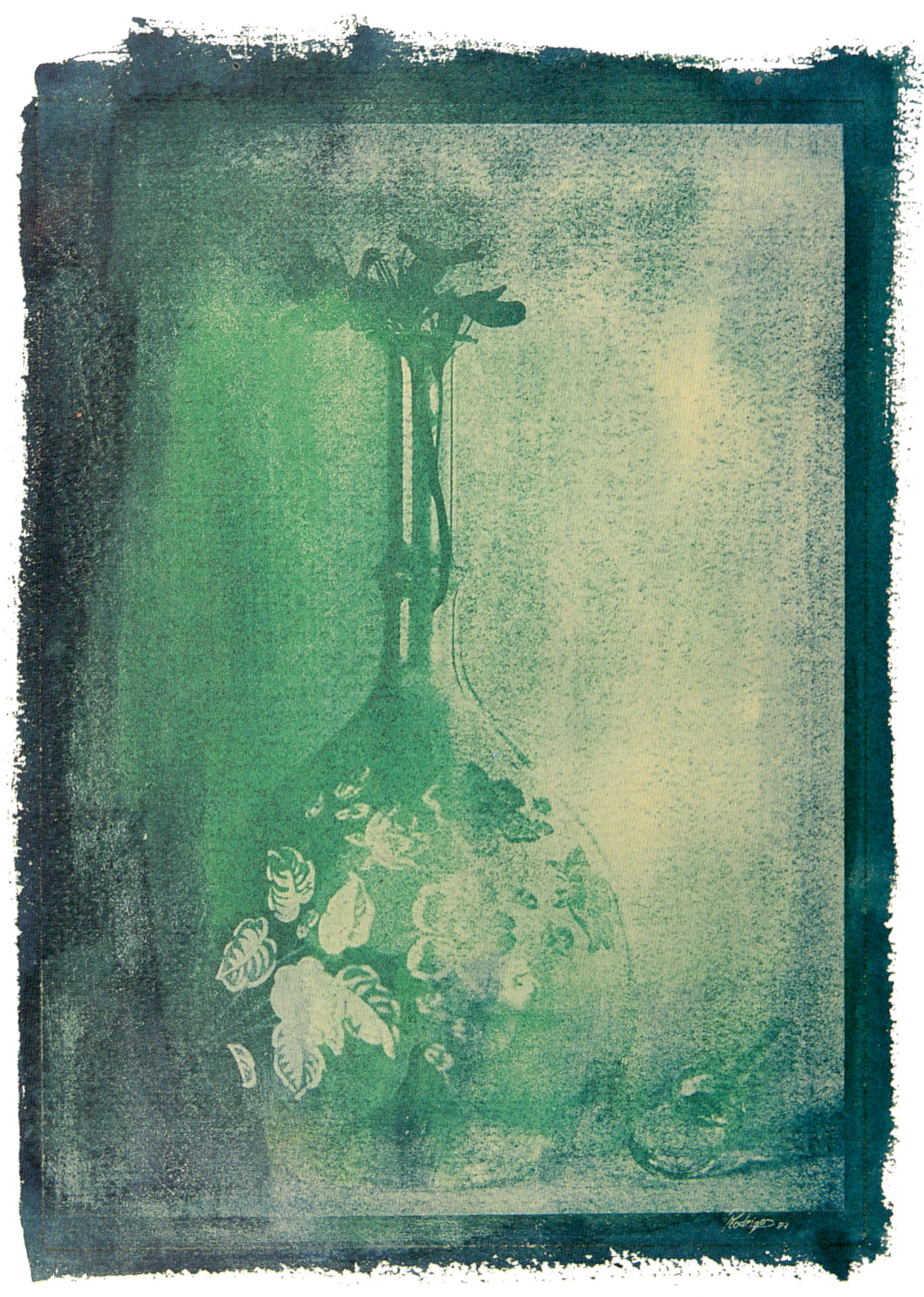

Pomo Veneciano

1988

Bicromatado

30 x 40 cm.

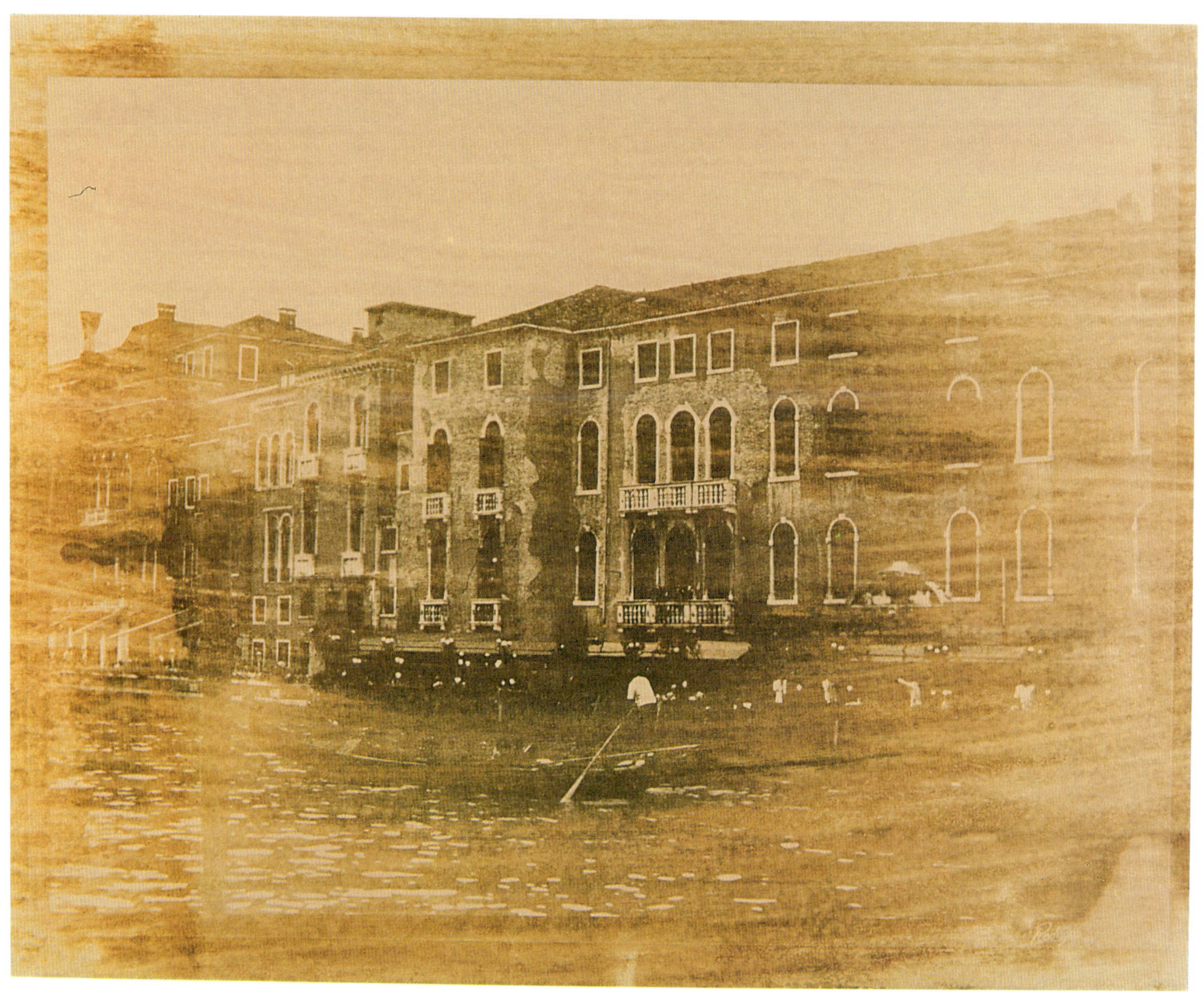

Venecia, 1981

1981

Van Dyke

30 x 40 cm.

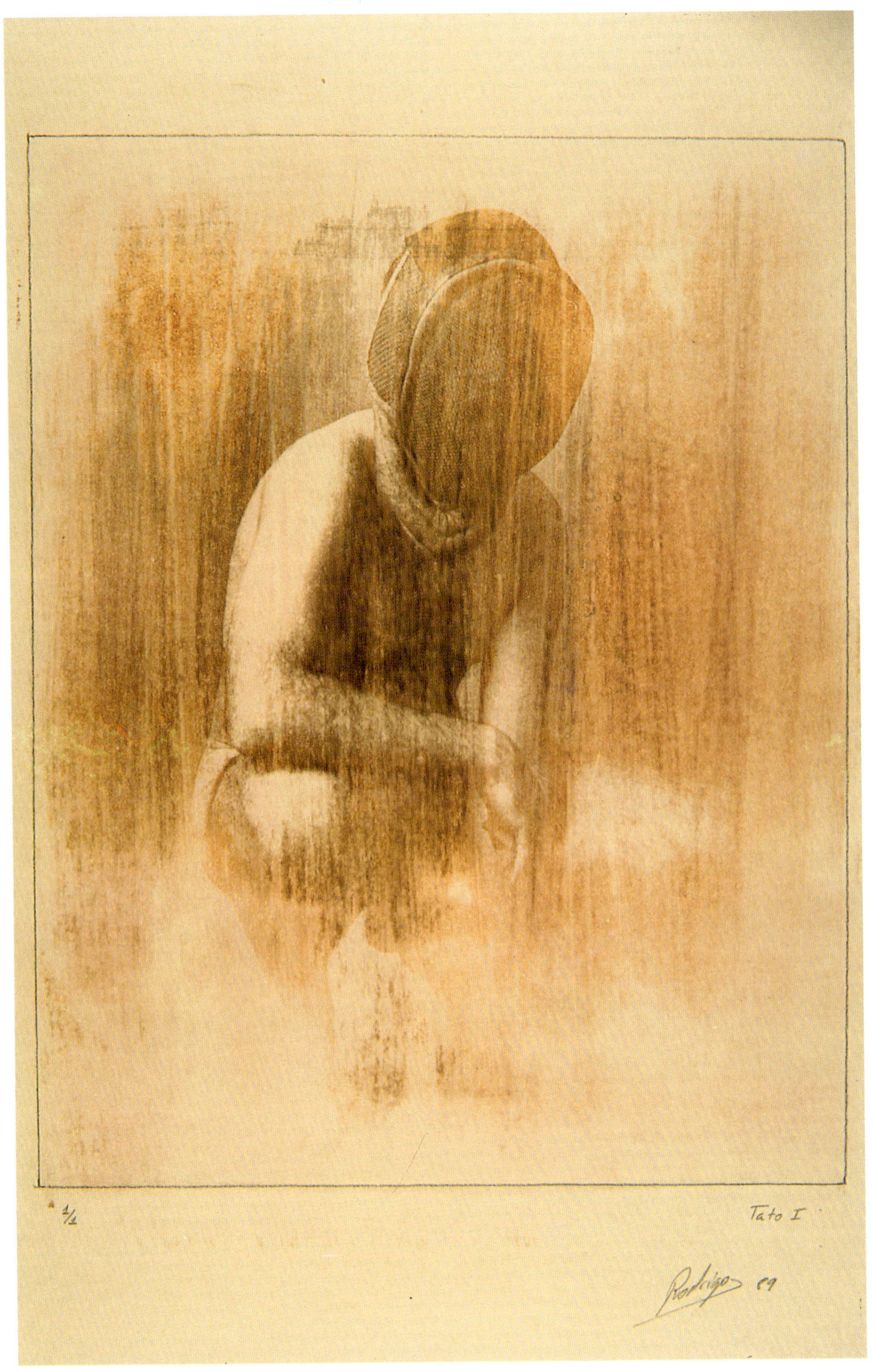

Tato I
1989
Van Dyke
30 x 40 cm.

ISABEL MUÑOZ

Born Barcelona, 1951 / Nació en Barcelona, 1951

Individual Exhibitions
Exposiciones individuales

1986   "Toques". Instituto Francés. Madrid,
        España.
1987   "América, América". Asociación Cultural
        Hispano-Norteamericana. Madrid,
        España.
1989   Galería Spectrum. Zaragoza, España.
        "Primeros Encuentros de la Fotografía".
        Villa de Leganés, Madrid, España.
1990   "Tango". Galería Jean-Pierre Lambert.
        París, Francia.

Group Exhibitions
Exposiciones colectivas

1989   "Cuando uno y uno son más de dos".
        Asociación Cultural Hispano
        Norteamericana. Madrid, España.

Photographs included in the exhibition
Fotografías contenidas en la exposición

1. Tango. # 1. 1989. Platinotipio. 98 x 98 cm.
2. Tango. # 3. 1989. Platinotipio. 24 x 36 cm.
3. Tango. # 6. 1989. Platinotipio. 38 x 56 cm.
4. Tango. # 13. 1989. Platinotipio. 43 x 46 cm.
5. Tango. # 14. 1989. Platinotipio. 38 x 56 cm.

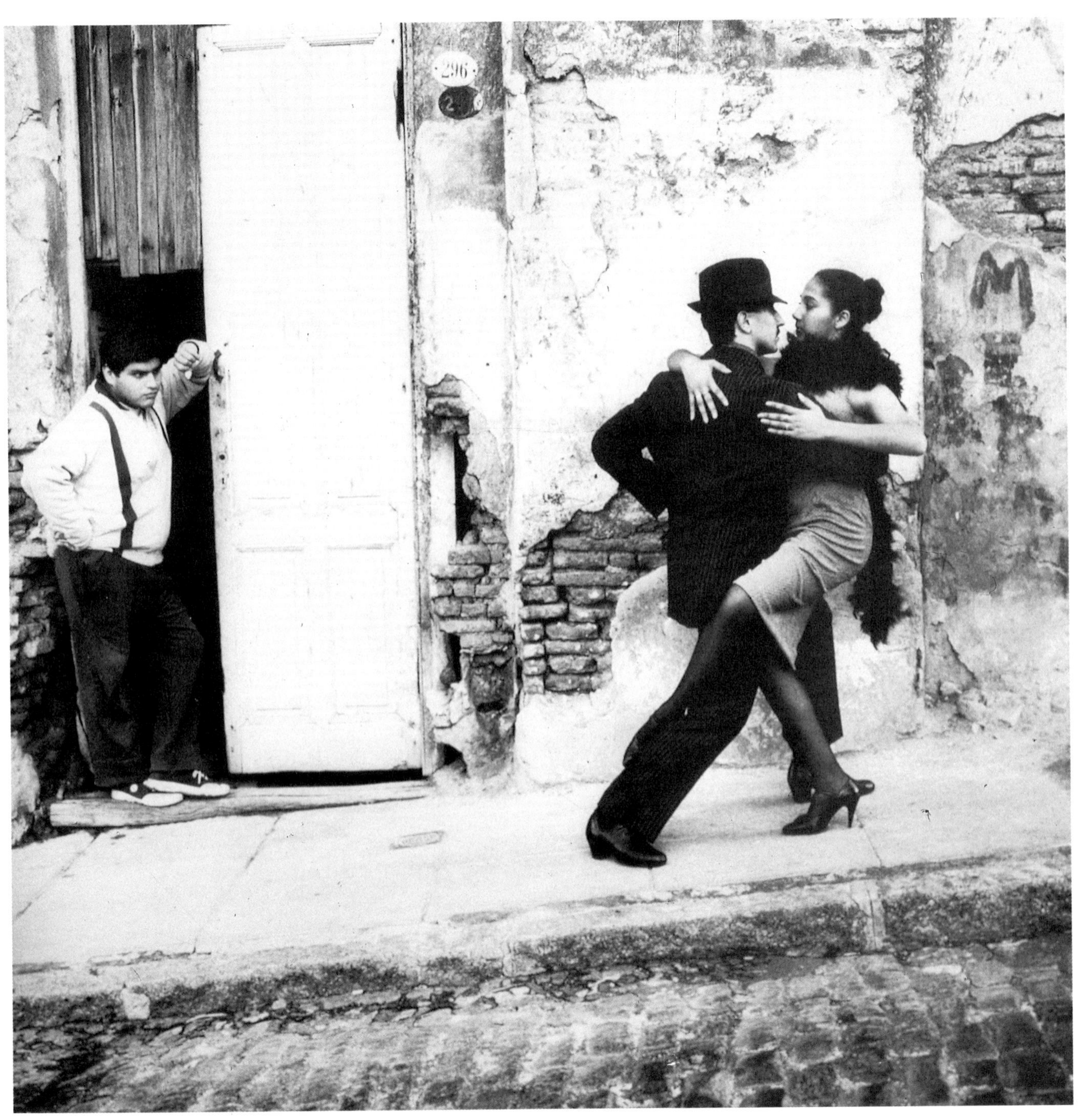

Tango
1989
Platinotipio
98 x 98 cm.

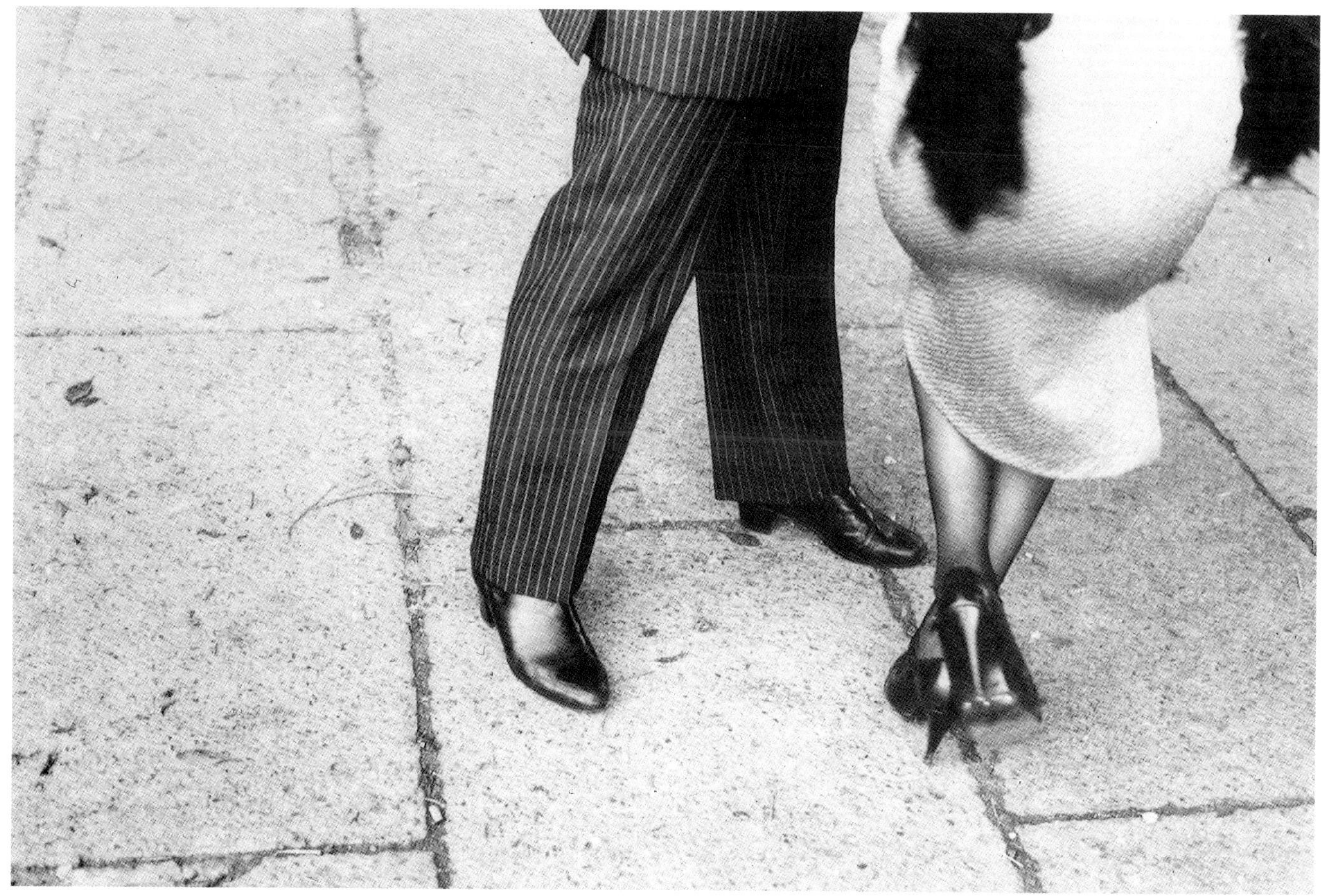

Tango
1989
Platinotipio
24 x 36 cm.

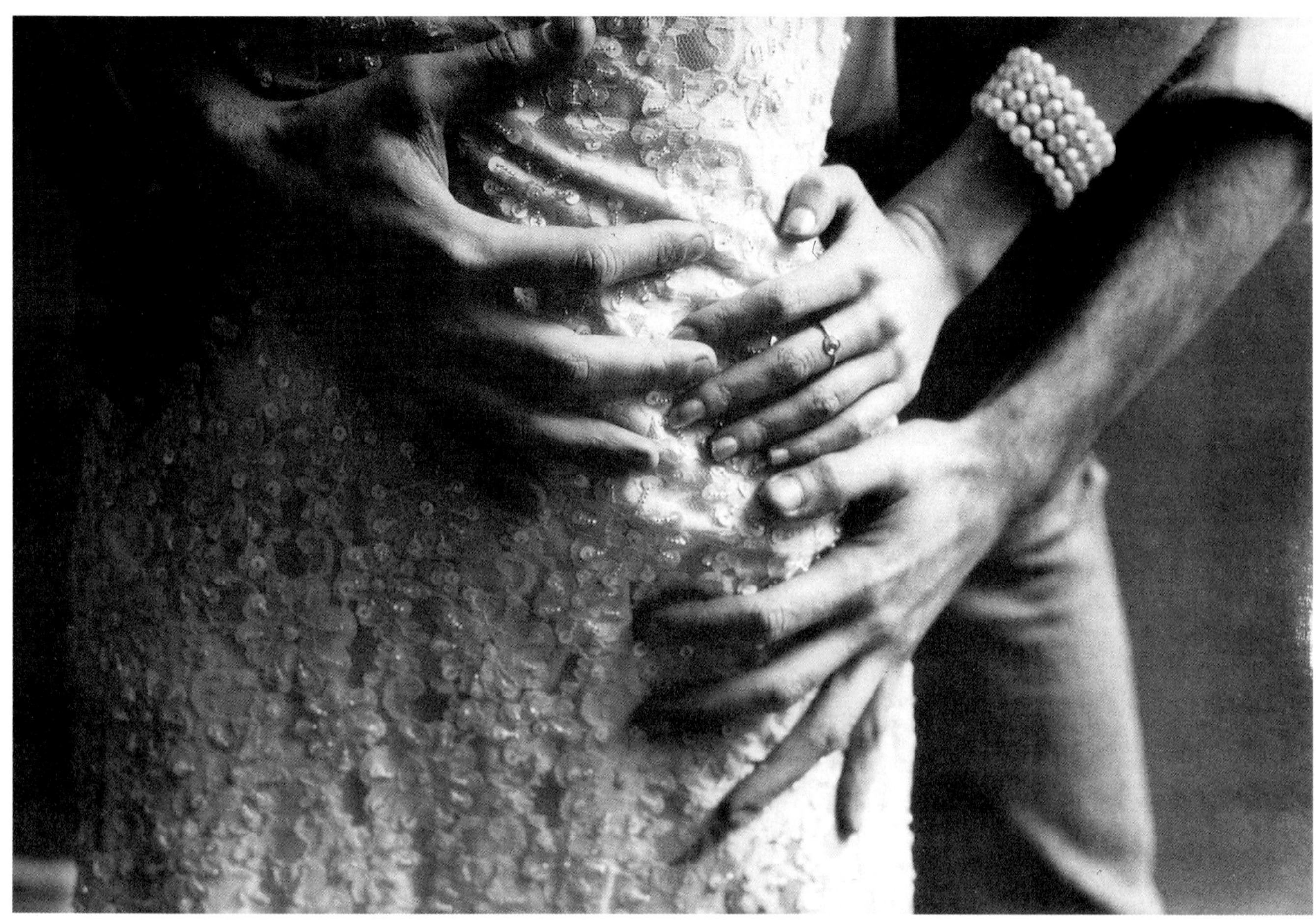

Tango
1989
Platinotipio
38 x 56 cm.

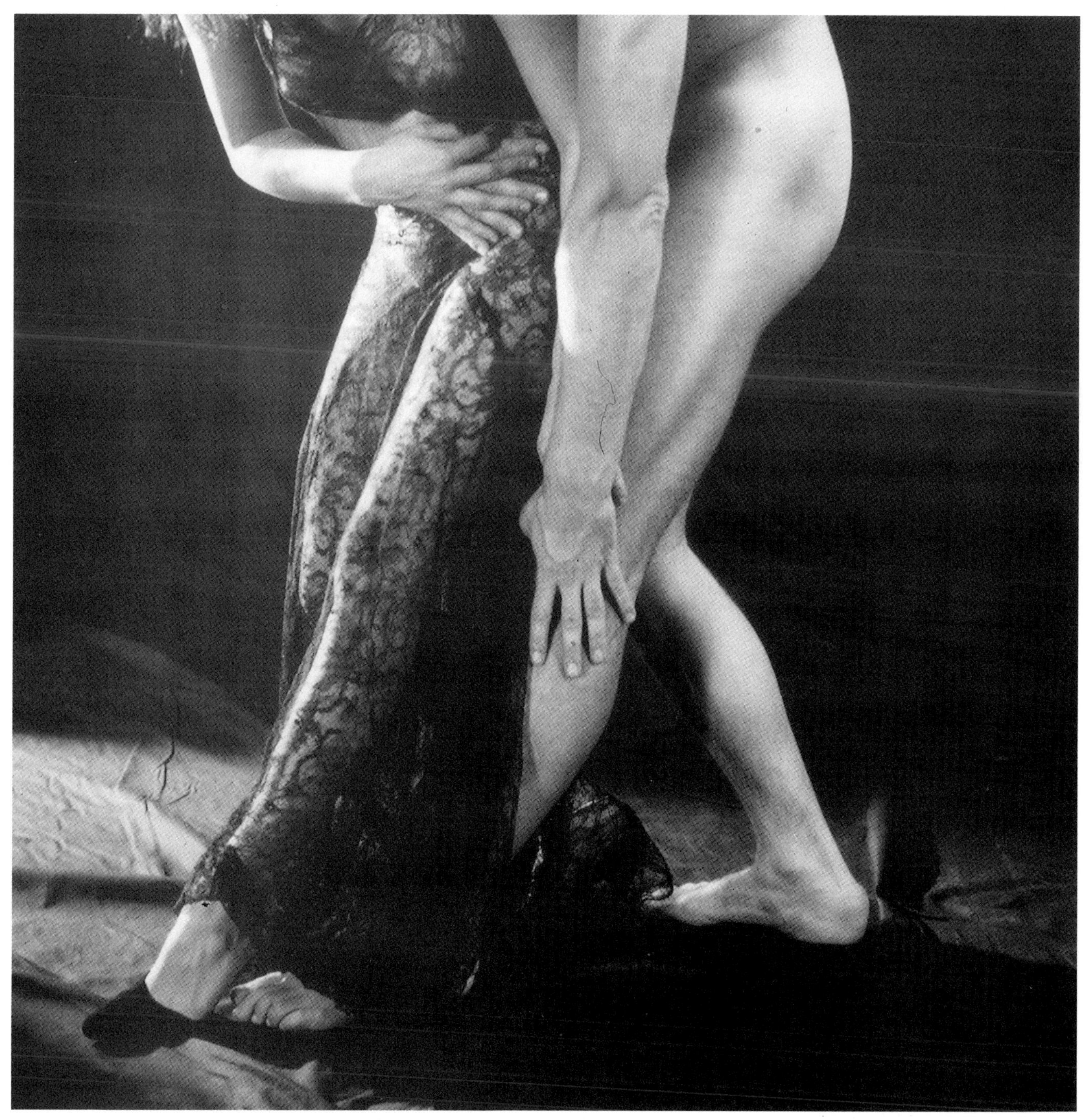

Tango
1989
Platinotipio
43 x 46 cm.

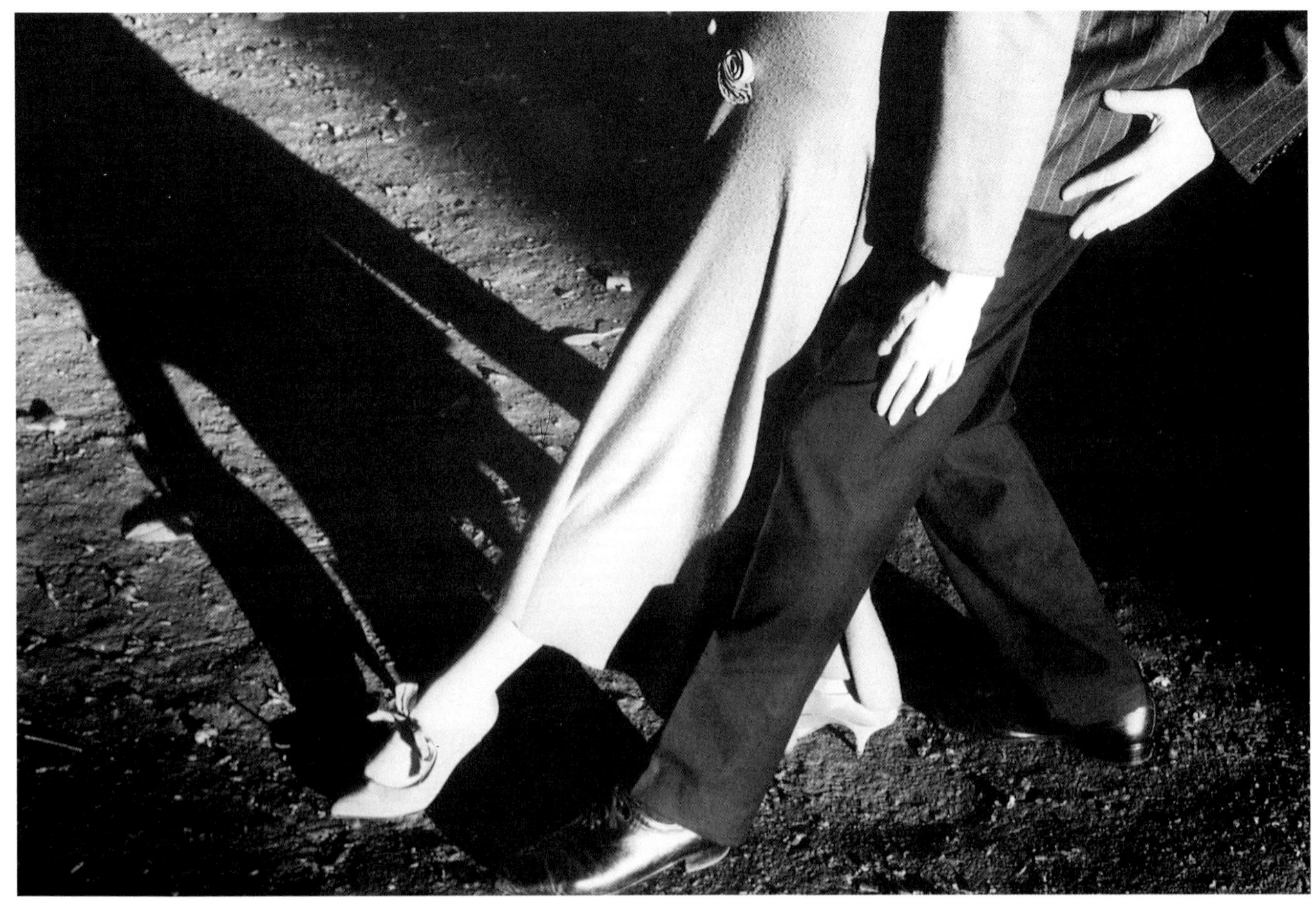

Tango
1989
Platinotipio
38 x 56 cm.

RAFAEL NAVARRO

Born Zaragoza, 1940 / Nació en Zaragoza, 1940

Main Individual Exhibitions
Principales Exposiciones individuales

1979   Canon Photo Gallery. Amsterdam,
Holanda.
The White Gallery. Tel Aviv, Israel.

1980   Paole Piaj Galerij. Antwerpen, Bélgica.
Photogalleriet. Oslo, Suecia.

1982   Il diafragma. Milano, Italia.
Galería Album. Sao Paulo, Brazil.
La Chambre Claire. París, Francia.

1984   Museum fur photographie. Braunschweig,
Alemania.

1985   Zur Stocheregg. Zurich, Suiza.

1987   Museo de Bellas Artes. Bilbao, España.
Museo Español de Arte Contemporáneo.
Madrid, España.
Perimeter Gallery. Chicago, Illinois,
EE.UU.

1989   Le Chateau d'Eau. Tolouse, Francia.
Teatro Municipal San Martín. Buenos
Aires, Argentina.
Centre de la Photographie. Gèneve,
Suiza.

1990   Museo Jovellanos. Gijón, España.

Main Group Exhibitions
Principales Exposiciones colectivas

1978   Art'78. Kunstmesse, Basel.
9èmes Rencontres Internationales Phot.
Arles, Francia.

1981   Salón Invitados. II Coloquios
Latinoamericanos de Fotografía. Palacio
de Bellas Artes. México D.F., México.

1983   Arbes. Centre Popidou. París, Francia.
European Photography. Northeastern
University. Boston, Massachusetts,
EE.UU.

1984   Multiple Images. The Photographer's
Gallery. London, Inglaterra.

1986   Foto Fest'86. Benteller Gallery. Huston,
Texas, EE.UU.
Contemporary Spanish Photography.
University Art Museum. Albuquerque,
Nuevo México. EE.UU.

1987   "After Franco". Marcuse Pfeiffer Gallery.
Nueva York, EE.UU.
"Facets of the Collection". Museum of
Modern Art. San Francisco. California,
EE.UU.
"Le temps d'un mouvement". Palais de
Tokio. París, Francia.

1988   ARCO 88. Madrid, España.
"Création Photographique en Espagne".
Musée Cantini. Marsella, Francia.

Photographs included in the exhibition
Fotografías contenidas en la exposición

1. Homenaje a siglo y medio. # 1 . 1989. Plata. 40 x 59,9 cm.
2. Homenaje a siglo y medio. # 3. 1989. Plata. 40 x 59,9 cm.
3. Homenaje a siglo y medio. # 4 . 1989. Plata. 40 x 59,9 cm.
4. Homenaje a siglo y medio. # 5 . 1989. Plata. 40 x 59,9 cm.
5. Homenaje a siglo y medio. # 7 . 1989. Plata. 40 x 59,9 cm.

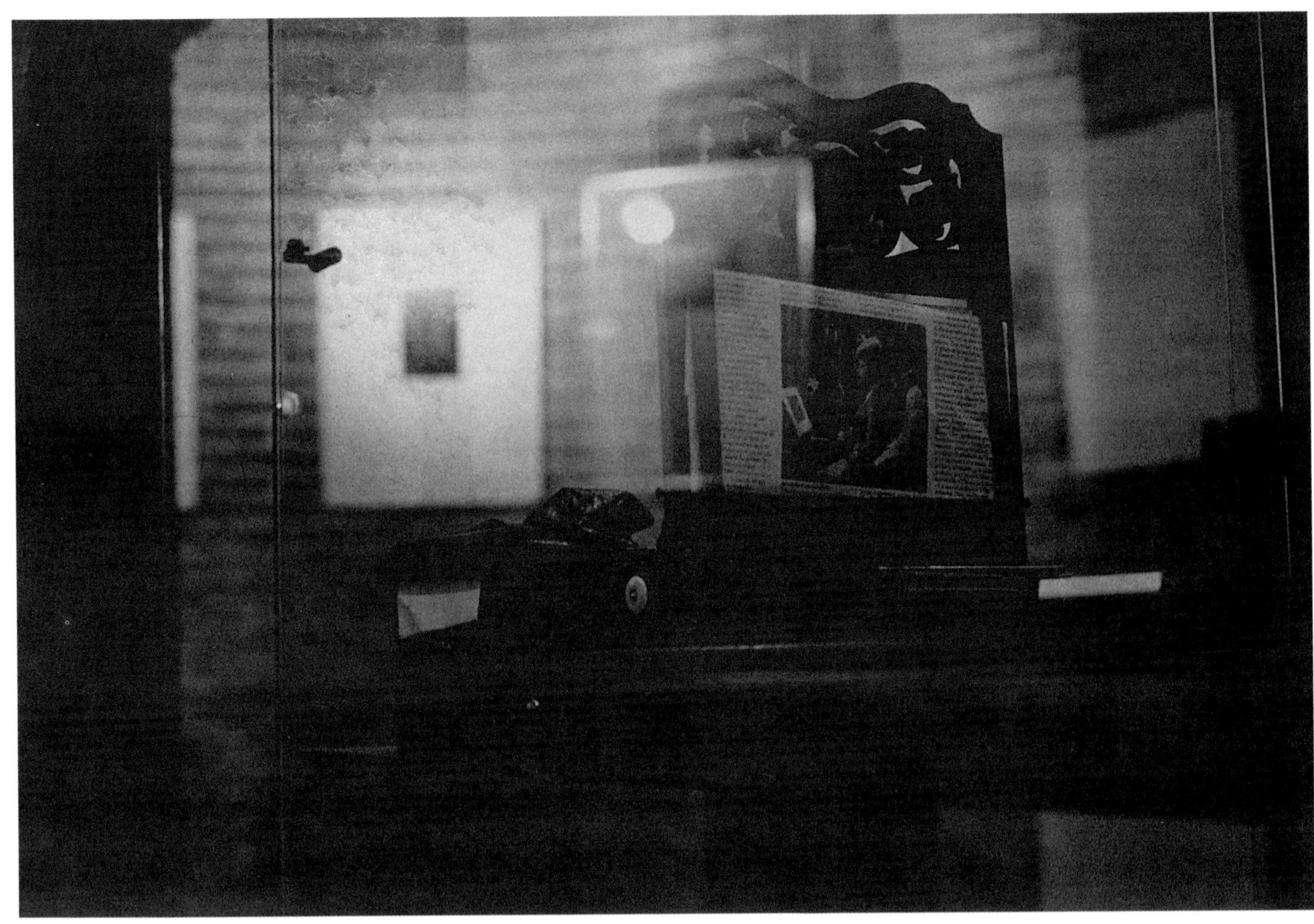

Homenaje a siglo y medio
1989
Plata
40 x 59,9 cm.

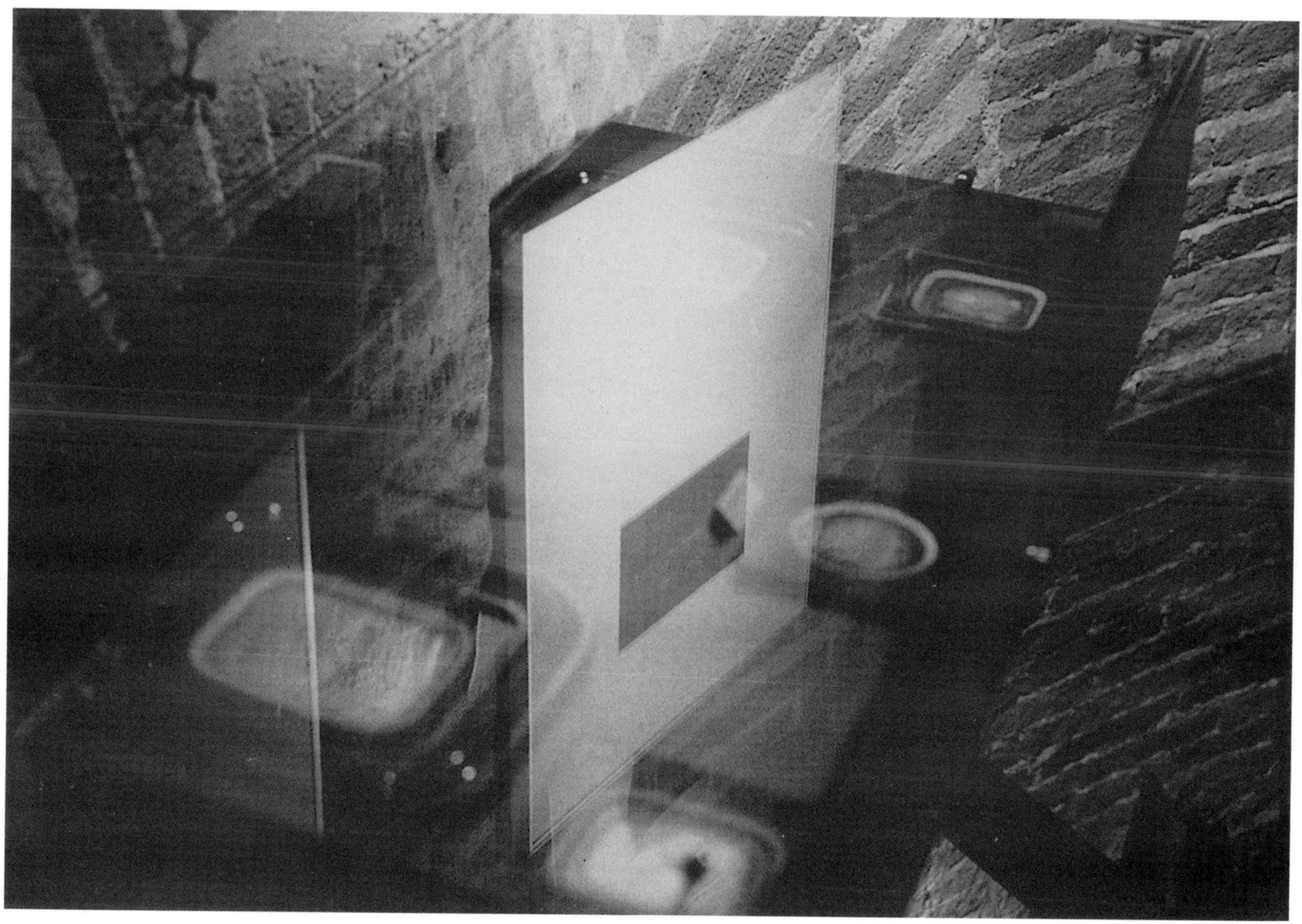

Homenaje a siglo y medio

1989

Plata

40 x 59,9 cm.

Homenaje a siglo y medio
1989
Plata
40 x 59,9 cm.

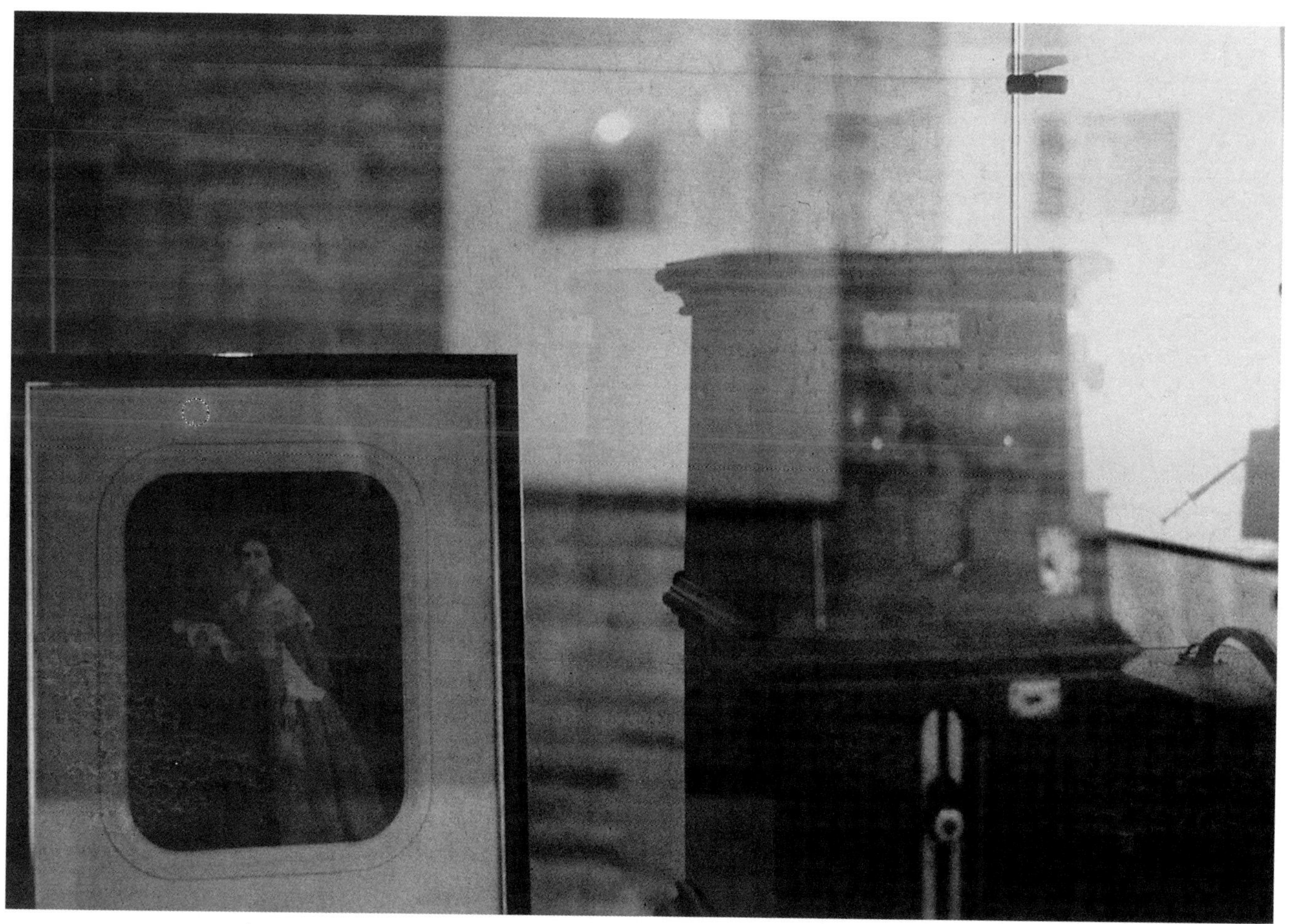

Homenaje a siglo y medio

1989

Plata

40 x 59,9 cm.

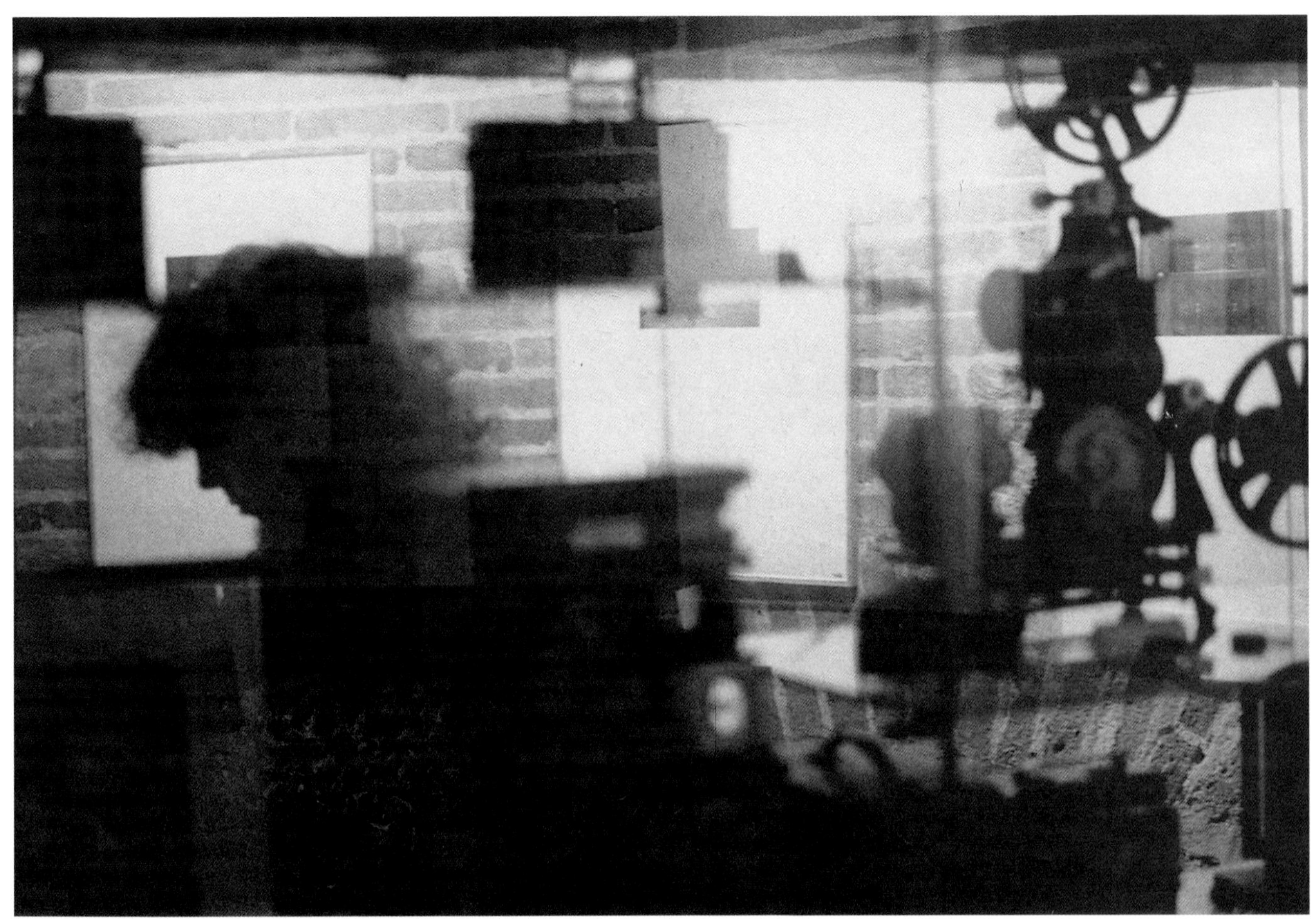

Homenaje a siglo y medio
1989
Plata
40 x 59,9 cm.

OUKA LELE (BARBARA ALLENDE)

Born Madrid, 1957 / Nació en Madrid, 1957

Individual Exhibitions
Exposiciones individuales

1980	"Peluquería". Galería Redor. Madrid, España.
1984	Galería Moriarty. Madrid, España.
1985	Museo de Bellas Artes. Málaga, España. Galería Forum. Tarragona, España.
1986	ARCO 86. Galería Morirty. Madrid, España.
1987	"Retrospectiva Ouka Lele". Museo Español de Arte Contemporáneo. Madrid, España.
1988	Sala Vanguardia. Bilbao, España. Sala Vinçon. Barcelona, España. Fondation Cartier. Diseños de Philippe Model. París, Francia. Sala de Arte Nicanor Piñole. Gijón, España.
1989	Círculo de Bellas Artes. Tenerife, España. Shibuya Seibu. Tokyo. Japón. "Ouka Lele pour Philippe Model". Palacio de la Magdalena. Santander, España.

Group Exhibitions
Exposiciones colectivas

1978	"IX Recontres Internationales de la Photographie". Arles, Francia.
1984	"259 Imágenes. Fotografía Actual en España". Círculo de Bellas Artes. Madrid, España.
1985	"Aspects de la jeune photographie espagnole". Galería Seguier. París, Francia.
1986	"Mois de la Photo". Kodak. París, Francia.
1987	"After Franco". Galería Marcuse Pfeiffer. Nueva York. EE.UU.

Bienal Internacional de Arte Contemporáneo. Sao Paulo, Brasil.

1988	ARCO 88, Galería Moriarty. Madrid, España. 2.º Encontros de Imagen. Associaçao Cultural de Fotografía de Braga, Portugal. "Audiovisual Lisboa 88". Portugal.
1989	"10 Fotógrafos Españoles". Palacio de Sástago. Diputación de Zaragoza. Zaragoza, España. "ART LA 89". Galería Moriarty. Los Angeles. California, EE.UU.
1990	ARCO 90. Galería Moriarty. Madrid, España. "Dún art, l'autre". Centre de la Ville Charité. Marsella, Francia. "Gitanos". París, Francia. "Spanish Fine Art Photography". The Special Photographers Company. Londres, Inglaterra.

Photographs included in the exhibition
Fotografías contenidas en la exposición

1. Autoretrato con agua. 1980. Copia en cibachrome de un original en blanco y negro coloreado a mano. 1980. 30 x 40 cm.
2. Hoy viene mi psiquiatra. 1980. Copia en cibachrome de un original en blanco y negro coloreado a mano. 1980. 30 x 40 cm.
3. Inocencia y juventud. 1984. Copia en cibachrome de un original en blanco y negro coloreado a mano. 1980. 40 x 30 cm.
4. Angela y Siro. 1984. Copia en cibachrome de un original en blanco y negro coloreado a mano. 1980. 40 x 30 cm.
5. Mis vecinos. 1984. Copia en cibachrome de un original en blanco y negro coloreado a mano. 1980. 40 x 30 cm.

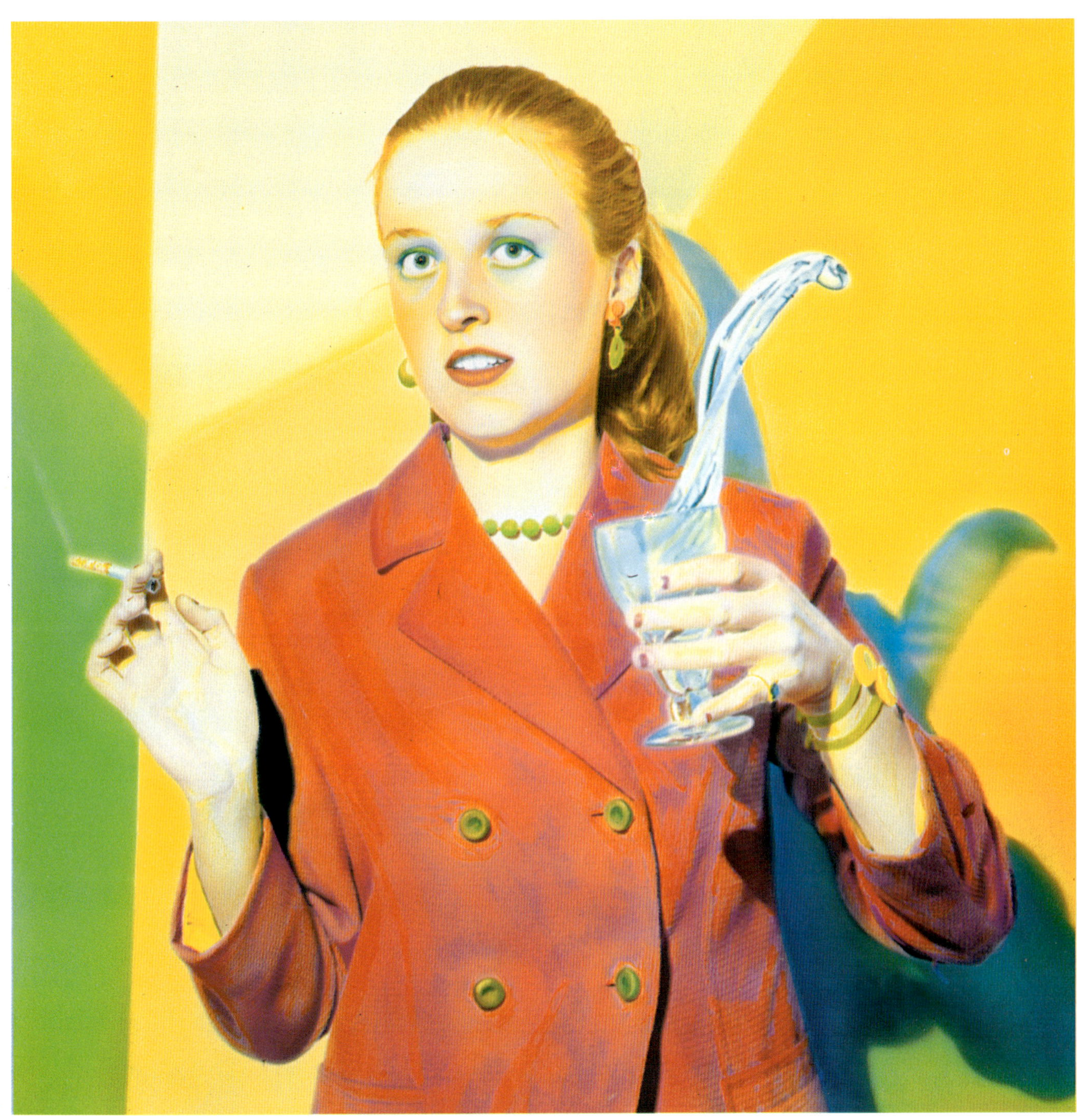

Autoretrato con agua

1980

Copia en cibachrome de un original en blanco y negro coloreado a mano

30 x 40 cm.

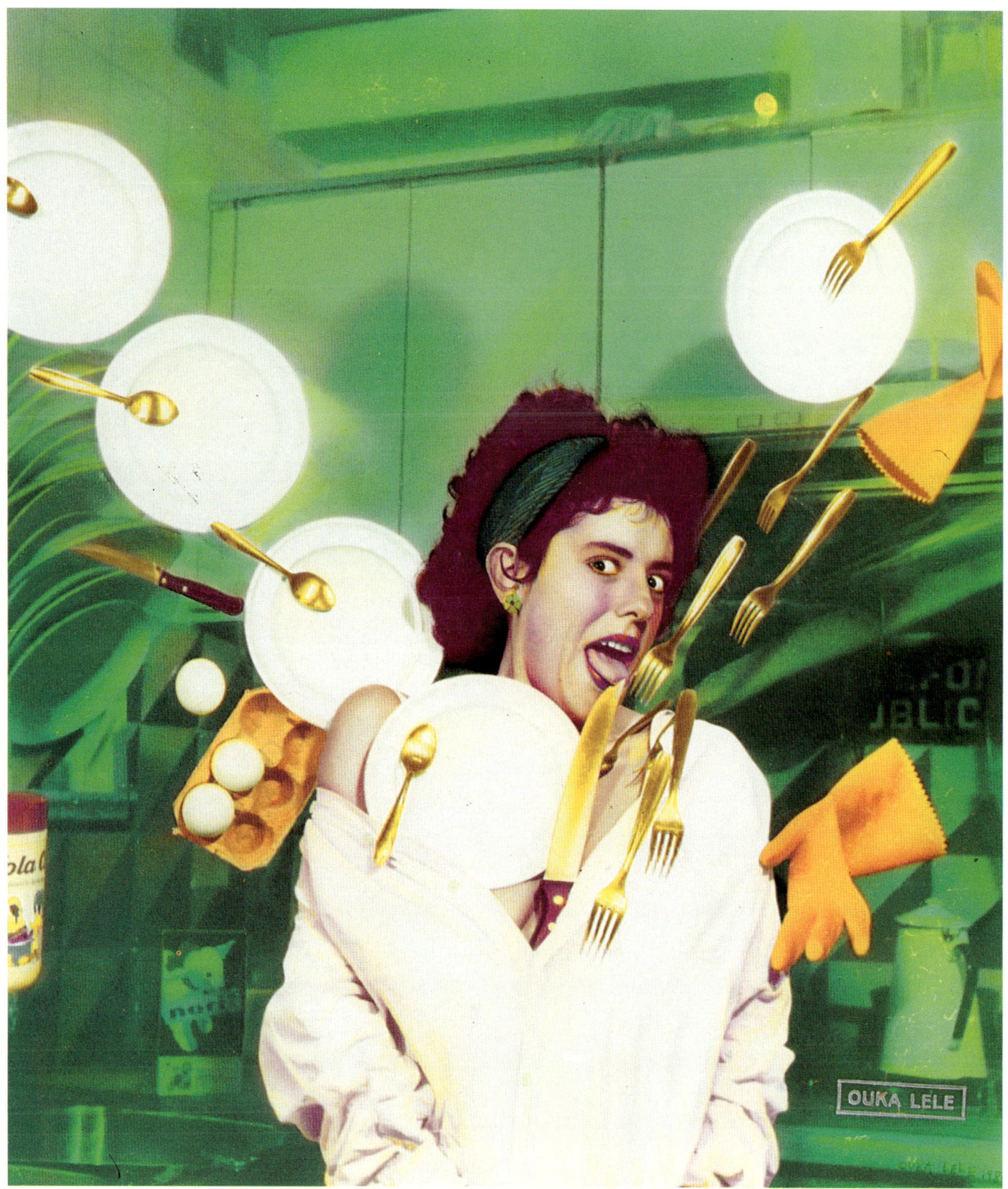

Hoy viene mi psiquiatra

1980

Copia en cibachrome de un original en blanco y negro coloreado a mano

30 x 40 cm.

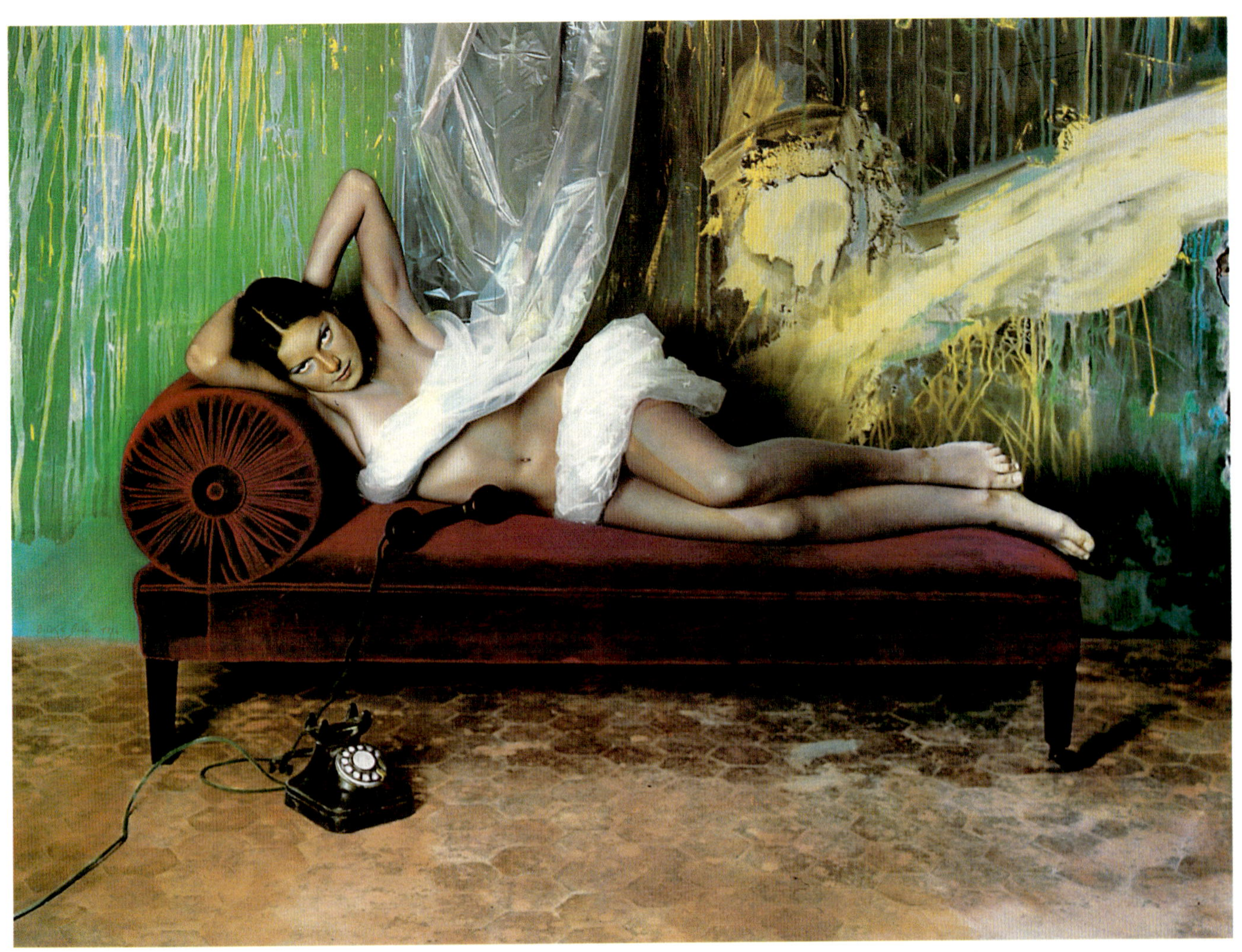

Inocencia y juventud

1984

Copia en cibachrome de un original en blanco y negro coloreado a mano

40 x 30 cm.

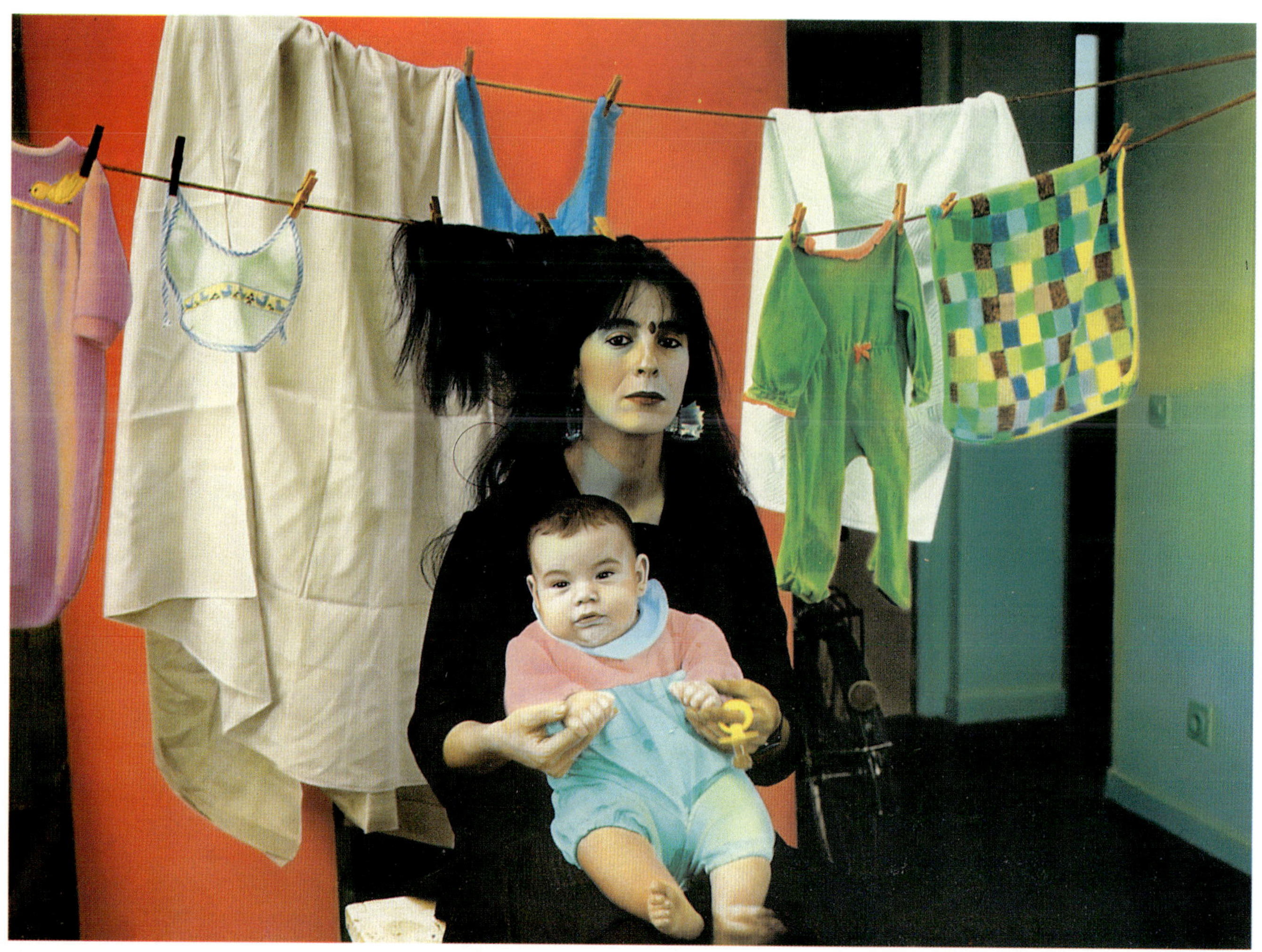

Angela y Siro

1984

Copia en cibachrome de un original en blanco y negro coloreado a mano

30 x 40 cm.

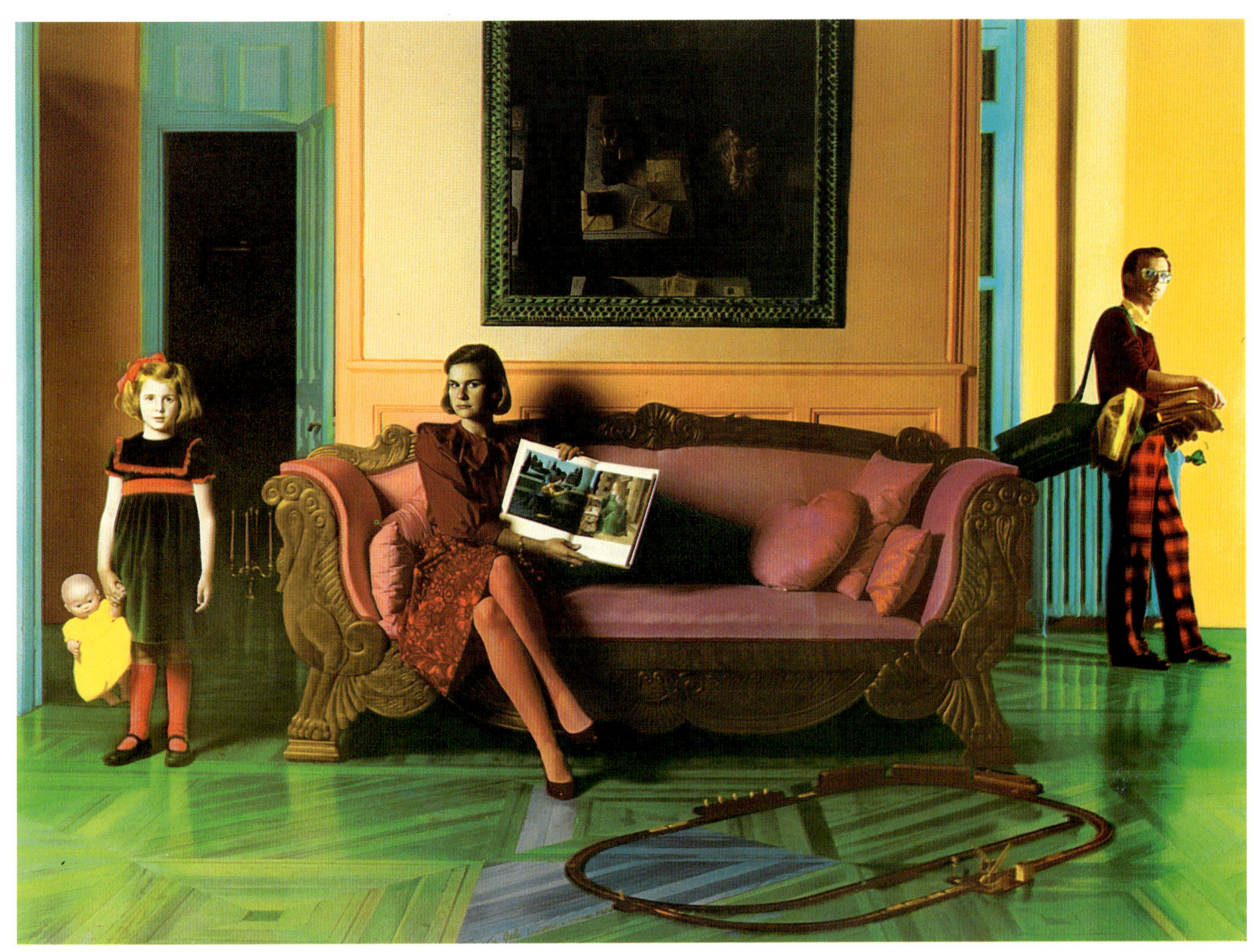

Mis vecinos

1984

Copia en cibachrome de un original en blanco y negro coloreado a mano

30 x 40 cm.

PABLO PEREZ MINGUEZ

Born Madrid, 1946 / Nació en Madrid, 1946

Individual Exhibitions
Exposiciones individuales

1973   "Juegos Cerrados". Galería Amadís.
        Madrid, España.
1974   "Propuesta fotográfica". Galería Redor.
        Madrid, España.
1980   "Foto Poro". Galería Baudes. Madrid,
        España.
1982   "Dioses y reinas", "Héroes", "Vírgenes y
        Mártires". Galería SEN. Madrid, España.
        "Primavera Fotográfica". Barcelona,
        España.
1983   "Primavera Fotográfica". Barcelona,
        España.
        "FOT/OLA". Sala Rock-Ola. Madrid,
        España.
1985   "Lo hipnótico es estético". Galería
        Spectrum. Zaragoza, España.
1986   "Foto Movida". Galería Palace.
        Granada, España.
1989   "Estética mística". Madrid y Barcelona,
        España.

Group Exhibitions
Exposiciones colectivas

1983   "259 imágenes fotografía actual".

        Círculo de Bellas Artes. Madrid,
        España.
1986   "50 años de fotografía moderna en
        color". Photokina. Colonia, Alemania.
        "18 fotógrafos y la moda". Sevilla,
        España.
1987   "Escenarios de la guerra civil española".
        Una visión de la fotografía actual. Sala
        exposiciones del Canal de Isabel II.
        Madrid, España.
1988   "Questioning Europe". bienale
        Fotografie. Rotterdam, Holanda.
1989   "35 fotógrafos españoles". Marsella,
        Francia.
        "El conepto manipulado". Mes de la foto.
        Reims, Francia.
        De Messidor a Termidor. 1789-1989.
        Galería Seiguer. Madrid, España.

Photographs included in the exhibition
Fotografías contenidas en la exposición

1. "Radio Futura". 1984. Cibachrome. 35 x 40 cm.
2. Santa Fé (Estética mística). 1989. Cibachrome. 35 x 40 cm.
3. Almodóvar místico. 1981. Cibachrome. 35 x 40 cm.
4. Gitana con niña (Estética mística). 1987. Cibachrome.
   35 x 40 cm.
5. Gitana mulata. 1982. Cibachrome. 35 x 40 cm.

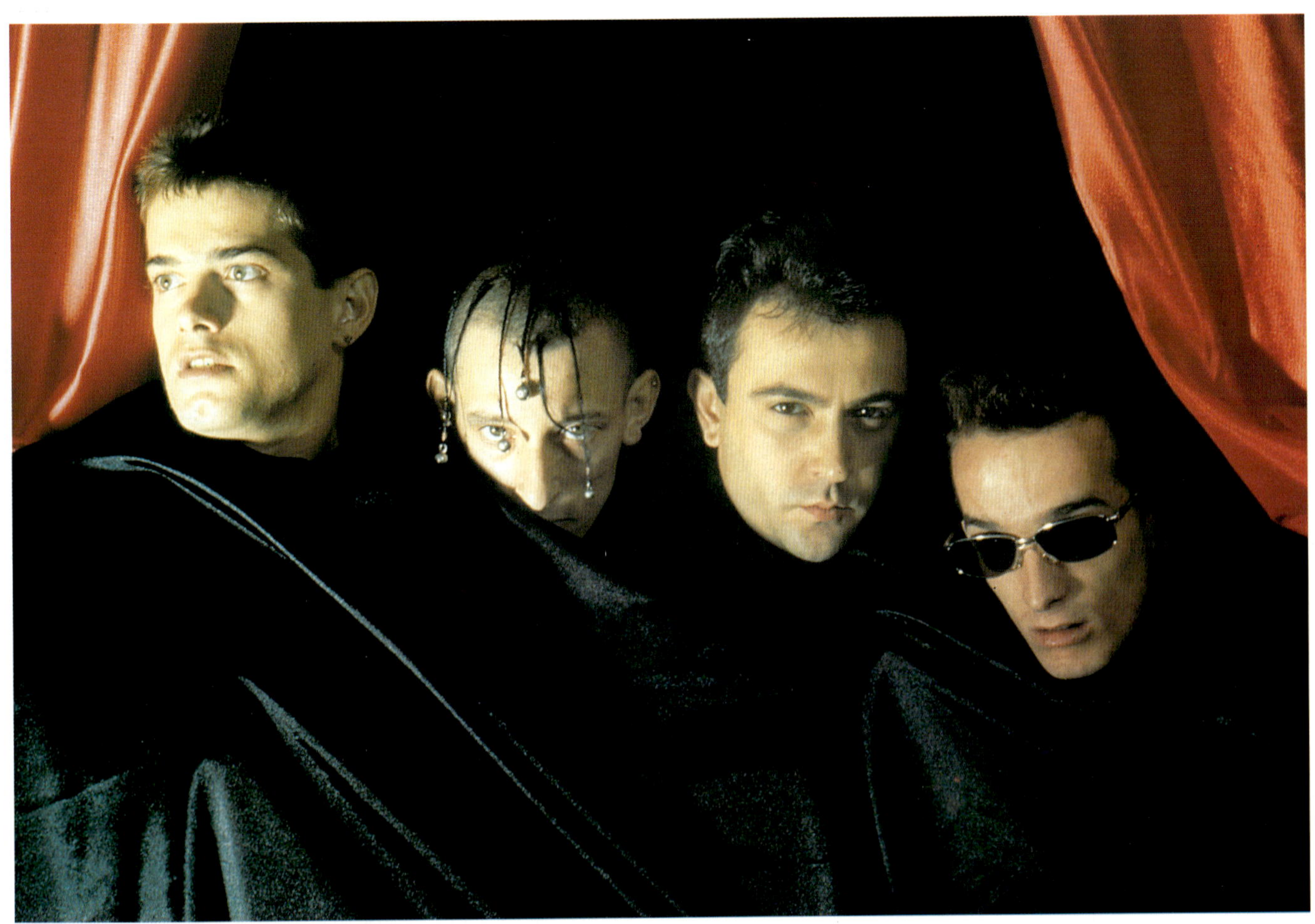

"Radio Futura"

1984

Cibachrome

35 x 40 cm.

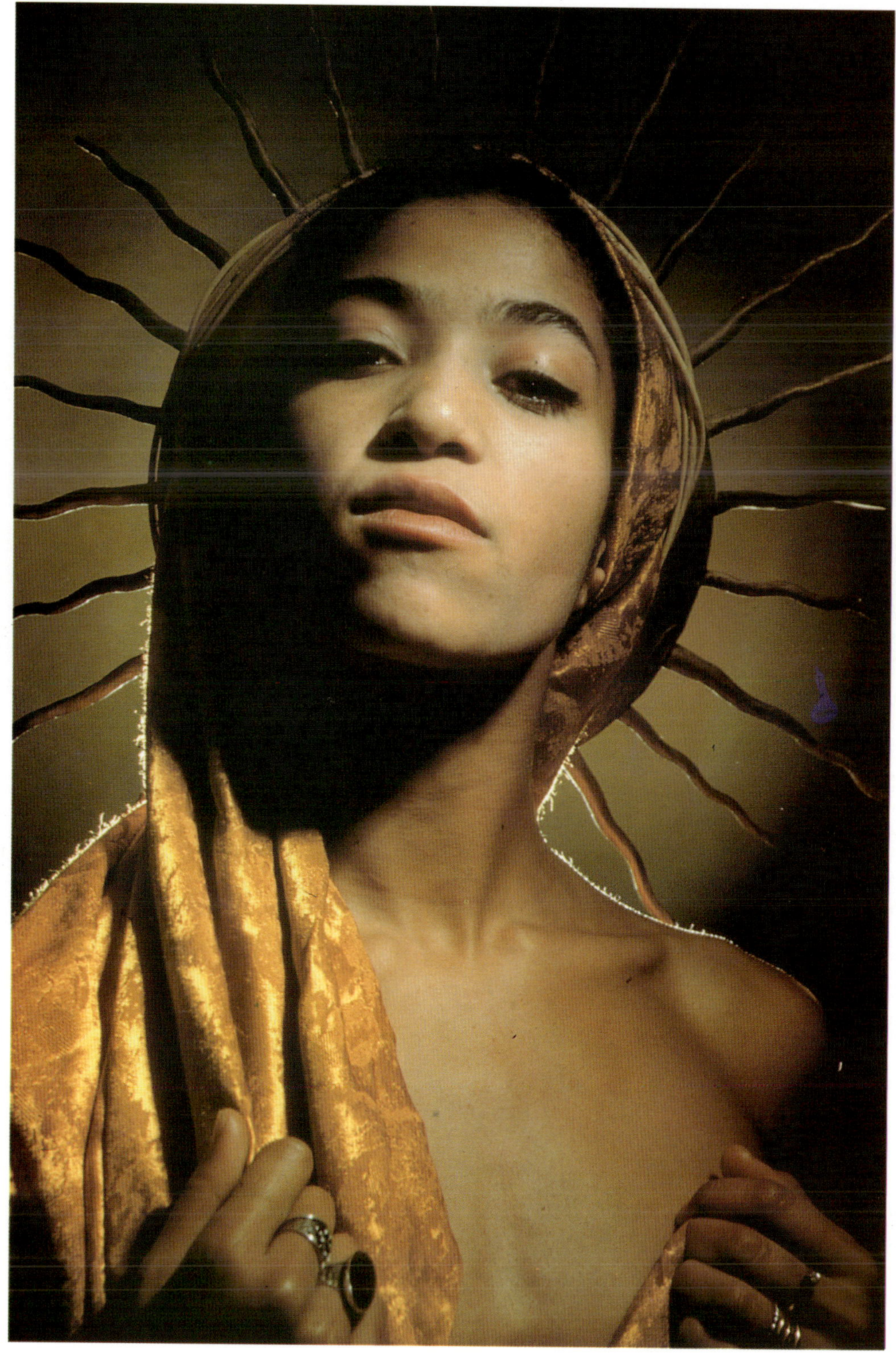

Santa Fé (Estética Mística)

1989

Cibachrome

35 x 40 cm.

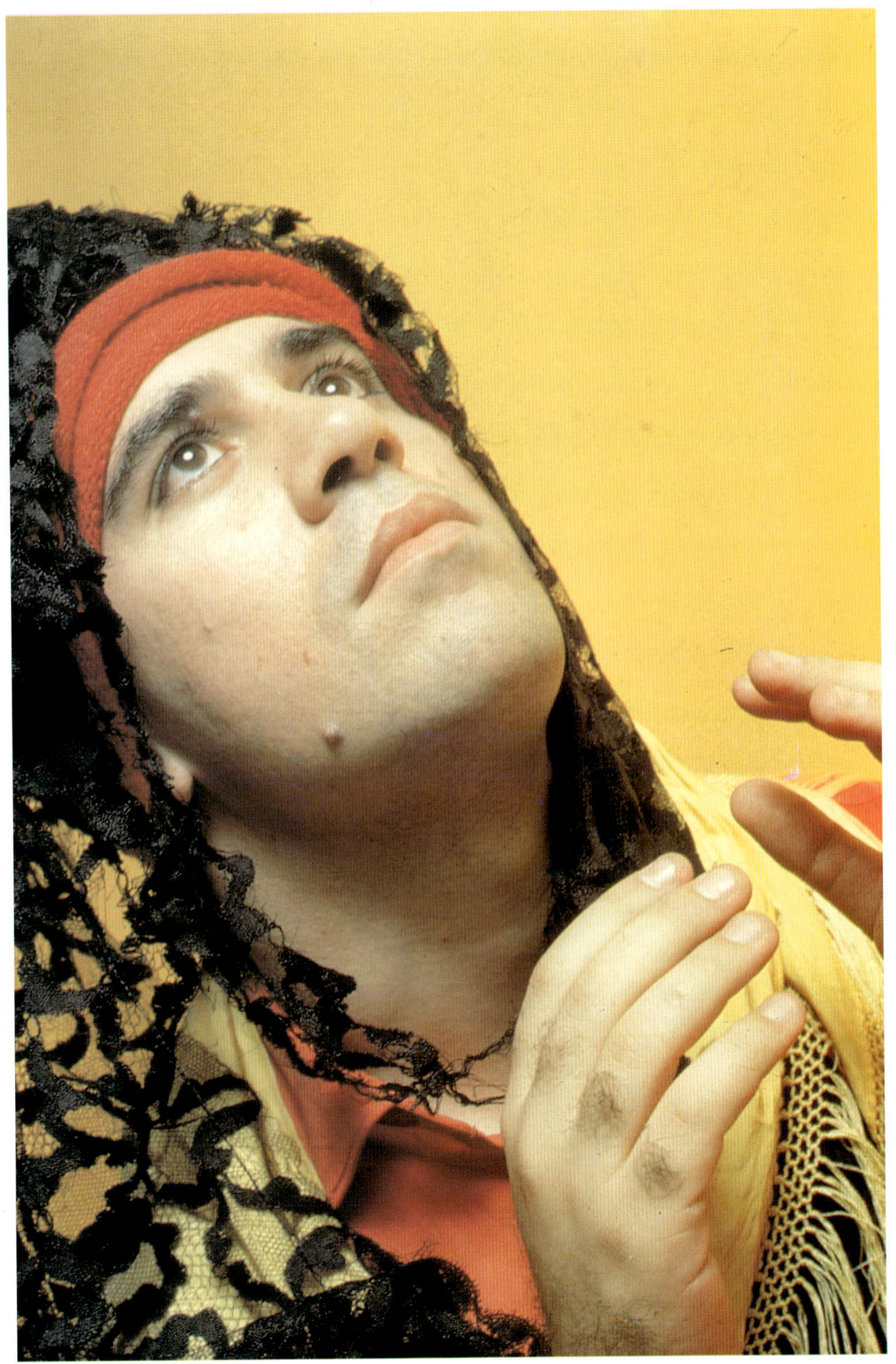

Almodóvar místico

1981

Cibachrome

35 x 40 cm.

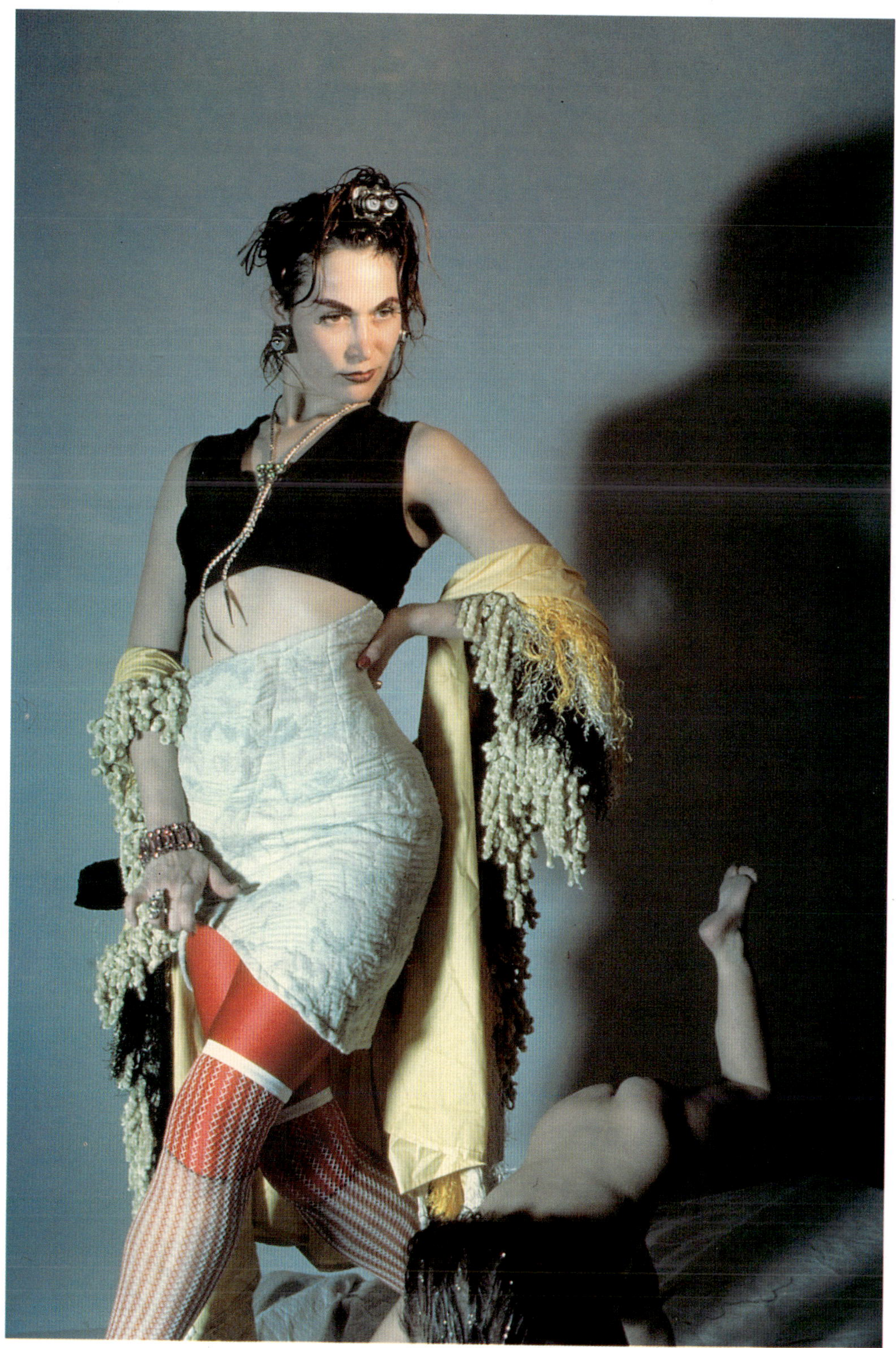

Gitana con niña (Estética mística)

1987

Cibachrome

35 x 40 cm.

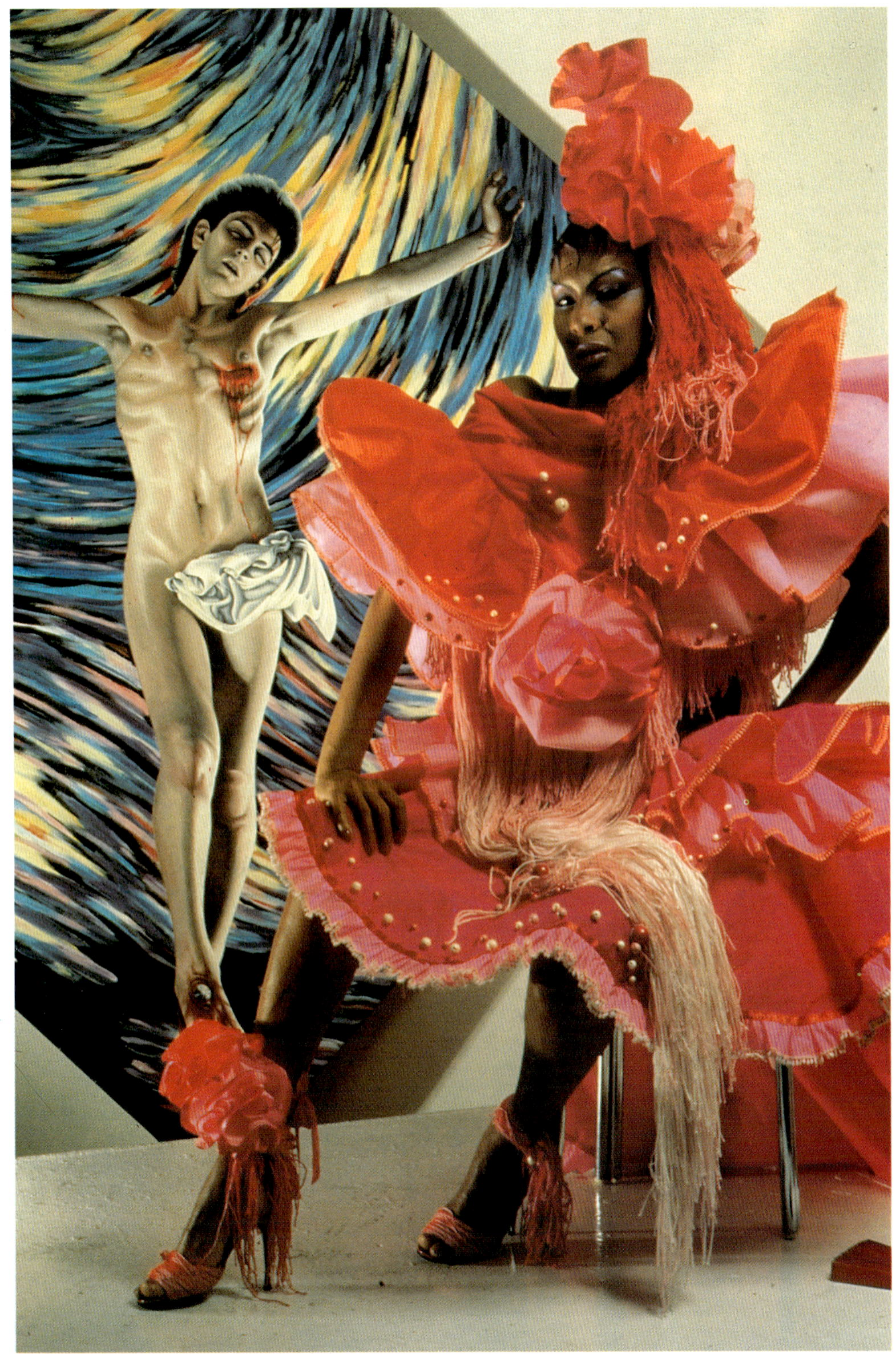

Gitana mulata

1982

Cibachrome

35 x 40 cm.

JORGE RUEDA

Born Almería, 1943 / Nació en Almería, 1943

Individual Exhibitions
Exposiciones individuales

Madrid. Barcelona. Sevilla. Granada. Ibiza. Guadalaja. Almería. Vigo. Murcia, Lérida. Toledo. Málaga. Gijón. París. Londres. Roma. Berlín. Nueva York. Arles. Bonn. Amsterdam. Oslo. Milán. Essen. Narbonne. Boston. Royan. Harlem. Kassel. Estocolmo. Ginebra. Tokio. Marsella. Almería.

Photographs included in the exhibition
Fotografías contenidas en la exposición

1. Mullflor. 1984. Montaje óptico. 28 x 20 cm.
2. Neumonia. 1973. Montaje óptico. 28 x 20 cm.
3. Blanbiz. 1982. Montaje óptico. 28 x 20 cm.
4. Curbosq. 1974. Montaje óptico. 28 x 20 cm.
5. Pepino. 1975. Montaje óptico. 28 x 20 cm.

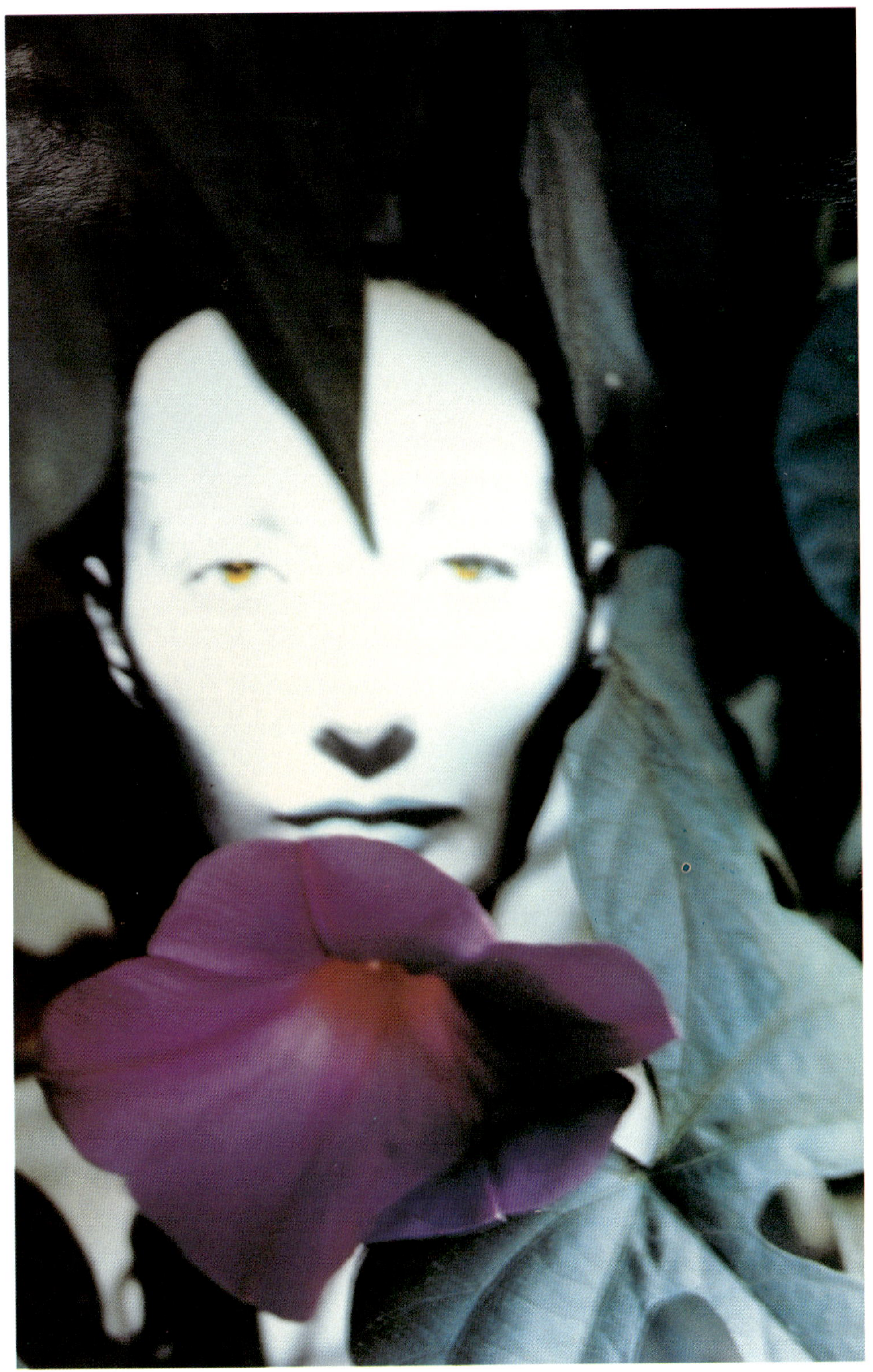

Mullflor

1984

Montaje óptico

28 x 20 cm.

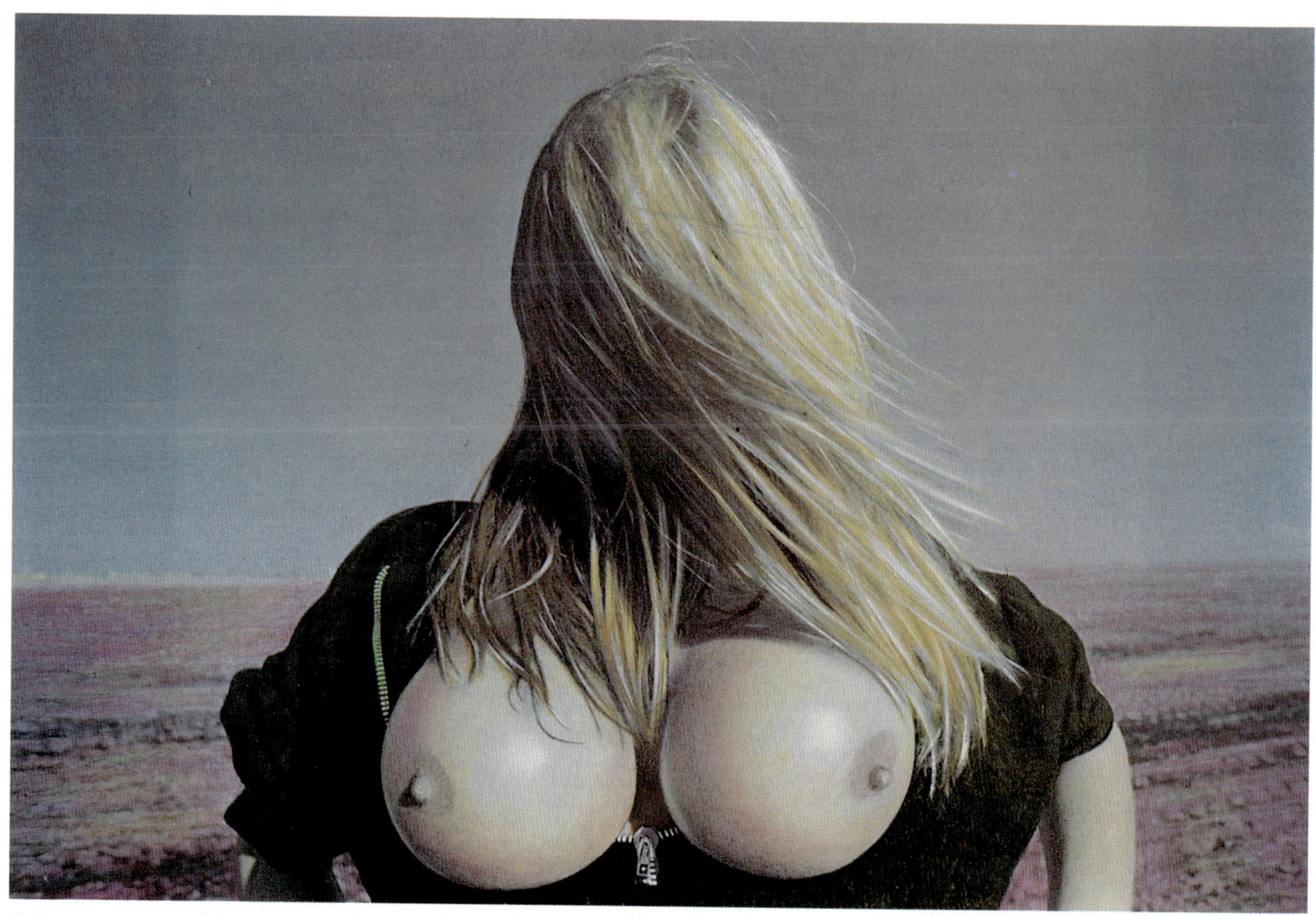

Neumonia

1973

Montaje óptico

28 x 20 cm.

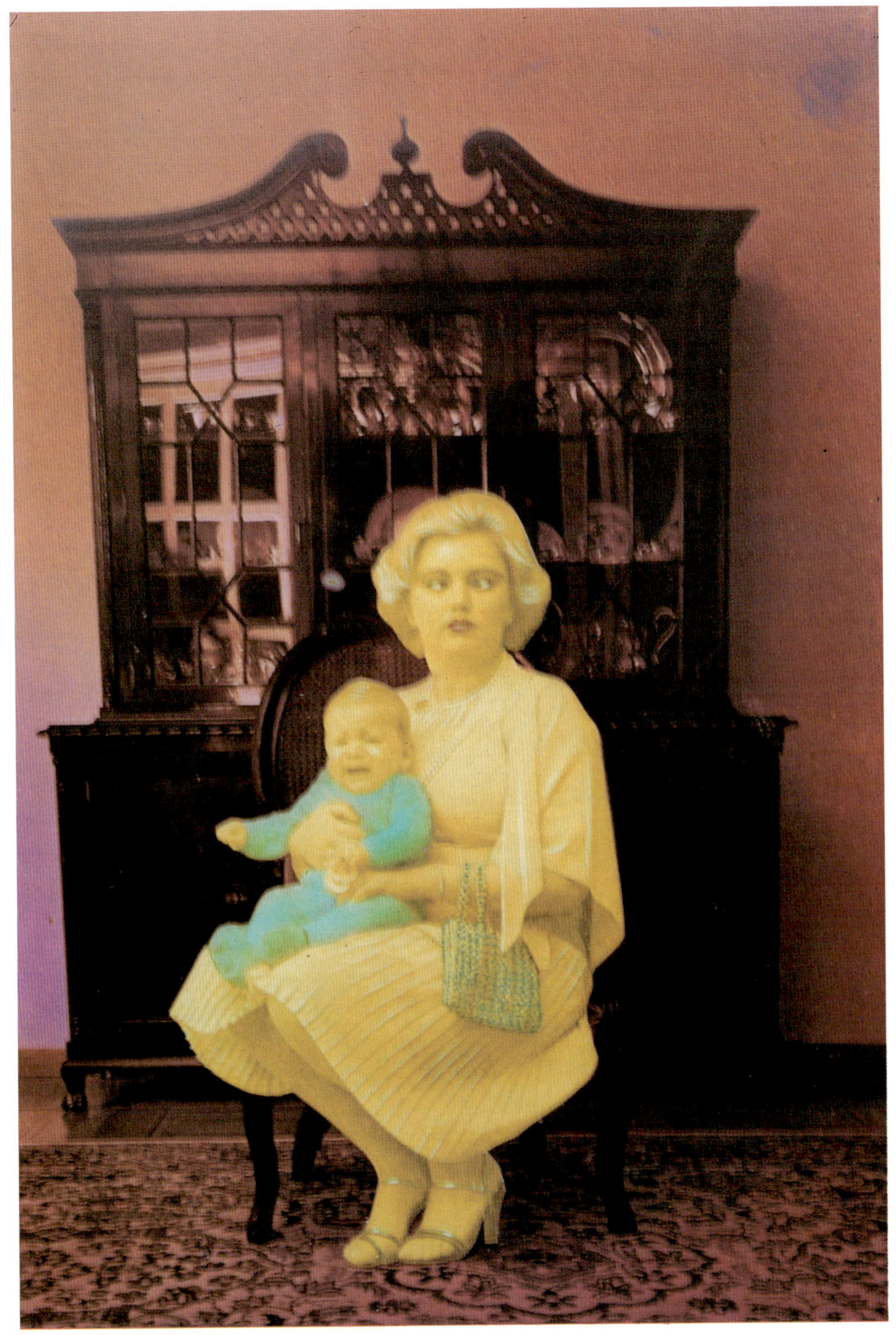

Blanbiz

1982

Montaje óptico

28 x 20 cm.

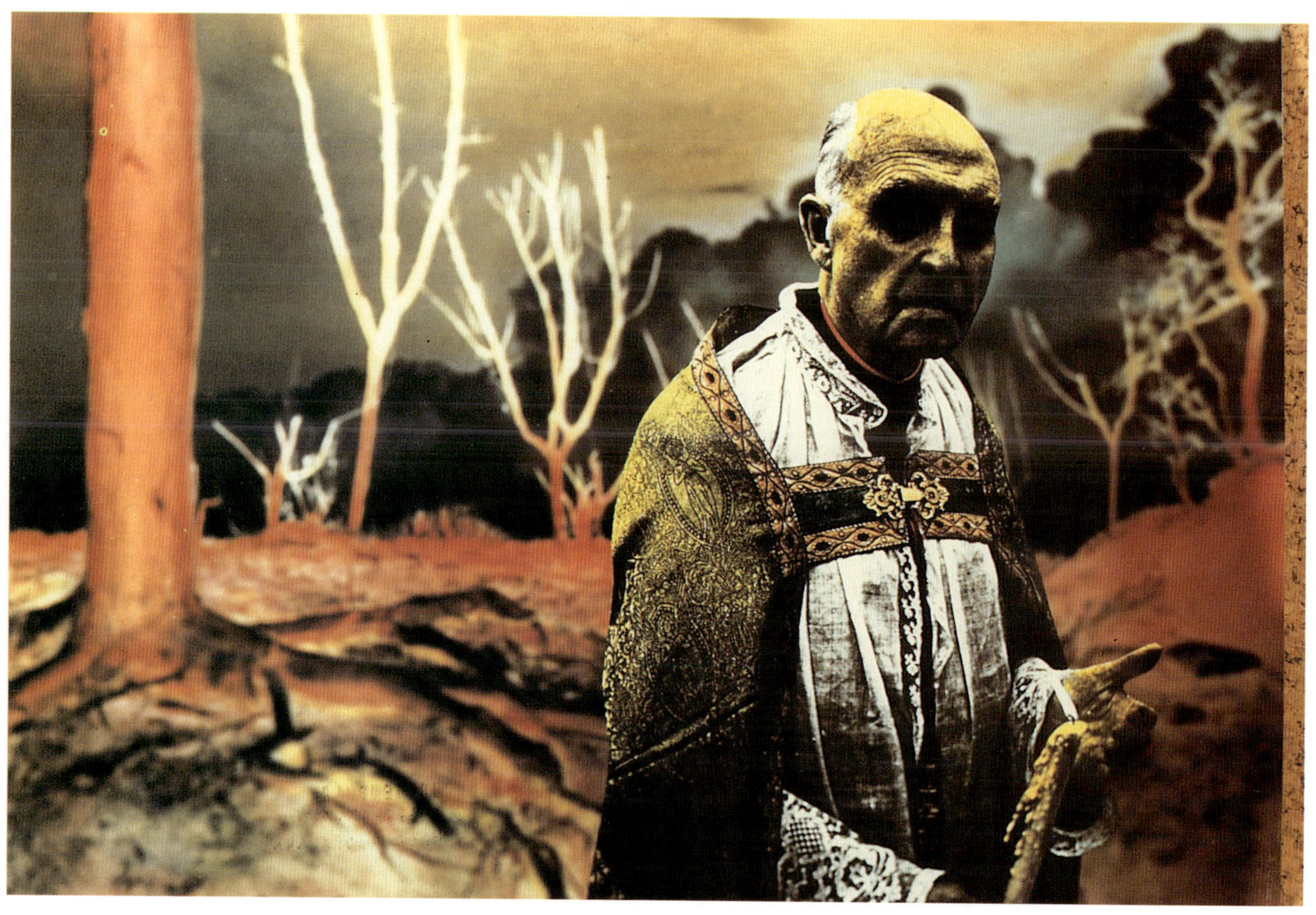

Curbosq

1974

Montaje óptico

28 x 20 cm.

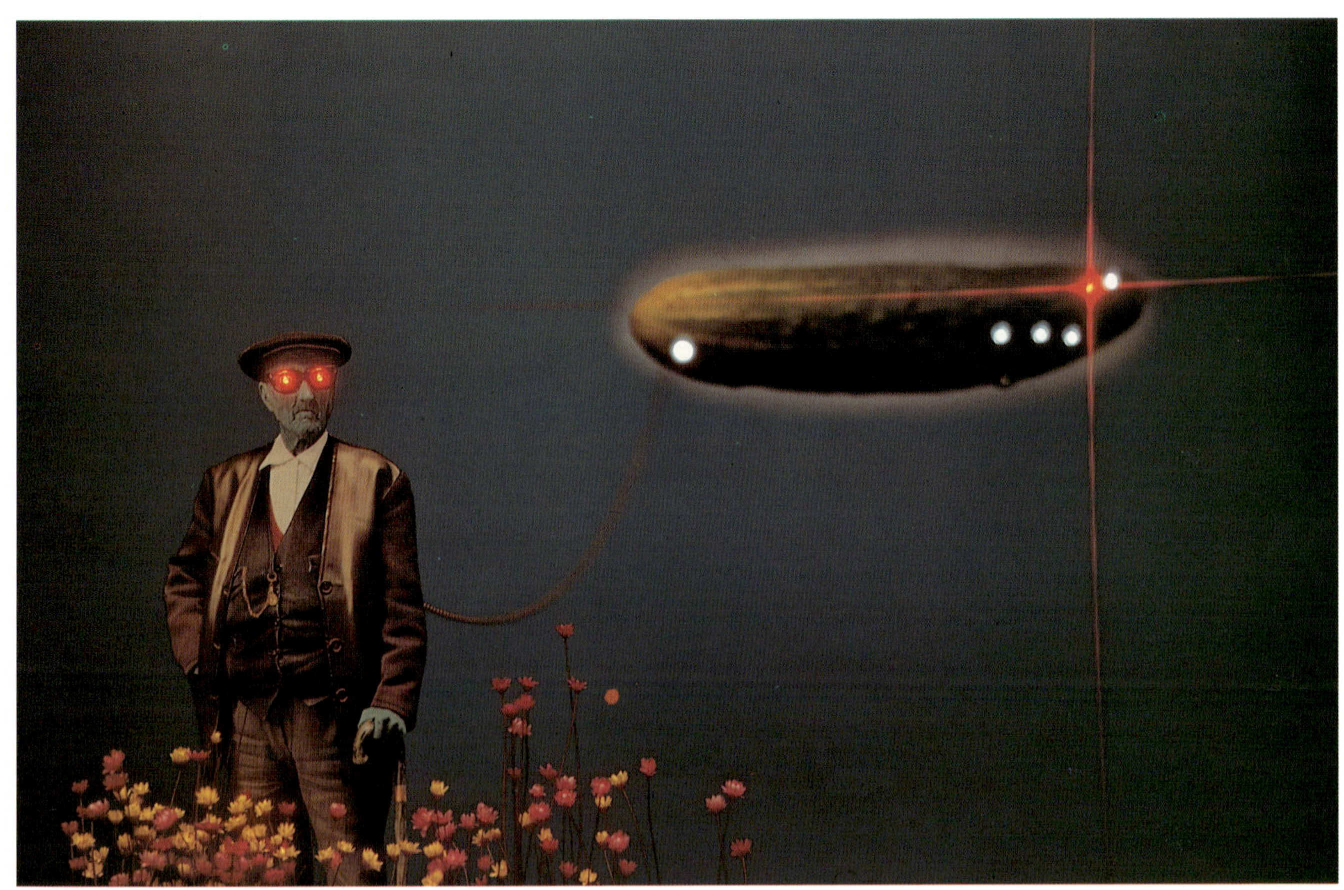

Pepino
1975
Montaje óptico
28 x 20 cm.

ALBERTO SCHOMMER

Born Vitoria, 1928 / Nació en Vitoria, 1928

Individual Exhibitions
Exposiciones individuales

1976   "La dulce violencia/Tierra fermentada.
        Galería Tambor. Madrid, España.

1977   Chateau D'Eau. Toulose, Francia.

1978   Shaday Gallery. Tokio, Japón.

1983   Visual Studies Worksop. Rochester.
        Nueva York, EE.UU.

1985   "Femento y Máscaras". Galería Juana
        Mordó. Madrid, España.

1987   "Civilizaciones". Galería Juana Mordó.
        Madrid, España.
        Museo de Arte Contemporáneo. Bilbao,
        España.
        Museo de Arte Moderno. Vitoria,
        España.
        Museo de San Telmo. San Sebastián.
        España.
        Escuela de Arquitectura. Zaragoza,
        España.

1989   "Retratos". Círculo de Bellas Artes.
        Madrid, España.

1990   "Civilizaciones". Weisbaden, Alemania.
        "Cascografía". Galería Céramo. Vitoria,
        España.
        "Retratos". Centre d'Art George

Pompidou. París, Francia.

Main Group Exhibitions
Principales Exposiciones colectivas

1958   Colectiva AFAL. Exposición itinerante.
        París, Francia.

1963   Sonimag. Barcelona, España.

1966   Fotógrafos Españoles. Colonia,
        Alemania.

1967   Expo-67. Montreal, Canadá.

1983   259 imágenes. Círculo de Bellas Artes.
        Madrid, España.

1988   Center for Creative Photography. Tucson,
        Arizona, EE.UU.

1989   Topan Collection. Museo Metropolitano
        de Tokio. Japón.

Photographs included in the exhibition
Fotografías contenidas en la exposición

1. Glacial del sonido. 1987. Cibachrome. 40 x 50 cm.
2. Corte terrestre. 1987. Cibachrome. 40 x 50 cm.
3. Formación de un planeta. 1987. Cibachrome. 40 x 50 cm.
4. Fragmentos de Cataluña. 1987. Cibachrome. 40 x 50 cm.
5. Apocalipsis. 1987. Cibachrome. 40 x 50 cm.

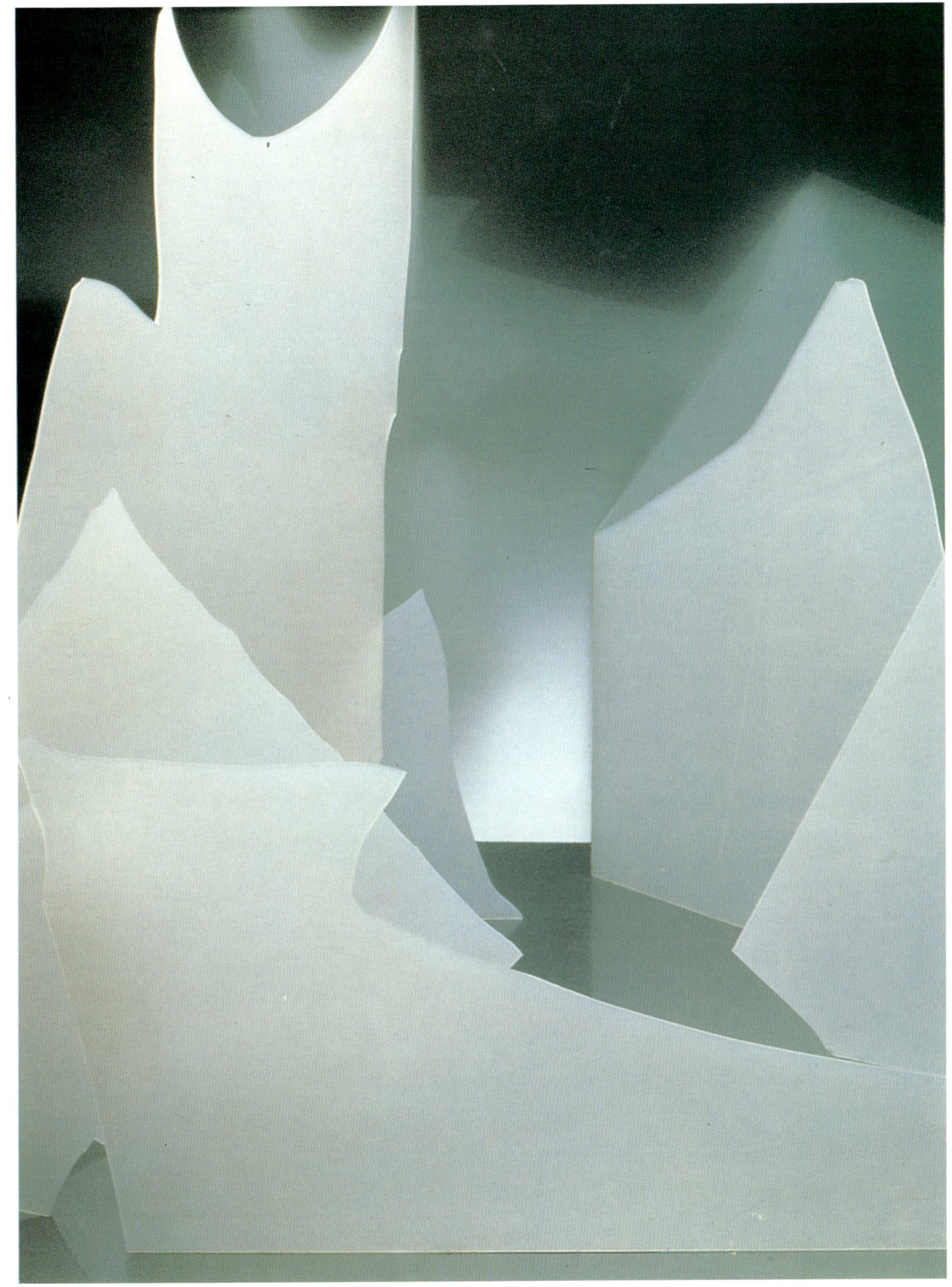

Glacial del sonido

1987

Cibachrome

40 x 50 cm.

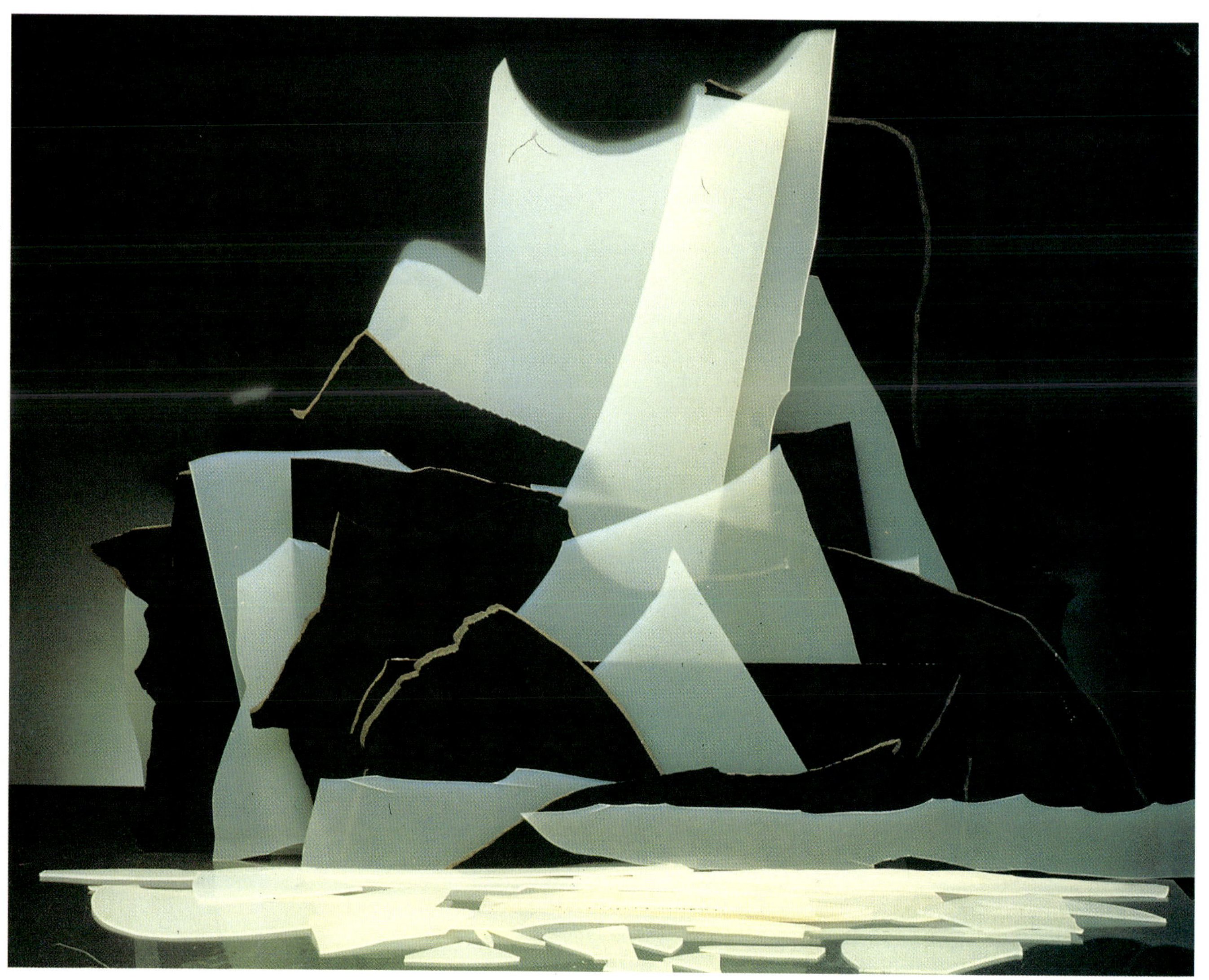

Corte terrestre

1987

Cibachrome

40 x 50 cm.

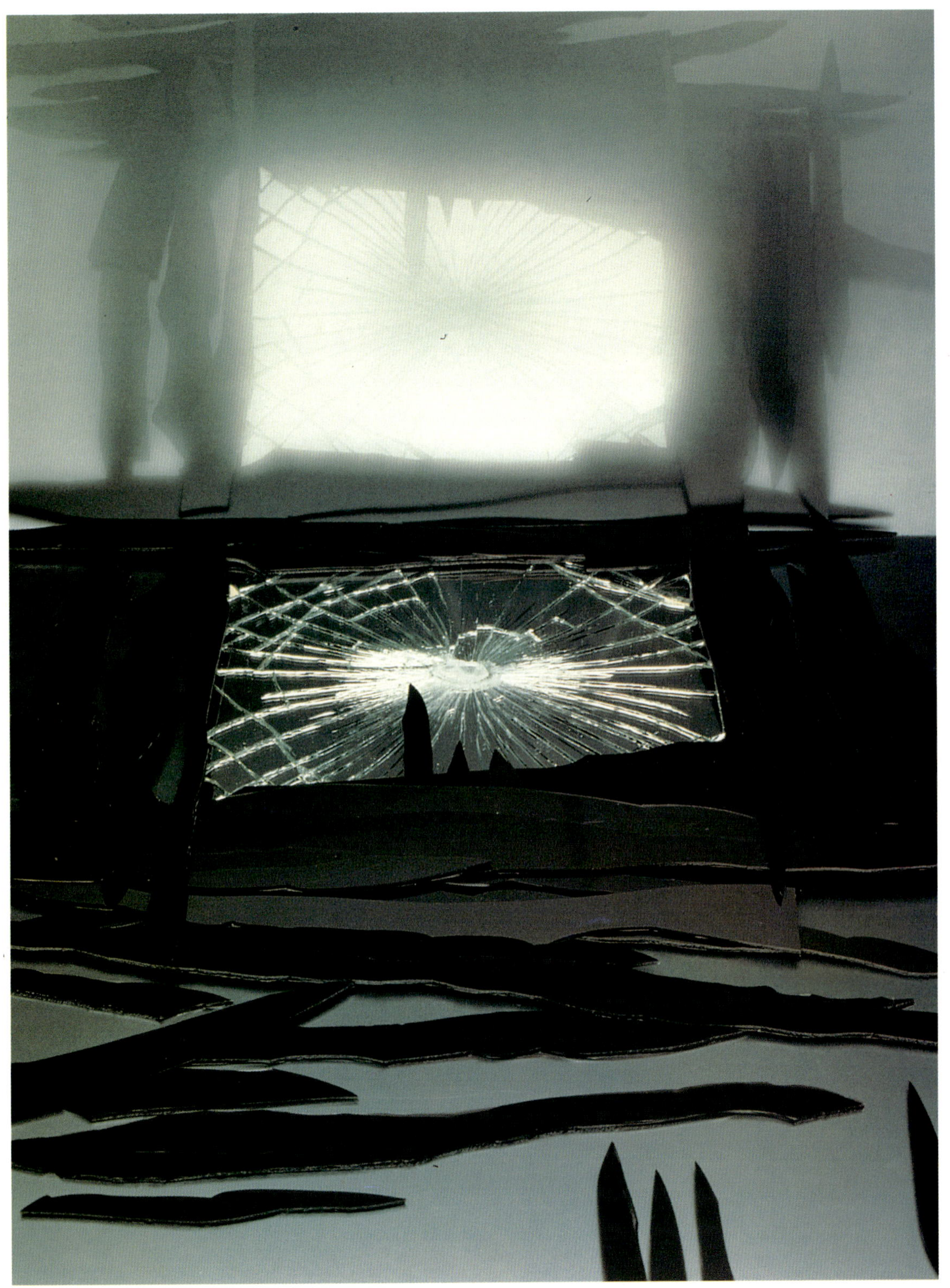

Formación de un planeta

1987

Cibachrome

40 x 50 cm.

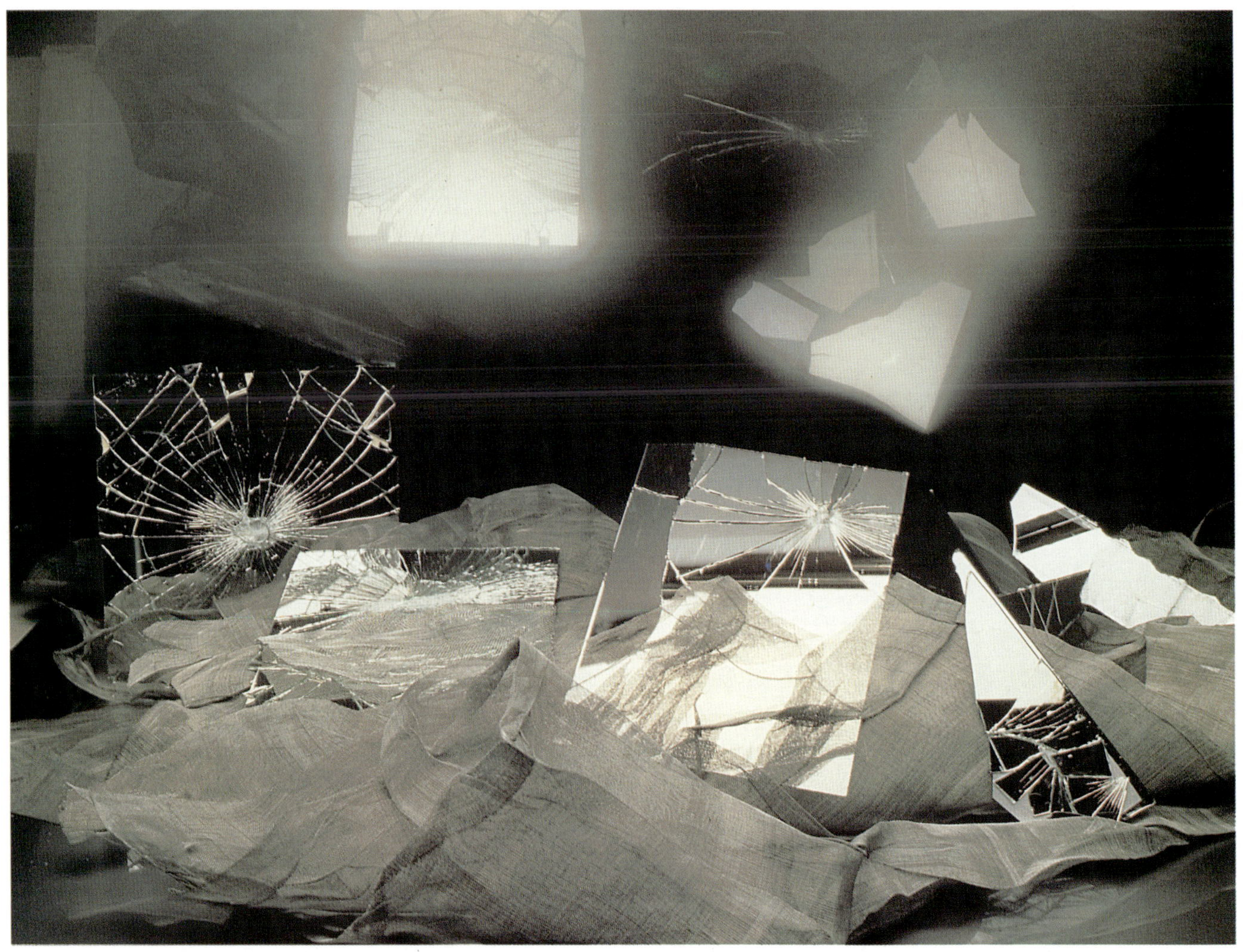

Fragmentos de Cataluña

1987

Cibachrome

40 x 50 cm.

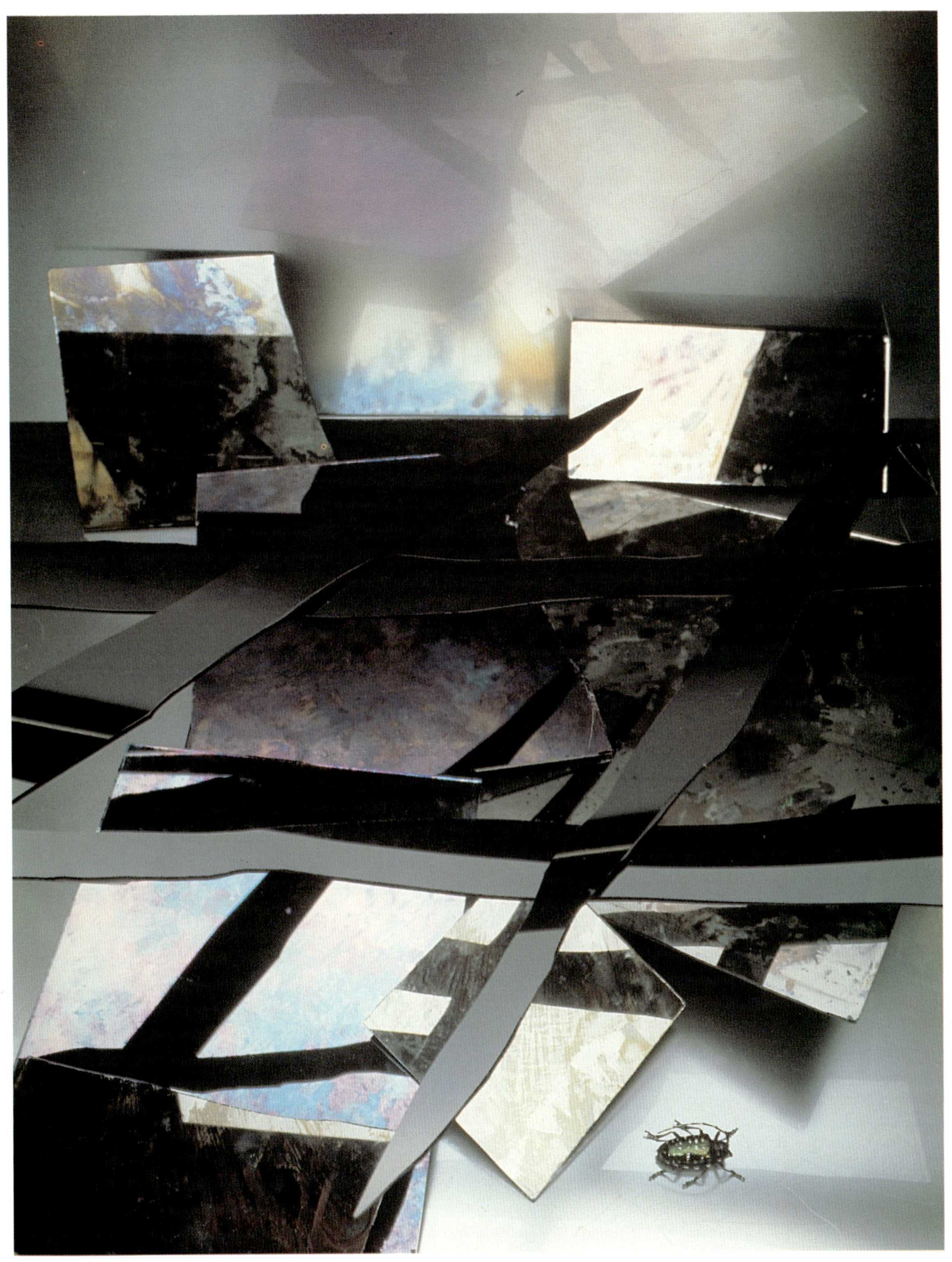

Apocalipsis

1987

Cibachrome

40 x 50 cm.

NESTOR TORRENS

Born Tenerife, 1954 / Nació en Tenerife, 1954

Individual Exhibitions
Exposiciones individuales

1982   "Salinas". Centro de Arte Ossuna, La
        Laguna. Tenerife, España.
        Galería El Aljibe. Lanzarote, España.
1986   "A cielo abierto". Edificio de Usos
        Múltiples. Consejería de Cultura del
        Gobierno de Canarias. Las Palmas,
        España.
1989   "Interiores-Exteriores". Círculo de Bellas
        Artes. Madrid, España.
        "Interiores-Exteriores". Círculo de Bellas
        Artes. Madrid, España.
        Sala Caja de Ahorros, La Laguna.
        Tenerife, España.
        Sala dos Peiraos. Concellería Cultural
        Concello de Vigo, España.

Main Group Exhibitions
Principales Exposiciones colectivas

1983- 1986 Colectiva del Colegio de Arquitectos de

Canarias. Sta. Cruz de Tenerife, España.
"La reinveció del paisatge". Fundació
Caixa de Barcelona. Barcelona, España.
"20 años de fotografía española".
Museo Contini. Marsella, Francia.
1989   "Tres fotógrafos". Galería Radach
        Novaro. Las Palmas, España.

Photographs included in the exhibition
Fotografías contenidas en la exposición

1. Sin título. s.f. Cibachrome. 31 x 41 cm.
2. Sin título. s.f. Cibachrome. 36 x 51 cm.
3. Sin título. s.f. Cibachrome. 30 x 40 cm.
4. Sin título. s.f. Cibachrome. 28 x 38 cm.
5. Sin título. s.f. Cibachrome. 37 x 51 cm.

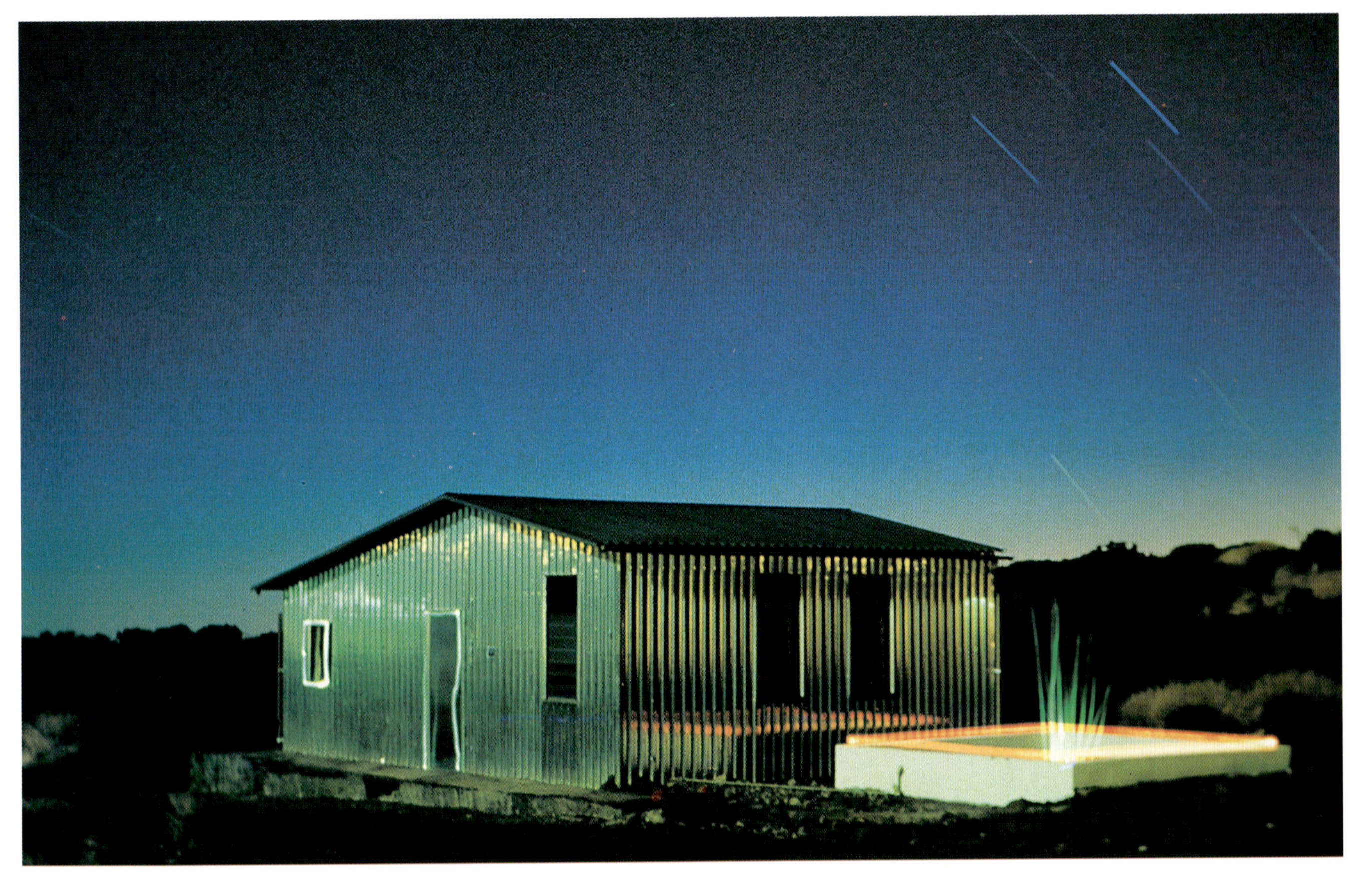

Sin título

Cibachrome

31 x 41 cm.

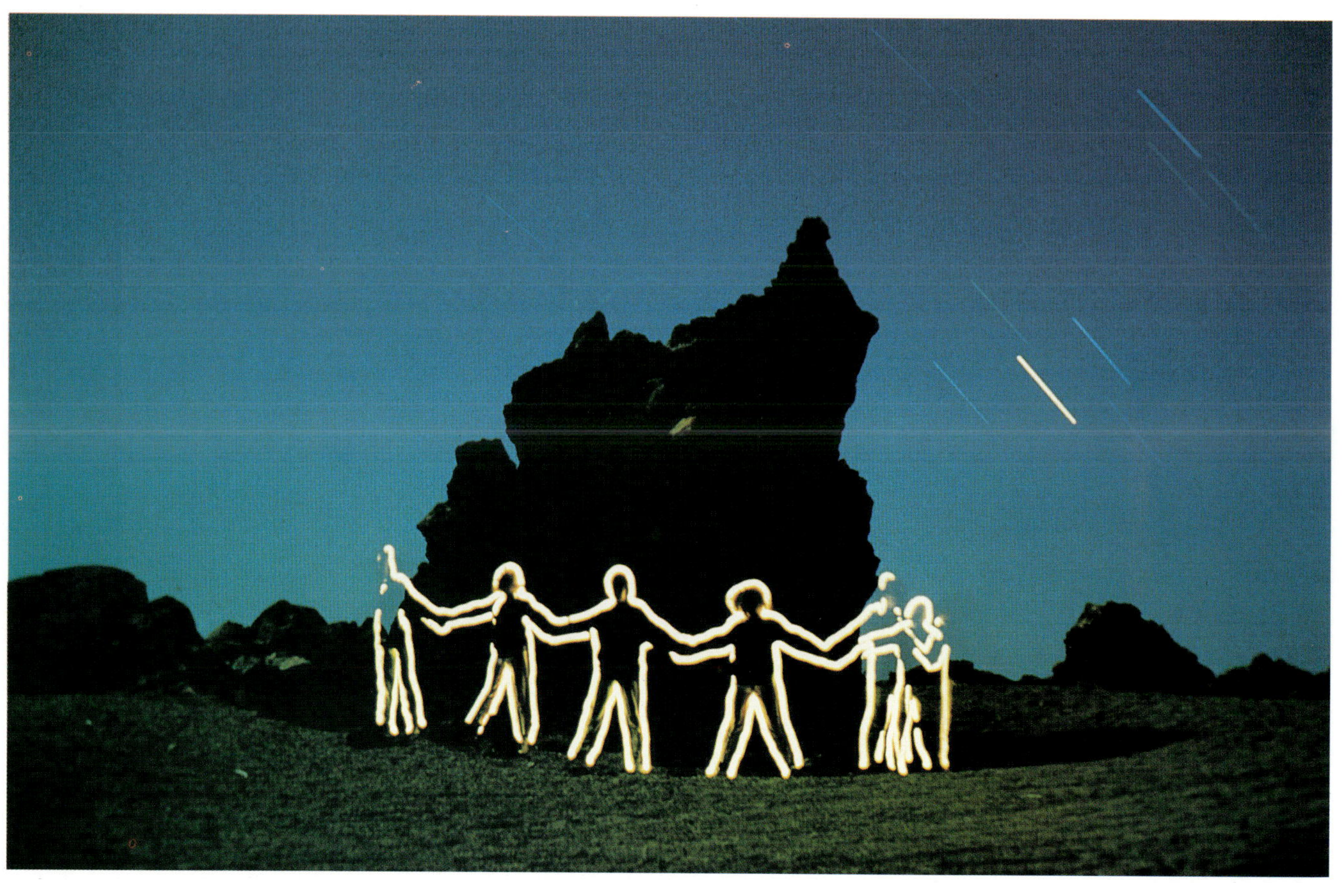

Sin título

Cibachrome

36 x 51 cm.

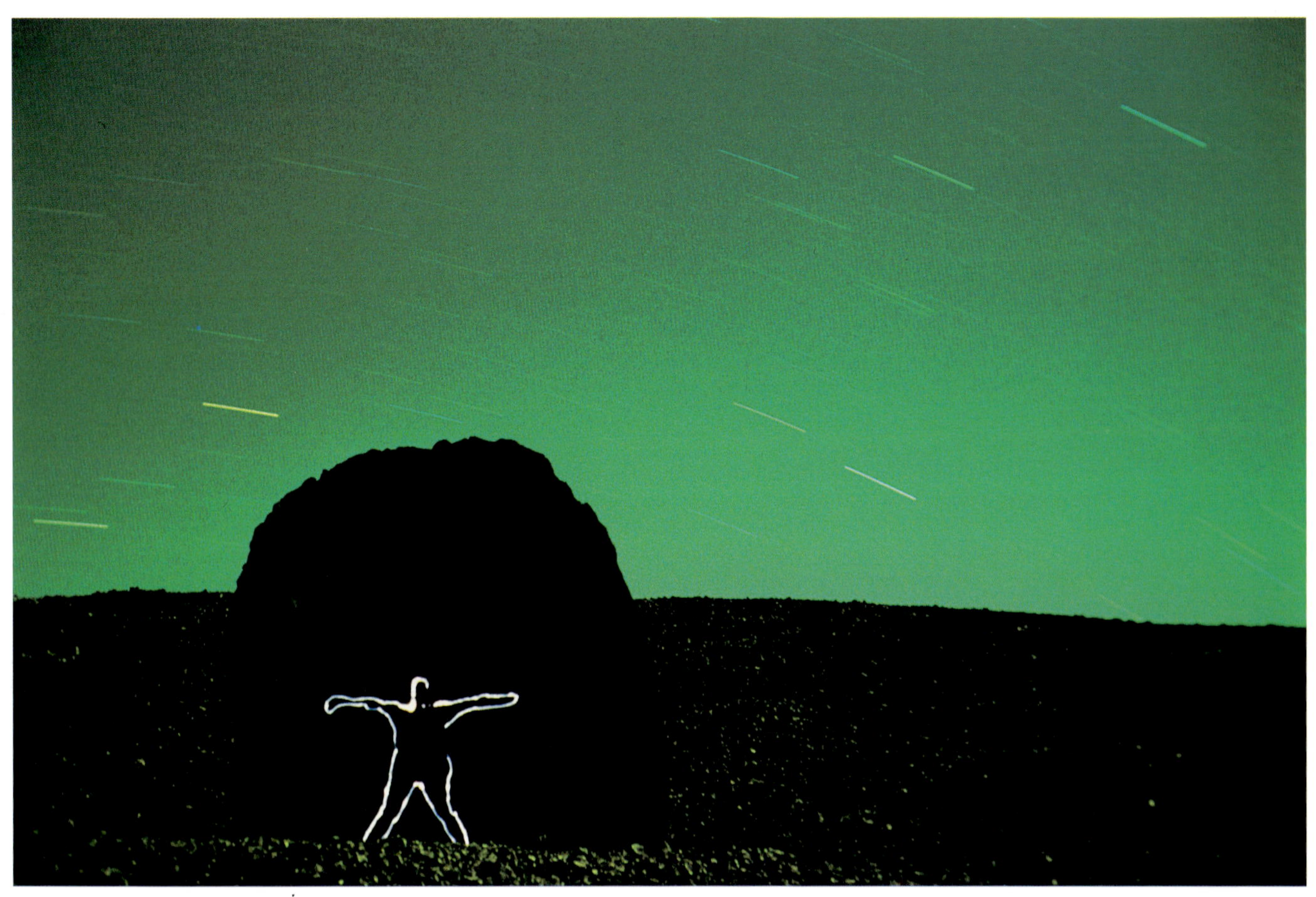

Sin título

Cibachrome

30 x 40 cm.

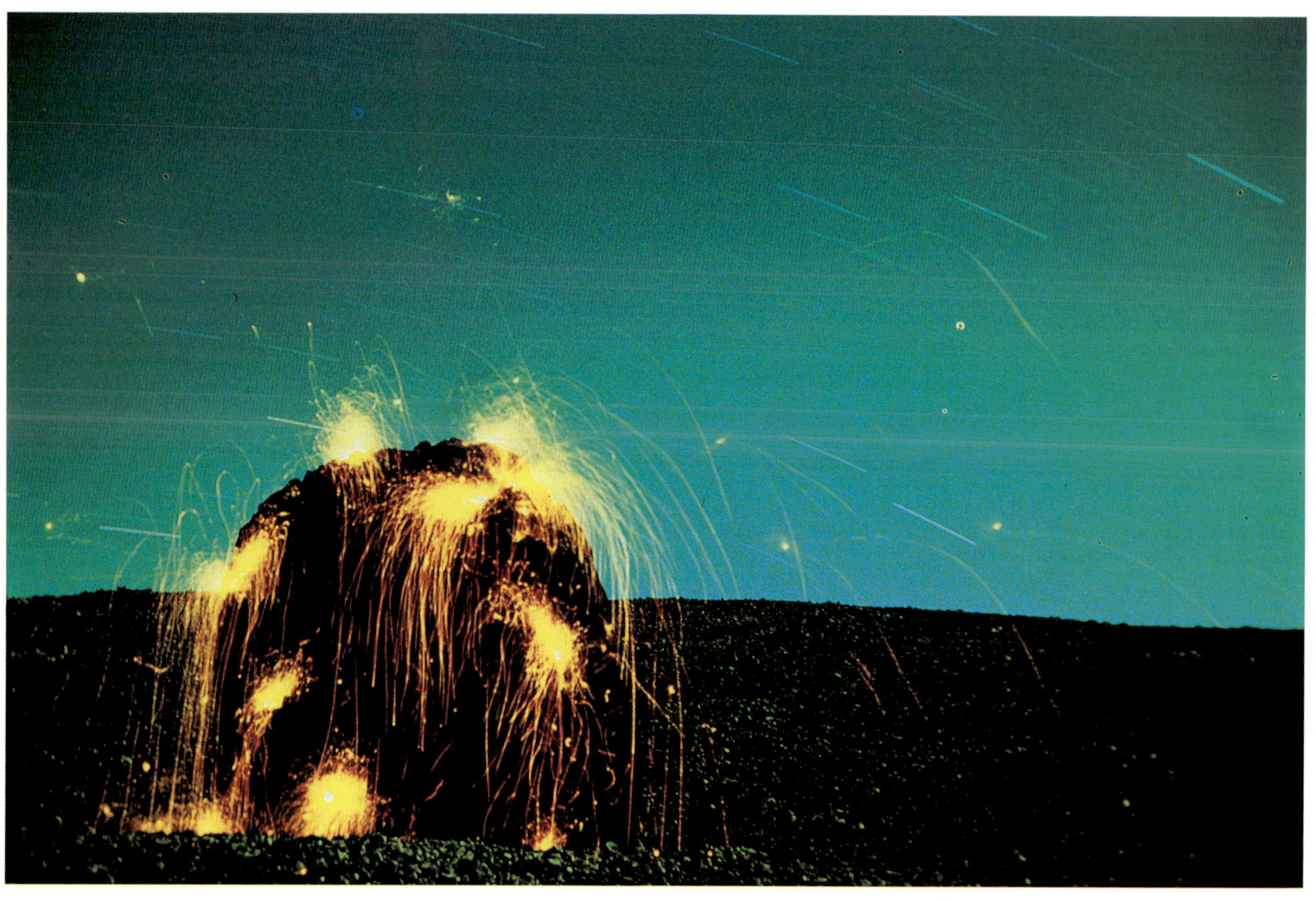

Sin título

Cibachrome

28 x 38 cm.

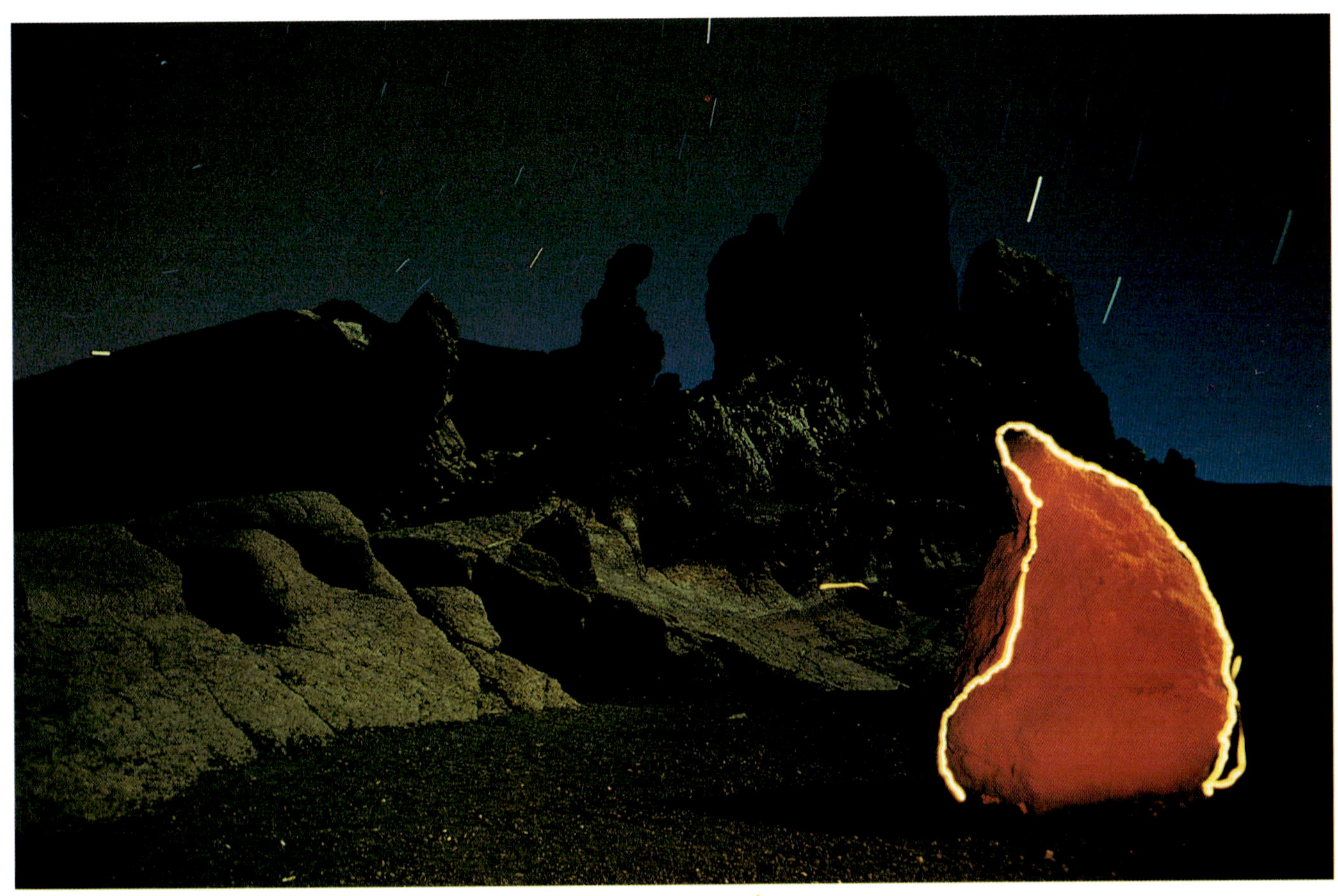

Sin título

s.f.

Cibachrome

37 x 51 cm.

RAFAEL VARGAS

Born Barcelona, 1959 / Nació en Barcelona, 1959

Individual Exhibitions
Exposiciones individuales

1985   "La nit". Foto Bar Ultimatum. Barcelona,
        España.
1986   Retrats. Fotogalería Railowsky. Valencia,
        España.
1987   Retrats. Sala Clixé. Aula de Cultura de
        Bellvitge. España.
1989   Bienal de Córdoba. Palacio de Viana.
        Córdoba, España.
1990   Fotografías. Sala Minerva de Fotografía.
        Círculo de Bellas Artes. Madrid, España.

Main Group Exhibitions
Principales Exposiciones colectivas

1986   Colectiva Aula 4. Galería Contraluz.
        Barcelona, España.
        Galería La Lune Vague. Toulouse, Francia.
1987   "Jove Fotógrafs". Sala Montcada. Caixa

de Pensiones. Barcelona, España.
"Echos d'Espagne". Burdeos, Francia.
"Fotografía Jove Catalana". Galería
Sotta. Venecia, Italia.

1988   "Fotografía Contemporánea Española".
        Milán, Italia.
        "Creatión Photographique en Espagne".
        Musée Cantini. Marsella, Francia.
1989   "Jóvenes Fotógrafos". Sala Amadís.
        Madrid, España.
1990   I Muestra Internacional de Fotografía.
        Salamanca, España.

Photographs included in the exhibition
Fotografías contenidas en la exposición

1. Esperanza Abad. s.f. 40 x 50 cm. B/N.
2. César Magdaleno. s.f. 40 x 50 cm. B/N.
3. Ricardo del Fresno. s.f. 40 x 50 cm. B/N.
4. José Antonio. s.f. 40 x 50 cm. B/N.
5. Canca. s.f. 40 x 50 cm. B/N.

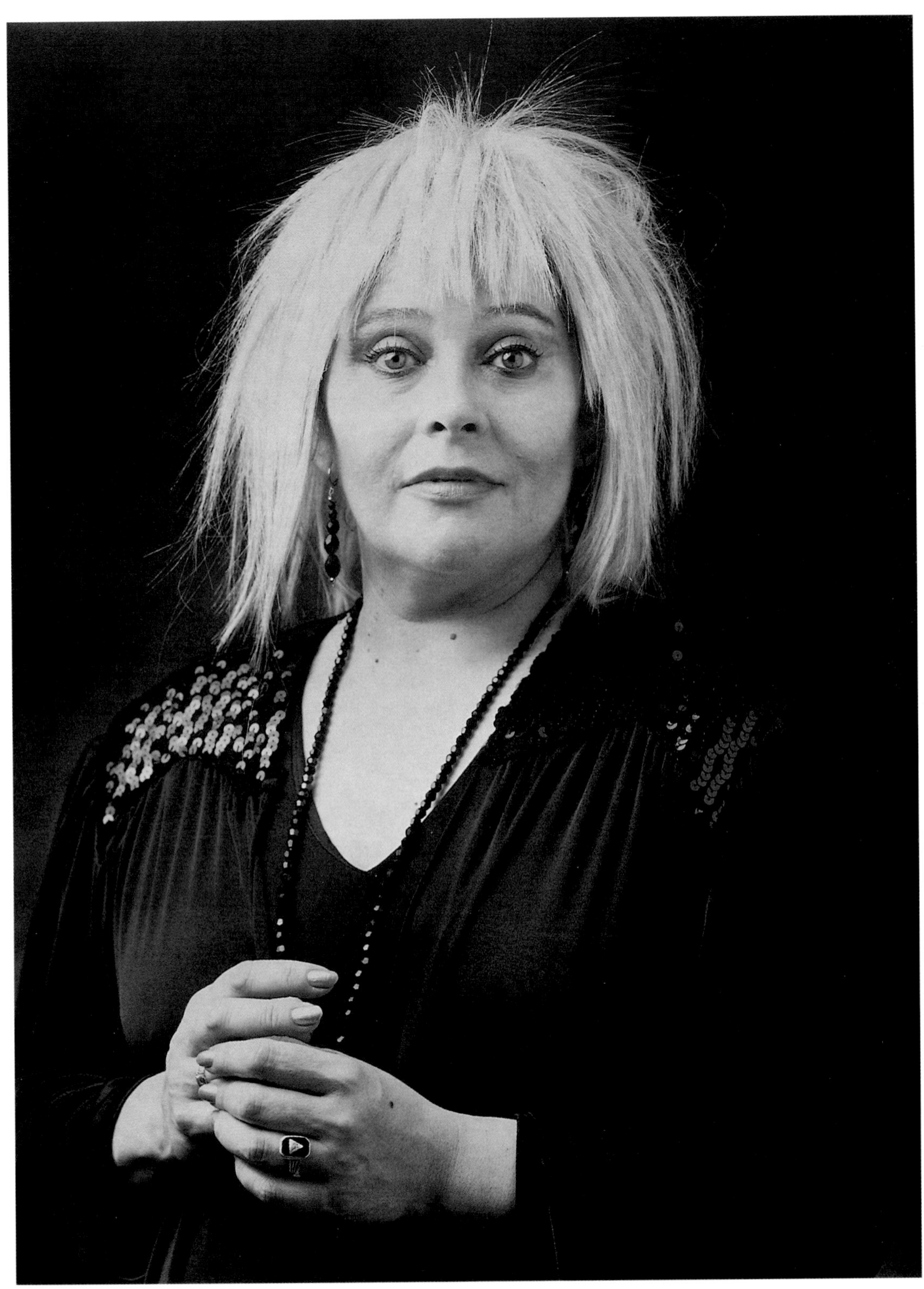

Esperanza Abad
s.f.
40 x 50 cm.

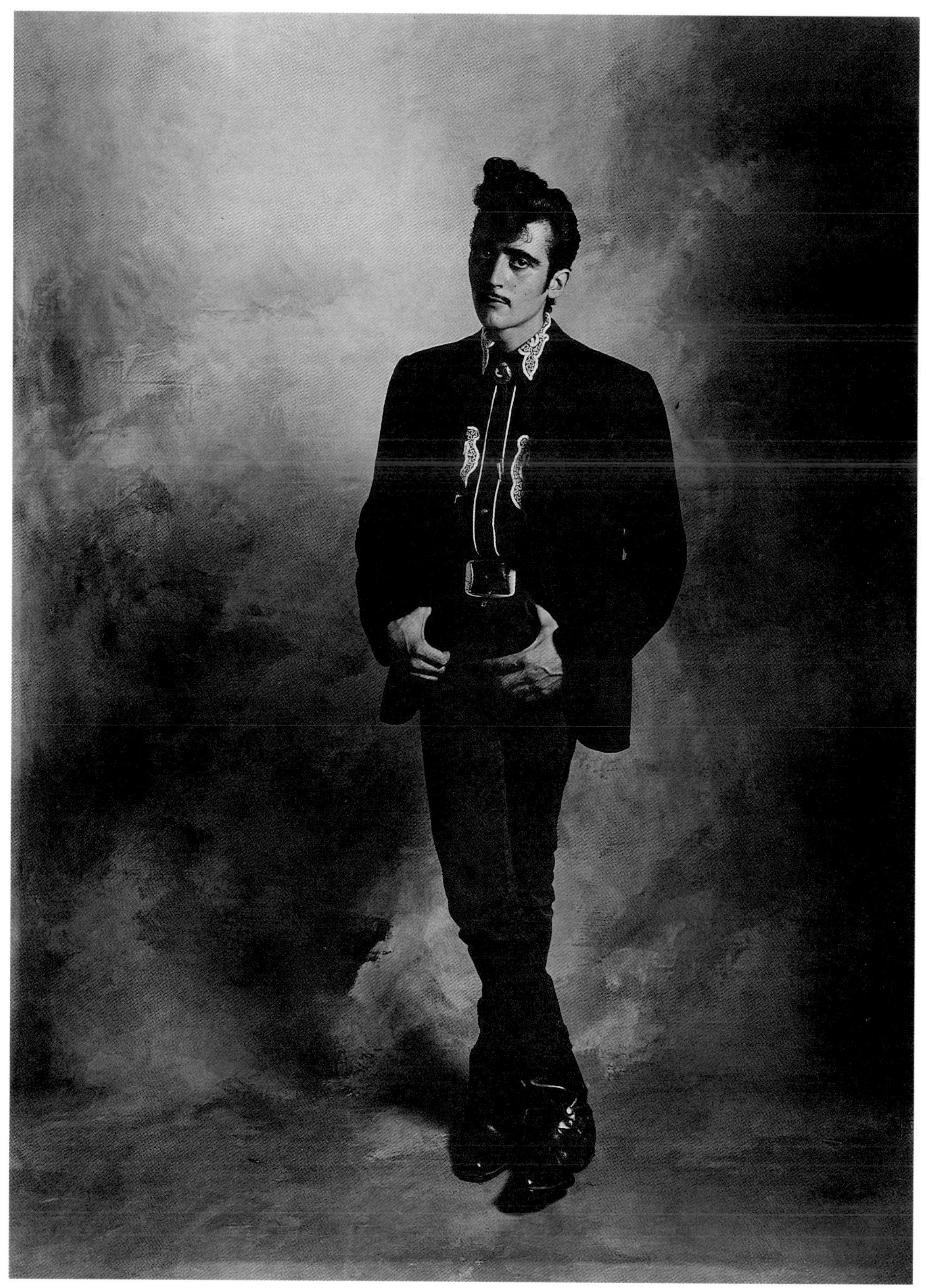

César Magdaleno
s.f.
40 x 50 cm.

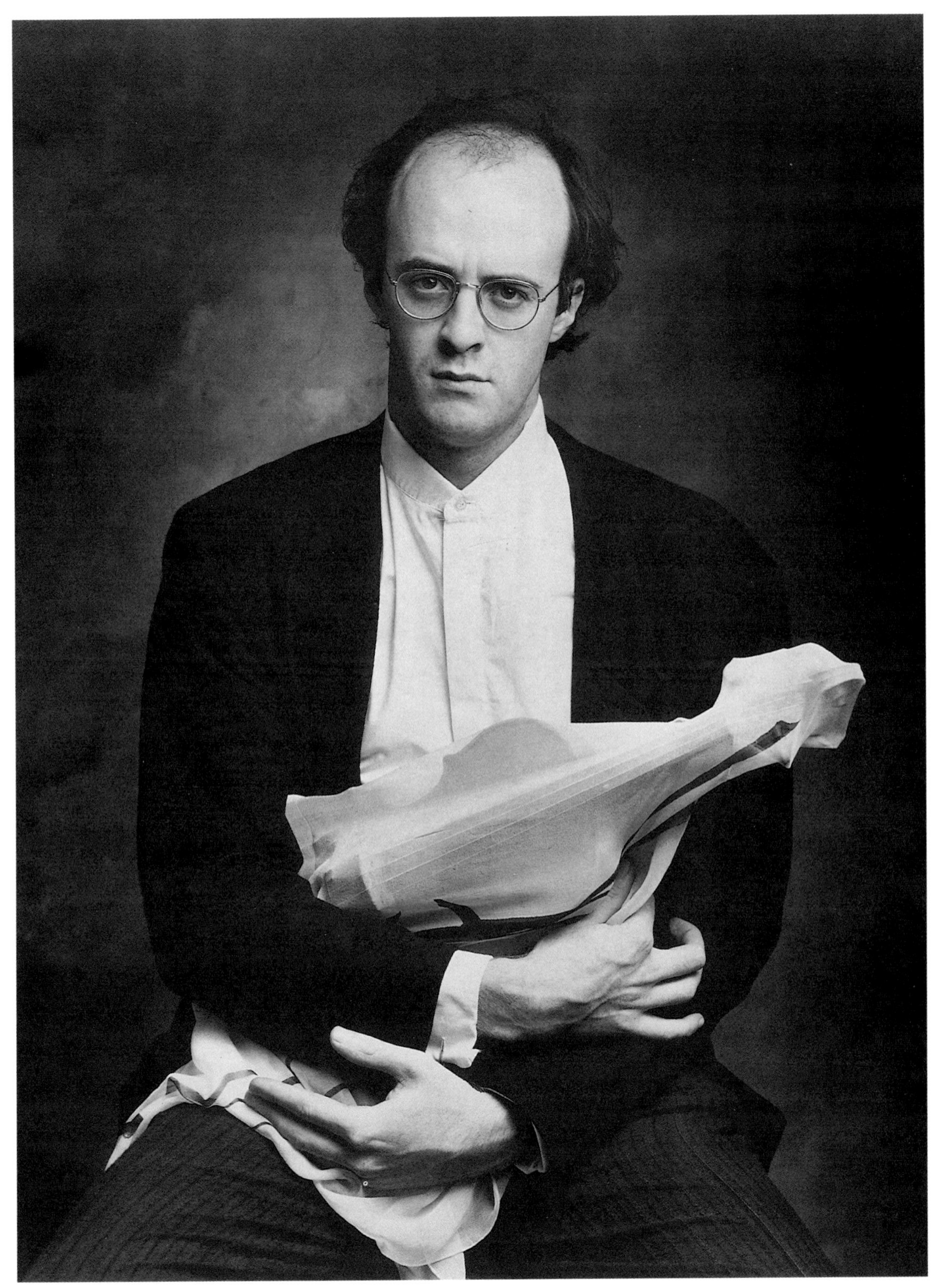

Ricardo del Fresno
s.f.
40 x 50 cm.

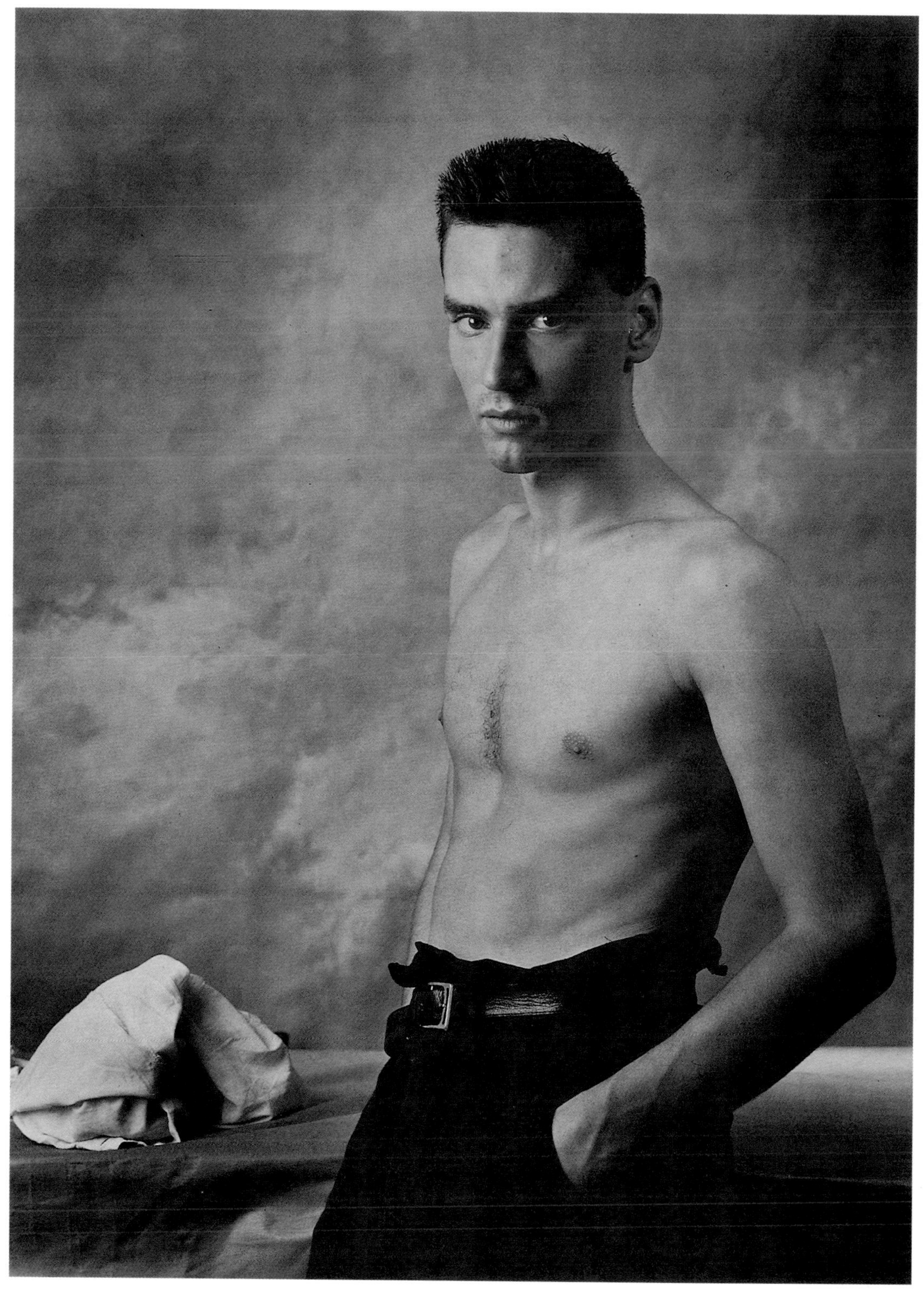

José Antonio
s.f.
40 x 50 cm.

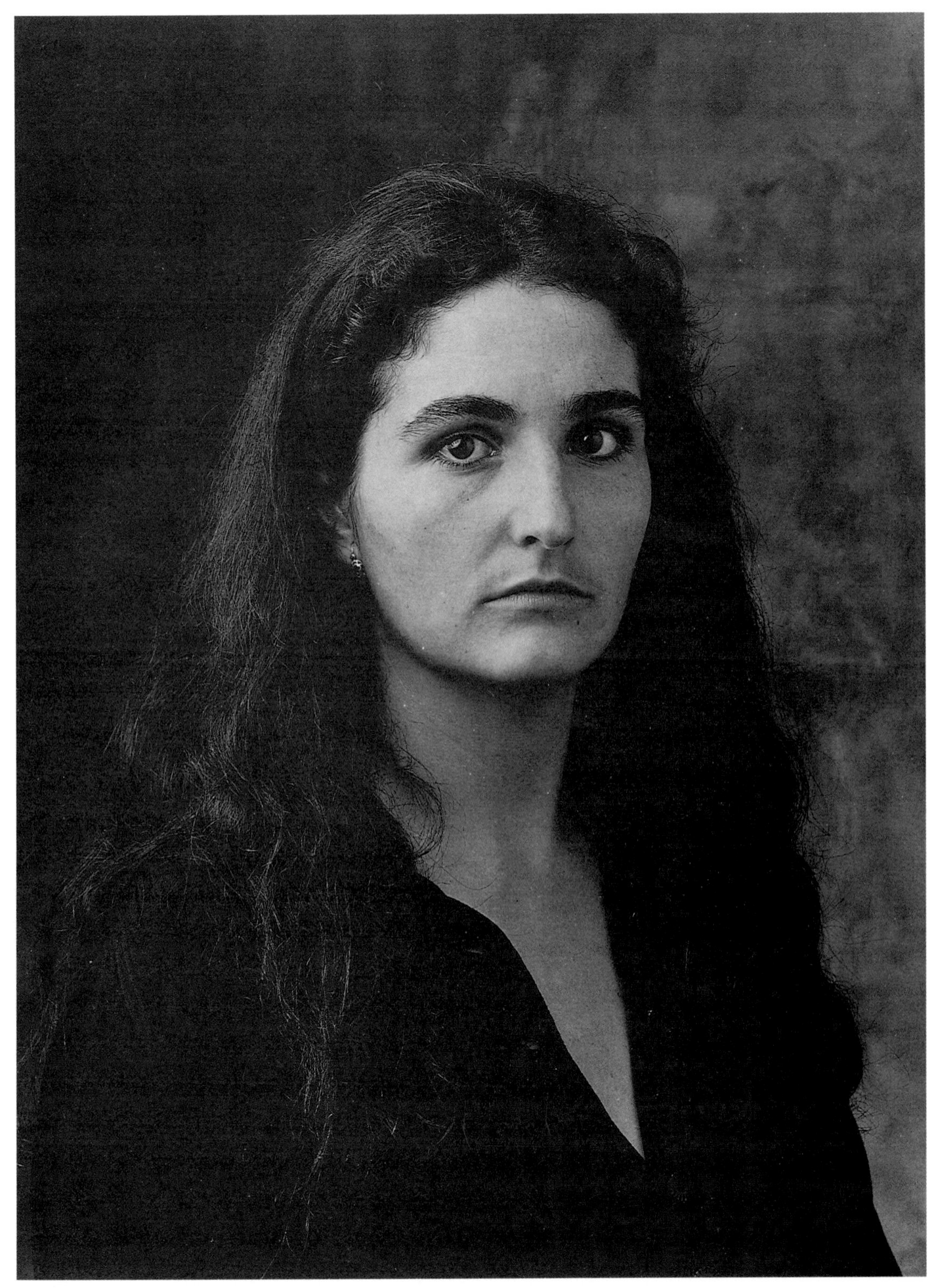

Canca

s.f.

40 x 50 cm.

GERARDO VIELBA

Born Madrid, 1921 / Nació en Madrid, 1921

Individual Exhibitions
Exposiciones individuales

1961 Real Sociedad fotográfica. Madrid,
    España.

Group Exhibitions
Exposiciones colectivas

1953 Salón Nacional de Fotografía Artística.
    Círculo de Bellas Artes. Madrid, España.
1959 V Salón Nacional de Fotografía Artística.
    Real Sociedad Fotográfica. Madrid,
    España.
1960 XI Salón Fotográfico del Mar.
    Agrupación Fotográfica Almeriense
    (AFAL). Almería, España.
    I Gran Concurso Internacional Perutz.
    Galerías Preciados. Madrid, España.
1961 Noir et blanc. Casino Biarritz, Francia.
1962 Premio de Bellas Artes. Biblioteca
    Nacional. Madrid, España.
    V Mostra Internazzionales de Fotografía.
    Círculo Fotográfico "La Góndola".
    Venecia, Italia.
1963 II Salon Europeen d'Art Photographique.
    Estrasburgo, Francia.
    "Alegría de vivir". Photokina 63.
    Colonia, Alemania.
1964 Europea Foto 64. Hamburgo, Alemania.
    V Bienal de la Fotografía Española.
    Sabadell, Barcelona, España.
1966 I Concurso Internacional de Fotografía.
    Guadalajara, España.
1968 14 Fotógrafos Españoles. Sala Carreño.
    Madrid, España.
1970 Antológica de la Real Sociedad
    fotográfica. Madrid, España.

1974 Fotomuestra S.F.L. de Lérida. Lérida,
    España.
1975 "El retrato de Fotografía". Instituto de
    Cultura Hispánica. Madrid, España.
1976 I Muestra de la fotografía española.
    Galería Multitud. Madrid, España.
1980 Semana de la fotografía española.
    Guadalajara, España.
1981 I Jornadas universitarias de fotografía.
    Colegio Mayor Elías Ahuja. Madrid,
    España.
1983 Humanizar la tierra. Banco de Bilbao.
    Madrid, España.
1985 La escuela de Madrid. Semana
    Internacional de la fotografía.
    Guadalajara, España.
1986 Historia de la fotografía española
    contemporánea. Sevilla, España.
1987 "Echos d'Espagne". Troisienne
    Quinzainee Internationales de
    photographie. Merignac, Francia.
1988 Fotógrafos de la Escuela de Madrid.
    Museo Español de Arte Contemporáneo.
    Madrid, España.
    La fotografía Spagnola dal 1950 al
    Giorni Nostri. Bari, Italia.
1989 150 Years of Photography. Nueva Delhi.
1990 Propuesta para una colección. Candas,
    Gijón, España.

Photographs included in the exhibition
Fotografías contenidas en la exposición

1. Paseo en el muelle en el atardecer. 1973. Bromuro. 20 x 30 cm.

2. Retrato en el carguero. s.f. Bromuro. 30 x 40 cm.

3. "Así de Grande". s.f. Bromuro. 30 x 40 cm.

4. Retrato en dos tiempos, Laredo. s.f. Bromuro. 28,5 x 40 cm.

5. Mañanita de María. 1990. Bromuro. 25 x 30 cm.

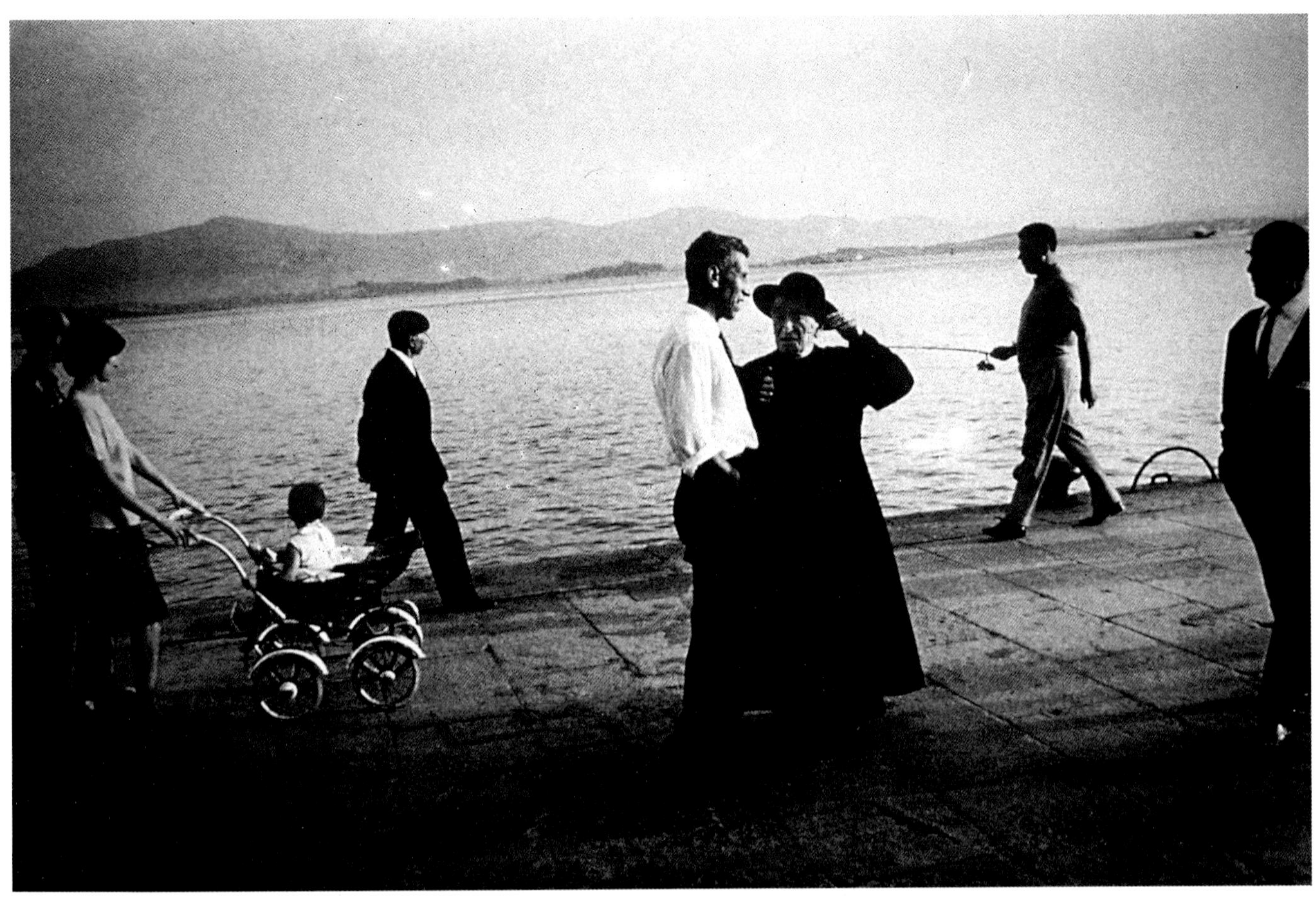

Paseo en el muelle en el atardecer

1973

Bromuro

20 x 30 cm.

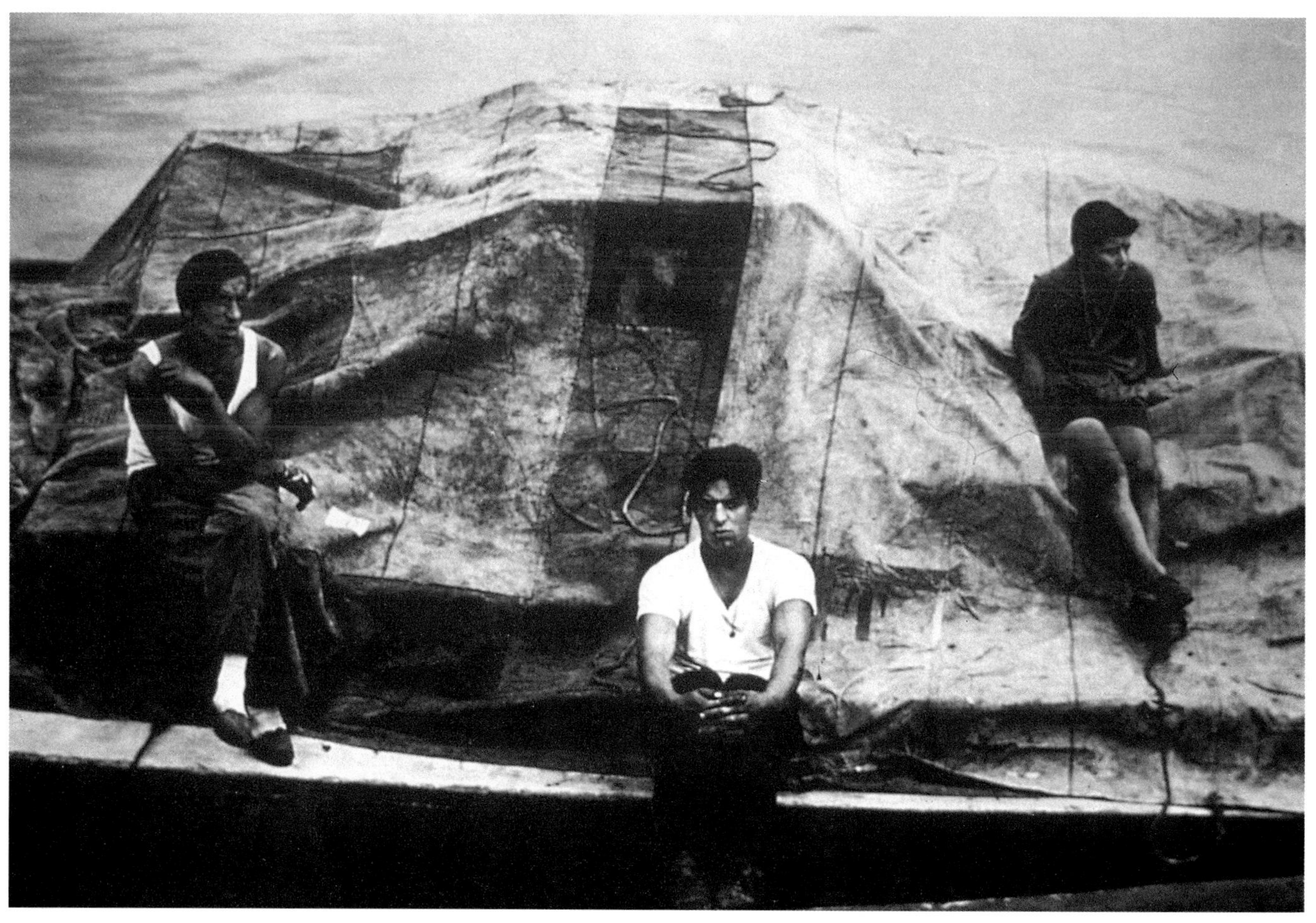

Retrato en el carguero

s.f.

Bromuro

30 x 40 cm.

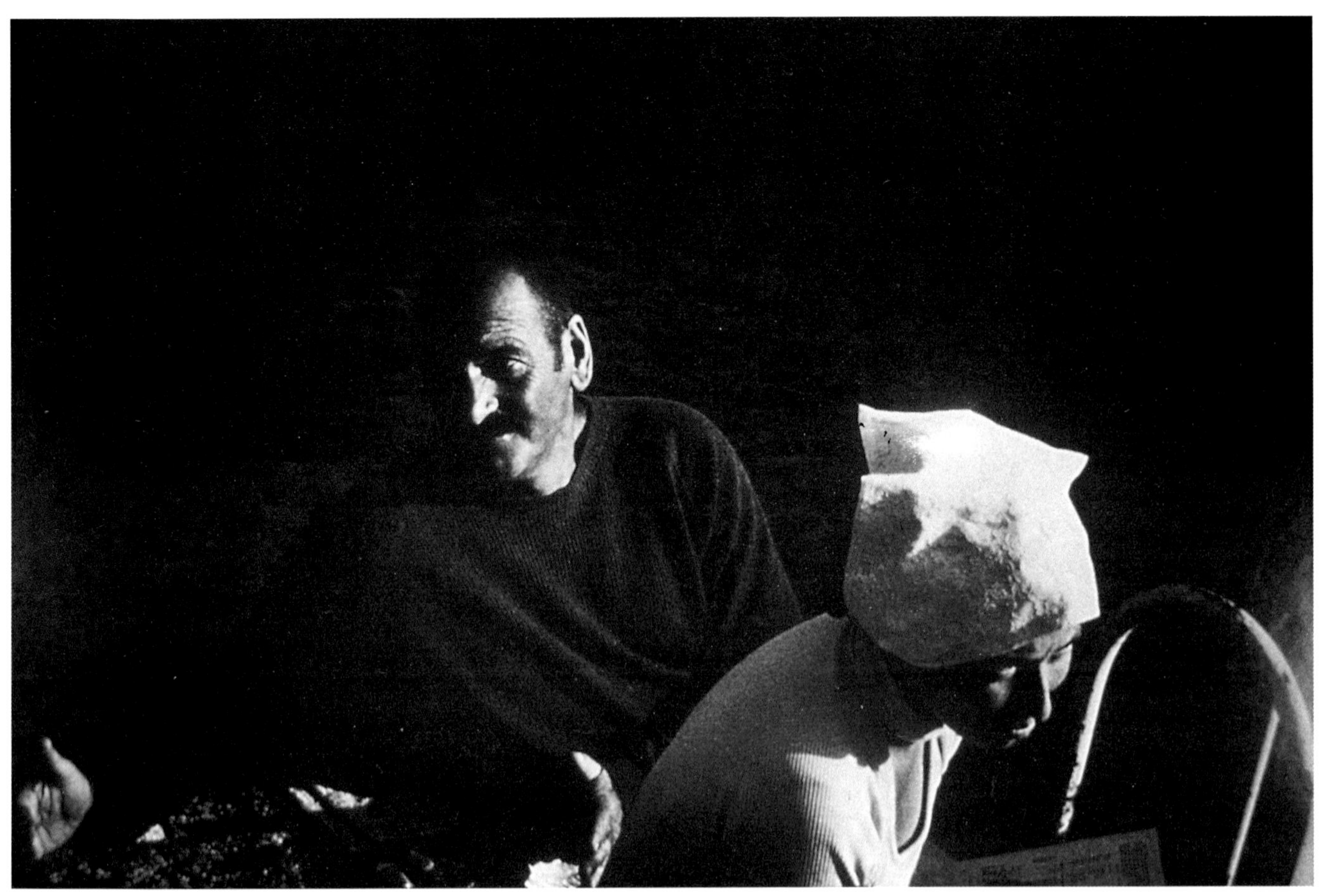

"Así de Grande"

s.f.

Bromuro

30 x 40 cm.

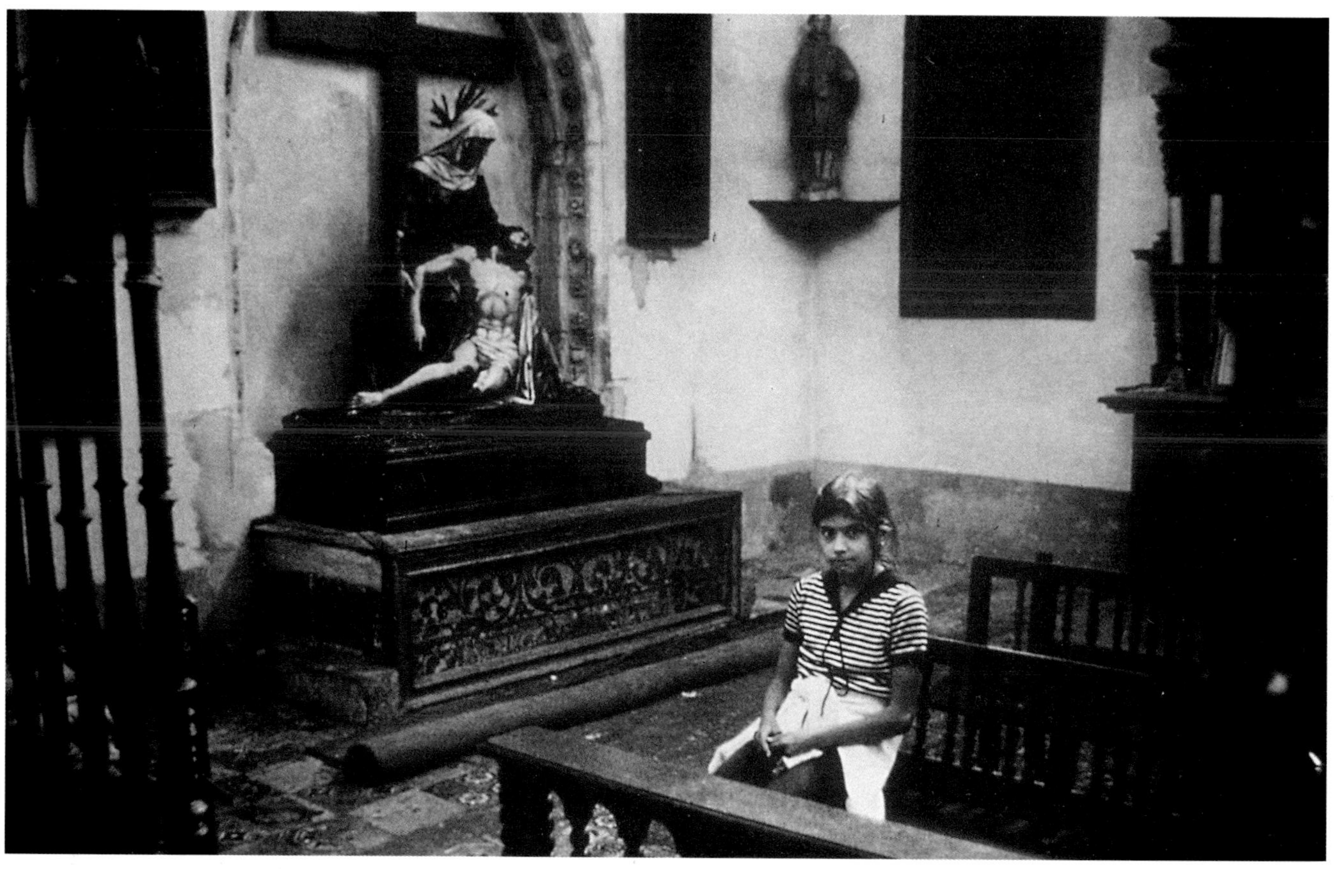

Retrato en dos tiempos, Laredo

s.f.

Bromuro

28,5 x 40 cm.

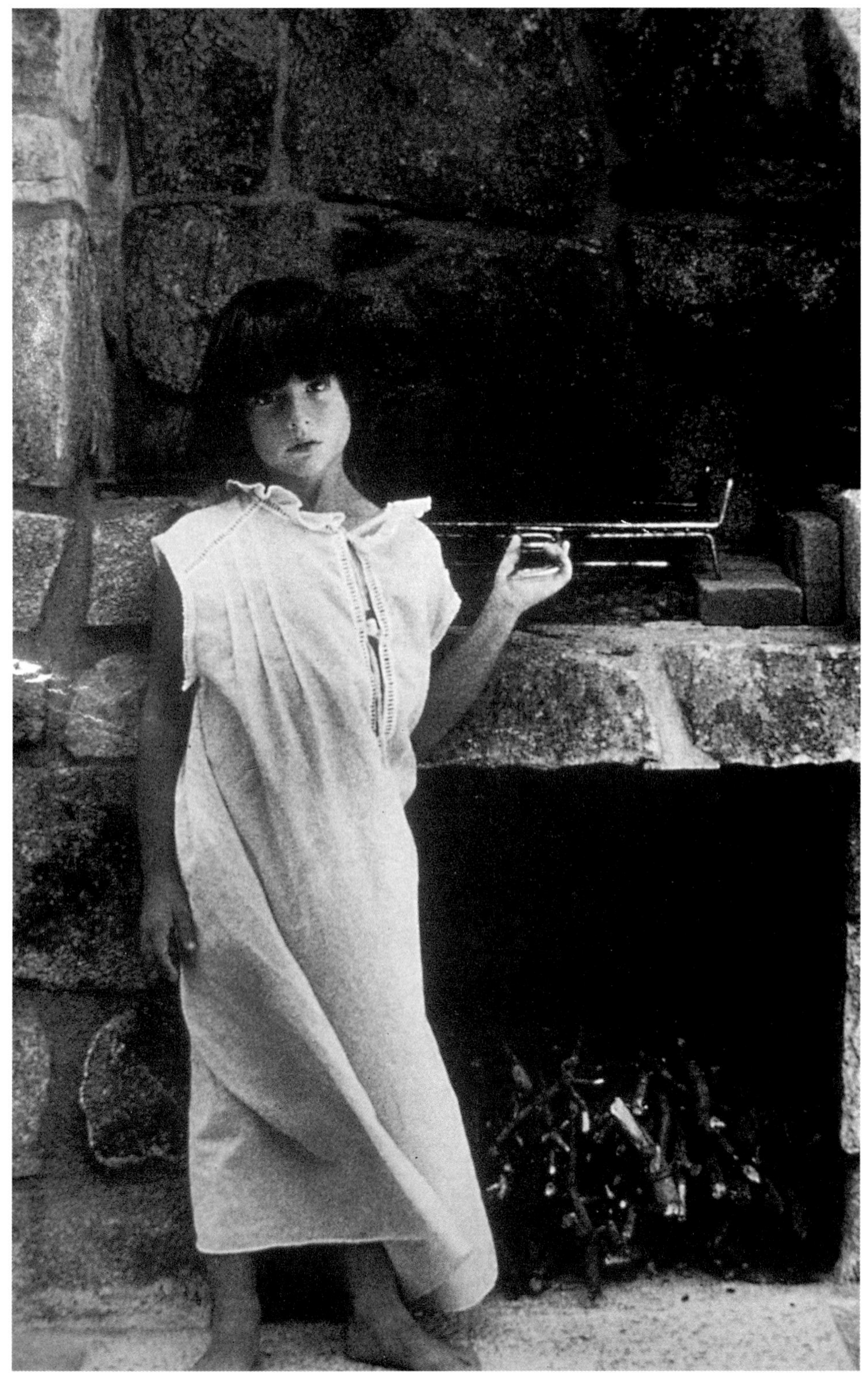

Mañanita de María

1990

Bromuro

25 x 30 cm.

MIGUEL ANGEL YAÑEZ POCO

Born Sevilla, 1940 / Nació en Sevilla, 1940

Individual Exhibitions
Exposiciones individuales

1975	Imagen 2. Sevilla, España.
1978	Museo de Arte. Palma de Mallorca, España.
	Artefiera. Bolonia, Italia.
	Galería Tau. San Celoni. Barcelona, España.
1979	Rectorado de la Universidad. Sevilla, España.
1982	Lincoln Art Centre. Denver, Colorado, EE.UU.
	Camera oscure. Denver, Colorado, EE.UU.
1987	Posada del Potro. Córdoba, Sevilla, España.
1988	Gallerie Foto-Husset. Gotemburgo, Suecia.
	Galería Vink. Valladolid, España.
1988	Caja de Ahorros. Valencia, España.
1989	Galería Hautefeuille. París, Francia.
1990	"Taurus Versus Ars". Museo Taurino. Córdoba, España.

Group Exhibitions
Exposiciones colectivas

1975	Casa del Mar. Cádiz, España.
1977	Galería Spectrum Canon. Barcelona, España.
1978	Museo de Arte Contemporáneo. Sevilla, España.
	Fotografía Fantástica a Europa i EE.UU. Fundación Joan Miró. Barcelona, España.
1979	Encuentros Fotográficos en Andalucía. Palacio de la Cónsula. Málaga, España.
1981	13 Fotógrafos Españoles Contemporáneos. México D.F., México.
1983	4emes Journées Internationales de la Photographie. Montpellier, Francia.
	259 Imágenes. Círculo de Bellas Artes. Madrid, España.
1984	Muestra de la Fotografía Andaluza. Utrera, España.
1985	Europalia. Bélgica.
	Fotoplín. Málaga, España.
1986	Historia de la Fotografía Española Contemporánea. Sala de Arte. Chicarreros. Sevilla, España.
1988	Creación Fotográfica en España. Musée Cantini. Marsella, Francia.

Photographs included in the exhibition
Fotografías contenidas en la exposición

1. Necrománticos de hoy. 1982. Clastotipo. 30,5 x 41 cm.
2. "Zeit und sein", retrato de Brahms. 1987. Clastotipo. 51 x 60,5 cm.
3. Trini la salerosa. 1988. Clastotipo. 30 x 40 cm.
4. La dama del velo. 1988. Clastotipo. 30,5 x 40,5.
5. La guerra, vida mía. 1983. Bromuro. 51 x 60,5 cm.

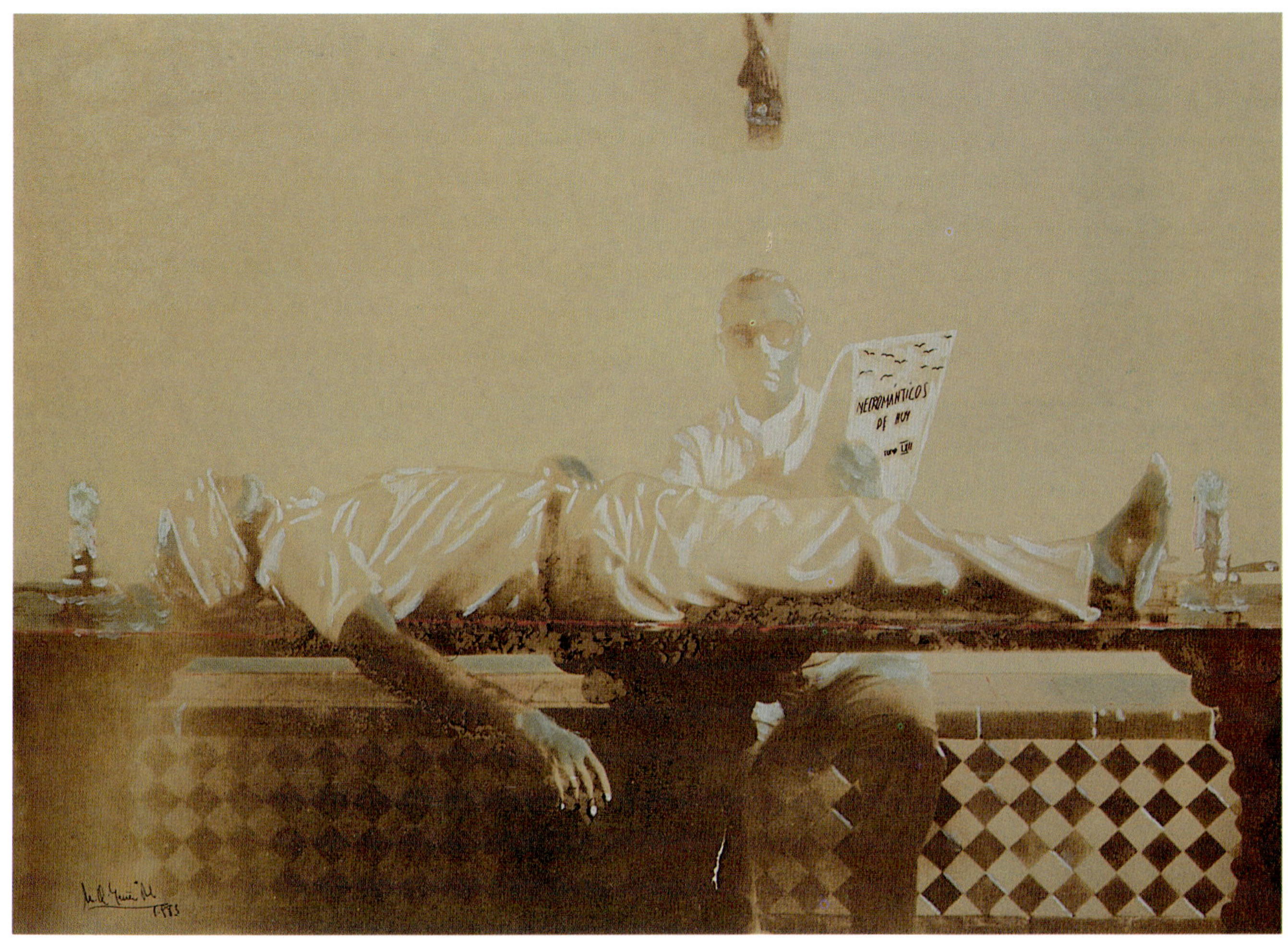

Necrománticos de hoy

1982

Clastotipo

30,5 x 41 cm.

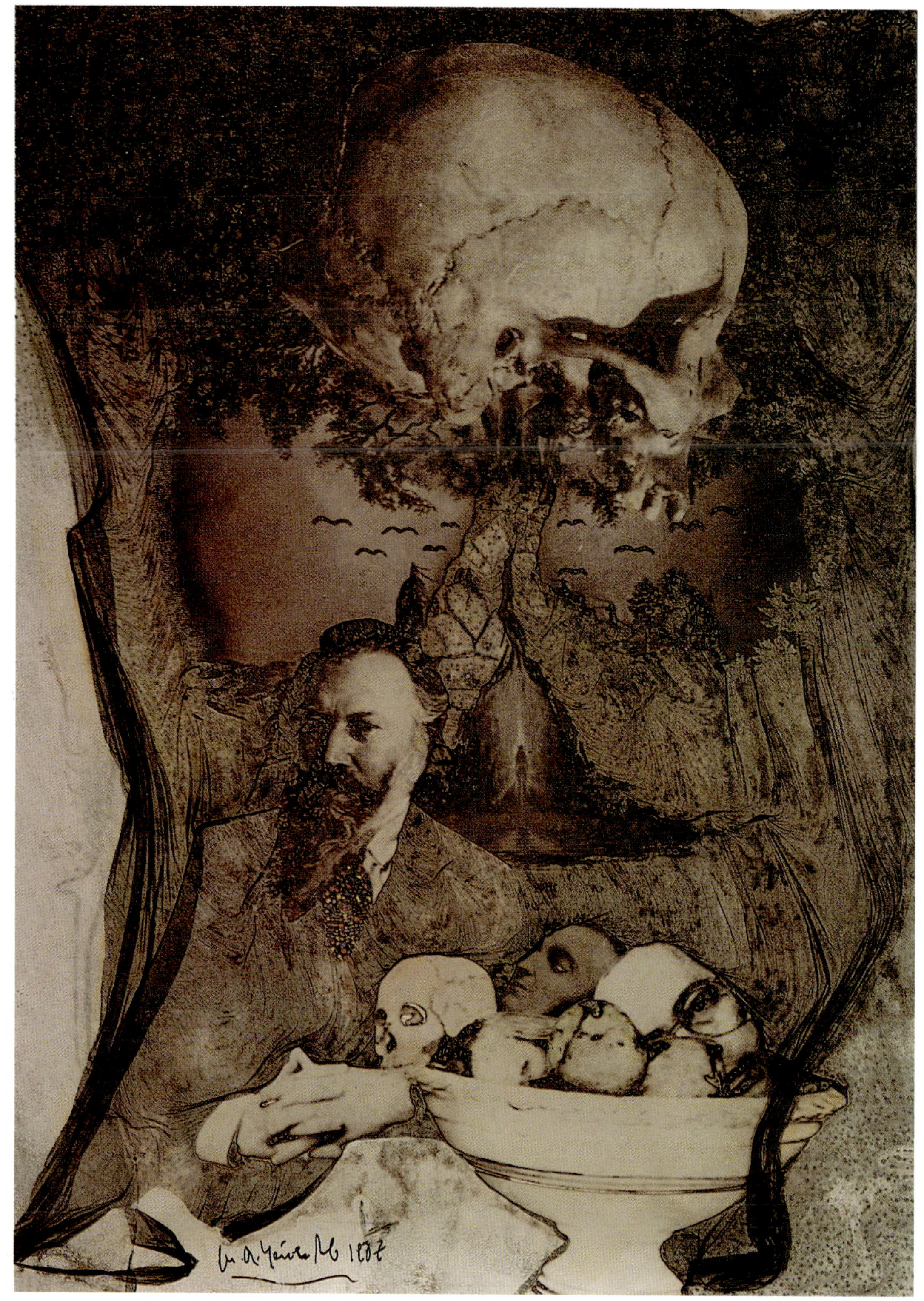

"Zeit und sein", retrato de Brahms

1987

Clastotipo

51 x 60,5 cm.

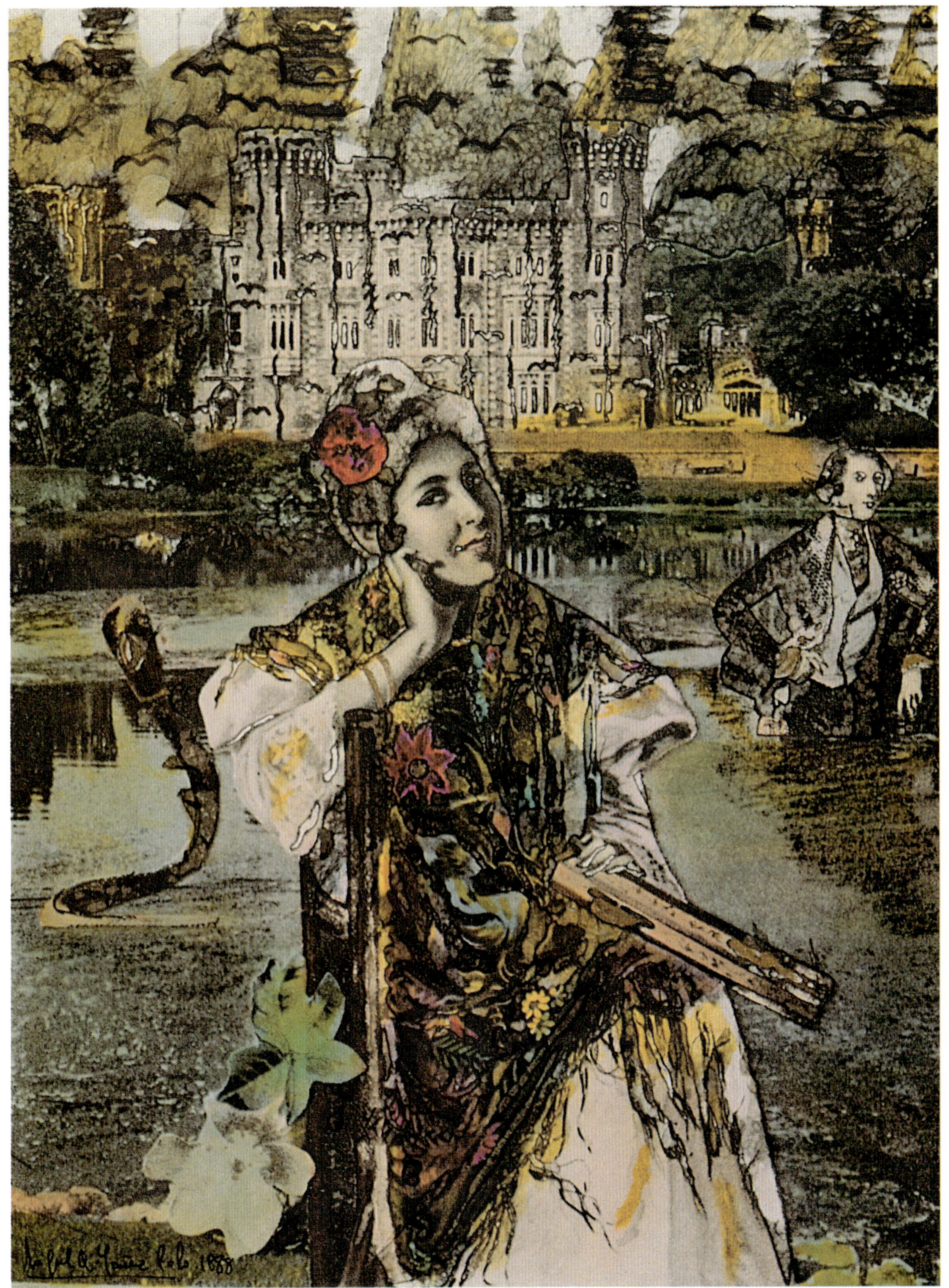

Trini la salerosa

1988

Clastotipo

30 x 40 cm.

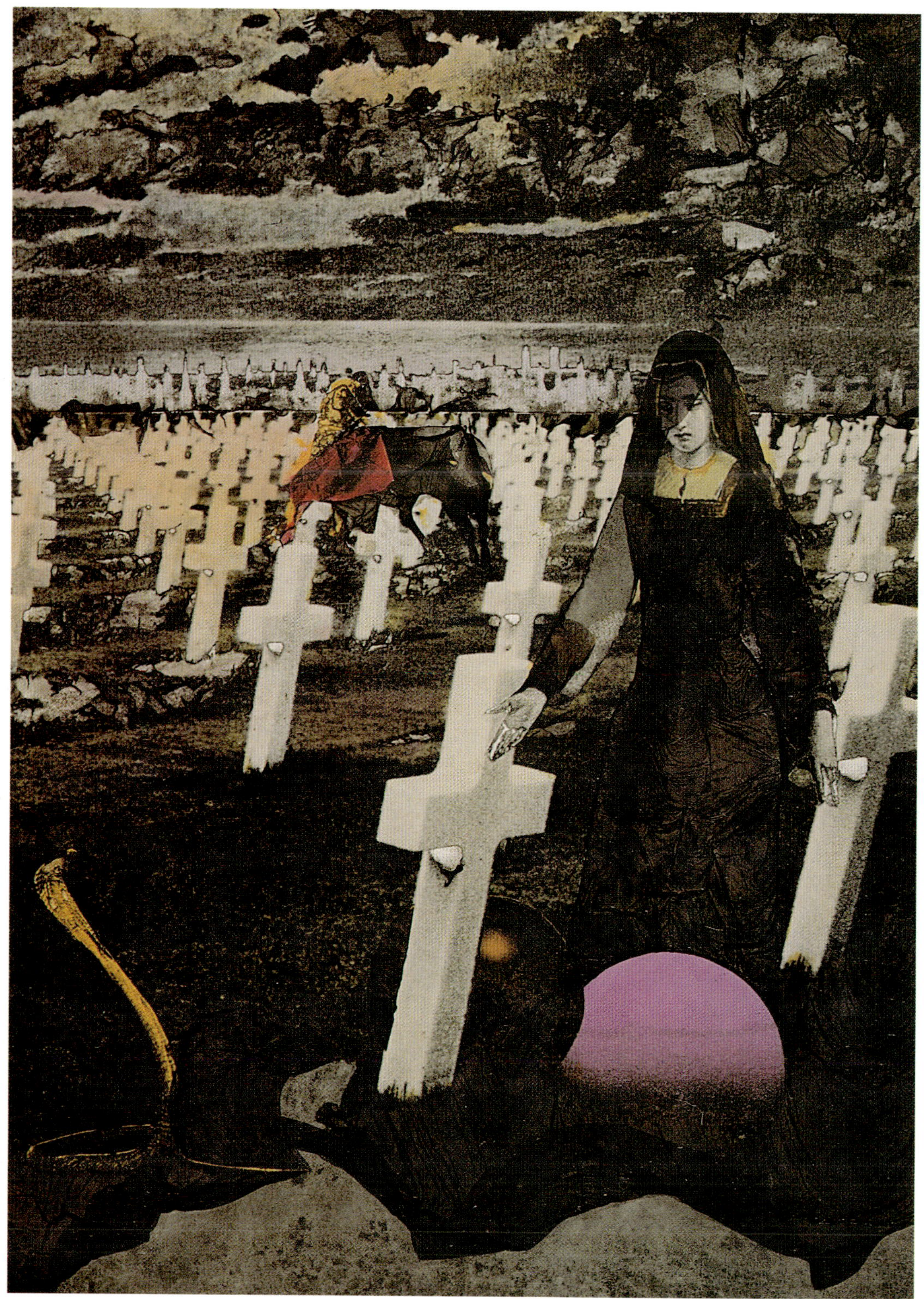

La dama del velo

1988

Clastotipo

30,5 x 40,5 cm.

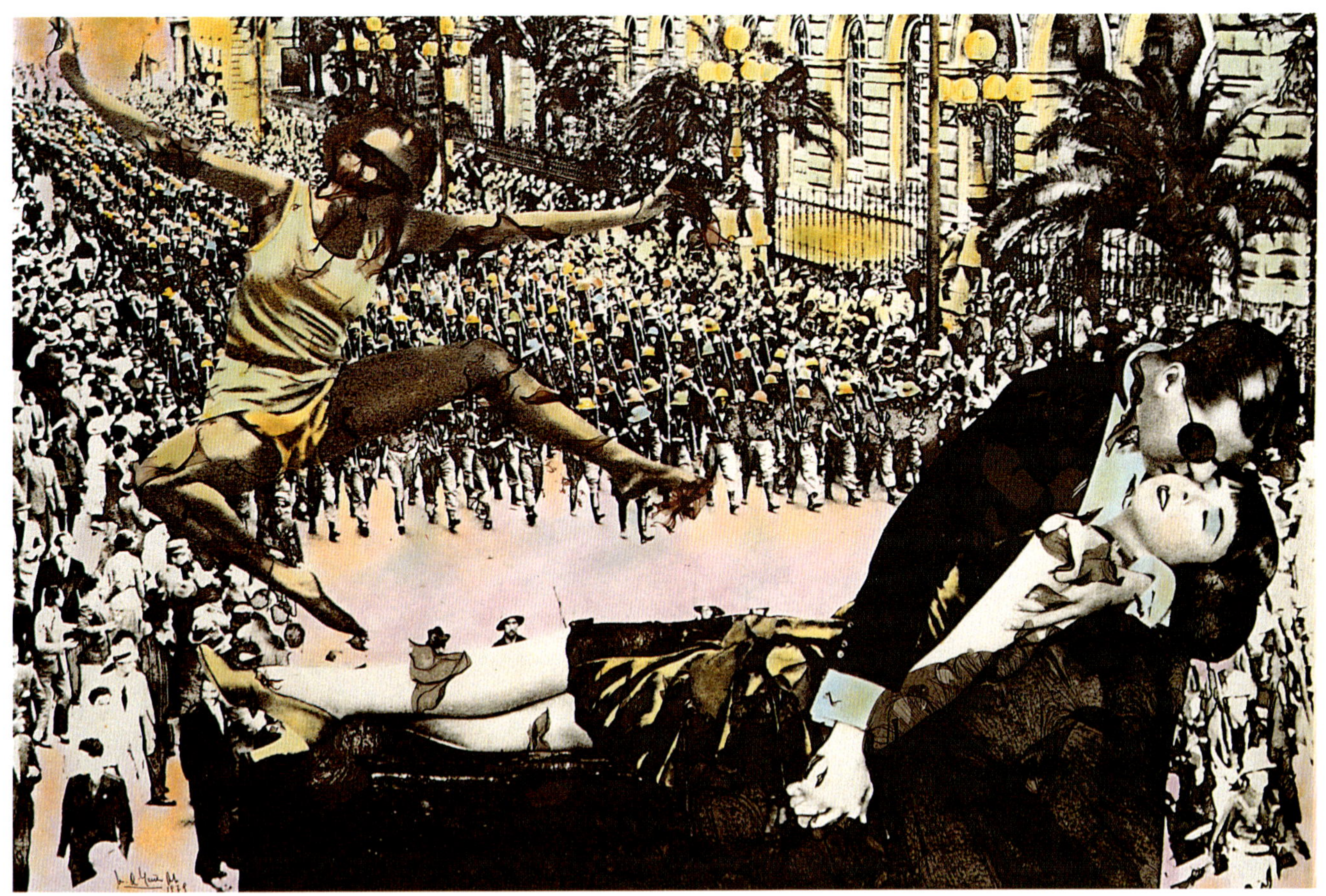

La guerra, vida mía

1983

Bromuro

51 x 60,5 cm.

JUAN RAMON YUSTE

Born Madrid, 1952 / Nació en Madrid, 1952

Individual Exhibitions
Exposiciones individuales

1983   "Madrid Me Mata". Galería
        Pentaprisma. Barcelona, España.
1984   "Dibujos de Luz". Galería Spectrum.
        Zaragoza, España.
        "Dibujos de Luz". Galería Moriarty.
        Madrid, España.
        Casa de Cultura. Elgóibar, España.
1985   "Primavera Fotográfica". Palacio de
        Exposiciones y Congresos. Madrid,
        España.
1987   "El color de la Luz". Galería Caja Rural.
        Córdoba, España.
1989   "O final da Realidade". Kiosko Alonso.
        La Coruña, España.
        "Retratos de Teatro de Bolsillo". Casa de
        Vacas. Madrid, España.
        Sala Municipal de Exposiciones. Cádiz,
        España.

Group Exhibitions
Exposiciones colectivas

1979   "Exposición Límite". Oficina Española de
        Turismo. Nueva York, EE.UU.
1981   "Jóvenes Becarios". Museo Español de
        Arte Contemporáneo. Madrid, España.
1982   "Por la Libertad de Conciencia". Centro
        Cultural de La Villa de Madrid. Madrid,
        España.
        "De Madrid al Frío". Galería
        Pentaprisma. Barcelona, España.
1983   "Fotografía Actual Española". Círculo de
        Bellas Artes. Exposición itinerante por
        Madrid, Albacete y Atenas.
        "La Luna". Galería Sen. Madrid,
        España.
1984   "Seis Fotógrafos Españoles de Color".
        Galería F. Atenas, Grecia.

"Madrid-Madrid-Madrid". Centro Cultural
de La Villa. Madrid, España.
"Tangentes". Dirección General de la
Juventud del Ministerio de Cultura.
Madrid, España.
"Foto-Picnic". Dirección General de
Cultura. Comunidad de Madrid, España.
"Imágenes Eróticas". Galería Moriarty.
Madrid, España.
1985   "Eklektiko". UIMP. Pabellón Mudéjar.
        Sevilla, España.
        "Jóvenes Fotógrafos Madrileños". Galería
        I.A.G. Nuremberg. R.F.A.
        "Fotoplín". Diputación Provincial.
        Málaga, España.
1986   "Photokina 86". Kunsthalle. Colonia,
        R.F.A.
        "Supertangibles". Instituto Francés.
        Madrid, España.
        "La Fotografía en el Museo". Museo
        Español de Arte Contemporáneo.
        Madrid, España.
        "Cómete al Cometa". Galería Ovidio.
        Madrid, España.
1987   "Escenarios de la Guerra Civil".
        Comunidad de Madrid. Madrid, España.
1988   "Todo Fluye". Canal de Isabel II. Madrid,
        España.
1989   "Fotografía Actual española". Museo
        Cantini. Marsella, Francia.
        "Spanish Eyes". Clarence Kennedy
        Gallery. Boston, Massachusetts.

Photographs included in the exhibition
Fotografías contenidas en la exposición

1. Autorretrato. 1974. Cibachrome. 30 x 30 cm.
2. Autorretrato. 1975. Cibachrome. 30 x 30 cm.
3. Autorretrato. 1976. Cibachrome. 30 x 30 cm.
4. Fermeture Éclair. 1976. Cibachrome. 30 x 38 cm.
5. Autorretrato. 1985. Cibachrome. 30 x 36 cm.

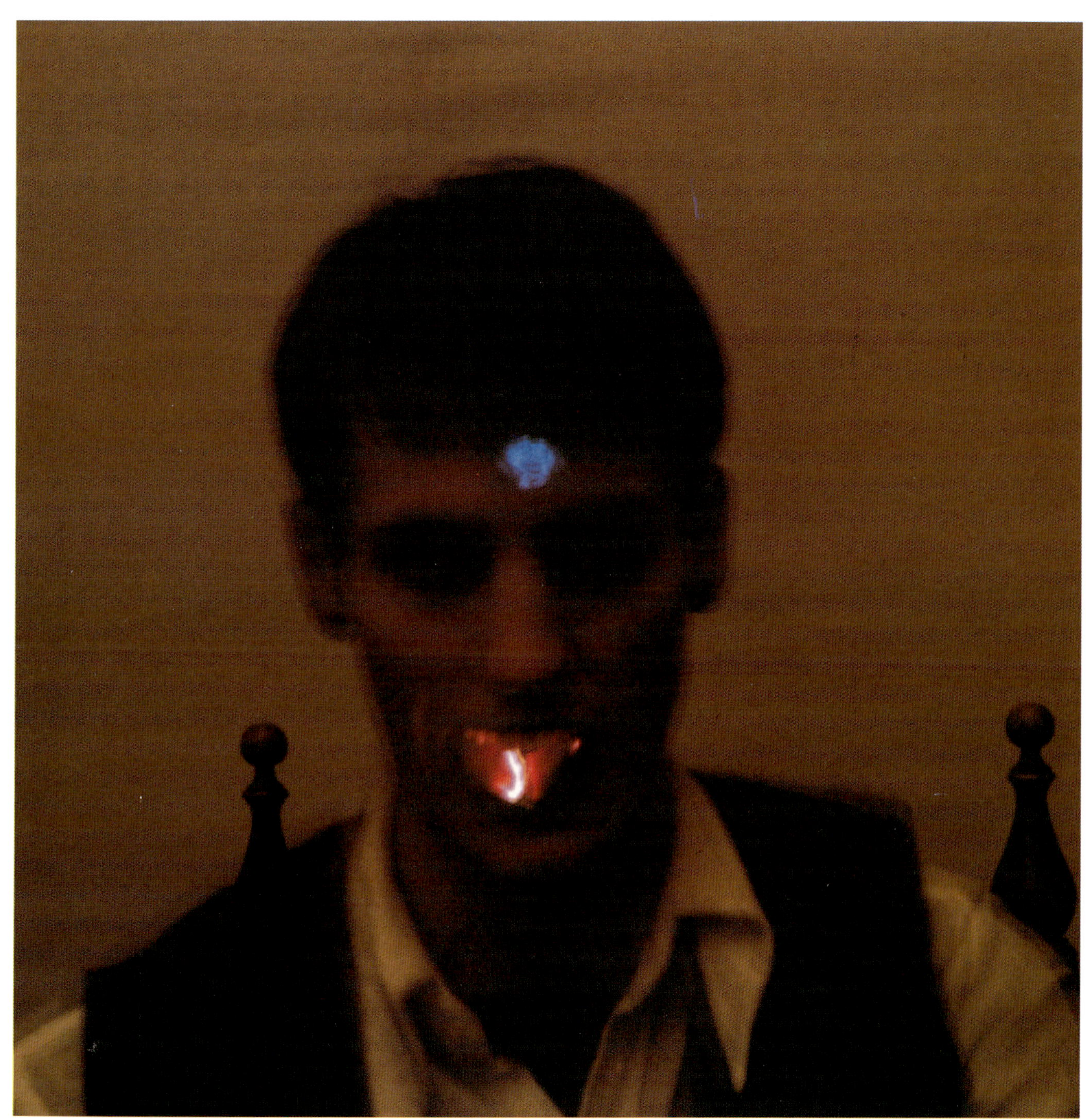

Autoretrato

1974

Cibachrome

30 x 30 cm.

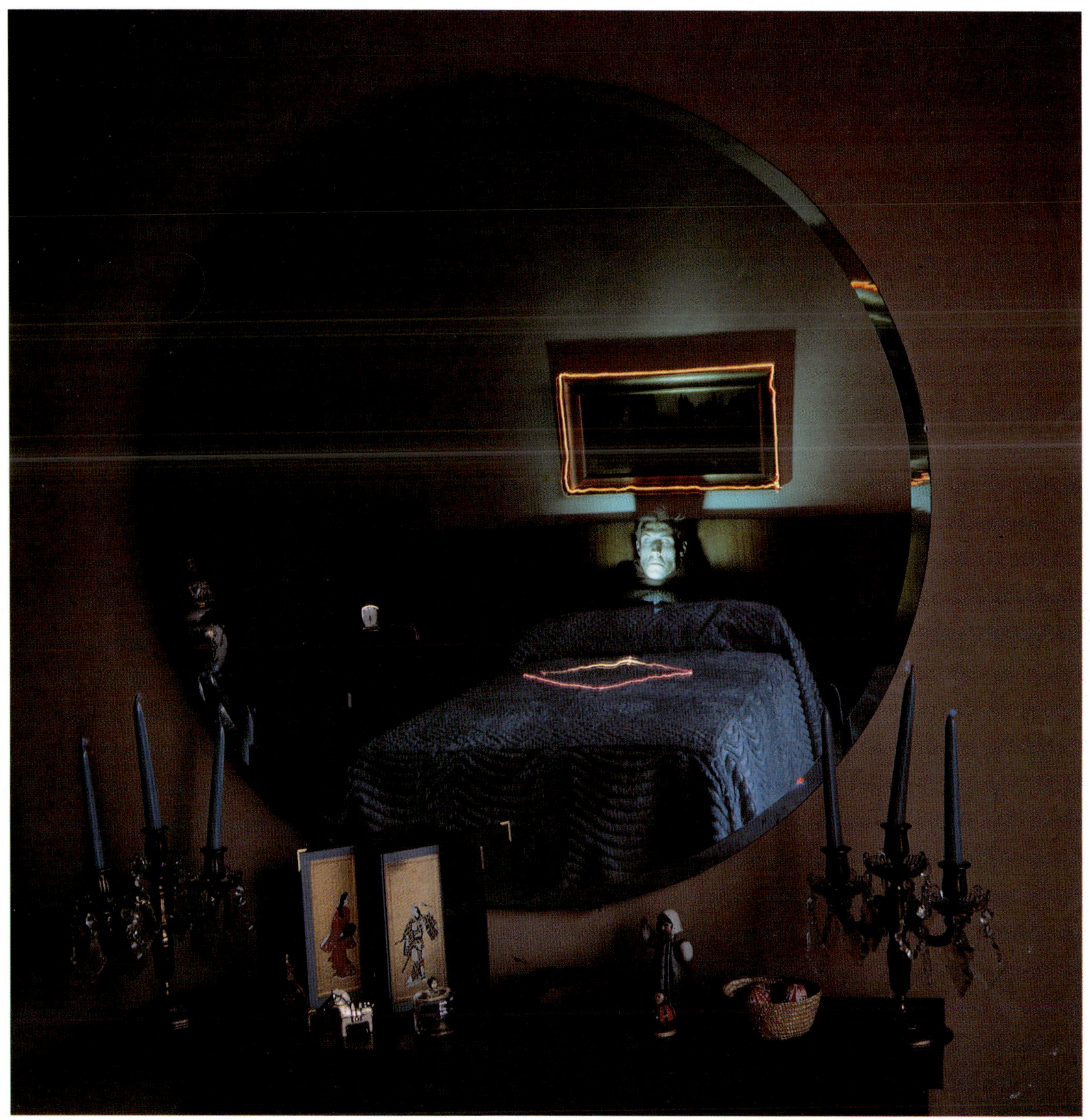

Autoretrato

1975

Cibachrome

30 x 30 cm.

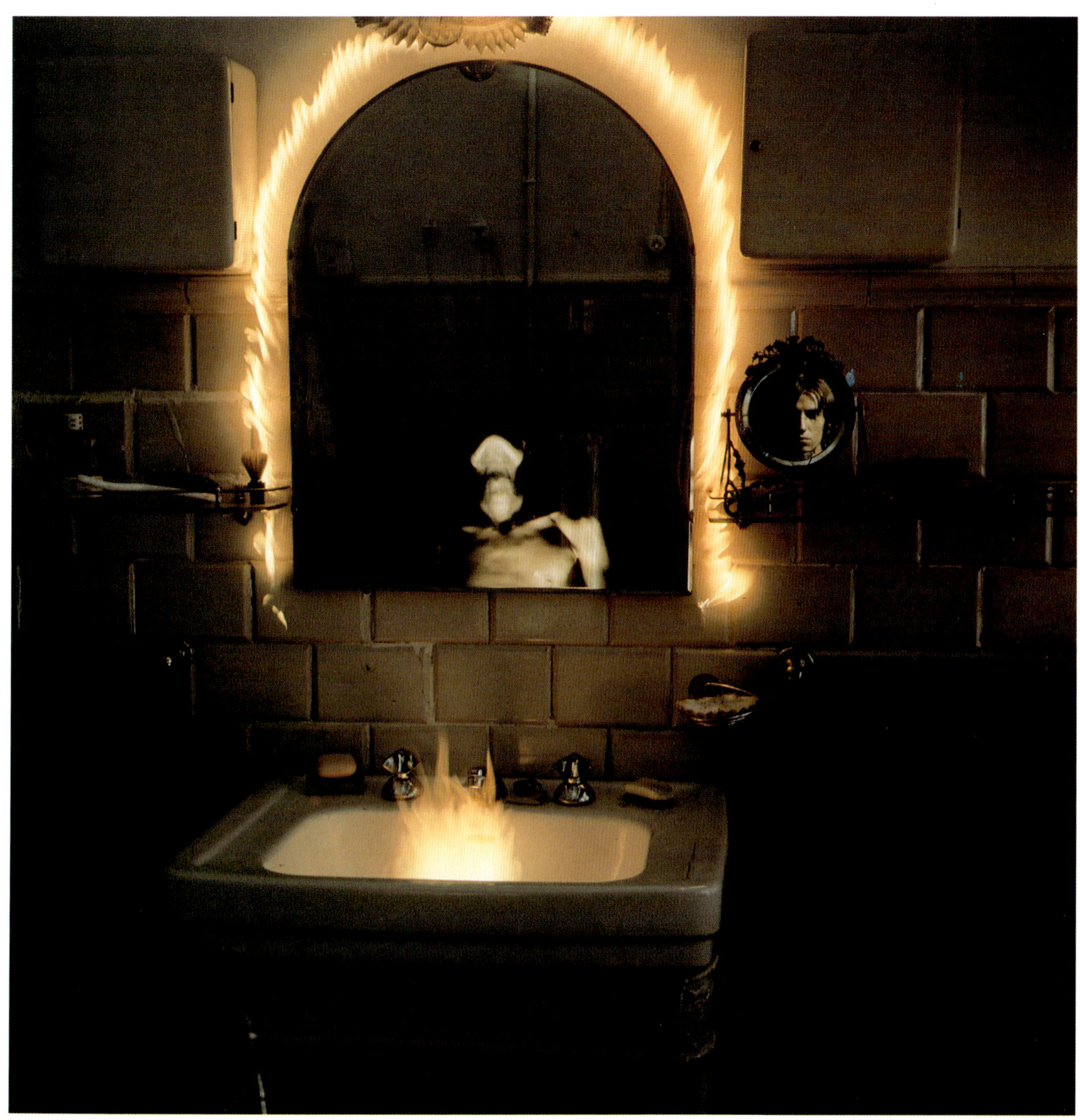

Autoretrato

1976

Cibachrome

30 x 30 cm.

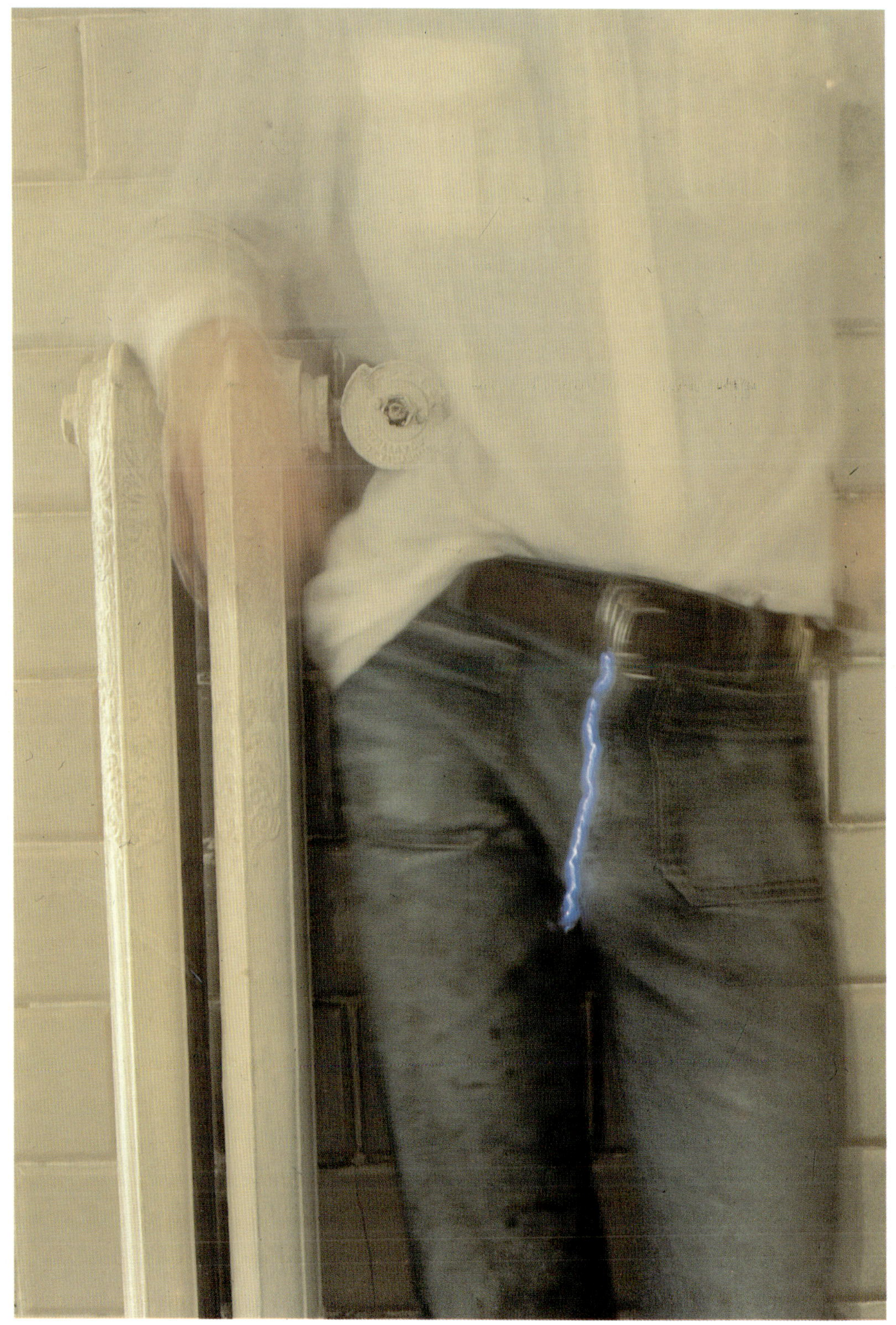

Fermeture Éclair
1976
Cibachrome
30 x 38 cm.

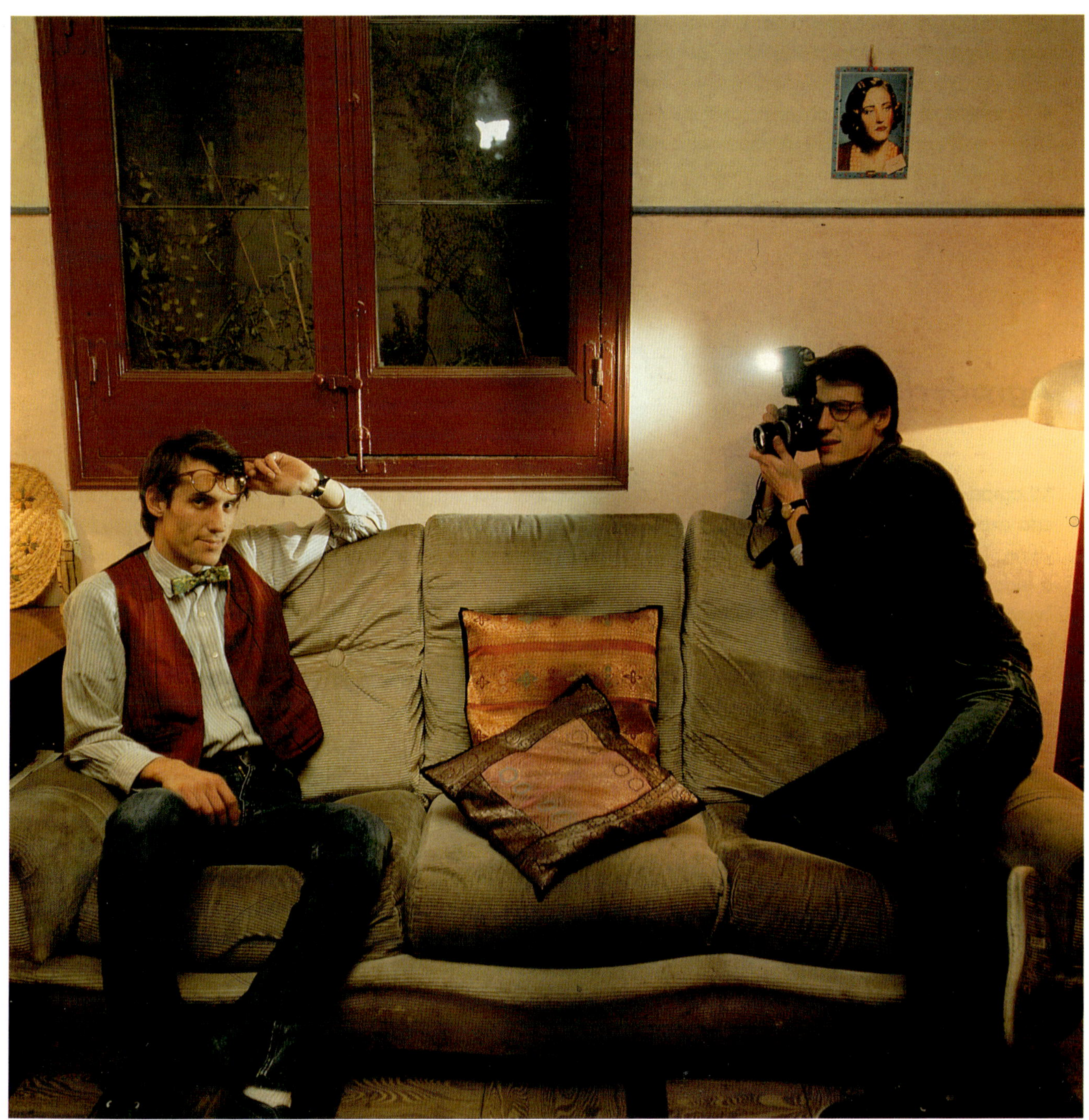

Autoretrato
1985
Cibachrome
30 x 36 cm.